Routledge Companion to Real Estate Investment

Real estate represents an increasingly significant global asset class and its distinctive characteristics must be understood by investors and researchers.

The *Routledge Companion to Real Estate Investment* provides an authoritative overview of the real estate asset class. The *Companion* focuses on the current academic research and its relevance for practical applications.

The book is divided into four parts, each containing specially written chapters by international experts in the relevant field. The contributors cover the institutional context for real estate investment, the main players in real estate investment, real estate appraisal and performance measurement, and real estate portfolios and risk management.

This *Companion* provides a comprehensive reference for students, academics and professionals studying, researching and working in real estate investment, finance and economics.

Bryan D. MacGregor is the MacRobert Professor of Land Economy and Executive Dean at the University of Aberdeen Business School, UK. He is editor of the *Journal of Property Research*.

Rainer Schulz is Senior Lecturer in Real Estate at the University of Aberdeen Business School, UK.

Richard K. Green is the Director of the University of Southern California's Lusk Center for Real Estate. He holds the Lusk Chair in Real Estate and is Professor in the USC Sol Price School of Public Policy and the Marshall School of Business.

Routledge Companion to Real Estate Investment

Edited by Bryan D. MacGregor, Rainer Schulz and Richard K. Green

First published 2019 by Routledge

2 Park Square, Milton Park, Abingdon, Oxon OX14 4RN
605 Third Avenue, New York, NY 10017

First issued in paperback 2021

Routledge is an imprint of the Taylor & Francis Group, an informa business

Publisher's Note
The publisher has gone to great lengths to ensure the quality of this reprint but points out that some imperfections in the original copies may be apparent.

British Library Cataloguing-in-Publication Data
A catalogue record for this book is available from the British Library

Library of Congress Cataloging-in-Publication Data
Names: MacGregor, Bryan, editor. | Schulz, Rainer (Economist), editor. |
Green, Richard K., editor.
Title: Routledge companion to real estate investment / [edited by]
Bryan MacGregor, Rainer Schulz and Richard K. Green.
Description: Abingdon, Oxon ; New York, NY : Routledge, 2018. | Includes index.
Identifiers: LCCN 2018034191 | ISBN 9781138020788 (hardback) |
ISBN 9781315775579 (ebook)
Subjects: LCSH: Real estate investment.
Classification: LCC HD1382.5 .R685 2018 | DDC 332.63/24–dc23
LC record available at https://lccn.loc.gov/2018034191

ISBN 13: 978-1-03-209424-3 (pbk)
ISBN 13: 978-1-138-02078-8 (hbk)

Typeset in Times
by Out of House Publishing

Contents

Figures

Tables

Contributors

Shaun Bond
University of Cincinnati, USA

Kwong Wing Chau
University of Hong Kong

Neil Crosby
University of Reading, England, UK

Ciara Cunningham
Northern Ireland Statistics & Research Agency and Land & Property Services, Northern Ireland, UK

Éamonn D'Arcy
University of Reading, England, UK

Steven Devaney
University of Reading, England, UK

Robert Edelstein
University of California at Berkeley

Ong Seow Eng
National University of Singapore

Mark J. Eppli
University of Wisconsin, USA

Robin Goodchild
LaSalle Investment Management, London, England, UK

Richard K. Green
University of Southern California, USA

Norman Hutchison
University of Aberdeen, Scotland, UK

Colin Jones
Heriot-Watt University, Edinburgh, Scotland, UK

Jiancong Liang
University of Hong Kong

Kenneth Lusht
Florida Gulf Coast University, USA

Bryan D. MacGregor
University of Aberdeen, Scotland, UK

Pat McAllister
University of Reading, England, UK

William McCluskey
University of Pretoria, South Africa

Paul McNamara
Linden Parkside, St Albans, Hertfordshire, UK

Alex Moss
Consilia Capital, London, City University, London, and University of Reading, UK

David Parker
University of South Australia, Australia

Carolin Pommeranz
RWTH Aachen University, Germany

Rainer Schulz
University of Aberdeen, Scotland, UK

Tien Foo Sing
National University of Singapore

Bertram I. Steininger
KTH Royal Institute of Technology, Stockholm, Sweden

Simon Stevenson
University of Washington, USA

Charles C. Tu
University of San Diego

Michael White
Nottingham Trent University,UK

Siu Kei Wong
University of Hong Kong

Shi Ming Yu
National University of Singapore

Yuan Zhao
University of Aberdeen, Scotland, UK

Si Zhou
University of Southampton, England, UK

Introduction

1 Introduction to real estate investment

Bryan D. MacGregor, Rainer Schulz and Richard K. Green

This companion contains 16 main chapters which provide an introduction to topics that are currently important for the real estate investment industry. The chapters are written by real estate practitioners and academics working on different continents and in different countries. Accordingly, the authors have different perspectives on the industry. It also means that there is some variation in the use of terms; for instance, some authors prefer to use the term property instead of real estate. As editors, we have kept such variations largely untouched.

For each topic area, we selected contributors who could give an informed and detailed discussion of the assigned topic. It is to be expected that authors will focus their discussion on markets and segments they are most familiar with. We do not claim that our selection of coverage is perfect, because the focus lies mainly on real estate markets in developed countries. It is also obvious from the affiliations of the authors that most of them work in the UK and the US. This is no accident, as these are two of the most transparent and active real estate investment markets in the world. Both countries also have universities with long-established real estate departments.

In designing the companion, it was important to us that it would be useful to practitioners, academics, and students alike. A recurring theme of the chapters is current research and its relevance for practical applications. However, given the different topics, some chapters are more descriptive and others are more analytical.

The companion is divided into four parts. Part I provides an overview of institutional similarities and differences of the real estate investment industry in different countries. Chapter 2 by Goodchild and D'Arcy discusses how important it is for real estate investors and researchers to understand the institutional background of real estate markets. Direct real estate investments require, for instance, a full understanding of the country-specific legal ownership rights, the planning laws and the corresponding decision-making processes, and the national tax system.

Investors in real estate can delegate some of these tasks to fund managers. As Chapter 3 by Steininger *et al.* discusses, once investors delegate, they must understand how these managers are regulated, what their duties and responsibilities are and how investors can ensure that managers act on their behalf. The same applies to the investment vehicles that can be offered to different investors. National financial authorities will regulate investment vehicles strictly if these are targeted at retail investors. International agreements, for instance through EU legislation, have brought a standardisation that makes it easier for fund managers to market their products in other countries. In contrast, more contractual freedom exists if vehicles are targeted at professional investors, such as institutions and wealthy families. In these cases, contracts are based on private law and are less standardised. For instance, hedge funds are usually set up in such a manner that regulation and publicity requirements can be avoided. One area where regulation of investment vehicles matters is with respect to the use of leverage. While leverage has a positive effect on the expected return of equity, it also increases its risk. Investment vehicles targeted at retail investors are, therefore, often restricted in the magnitude of leverage they can use. This is different for private vehicles, where the manager of a fund has often some leeway with respect to the use of debt.

Chapter 4 by Green considers the relationship between real estate and banking, and reviews the various roles that banks play as part of the real estate lending process. With a particular focus on the US, the chapter provides details on the different loan products that are relevant for the development and acquisition of commercial real estate. Real estate loans are important assets on bank balance sheets but banks also originate loans and then distribute them to capital markets. The chapter also considers the regulation of banks, particularly with respect to capital, and how capital standards might or might not change the cost of lending.

Chapter 5 by Jones discusses the factors that influence the supply of new buildings, both commercial and private housing, much of which in developed countries is provided speculatively. The creation of new supply can also include buying an existing, but outdated, building and refurbishing it with the intention of selling. Development finance is crucial and can be distinguished as short or long term, although the distinction is increasingly arbitrary, so the chapter discusses investment vehicles, such as private equity funds. Development can also be triggered by tax incentives or partnerships with the public sector.

Part II of the companion focusses on two essential groups of players in the real estate investment market. Chapter 6 by Goodchild *et al.* focusses on fund managers and discusses the investment products and services they provide for clients. It provides a comprehensive review of the diverse ways in which property is managed and offered as an equity investment held within a fund, and distinguishes between private, unlisted entities and public, listed vehicles. Within these main categories, various sub-categories are considered, including open or closed end funds, real estate investment trusts (REITs) or non-REITs, and specialist or broad platform managers. The chapter concludes by evaluating the future of the industry.

Chapter 7 by Edelstein and Green focusses on the important group of real estate agents and brokers. While most research in the area concentrates on residential real estate, the insights from this research is also relevant to investors in the commercial real estate sectors. The chapter briefly reviews the industrial organisation of the real estate brokerage industry in the US and discusses the literature on brokerage and contracting. As real estate transactions involve lumpy, heterogeneous products in markets with asymmetric information and high search costs, buying and selling of real estate is complicated so buyers and sellers rely heavily on brokers. The principal–agent problem creates problems for including appropriate incentives in contracts for the sale and lease of real estate.

Part III of the companion focusses on appraisals and the measurement of the performance of direct real estate. Securitised real estate, such as the REIT, is usually listed in public markets, so that prices can be observed directly. Index construction is thus straightforward. In comparison with financial assets, individual buildings are traded seldom and in private markets. Thus, valuations play an important role for those who want to invest in direct real estate, be it because they want to buy or sell buildings or because they need valuations for their operations, as it is the case for open-ended funds.

Chapter 8 by Crosby *et al.* gives an overview on the need for valuations for real estate investments. This is followed by a detailed account of the organisation of the valuation profession in several different countries. As self-regulated professions, the standardisation of methods and techniques has always been an important aspect in valuation, and this has gained further momentum through the integration of investment markets, for instance in Europe. Fund managers are not only interested in valuation for specific buildings that they own or want to buy, but are also interested in a measure of the overall asset class. Such information is offered by specialised index providers.

Chapter 9 by Crosby and Devaney discusses indices that rely on valuations for the computation of the performance of direct real estate. These indices have the advantage that relatively many data points are observable, but these data points might suffer from measurement error caused by the valuation process. Reasons and potential solutions for this measurement problem are discussed. The chapter also discusses some of the choices developers of indexes must make; for example, whether to use a value weighted or transaction based index. Chapter 10 by Chau *et al.* discusses the construction of real estate price indices using transaction prices. As transaction prices for commercial real estate are difficult to obtain and studies in this area are sparse, the focus of the chapter is on residential real estate.

Part IV of the companion broadens the perspective on real estate asset investments. In capital markets, real estate competes with many other assets for investors' attention. A portfolio perspective is required to understand why investors can benefit from investing in real estate assets and how much they should pay for such opportunities. Chapter 11 by MacGregor *et al.* discusses asset pricing models and how these models explain prices in equilibrium. All models share the insight that the asset price should be related positively with asset's diversification potential in the investor's portfolio. Several different models are presented and their relevance is discussed.

Direct real estate provides the owner with great flexibility so Chapter 12 by MacGregor *et al.* discusses how option theory can be used to model and understand this flexibility. Real option theory is an area that has gained momentum within the industry. Real options can mean that property is more valuable than a standard cash flow model might imply. Land development, for instance, can be postponed, the use of a building can be changed, rents can be adjusted, and lease contracts can be extended or terminated. Equipped with an understanding of these models, the chapter discusses studies that test real option models with data from real estate applications.

Another growth area is behavioural finance, which is the topic of Chapter 13 by White. Behavioural finance is based on the insight that participants in financial markets, such as investors and fund managers, do not always react in a fully rational manner to new information. In real estate, the valuation process may be subject to the anchoring and representativeness heuristics that induce slow and inaccurate adjustment of value perceptions. The chapter considers anchoring on comparables, over-confidence and regret avoidance that cause investors to trade excessively and to hold loss-making assets. Investors also tend to pay too much attention to recently observed prices when forming return expectations. Trend chasing behaviour and over-confidence exist, and tend to increase in boom periods, creating an illusion of validity to investment decision making. Investors are loss averse and tend to sell well-performing assets and retain poorly performing assets. The characteristics of real estate assets suggest that behavioural approaches could help to explain processes and outcomes in this market.

Chapter 14 by Eppli and Tu discusses the role that real estate – in particular, direct real estate – can play in mixed asset portfolios. This is exemplified with US data. As bond yields have fallen over the first two decades of the twenty-first century, investment advisers have been pushed into investing in higher-risk securities to maintain target returns. Direct investment in commercial real estate maintains relatively high returns and the greatest opportunity for diversification benefits in portfolios with stocks, bonds and other investments.

As direct real estate is a real asset, it is exposed to risks that are of less or no importance for financial assets. This includes liquidity and operational risks. For instance, owning a building and acting as landlord exposes the owner to operational risk. Examples include the loss of an important tenant or the loss of a location advantage because planning authorities permit new development nearby. Chapter 15 by Bond and Stevenson gives an account of these risks and how they can be managed. Particular emphasis is given to real estate index derivatives that allow the management of the price risk of buildings in the portfolio. Such derivatives also allow synthetic restructuring of a portfolio, where short positions are taken in segments that are expected to underperform and long positions in segments that are expected to outperform. As with most derivative contracts, real estate index derivatives are exposed to liquidity, pricing and basis risk. It remains to be seen whether such contracts become a standard risk management tool in the industry.

As most professional investors invest in real estate through fund managers, the companion closes with two chapters on fund manager performance and behaviour. Chapter 16 by Schulz *et al.* discusses the approaches that exist to evaluate the performance of fund managers. While it is fairly straightforward to establish whether a passively managed fund achieves the performance of the index it is matching, matters are more complicated for actively managed funds. Managers of active funds act in a risky environment that makes it difficult to separate skill – if the manager has any – from luck. The environment necessitates that the performance is assessed relative to the risk taken and the fair compensation investors require for this exposure. This links back to asset pricing models that can provide such required return rates. A statistical framework is required to account for the stochastic elements of return rates. The evidence on fund manager performance is overall quite clear. While some managers may indeed have skills, these skills are difficult to spot and investors do not usually benefit after cost. This outcome is to be expected, given the highly competitive fund management industry. The empirical evidence does not imply that the fund management industry is without merit. It indicates, however, that active strategies might be of less value than manager might want to make us think.

Chapter 17 by McAllister looks at the behaviour of fund managers. There have been several recent cases where fund managers intentionally defrauded their investors. But besides such criminal cases, there is a classical principal–agent conflict where the investors, as principals, are likely to have less information than the manager and also find it difficult to observe all the actions that the manager, as agent, takes or does not take. Effective monitoring of fund managers requires good reporting standards and the incentive for investors to use this information effectively. Giving managers a stake in the profits of a fund, as is implemented by many private vehicles, can deliver high-power incentives to work hard for investors' and the manager's own benefit. Ethical standards and codes of conduct might be a valuable complement to such monetary incentives.

Finally, we do not claim that the companion is comprehensive, so in closing, we identify some areas that are becoming important in the industry but which have not been covered in the companion. One area relates to the availability of data for investment analysis. Several professional data providers have entered the market and offer to their data subscribers detailed information on individual buildings and transactions. This information will make real estate markets more transparent. It should also speed up the diligence and sale process. Another relevant area is infrastructure investments. Given tight public budgets, national and local governments are keen to involve the private sector in infrastructure investments. While this brings opportunities for investors, it also brings risks. For instance, as most infrastructure projects have a large unit size, most investors will face single-address risk. It is also essential to understand the contractual relationship with the respective government body and the impact that regulation can have on the returns of such investments. The companion also does not discuss green buildings. While the evidence is mixed that sustainable buildings pay off for investors, there is reason to believe that environmental standards and technological progress can affect the success of building investments. Despite these omissions, we hope that the 16 main chapters that follow will provide a valuable resource for a wide and diverse readership.

Part I

The institutional context

2 An international overview of real estate markets

Similarities and differences

Robin Goodchild and Éamonn D'Arcy

Introduction

Real estate has become a global asset class only relatively recently. The development of the industry is described elsewhere but the global element began to emerge from 1980 when Middle Eastern and Japanese institutions started investing in UK and US property; this accelerated during the 1990s with the arrival of the German open-ended funds followed by principally US investment managers offering closed-end funds for investment around the world.[1] These investors needed to learn how to navigate their way around different real estate markets. While some aspects may have appeared familiar, for example, the same international banks and accountants occupying major central business district offices in different financial centres, alien legal systems and different market practices presented new challenges. This chapter provides an overview of the challenges that real estate investors face when they move outside the domestic market within which their knowledge and experience has been learnt. In particular, the analysis seeks to distinguish between the learning that can be applied without adjustment, because markets do work similarly, and the elements that an investor should expect to be different. Predictably, there is much more focus on the latter.

Over the first two decades of the twenty-first century, global real estate investing has become more common place. While, inevitably, strategies that reflect a domestic bias remain a material force, a number of factors have enabled cross-border or global strategies to become a much more viable part of the investing landscape. In particular, a key driver has been the 'revolution' in the availability and quality of the information necessary to support cross-border investment decision making. This revolution has taken place at a number of levels from the increasing availability of consistent performance data for a wide variety of property sectors and markets through the activities of organisations such as Investment Property Databank (IPD), now MSCI, to better overall market information on a wider set of locations as a result of the emergence of global delivery platforms in real estate services (D'Arcy, 2009). A key impact of this revolution has been a significant reduction in the importance of information costs as a barrier to international investing. A further factor worth noting has been the changes brought about in the structure of investment markets as a result of the evolution of the 'indirect' market, both listed and especially non-listed. The expansion of the latter has favoured the creation of cross-border and even global non-listed property investment vehicles. As a practical illustration of such trends, over 50% of City of London office stock was in foreign ownership in 2011 (Lizieri *et al.*, 2011) and that proportion has increased further since then, with the arrival of Chinese and other Asian institutions.

The danger is that investors and professionals forget that real estate is accessed through local markets with their own unique characteristics. An example of this danger is well illustrated by a subtle case study (Bao and Feng, 2014). Students are provided with data on 600 land transactions between 2004 and 2011 around Beijing and asked to advise a European investor contemplating investing speculatively in development land. The temptation is for all the effort to go into analysing the 600 transactions to discern price trends. However, the best students would recognise that the land parcels actually may not be tradeable, without first carrying out any development, because the ownership rights could be cancelled by the municipal authorities without compensation to discourage speculative 'flipping' of undeveloped sites, particularly by foreigners.[2]

The classic texts in real estate economics all stress that the market deals in property rights and those rights have unique elements (see, for example, Ely and Wehrwein, 1940 or Turvey, 1957). The first task of a valuer or appraiser when instructed to value an asset is to establish, as precisely as possible, the property rights held by its owner, both their spatial extent and the legal rights attached to that space. This truism cannot be assumed away with the move to global real estate. Moreover, the nature of those property rights materially influences the rules of the market; effective players have to understand these rules. Investors and property professionals, therefore, need to establish how these rules are likely to affect their objectives in each new location into which they enter.

It is not practicable to provide a guide to the operation of every real estate market globally in a single chapter. Instead, this chapter provides a framework for understanding how individual market rules impact on the operation of markets and thereby either facilitate or constrain the objectives of specific market players. The chapter includes examples focussing principally on factors that affect investment returns, either directly by affecting cash flows or indirectly through their impact on market dynamics.

A simple market model

Real estate markets are driven by three broad interacting forces:

- economic drivers – local, national and global;
- capital markets; and
- new supply operating through local institutional frameworks.

The state of an economy, which itself is a function of local, national and global forces working in combination, is the principal determinant of the local demand for space from firms and households in any given market. The capital markets determine the level of interest rates, sentiment towards real estate as an investment relative to other options (such as stocks) and the general market level of risk aversion/tolerance, often described as the balance between 'greed' and 'fear', that influences the risk premium. As a result, capital markets have a major influence on investment flows to real estate and levels of liquidity. When flows are increasing, property yields tend to compress as prices are bid up and liquidity levels normally increase as more owners choose to capture profits. When flows dry up, vendors need to be prepared to reduce their asking price to attract bids. Moreover, capital market sentiment can change very quickly, causing yields to move sharply, so they are a major influence on the whole real estate market.

New supply is normally one of the most predictable elements of a real estate market because the construction process takes time, so accurate estimates can be made of, for example, new office supply for the next 18–24 months. Forecasts are also made for longer time periods but these are usually less reliable because new projects can be added to the

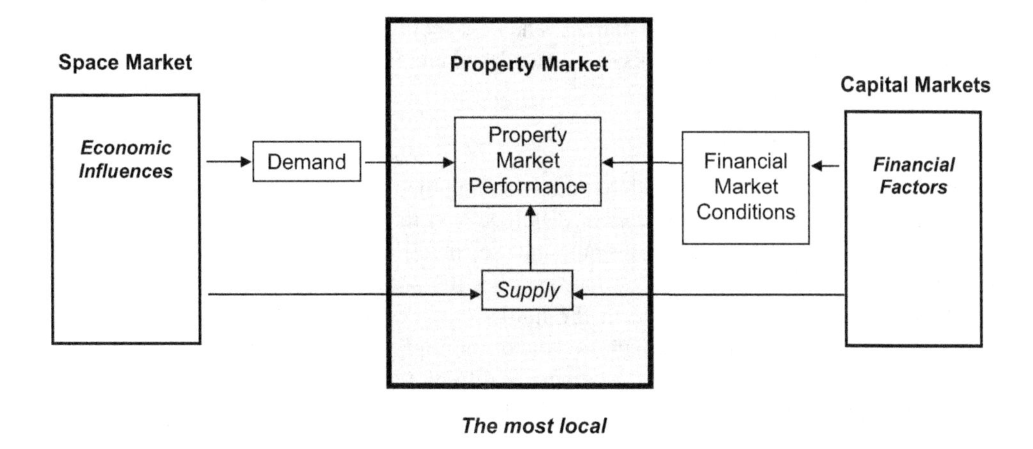

Figure 2.1 A simple model of real estate markets
Source: Higgins adapting Archer and Ling (1997).

pipeline or expected projects delayed. Within the 18–24 month period, construction work will have actually commenced, so the likelihood of projects not proceeding to completion is much reduced. Thus, real estate service providers publish 'crane surveys' for specific markets that highlight where new projects are underway and the overall scale of the pipeline.

This simple model is shown graphically in Figure 2.1. The model is universal and can be applied to any real estate market. Occupier demand for real estate is always a function of economic forces – whether local, national or global; thus, gross domestic product (GDP) is invariably a material independent variable in any econometric model that forecasts commercial property rents and capital values. Capital markets, in any location, are always liable to sudden changes so are a major source of volatility in capital flows and liquidity. The relative importance of key capital market actors among banks, insurance companies, pension funds, high net worth individuals, mass retail funds, endowments and sovereign wealth funds can and does vary from market to market, so investors need to identify the key players that are likely to have the biggest influence in any specific market. In Germany, for example, the high net worth and mass retail funds play a more important role than the local pension funds, while in Asia, public market entities, both real estate investment trusts (REITs) and listed property companies, are a much more significant force than their counterparts in Europe. Notwithstanding this variation, investors should always be wary of the capital market's ability to affect levels of liquidity, whether by design through, for example, a central bank changing interest rates or more randomly when sentiment changes as a result of an economic or other shock.

While new supply is always predictable because development is unavoidably time consuming, so that the pipeline can be identified, the way in which that supply is created and how the finished space is offered to occupiers is determined by a set of local rules and practices specific to each market. Thus, the institutional framework within which a property market operates is local and profoundly affects how that market functions, including how the capital markets and occupier demand interact. Investors and property professionals need to understand the nature of institutional frameworks so they know what to expect in terms of the likely impacts on the market objectives they are seeking to achieve.

This chapter focusses on how institutional frameworks can be assessed from a real estate perspective and their effects on the market. The next section provides a theoretical perspective on how institutional frameworks can be analysed and understood.

Institutional economics

An institutional economics approach to understanding the real estate market is very relevant as a means of interpreting the *origins* of differences in the structure of real estate markets and the range of market objectives spanning use, investment and development that they accommodate. For example, such an approach has the potential to provide useful insights into how the rules governing trade in the market have evolved over time, which groups of market actors have influenced such rules and, by implication, the extent to which these rules facilitate or even hinder the achievement of different market objectives. Moreover, this framework can be extended to develop an analysis of how institutional change can, over time, alter the rules.

Over time, real estate markets have evolved specific sets of institutional arrangements for the transactions environment[3] and that facilitate market actors in achieving their individual real estate market objectives. These institutional arrangements inevitably reflect the wider institutional environment – social, economic and political – where the real estate market in question is located. These wider influences shape market-based institutions, influence their legitimacy and contribute to institutional resistance or acceptance of change. In very simple terms, the institutional structure of any market may be viewed as the set of rules governing the operation of that market (Coase, 1972, 1984; Eggertsson, 1990; Hodgson, 1994; Samuels, 1995). Obviously, these rules also reflect the wider institutional norms, economic, social and political, of the country within which the market is located. At a market level, while the economic rationale for such rules should be the reduction of transaction costs, the reality might also reflect the historical influence of various market actors seeking to facilitate their market objectives to the exclusion of other groups and their objectives. In fact, there may even be no obvious economic rationale but rather an explanation in terms of power relationships which existed at some point in time and have, for better or worse, persisted ever since.

Rules, once established, may be difficult to abandon because of simple inertia. These rules define the transactions environment and structure the transaction incentives for market participants. Some rules may be very formal and have legislative force, while others may reflect market practices, the original basis for which may have long been forgotten. These rules both constrain and facilitate the objectives of market actors at any time. The current institutional structure of a market will be optimal for some market participants because they can achieve their market objectives. For others, it may be sub-optimal and may constrain them from realising their goals. Some actors may have been in a dominant market position at one time, sufficient to influence the institutional structure of the market so that they could readily achieve their objectives. As a result, the current institutional form of a market may embody redundant or even restrictive practices designed to exclude other market participants. Again, this highlights the relevance of understanding power relationships and their market legacies as a means of interpreting the institutional structure of any market.

Institutional change comes about as a result of some form of dissatisfaction with the current institutional structure of a market and the outcomes it generates. Pressures for change may be internal or external to the market concerned. Changes in power relationships provide a useful illustration of institutional change internal to the market. New players may displace established players and disrupt long-standing relationships. External pressures for change are likely to reflect wider changes in the structure of the economy and society brought about by factors such as the revolution in information and communication technologies, or by the need to incorporate new business practices or market requirements, such as supporting internationalisation. In some cases, externally driven change may take the form of government intervention if market outcomes are deemed to be socially unsatisfactory or if the market has failed.

It is important to note that institutional change and the resulting new institutional arrangements will not necessarily be efficient in the strict sense of neoclassical economics. They may reduce transactions costs or they may not. There may be winners and losers. Some new or existing actors may be better able to achieve their objectives while others may face new constraints. Very powerful actors may be able to bypass institutional change because their specific power relationships remain undiminished. To survive, other market participants may have to change their core activities and, hence, their market objectives. For example, internationalisation is likely to expose many existing domestic actors to new sources of competitive pressure; for others, it will provide significant new market opportunities. The efficiency of any given process of change needs to be judged not from the perspective of an entire market, but rather from the perspective of specific participants and the objectives they seek to achieve (Keogh and D'Arcy, 1999). As a result, the market may be efficient for some but not for others. The efficiency of the market then becomes contingent on the set of objectives that actors seek to achieve.

Processes of institutional change are most likely to be gradual in nature, involving continuous marginal adjustments. As a result, most markets are likely to governed by a mixture of potentially conflicting institutions (North, 1990), some of which may be in direct conflict with others. The current institutional structure of any market, and the specific arrangements which support it, will inevitably exhibit some elements that reflect from where and how it started, that is 'path dependency'. This concept suggests that, as markets evolve, their nature and the changes that have occurred are a function of their unique social, economic and political history (David, 2000). In short, this suggests that initial conditions matter and markets get 'locked-in' by historical events (Arthur, 1994), which has implications for market outcomes, issues of market failure, processes of institutional change and judgements about market efficiency. Unsurprisingly, path dependency concepts have an obvious relevance within such frameworks for market analysis. The current institutional structure of any market inevitably exhibits some element of path dependency or sensitivity to starting points.

It is likely that some institutional rules and arrangements, once established, will persist and have future consequences for a market's evolutionary path. For example, market elites or simple 'inertia' may guarantee the regurgitation of institutional forms which have become unsuitable for current market requirements. The arguments made previously about redundant practices can be interpreted in a similar manner. These inevitably reflect some degree of path dependency' As a result, issues relating to potential sources of path dependency cannot be ignored as they are central to an understanding of any market's evolution, structure, outcomes and processes of institutional formation and change.

So, what is the benefit of using such an approach to markets and market change in the context of the real estate market? In short, it provides important insights into the rationale for current market processes, a market's evolutionary path, the objectives it accommodates as well as the objectives it does not, and how and why institutional change takes place (Keogh and D'Arcy, 1994, 1999). It shifts the focus from an attempt to rationalise change and its drivers at the aggregate level of 'the market' to understanding change from the perspective of market participants, both old and new, in pursuit of their particular goals. The approach also has the advantage that it does not assume that change will necessarily be efficient for all. It permits a consideration of how markets are inevitably constrained by their history and how certain groups of market participants exhibit considerable inertia to change as they cling to outdated market practices which promote their specific objectives. The approach also has sufficient flexibility to consider the issue of power structures in markets and the wider institutional environment in terms of being able to identify the origins of change at different levels, both from within a market itself and outside.

Institutional formation

In addition to the issues raised above, it is also necessary to consider explicitly the topic of institutional formation within this framework. To be able to interpret the evolution of new institutional arrangements through institutional change, it is necessary to understand something about the potential rationale for the formation of such arrangements and ultimately their reproduction over time. Mahoney (2000) suggests that such explanations fall within four broad categories.

First, utilitarian explanations suggest that market actors will support the formation of new institutional arrangements, even inefficient ones, as long as the benefits of change are outweighed by the costs. Implicit within this is the key assumption that the resulting distribution of benefits would be favourable to all. If the distribution of benefit is not universal then market actors who will not benefit have no incentive to support the new institutional arrangements. The existence of appropriate supporting organising institutions, information networks and actor proficiencies combine to lock in such new institutional arrangements. Changes to these arrangements, once established, will only take place when there is no longer any benefit to the key actors involved in continuing with the existing arrangements. New competitive pressures and learning processes such as those associated with, for example, improvements in technology, are likely to be the key triggers of change within this explanation.

A second explanation suggests a functionalist account of institutional formation. The focus here is on the wider market system with the formation of individual institutions taking place because of their perceived functional importance within the wider system. This may result in the formation and survival of sub-optimal institutions. In these circumstances, change will only take place through exogenous shocks to the overall market system which, in turn, can make the operations of the individual institution redundant, so they go out of business. Examples in this context might include legal rules, accepted market conventions and even, in some cases, the continued existence of particular types of professional bodies or business entities. This explanation in particular stresses the importance of the wider institutional environment as an influence on market specific organisations with their persistence depending on their continued functionality within it.

Explanations based on the power of elite groups provide a third category of justifications for institutional formation and reproduction. In these explanations, institutional formation favours the interests of an elite group that is able to influence this process because of its position of power. The resulting institutional arrangements will favour the objectives of this group above others. These institutions will then be very efficient for the elite group, providing a clear rationale for institutional reproduction, even though they may be very inefficient for other groups. Change will take place if the power of the elite groups diminishes over time or the power of subordinate groups or of new entrants increases. A good example in this context might be the traditional structure of commercial leases in the UK which have favoured the interests of investors over those of occupiers.

A final category of explanation centres on the idea of legitimation. In this case, institutional formation takes place because actors view an institution as legitimate and voluntarily opt for its reproduction. Indeed, in this case, reproduction and, ultimately, longevity also reinforce legitimacy. For change to take place, the subjective or moral views and values of the actors concerned have to change, which results in a questioning of the legitimacy of existing institutional arrangements and, thus, a desire for change. As an example, the continued existence of a long-standing professional body like the Royal Institution of Chartered Surveyors (RCIS) reflects this idea of legitimation. The Institution has changed very considerably since its creation as the Surveyors' Institute in 1868, in response to myriad market changes. The global reach it has today would be inconceivable to its founders.[4]

A systems approach

A further strand of analysis, which again is concerned with the institutional structure of markets, is a systems approach to the interpretation of market structures and activities. Following the approach of Casson (1990, 1995), the economy can be considered as an information system rather than the more conventional treatment of it as a system of materials or product flows. The focus is on handling information relating to goods and services rather than on the handling of final or intermediate products. Within this system, economic institutions, markets or firms evolve to allocate decision-making responsibilities and structure information flows. This highlights the importance of information, its characteristics and costs, as drivers of institutional formation and evolution. Focus is placed on information intermediation through market making, with the market maker performing a key role in adding value and reducing information costs by structuring information flows and creating an information synthesis.

Within this framework, the form that market institutions take might reasonably reflect information costs, its collection and communication, as well as the potential for information asymmetries. The structure of institutions themselves becomes a direct response to the magnitude of the information problems exhibited. As information costs change due, for example, to improvements in communications technology, the structure of these institutions changes to reflect this. For example, institutional change driven by falling communication costs might, over time, increase the geographical scope of firms and markets. Likewise, changes in the information requirements of market activities prompt institutional change through the requirement for new market-making roles and new categories of information flow. From a real estate market perspective, the evolution of global delivery platforms in real estate services since 2000, combined with the emergence of bespoke information providers, provide notable cases in point. Another very relevant example is the explosive growth of non-listed real estate investment vehicles which have generated many new information requirements and new forms of information flow.

The institutional structure of a real estate market broadly reflects its information costs and potential problems of information asymmetries. This, in particular, is reflected by the active market participation of a wide range of professional experts and service providers whose primary function is to reduce information costs through intermediation activities. Experts in a real estate market collect information relevant to real estate involvements, structure information flows, add value to it through its interpretation and communicate it to various groups of market actors, such as occupiers, investors and developers. They, in turn, use this information to achieve their market objectives, such as the growth and development of their business models. Given the value of information, some actors have a clear incentive to become monopolists in its provision. As markets evolve, they create new information requirements and result in the entry of new types of professional expert, which raises the possibility of some established experts becoming redundant. Existing experts have a clear incentive to impose barriers to entry on new entrants as a means of avoiding such an outcome. The advent of mass appraisal systems substituting for individual property valuations and the competition from online brokerages to traditional high street estate agencies are two real estate examples where there is high likelihood of redundancy. Existing professional experts in the real estate sector may also be under threat from the application of 'big data' to a wider range of real estate functions and the evolution of more sophisticated forms of 'proptech'. The need to support internationalisation and its new information requirements provides another important case in point (D'Arcy, 2009). In particular, this creates opportunities for market experts who reduce the information costs of international real estate involvements and provide the information requirements necessary for actors to realise their internationalisation objectives. Likewise 'disruptive technologies' and associated disruptive business models like the 'sharing economy' will create new opportunities through driving new information requirements for a range of property involvements.

Key market characteristics

As highlighted above, the institutional framework for a real estate market is multi-facetted and complex. Each market has developed into its current form through its own history and changes in power structures. It is not the object of this chapter to attempt a comprehensive analysis of even a single aspect of a specific market's institutional framework. Instead, the analysis is limited to five key supply-side factors which are:

- tax and legal;
- market transparency;
- lease terms;
- planning and land use controls; and
- terms of trade between investors and developers.

This list is not claimed to be exhaustive, but it does cover a range of factors that provide helpful insights into the contrasting ways in which different national markets can operate. Market liquidity, for example, is also highly relevant; however, there is a strong correlation between liquidity and market transparency with international capital especially attracted to transparent markets which they can understand more readily, so liquidity is not considered separately.

Tax and legal

Real estate is subject to a myriad of local and national, general and specific taxes. Investors need to research carefully the impact those taxes will have on prospective investments. Unfortunately, each investor's tax status is personal and has to be analysed as such because legal structures matter for tax purposes. Often, a legal structure is designed to mitigate specific taxes but it is rarely effective at avoiding or reducing other taxes, so a new solution is required. This also applies to funds. A fund structure designed to be tax efficient for, say, Dutch and US institutions to invest in real estate in Central and Eastern Europe is likely to require considerable adaptation (assuming it is possible) if it is to be tax efficient for German investors as well. The actions of German investors are highly regulated, so it is often much more practical for them to invest in domestic vehicles specifically designed for the local regulatory environment, even for international investing.

Many institutional investors, such as pension funds, enjoy tax concessions when investing in their domestic real estate market. Concessions are rarely available when investing internationally, except for some sovereign wealth funds. Thus, investors who are used to operating tax free at home have to adjust to becoming taxpayers and this can be a major disincentive to diversifying internationally. Moreover, returns need to be measured net of tax to appraise investments appropriately for comparisons to be made with other opportunities.

One of the most common ways to mitigate tax for real estate investments is to introduce debt into the structure. Interest payments can normally be offset against rental income for tax purposes so reducing the tax liability. Moreover, interest payments are often taxed at a lower rate than rents from residential or commercial property, which are usually taxed as 'profits', and this feature is frequently used in tax planning. The downside, at least for some investors, is that their foreign real estate holdings are geared. Many European pension funds invest directly in domestic real estate without debt, so having to understand the effects of gearing is another challenge that those investors have to come to terms with before venturing overseas.

The REIT entity, which is now available in many countries, is unusual in that it is a tax exempt structure. REITs were created in the United States in 1960 as a publicly listed entity that was not liable for income or capital gains tax as long as 80% of the net income, which would otherwise be taxable, is distributed as a dividend to unit holders. Unit holders pay tax on that dividend in accordance with their normal entitlements. As a result, the income is not taxed twice, once at the entity level and again with the unit holder. Thus, the tax position is the same as if a unit holder owned the whole property, paying tax on the income once. It took over 30 years before the US REIT structure was finessed, enabling its widespread use, but, since the 1990s, their market capitalisation has increased many fold. This encouraged most other developed nations to create their own REIT structures. While all have their own unique features and are designed to work with local corporate taxes, they all have the common feature of tax neutrality as long as most of the net revenue is distributed to unit holders. As a result, the global REIT market has grown to a market capitalisation of over US$1.2 trillion spread across around 40 national markets and has become an excellent tax-efficient means for many investors to secure exposure to commercial real estate globally. It is especially appropriate for households and small institutions, for whom liquidity considerations are usually more important.

The main taxes that investors are seeking to mitigate are income taxes and capital gains tax. The former is normally mitigated by making full use of all allowances, for example, on debt interest and depreciation. It is usually harder, though, to mitigate capital gains taxes, except in the UK, where foreign investors have been exempt – to encourage inward foreign direct investment in general, not just in real estate. Transfer taxes, like the stamp duty land tax (payable in England, Wales and Northern Ireland), also need to be considered. Sometimes, these taxes can be mitigated through using a corporate structure where the sale of units/shares attracts a much lower tax rate. One example is in Belgium, where the transfer tax for real estate is 12.5%. However, this is rarely paid because transactions can be structured as share deals paying just 0.5%. But, even though significant savings can be generated at the time of purchase, owning through a corporate structure has a downside. The special-purpose vehicles created to hold the property can both generate significant administration costs and reduce future flexibility through closing off sale options.

While it is dangerous to generalise, Australia and Canada are generally viewed as high tax locations for most institutions investing internationally. In the case of Canada, increased taxation on foreign capital investing in its real estate has been used as a way to ensure that US investors do not dominate its market. Ironically, in the 2010s, Canadian institutions have become major players in the global real estate market including in the United States, thanks to their abundant wealth of natural resources. The United States itself has also been a difficult market to penetrate for overseas capital if investors seek majority ownership of properties. Until recently, most international capital has effectively been limited to taking minority interests (that is, up to a maximum of 49%) to invest in individual assets because of the Foreign Investment in Real Property Tax Act. This Act is currently being modified, which should make it practicable for foreign capital to own single assets outright. In the meantime, international investors can hold US REITs tax efficiently.

International investors need to be especially wary in respect of tax matters when investing in residential property. The provision of housing is always of interest to politicians. Most housing markets are affected by different tax incentives between the tenures, which can create counterintuitive forces. Owner occupation is generally encouraged in most developed markets. However, in Germany, the tax system encourages private renting more than owner occupation, with a number of people being both tenants and landlords. The role and scale of social housing can also have an important influence on the overall housing market. During the 2000s, large portfolios of social housing were sold by German municipalities, principally to US private equity funds. Those funds expected to profit from their investment through selling apartments to the occupying tenants at a discount to their market value, so the occupiers would immediately enjoy a capital gain. However, this strategy was not successful because most tenants were not interested in becoming home owners; they preferred their current tenure.[5]

Thus, investing internationally in residential property can be more challenging than commercial because of the different ways in which tax and social policy affect local markets. Commercial property tends to attract less political attention, so it is rarely subject to the same degree of market intervention and, as importantly, frequent changes in government policy which affect market behaviour.

Taxation and legal systems are naturally local, resulting from a myriad of institutional forces from the past. They are also subject to significant inertia that does at least gives investors and property professionals a better chance to understand the rules within which they operate. Different tax and legal systems present a significant challenge to global real estate investors, which cannot be avoided. However, learning about a market is a one-off 'cost'. It should encourage global investors to restrict their activity to a manageable number of locations, focussing principally on those markets that have sufficient scale to provide a meaningful pipeline of attractive opportunities. Those locations are likely to be the more transparent and open markets. The nature of, and data on, market transparency are discussed in the next section.

Market transparency

Investment decisions and strategies are heavily dependent on the quality, availability and accessibility of the information that drives the trading process. However, the availability of, and access to, information on the investment characteristics of commercial real estate markets vary greatly from country to country. As outlined above, the process of information generation will reflect the institutional structure of the market concerned. The essence of market transparency is the ability of market participants to access and observe all the information required to understand and participate in property transactions within a stable trading framework. Lack of transparency increases significantly the probability that expectations for investment performance will not be achieved and thus raises the cost of capital destined for a particular economy and investments within it.

The term 'transparency' is used in a variety of contexts including policy making, judicial decision making and corporate governance. Definitions of transparency used by international organisations (such as the Organisation for Economic Co-operation and Development, the World Bank and the International Monetary Fund) vary but, essentially, they come down to all market participants having access to all relevant information and being able to trade on a level playing field. A non-transparent market is one where there is an asymmetry of relevant knowledge or information, placing some participants (or potential participants) to a transaction at a disadvantage. From the perspective of investors, transparency can be characterised as clear unambiguous information on rules and procedures, as well as outcomes from, and accountability for, the decision-making process.

Recognising the importance of transparency and the crude nature of the 'country risk premium' approach adopted by investors in equities and fixed interest securities, JLL (formerly Jones Lang LaSalle) introduced its first Global Real Estate Transparency Index (GRETI) in 1999, covering 22 countries (see Gordon, 2000). The GRETI is compiled from a survey across the global business network of JLL and LaSalle Investment Management. The survey is refreshed every two years and GRETI 2016 represents the ninth edition covering 109 countries.[6]

The survey sets out to determine objectively relative real estate transparency across the world. It is broken into five major categories that address unique and separate factors affecting real estate transparency. These categories are:

- performance measurement;
- market fundamentals;
- governance of listed vehicles;
- regulatory and legal environment; and
- the transaction process.

These categories reflect the range of data and criteria that both investors and occupiers require to make informed decisions when entering a real estate market for the first time. Thus, historic performance data, which spans at least one complete property cycle, enables investors to determine whether a market is likely to deliver the returns they require from that market. Market fundamentals data provide an understanding of the occupational markets in leading metropolitan areas for the main property types. The quality of governance for listed and private vehicles enables a judgement to be made about the risks around investing indirectly. An understanding about the nature of a market's regulatory and legal environment enables investors to be aware of potential operational pitfalls, while access to the market through a transparent transaction process has a significant effect on the ease with which an investor can acquire property as a new player. The structure of the survey, together with the topics included within each category, is shown in Figure 2.2 (see also Appendix 2A for further details on the survey methodology).

Each national market is classified into one of five categories ranging from highly transparent to opaque. The top 15 most transparent markets in GRETI comprise the main English-speaking nations plus some continental European markets (Table 2.1). Australia, Canada, the

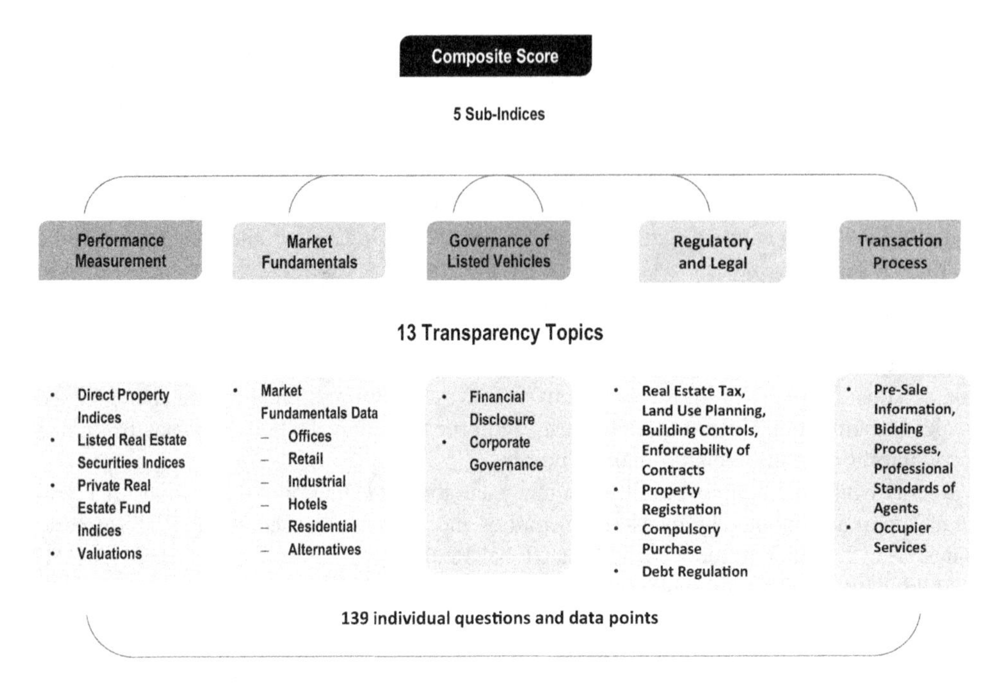

Figure 2.2 Global Real Estate Transparency Index components
Source: JLL, LaSalle Investment Management.

United States and the UK have dominated the rankings since the survey's inception. In fact, the UK has occupied the top spot since 2014, principally because of its excellent monthly performance data and market sensitive valuation services. The full list of countries in the survey and their classification is shown in Appendix 2B.

The dominance of the English-speaking nations merits some explanation. It reflects the higher status that the UK in particular has given to its property profession, whose origins can be traced back to the nineteenth century and the management of country estates for the aristocracy, followed by the land acquisition programmes required for constructing the railways.[7] There is no real equivalent to chartered surveyors in, for example, continental Europe, where, even today, many professionals move into real estate after initially training as engineers or architects. In contrast, surveying courses have been offered in the UK since 1919 and university degree courses since the Second World War. This tradition was exported to Australia and Canada. In the United States, property education has developed differently, with real estate offered as an option within business and finance courses. Both these models have been followed in the rest of the world, but the highest levels of real estate education now tend to be found in business schools, even in the UK. Thus, market transparency is a further reflection of the way in which local institutional frameworks have developed.

Since its inception in 1999, the Transparency Index has evolved and been refined to reflect the changing demands of cross-border investors and corporate occupiers. Specifically, in 2008, new questions were added to embrace the perspective of corporate occupiers relating to occupier service charges and facilities management. Questions concerning debt financing and the frequency and credibility of property valuations were also added.

Table 2.1 The world's most transparent real estate markets, 2016

	Global Rank	*Market*	*Composition score*
Highly transparent	1	United Kingdom	1.24
	2	Australia	1.27
	3	Canada	1.28
	4	United States	1.29
	5	France	1.34
	6	New Zealand	1.45
	7	Netherlands	1.49
	8	Ireland	1.60
	9	Germany	1.65
	10	Finland	1.66
Transparent	11	Singapore	1.82
	12	Sweden	1.82
	13	Poland	1.85
	14	Switzerland	1.86
	15	Hong Kong	1.89

Sources: JLL, LaSalle Investment Management.

In 2010, post the global financial crisis, the existing questions regarding debt financing were substantially revised to reflect more appropriately the key issues of debt transparency, relating to the availability of information on commercial real estate debt and the role of bank regulators in monitoring commercial real estate lending. There were also revisions to questions on the transaction process covering both pre-sale information, and the bidding and negotiating process.

In the 2012 Index, the importance of sustainability in real estate investing was first recognised and a separate index created. In the latest edition, 37 countries are ranked based on the status of financial performance indices for green buildings, green building reporting and certification systems, carbon reporting frameworks, energy consumption benchmarking systems, energy efficiency requirements for new and existing buildings, and green lease clauses. France, Australia, Japan and the UK are the top ranked markets in 2016 measured on sustainability.

Valuation practices are an important component of market transparency and they vary significantly around the world. Despite the RICS being one of the most recognised brands in real estate globally, the Red Book approach to valuations, which most UK professionals know well, is not followed in many parts of the world. Moreover, expectations of appraisers (using their US name) are generally lower than in the UK. Experienced professionals know that reported values normally lag the market principally because valuers put most weight on evidence from completed transactions to reach their conclusions. However, it can be argued that UK valuers are much more prepared to put some weight on a change in current market conditions and on transactions agreed, but not yet completed, than valuers elsewhere. This reflects, at least in part, that UK valuers generally work for firms that also provide other real estate services, such as agency. In some markets, for example in the United States, licensed appraisers are not permitted to operate in this way and solely offer valuation services. As a result, they have much less access to information about current deals in process but not completed.

Valuation practices in Germany are also noteworthy. The German concept of market value, *Verkehrswert*, does not differ materially from International Valuation Standards Council's definition which is adopted in the Red Book. However, in the experience of one of these authors, German valuers require more evidence that a market value has changed to adjust their assessment than does a UK valuer; furthermore, that evidence has to be from completed property transactions, not general financial or economic conditions.

Property valuations have long played an important role in the German financial system, particularly its mortgage market. The *Pfanbrief* market is a means for German banks to finance mortgage loans that meet strict loan-to-value criteria. This has been a highly successful and robust market, well regulated by government, for over one hundred years. Valuations for mortgage purposes are produced under statutory rules and require the valuer to assess a property's value over the life of the loan, not just at the valuation date as in the UK. Thus, the focus is on the long term and valuers are encouraged to disregard temporary market fluctuations within the scope of a 'prudent valuation'. The importance of mortgage valuations with their long-term outlook appears to colour German valuers' approach to market appraisals. As a result, for example, the German MSCI/IPD Index shows less volatility than is observed in other markets.

Real estate professionals working internationally need to be mindful of how valuation practices differ around the world. Even though the formal rules under which valuations are carried out may be very similar, local practice may result in very different outcomes. These differences can impact both the way in markets function, and in the degree to which valuations are 'smoothed'; that is, understate their true volatility.[8]

Low real estate market transparency is often associated with general corruption or the tolerance of conditions under which corrupt practices can flourish. The best known measures for the level of corruption around the world are Transparency International's Corruption Perception Index (CPI) and Bribe Payers Index.[9] Corrupt practices are not overtly measured in GRETI, yet the correlation between it and the CPI is high (0.60) and this has been a consistent feature of the results since the two surveys could be compared (Figure 2.3).

There is also a relationship between transparency and liquidity as measured by the volume of investment transactions relative to a country's GDP. 2016 results are shown in Figure 2.4.

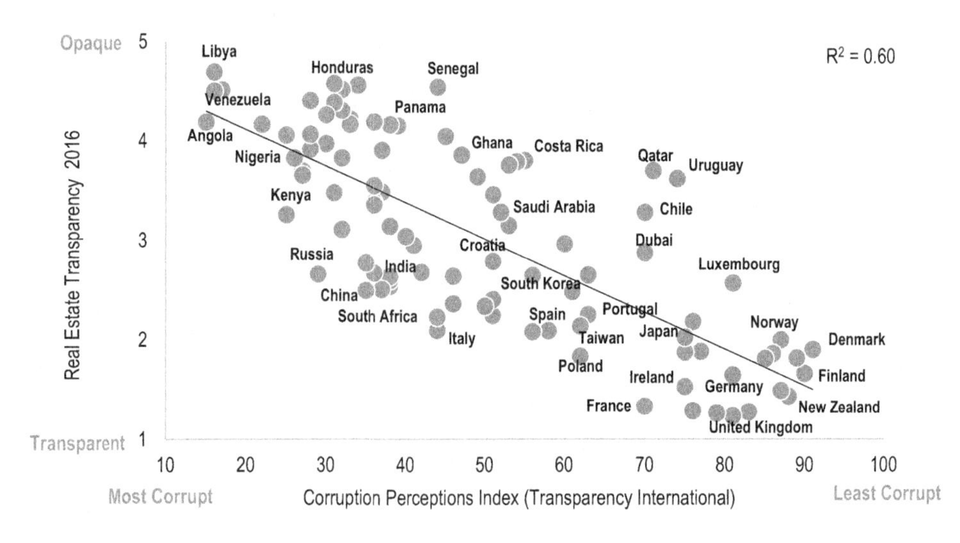

Figure 2.3 Real estate transparency and perceptions of corruption
Sources: JLL, LaSalle Investment Management, Transparency International.

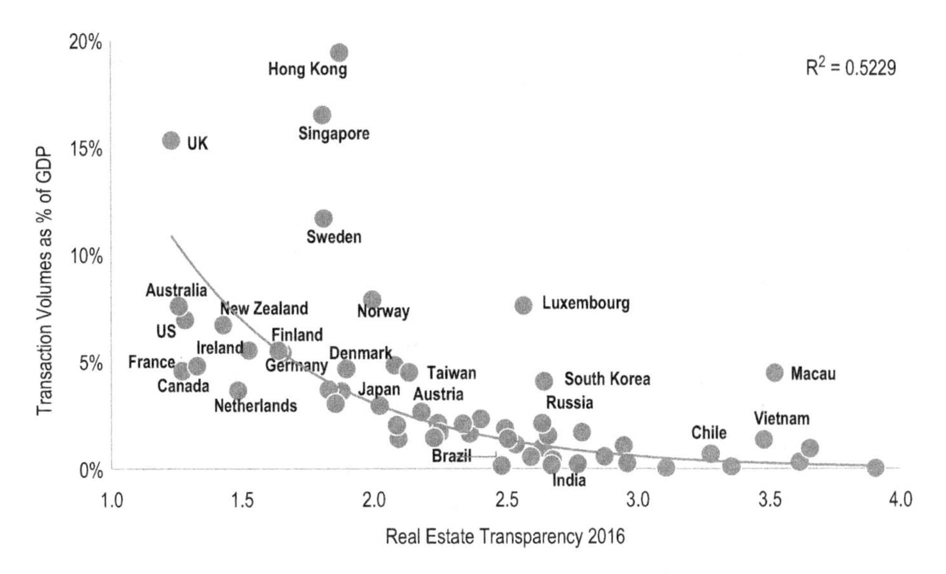

Figure 2.4 Real estate transparency and investment volumes
Note: Based on direct commercial real estate volumes, 2011–2015.
Sources: JLL, LaSalle Investment Management, Oxford Economics.

The correlation is lower than for the relationship with corruption but its non-linear form emphasises that liquidity only starts to rise materially once a market reaches 'transparent' status. This is further emphasised by 75% of all transactions in real estate investments globally occurring in the 10 'highly transparent' markets set out in Table 2.1, which comprises fewer than 10% of the countries in the survey (see GRETI, 2016).

Liquidity and transparency can be viewed as related because a greater volume of transactions results in more comparable evidence for valuers and increased revenue for service providers. These can act as the basis for better data provision generally. Recent research (McAllister and Nanda, 2016) shows that greater foreign investment in a real estate market causes yields to compress. Thus, local property owners can benefit by improving the transparency of their market to attract overseas capital. One example of this is South Africa where the local property owners' association, which included a number of insurance companies, came together to accelerate the creation of an IPD property index for that country. This index has successfully operated since 1995 and South Africa is ranked as a 'transparent' market in GRETI, making it the most highly placed developing economy. However, perceptions of corruption there are high (Figure 2.3) and the country has not, to date, attracted much international capital into its real estate market.

GRETI provides an excellent starting point for investors considering investing internationally. It captures the main elements of a market's institutional framework to permit a broad understanding of its functioning and, when combined with other international measures (for example, sovereign bond ratings) can be used to construct real estate country risk premiums. However, transparency is not the whole story; investors need to be aware of a number of other institutional differences, which can be quite subtle. They are described in the remainder of this chapter. Lease terms are one such factor.

Lease terms

Every country has its own form of lease for commercial real estate, which reflects its institutional history. In some markets, the form of lease is likely to be highly variable, reflected in uniquely negotiated contracts. In other markets, notably much of continental Europe, leases are in a proscribed form set by national law through the Civil Code. In these markets, the parties effectively 'fill in the blanks' in a pre-set contract where the blanks comprise (obviously) the rent, including any concessions, the parties, the start date and the duration. For professionals used to a common law system where every word of a contract can be amended, it can be quite a shock.[10]

Leases around the world vary in two key respects, both of which are crucial to the cash flow generated by a property investment. These are the typical duration of the lease and the proportion of the rent paid by the tenant that the owner can 'bank' as the income return from the investment. In real estate jargon, this latter sum is the 'net operating income'. Most professionals, especially those from the United States, are very familiar with this term, but it is much less familiar to those operating in the markets, such as the UK and Ireland, where tenants traditionally bear the full repairing and insuring costs of the property, in addition to their rental commitment.

Different lease structures are a good example of how institutional frameworks can be a function of power structures within which they have developed, and would be a good subject for specific research. It is noticeable that the UK is one of the few European countries where the landowning class has not experienced a period when its powers were severely constrained and significant redistribution of land occurred outside of the monarchy or aristocracy. This may explain why the UK is widely viewed as the most landlord-friendly real estate market in the world.

International data on these variables are set in Figures 2.5 and 2.6. Typical lease durations are shown in Figure 2.5. The UK has the longest lease terms, even if their duration has reduced significantly since 1990 when 25-year terms were the norm. Lease terms in Asia tend to be shorter than in the rest of the world. However, the average time for which a business occupies commercial floorspace may not be as variable as the difference in lease durations would suggest because leases are extended or renewed. Nonetheless, an investor's cash flow is still rendered less certain because of the greater risk of voids where leases are shorter.

Figure 2.6 shows the difference between gross and net yields for institutional office buildings for most of the major national markets across the globe. The norm is for an investor to bank around 90% of gross income, because the landlord generally carries some responsibility for structural repairs and insurance. The outliers are the UK and United States. The notorious UK full repairing and insuring lease results in owners of British real estate banking the whole rent cheque except for its cost of collection. In the United States, generally the owner not only bears most of the repair and insuring costs but is also responsible for property taxes. As a result, net operating income is typically around 60% of gross rent compared with 99% in the UK.

Other lease terms can have an effect on cash flow; for example, a tenant's alienation rights. Where a property has been acquired because of the tenant's robust credit quality, it is important to establish whether the occupier can transfer the lease to another entity whose covenant is weaker. If so, this can be a major threat to reliability of the cash flow from the asset in the future.

Investors entering a new market should, therefore, be forensic in understanding the local lease terms and their implications for cash flow. They should always seek to establish the

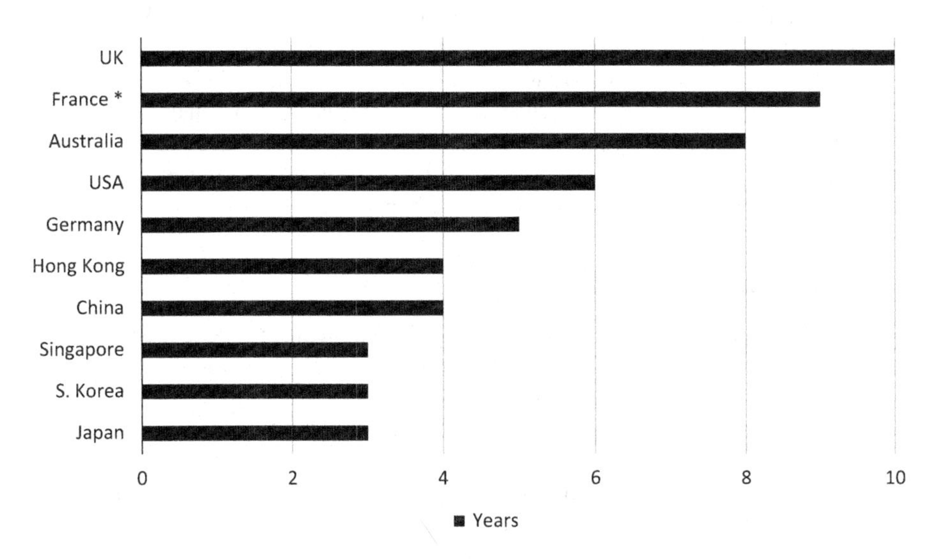

Figure 2.5 Typical duration for office leases in major global markets

Note: Figures quoted do not reflect existence of breaks. Where there are multiple typical lease lengths, the figures quoted are an average.

* Many French leases include tenant only break clauses every 3 years but for a new building a landlord would expect a 6- or 9-year term certain.

Source: JLLReal Estate Standards Index 2012.

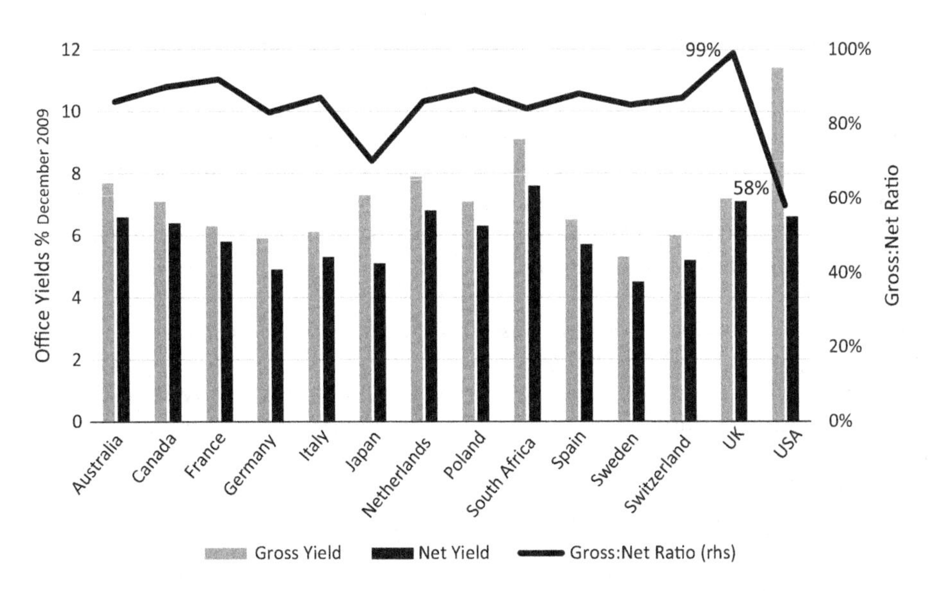

Figure 2.6 The margin between gross and net yields for offices – net operating income

Source: Investment Property Databank Multinational Index.

amount of net operating income that a property will deliver and how that figure is expected to fluctuate, rather than seeking to focus on the gross rent paid by tenants.

But knowledge of a market's relative transparency and the local lease terms are not sufficient for successful international property investing. Investors need to have an understanding of how markets are controlled and regulated, particularly in respect of development. These factors play an important role in affecting levels of land value, the amount of vacancy in office markets and even the structure of development industries.

The effect of planning systems on real estate markets

Virtually every developed country controls property development to some extent. In this section, the different ways in which some countries regulate land use are reviewed and their consequences for real estate investors examined.

Controls on property development are justified on either or both of two policy grounds:

- public health issues, because adjoining land uses can be incompatible, such as industry producing noxious fumes next to residential; and
- the economic concept of 'externalities', where the decisions of property owners in respect of their ownership can have adverse consequences for adjoining owners and occupiers but the cost of those consequences are not factored into the decision.

While many economists would regard the two points as essentially the same, most legal systems view them differently, with the state having a much longer history of controlling development that can have an adverse effect on public health; for example insanitary housing.

In the United States, where land use controls tend to be relatively light, the public health principle is used to justify land zoning to prevent incompatible uses locating close to one another. Because the restrictions are based on public health, the states are able to limit property rights, without compensation, which would otherwise be unconstitutional. The State of Texas, for example, has a system for zoning land but, by the standards of the rest of the world, it is permissive and has little, if any, effect on restricting land supply.

A more relaxed attitude to property development is clearly easier where land is plentiful, as is the case in much of the United States. Elsewhere, and especially in Europe where population densities tend to be higher, land use controls are generally stricter. As a result, land supply for all forms of urban development tends to be restricted because, generally, rural land is protected. This can be justified on three grounds:

- Once rural land is converted to an urban use, it is extremely expensive to reverse the use, so it is not a process to sanction lightly.
- Low-density urban sprawl can create its own externalities, particularly in respect of transport and sustainability issues, while higher-density development can better support mass transit systems.
- Most nations still wish to maximise their own domestic food production for security reasons, so do not wish to lose good agricultural land.

Each developed country has created its own institutional framework for land use planning that reflects both its own traditions in respect of controls on private sector activity and its confidence in the ability of public sector bodies to be efficient economic actors. These are heavily influenced by a nation's political history and ideology. Planning systems comprise a combination of 'plan making' that defines expected changes of use and an administrative apparatus for approving new developments. In some countries (for example Germany), detailed approved plans largely decide development outcomes. In the UK, while there are approved plans, they are often out of date, and the local politicians deciding a planning application have considerable discretion. As a result, the process tends to be less predictable and is prone to delays. The system in the United States, while varying from state to state, is principally plan based with zoning rules determining the form of development. However, getting consents has become progressively more time consuming since the 1970s, as neighbourhood groups and other stakeholders need to be consulted.[11]

Knowledge about the framework for land use decisions, however, may not be sufficient to understand how a system works in practice and the effect on its land market. The general attitude of decision makers towards development is vital. Systems which are managed to encourage development activity have very different effects on their land market than those operated to limit activity, even though the formal legal framework may be very similar. This is best illustrated by comparing the UK with the Netherlands. As is demonstrated below, Britain has the highest levels of land value in Europe while Dutch land values are much lower, yet these countries have similar population densities, both overall and in their most dense regions.

In the UK, the forces ranged against new development are very strong, with Green Belt policies, which limit the size of urban areas, having strong popular support, especially in Southern England where demand for housing is greatest. The Campaign for the Preservation of Rural England is a very successful charity and pressure group that opposes virtually all greenfield development. As a result, the local opposition to most developments is vocal and it is a challenge for local politicians (who seek re-election) to resist 'nimbyism',[12] especially as the immediate community receives little financial benefit from most schemes.

In contrast, in the Netherlands, land is regarded as a 'utility' to be made available as demand requires, just like water, gas and electricity (Needham, 2007). The Dutch are the world's leading experts at land reclamation, actually 'making' land. The pro-development approach has ensured that under-supply pressures have not built up and caused land values to rise disproportionately. This is illustrated by the level of office values in the UK provincial cities of Birmingham, Manchester, Edinburgh, Glasgow, Bristol and Leeds all exceeding the level of prime office values in Amsterdam, while values in Rotterdam, The Hague and Utrecht are less than half that of their UK counterparts.[13]

Differing attitudes to land and property development can have other consequences for markets. Land is not universally regarded as real estate that can be traded freely by private owners, as is the case in the UK and United States. In some emerging markets, the registration of land ownership rights may be embryonic, so that it can be difficult to identify the true beneficial owner or to untangle the web of interests claimed in a plot subject to multiple user rights. Moreover, some land, particularly mountains and forests, can be regarded as having 'sacred status', even though the land may not be formally protected by law. On a smaller scale, it is common for families to regard their ancestral land and home as inalienable and to be held in perpetuity.[14]

The way in which land use controls operate has a profound effect on land values and real estate markets. Three practical effects are reported on below:

- differing levels of vacancy rates in office markets;
- impacts on the level of land values; and
- effects on the structure of local development industries.

These are not claimed to be the only effects but are all supported by academic literature.

The evolution of average office vacancy rates for the Americas, Asia-Pacific and Europe are shown in Figure 2.7. This figure clearly demonstrates that the markets in America operate at a consistently higher vacancy level than in Europe and Asia and this conclusion is confirmed by Sanderson *et al.* (2006). The data for individual markets in Figure 2.8 add colour to this, with the tightest American markets at the 10% level while most European and Asian markets are below this level with a number less than 5%, despite some outliers. This structural difference is further reinforced by Figure 2.9, which shows the sub-markets JLL identified as showing 'severe shortages' at the end of 2015. In Europe and Asia, these markets have a vacancy rate of 5% or less, while all the ones in the United States are in the 6–10% range.

Analysis of the causes for this marked difference in regional office markets requires further research. Sanderson *et al.* (2006) focus on identifying the natural vacancy rates for a variety of cities rather than seeking to identify the reasons why the European and American markets behave so differently. Investors in North American real estate need to be aware that office markets there operate at higher natural vacancy rates than in Europe and much of Asia. Greater potential void costs need to be reflected in cash flows, both through an allowance for permanent structural vacancy (that is, the building is never assumed to be more than, say, 95% leased), as well as extra planned capital expenditure to ensure that the property remains attractive to occupiers in a highly competitive market.

A further example of the influence of planning systems on markets is provided by the level of prime warehouse rents across Europe. These are shown in Figure 2.10 and range from €42/square metre in Lisbon to €161/square metre in London. While the former is undoubtedly a remote European warehouse location, can London be regarded as the best? It is noticeable that its rental level is over three times greater than prime warehouse rents around Paris, yet both cities have similar levels of population and income per head.

Arguably the best warehouse locations in Europe are either close to the continental North Sea ports of Rotterdam and Hamburg, or Frankfurt, where the largest population can be

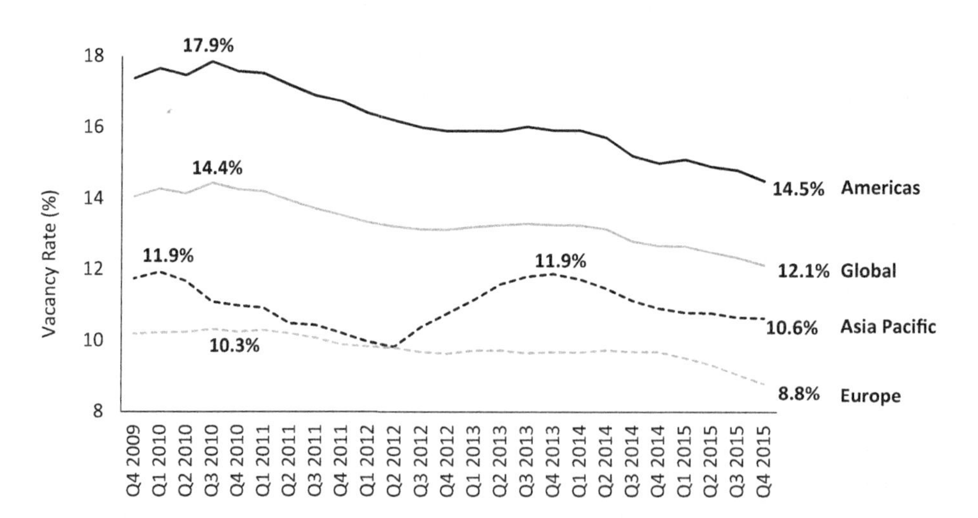

Figure 2.7 Global and regional office vacancy rates, 2009–2015
Source: JLL, 2016.

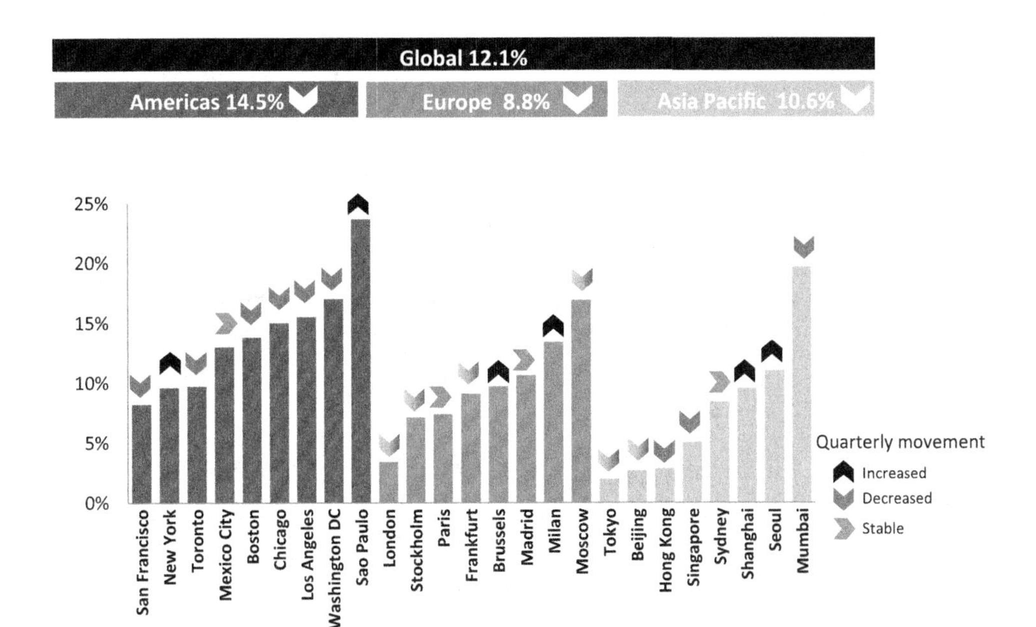

Figure 2.8 Office vacancy rates in major cities, fourth quarter 2015
Source: JLL, 2016.

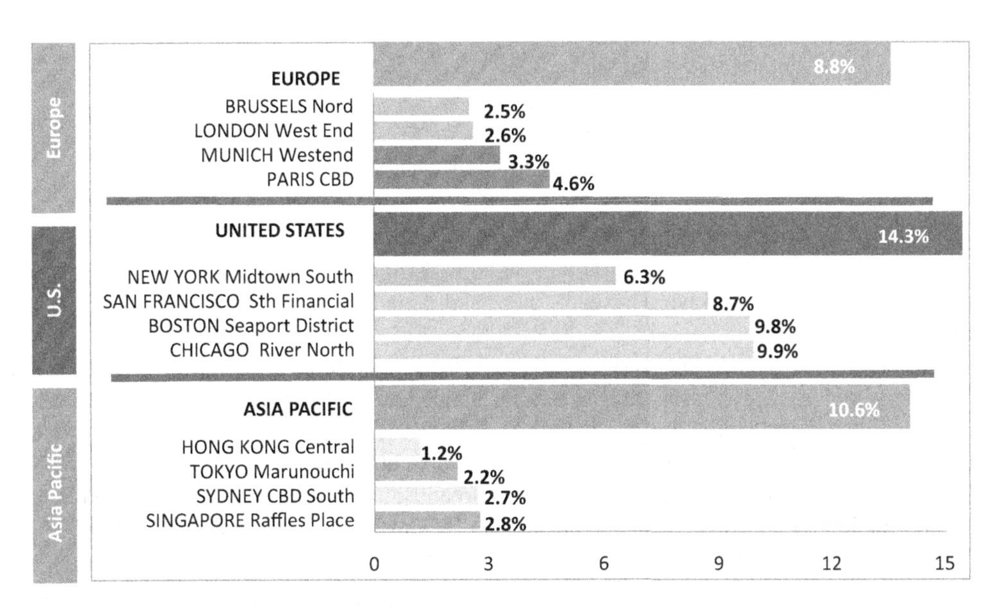

Figure 2.9 Vacancy rates in markets with 'severe shortages', fourth quarter 2015
Source: JLL, 2016.

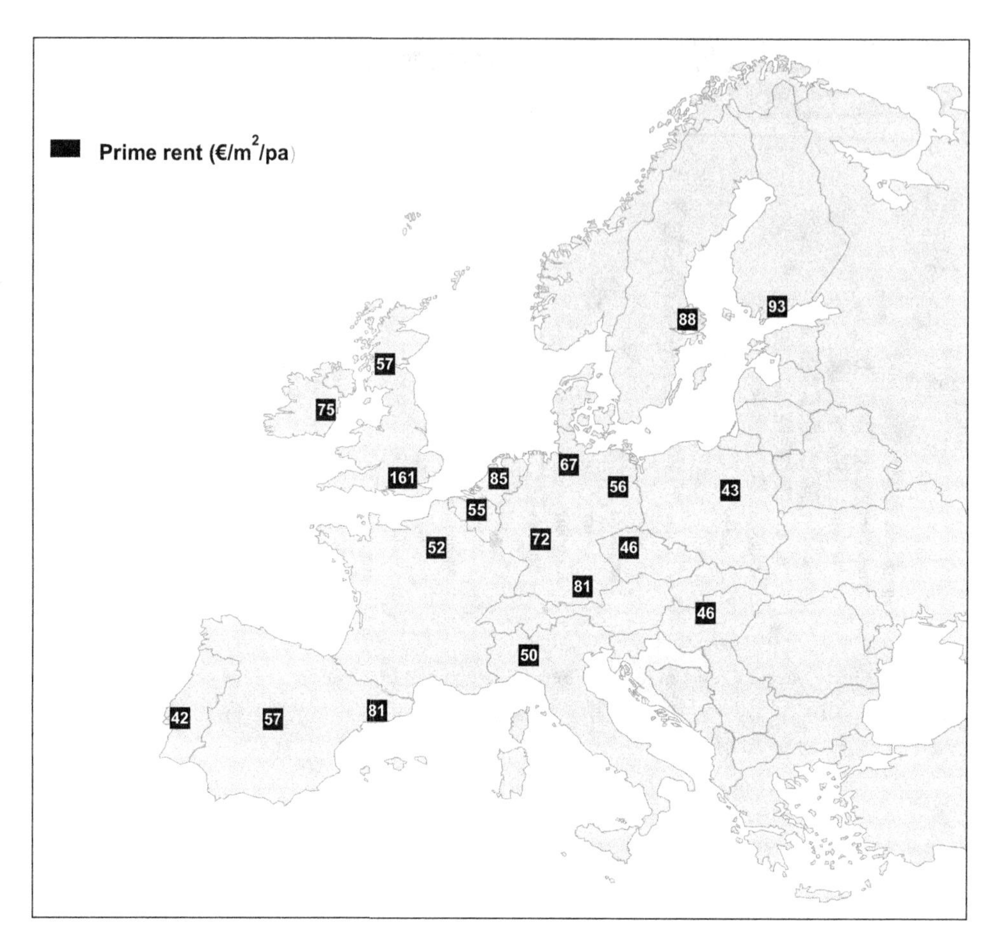

Figure 2.10 Prime warehouse rents across Europe, fourth quarter 2015
Source: JLL, 2016.

reached in a single day's drive. However, the rental pattern shown in Figure 2.10 does not support this.

So what does explain the levels of warehouse rents across Europe? Despite the large size of modern logistic warehouses, they are not a major land use at a city level. The largest urban land use is residential and the value of all other uses is affected by the price of land for housing. Thus, warehousing has to compete against other uses, particularly residential. The tight constraint put on land availability by Green Belt policies causes warehouse rents around London's Heathrow Airport to be so high. The work of Cheshire and Hilber (2008; Cheshire *et al.*, 2014; Hilber and Vermeulen, 2015) consistently shows that land use regulation in the UK has increased the cost for all types of space, both within the country (with London's West End being the most extreme) and relative to other European countries.

A further effect is identified by Ball (2013). His analysis shows that UK housebuilding is much more oligopolistic than in the United States and Australia, with the largest firms having a bigger market share than in any of the other markets. While this could be due to the smaller scale of the UK relative to his comparator markets, Ball believes that 'land shortages and the nature of the UK planning system encourage concentration and make it difficult for both new entrants and movement up the size hierarchy.'[15] The conclusion that the UK housebuilding industry is oligopolistic is also expressed by a number of experts who gave evidence at a recent parliamentary inquiry (House of Lords, 2016).

This phenomenon is probably caused by the way in which development land is identified through the planning process. While land is often allocated in a local plan, this usually occurs after a number of sites have been proposed by their owners as suitable to provide the number of homes that the planners estimate is required. This competitive process is complex and capricious, so most landowners enter into a partnership with a housebuilder to enable their site to be considered. If successful, the housebuilder will then acquire the land at a discounted price, normally 70–80% of its market value with planning permission for residential development, to reflect a return for their risk. This process makes it very hard for small developers to compete and get access to raw land, so reinforcing the oligopolistic nature of the market, as Ball describes.

Planning controls affect property markets in a variety of ways and every system has its own idiosyncrasies. This section has provided some examples of how markets can be affected differentially. The explanations for the differences may be more complex than has sometimes been portrayed but that is because rigorous analysis has still to be carried out, emphasising the rich field of comparative studies waiting to be researched. The key point is that there are differences that result from land use controls and international real estate investors need to be prepared for them.

The terms of trade between investors and developers

Development activity occurs in every market within its own institutional framework. A good illustration of the contrasting approaches is provided by Squires and Heurkens (2015), where experts from 11 countries describe the way in which development takes place in their markets. The countries covered range from the highly developed (United States, UK, Netherlands and Australia) to the newer markets of Hong Kong, Chile and the Gulf States plus the developing markets of China, Ghana and India. The emphasis is primarily on planning and macro outcomes rather than focussing on detailed financial arrangements but the book is a model for promoting the study of international real estate.

Development is normally carried out by local professionals because it requires a very detailed understanding of local laws and practices, as well as a deep network of professionals skilled in all the different technical disciplines required for completing a successful project. International developers are rare[16] and are mainly focussed on specialist property types, such as large-scale retail centres or logistic warehouses, where the occupiers tend also to be international. Even then, they may well partner with local players particularly to secure land. Thus, REITs like Unibail, Simon and Westfield develop shopping centres internationally, while ProLogis and SEGRO plc have built up portfolios of warehouses globally. The managers of large opportunity funds, like Blackstone, also participate in developments but normally by partnering with a local operator; they rarely act as the developers themselves.

The main emphasis in this section is narrow, focussing solely on the different ways in which institutional investors provide equity capital to developers, so they can finance an individual project and possibly retain ownership of the completed asset. The project in this context is typically a speculative office development for which an occupier (or occupiers) needs to be found, ideally before practical completion but, if not, as soon as possible after the building is finished. Once let, the investor may retain the property in its portfolio or choose to sell to capture a capital gain.

Once planning permission and other consents have been granted, speculative development comprises two main risks, each of which has a number of dimensions.[17] These are:

- construction: the risks are the possibility of cost and time overruns, plus that the completed building is constructed to the expected quality; and
- leasing: the risks are that the space is let for the expected duration on the anticipated terms at the budgeted rent, including incentives, within the expected time frame and to businesses of appropriate credit quality.

The agreement between investor and developer is designed to determine who bears these risks and who benefits, should the outcome exceed expectations. The typical development agreement involves a sharing of these risks, with the developer as well as the investor providing equity capital to ensure that their interests are aligned as much as possible. Usually the developer provides 5–10% of the total equity required, depending on the scale of the developer's business. This may be through not being reimbursed for the cost of the land until the project completes, with the investor paying for all construction works.

A major part of the agreement is devoted to how profits and losses are shared. If the completed investment is to be sold, that can simplify matters as each party then takes pre-allocated shares possibly with the investor receiving a minimum return on capital invested, with any surplus weighted towards the developer. Where the investor is retaining the completed development, the developer may receive an extra return if the property is let at a rent in excess of the budgeted level. If the development does not proceed as originally envisaged, the losses are shared between the parties, generally in line with the proportions of their equity capital.

There are two markets where these general risk-sharing terms of trade are not followed. In the UK, at times when institutional investors are keen to finance development, for example, during the mid-1980s and in 2005/06, developments are financed through a 'profit erosion' model. The key feature of this model is that the maximum loss the developer can bear in the deal is their projected profit only. However, the developer still expects to benefit from overage payments if the property lets at a higher rent than expected and if the yield on exit is lower than forecast, so increasing the capital value. As a result, the investor bears a disproportionate share of the losses if, for example, the property fails to let on the budgeted terms or if there are construction cost overruns.

In contrast, the typical terms for office development in France are much more attractive to the investor. There, developers commit to constructing a new building (to an agreed specification by a set date) for a fixed price to be paid on completion; that is, the developer takes on all the construction risk in exchange only for the investor providing a bank guarantee for the purchase price. Moreover, the developer normally provides a rent guarantee of 18–36 months after completion, if the building does not become fully income producing within that period. The investor, therefore, takes on the leasing risk only and, even there, a part is shared with the developer. But the big difference is that if rents rise, the investor enjoys all the benefits, because the developer does not receive any overage. This provides a very obvious illustration of the influence of power relationships within institutional structures. Investors in France achieve their objectives at the expense of developers relative to other markets, yet the latter appear to be content with the arrangement.[18]

Table 2.2 Terms of trade between investors and developers: some examples

Key terms	*Standard JV*	*UK*[a]	*France*
Name	Equity/profit share	'Profit erosion'	'VEFA'[b]
Investor price	Variable	Notionally fixed	Fixed
Developer overage	Yes	Yes	No
Developer capital	Yes, e.g. 10%	None	Land and construction
Developer maximum loss	Equity stake	Zero	Rent guarantee

a Not universal but common at market peaks.
b *Vente en l'état futur d'achèvement.*

This form of contract is known as a *vente en l'état futur d'achèvement* and it makes financing development in France a much more attractive proposition than elsewhere, but particularly in the UK, because investors can take on the risk they are best able to underwrite – leasing – and not have to share the upside with the developer. A comparison of the three models is set out in Table 2.2.

Why do these different models occur? There is no explanation in academic literature of which the authors are aware but we believe the answer comes from the way the respective planning and development processes operate. In France, the public sector frequently plays a major role in urban regeneration through carrying out the site assembly function. They then offer individual sites to the market with a planning brief. Crucially, bids are invited on the basis both of price and design, so what is to be developed is as important as the financial offer. As a result, the main bidders are construction firms (for example, Bouygues), which are primarily seeking a return from their building expertise and are content for the investor to take the leasing risk.

In the UK, the main skill for developers is in site assembly and securing planning permission, not in construction, so their business model is wholly different. Moreover, when institutional investors are especially keen to invest in real estate, at times when prices are rising sharply and there is keen competition for existing assets, securing a new property through financing development is a more certain way to acquire assets than bidding aggressively for standing investments. Thus, developers are able to exploit this extra demand to reduce the risks they carry.

This area is ripe for further comparative research. The French model (in the authors' experience) is unique to France. In most countries, the risks are shared in a manner similar to the typical joint venture. Investors operating internationally need to be aware that the terms of trade between developer and investor can vary significantly and focus on financing development projects in markets where the basis of risk sharing is reasonable. Elsewhere, development projects should be approached with great caution.

Summary and conclusion

The history of global real estate investing is quite short but it is increasingly accepted by pension funds, insurance companies and sovereign wealth funds as an appropriate component of a multi-asset portfolio. The risk with the rapid move to global is that the essentially local elements of real estate are overlooked. Each location has its own unique institutional framework within which its real estate market operates and that framework is a function of its history, particularly of its political economy. International investors must always be mindful of those frameworks and the precise nature of the property rights on offer. Frequently, tenure similar to freehold title is available, but not always (for example in China), so investors need to study each new market carefully.

It is not possible within a single chapter to cover comprehensively the institutional frameworks for even the major real estate markets of the world. Instead, the focus has been on specific features that have a material effect on the way in which markets function. These features are on the supply side of the equation and the specific characteristics focussed on are:

- tax and legal;
- market transparency;
- lease terms;
- planning and land use controls; and
- terms of trade between investors and developers.

The academic literature reviewed in the chapter provides an important interpretative context within which to make judgements about the potential market impacts associated with the specific features examined, some of which have not been analysed before. The literature highlights the importance of institutional structures and the constraints they place on the behaviour of market actors. It has also revealed how power relationships can shape institutional structures and how market practices, even redundant ones, can persist over time. Moreover, it provides a basic framework from which to begin to examine processes of institutional change and their origins.

Market transparency is a key characteristic and the JLL GRETI is recognised as a very helpful tool for understanding property markets internationally. Moreover, it is no coincidence that 75% of all real estate transactions take place in the 10 markets classified in GRETI as 'highly transparent' because investors can be much more confident that they know how those markets operate; and increased capital flows promote greater market transparency, so generating a virtuous circle as more liquidity is attracted.

Market transparency, however, is not sufficient for understanding the different nature of markets. Lease terms determine the cash flow from a real estate investment, both its duration and predictability. Each market has its own form of lease: a key issue is who pays for a property's upkeep and insurance. UK investors are used to the tenant bearing all the costs but this is exceptional and, in most markets, the landlord spends 10–20% of the gross rent on repairs and the like. New investors must, therefore, ascertain the level of net operating income that a property will deliver rather than focussing on the gross rent roll.

Planning and land use controls are exercised in different ways around the world and they have an impact on markets in a number of ways. Markets where land use controls are tight tend to operate with lower vacancy rates and have higher land values. In special circumstances, the same controls may also influence the terms of trade between developers and investors. Action by planners can affect the role a developer has to play in the process: if 'oven-ready' development sites are offered to the market, developers can concentrate on building the project. Where a developer's main focus is on site assembly and securing planning approval, the construction process is likely to be tendered to specialist builders and the developer expects to benefit from the increase in capital value created, rather than construction profits.

All these aspects relate to a market's institutional framework. There are, no doubt, other characteristics that can have important effects on a market's operations in addition to the ones identified in this chapter. The whole area of institutional frameworks is ripe for further research, which will benefit all global real estate investors as they navigate the growing number of markets that are open for their business.

Appendix 2A: Global Real Estate Transparency Index 2016 – methodology

Survey questions have been developed for each of the five main categories (performance measurement, market fundamentals, governance of listed vehicles, regulatory & legal environment, and transaction process) under 13 different topics, (Figure 2.2). The questions have a five-choice answer (1–5); answering '1' for a question means the market is highly transparent for that question; an answer of '5' corresponds to an opaque market. Unless specified, the survey is based on conditions in the principal city of each country. The exceptions are in Russia, India and China, where the survey differentiates between primary, secondary and tertiary cities (and in Brazil between primary and secondary).

The Composite Transparency Index is compiled from the weighted scores from the 133 questions. These include questions from the perspective both of domestic and non-domestic owners and corporate occupiers. Sub-index scores for each of the five transparency categories are calculated from the average scores of the relevant questions.

The Composite Transparency Index scores range on a scale from 1.00 to 5.00. A country or market with a perfect 1.00 score has total real estate transparency; a country or market with a 5.00 score has total real estate opacity. Countries/markets are assigned to one of five transparency tiers shown in Table 2A.1 (see www.jll.com/GRETI for further details).

Table 2A.1 Transparency tiers in the Composite Transparency Index

Tier	*Total composite score*
1: highly transparent	1.00–1.74
2: transparent	1.75–2.49
3: semi-transparent	2.50–3.49
4: low-transparency	3.50–4.49
5: opaque	4.50–5.00

Appendix 2B: Global Real Estate Transparency Index 2016 – scores for 109 countries

Transparency level	*2016 composite rank*	*Market*	*2016 composite score*	*Transparency level*	*2016 composite rank*	*Market*	*2016 composite score*
High	1	United Kingdom	1.24	Semi	56	Argentina	3.12
	2	Australia	1.27		57	Zambia	3.14
	3	Canada	1.28		58	Mauritius	3.16
	4	United States	1.29		59	UAE – Abu Dhabi	3.24
	5	France	1.34		60	Cayman Islands	3.25
	6	New Zealand	1.45		61	Kenya	3.27
	7	Netherlands	1.49		62	Chile	3.28
	8	Ireland	1.60		63	Saudi Arabia	3.28
	9	Germany	1.65		64	Peru	3.36
	10	Finland	1.66		65	Egypt	3.39
Transparent	11	Singapore	1.82		66	China – Tier 3	3.40
	12	Sweden	1.82		67	Bahrain	3.46
	13	Poland	1.85	Low	68	Vietnam	3.49
	14	Switzerland	1.86		69	Sri Lanka	3.49
	15	Hong Kong	1.89		70	Macau	3.52
	16	Belgium	1.90		71	Morocco	3.55
	17	Denmark	1.92		72	Uruguay	3.62
	18	Norway	2.00		73	Kuwait	3.64
	19	Japan	2.03		74	Qatar	3.64
	20	Czech Republic	2.10		75	Ukraine	3.66
	21	Italy	2.10		76	Puerto Rico	3.68
	22	Spain	2.11		77	Iran	3.70
	23	Taiwan	2.14		78	Russia – Tier3	3.73
	24	Austria	2.18		79	Jordan	3.75
	25	South Africa	2.23		80	Rwanda	3.79
	26	Hungary	2.26		81	Costa Rica	3.80
	27	Portugal	2.26		82	Bahamas	3.82
	28	Malaysia	2.35		83	Nigeria	3.82
	29	Slovakia	2.37		84	Ecuador	3.83
	30	Romania	2.38		85	Ghana	3.86

Semi	31	Israel	2.49		86	Colombia	3.91
	32	Mexico	2.51		87	Kazakhstan	3.92
	33	China – Tier 1	2.52		88	Pakistan	3.97
	34	Brazil – Tier 1	2.55	Opaque	89	Oman	4.04
	35	Luxembourg	2.58		90	Uganda	4.05
	36	India – Tier 1	2.61		91	Lebanon	4.06
	37	Greece	2.65		92	Panama	4.15
	38	Thailand	2.65		93	Tunisia	4.16
	39	India – Tier 2	2.65		94	Ethiopia	4.16
	40	South Korea	2.66		95	Myanmar	4.17
	41	Botswana	2.66		96	Algeria	4.19
	42	Russia – Tier 1	2.67		97	Angola	4.19
	43	Brazil – Tier 2	2.68		98	Dominican Republic	4.22
	44	Turkey	2.69		99	Tanzania	4.33
	45	Indonesia	2.69		100	Belarus	4.30
	46	Philippines	2.78		101	Mozambique	4.39
	47	Croatia	2.80		102	Guatemala	4.41
	48	UAE – Dubai	2.88		103	Iraq	4.50
	49	China – Tier 1.5	2.90		104	Ivory Coast	4.51
	50	Bulgaria	2.96		105	Venezuela	4.52
	51	Slovenia	2.97		106	Senegal	4.54
	52	India – Tier 3	3.00		107	Djibouti	4.56
	53	Serbia	3.04		108	Honduras	4.58
	54	Russia – Tier 2	3.09		109	Libya	4.69
	55	China – Tier 2	3.10				

Source: JLL, LaSalle Investment Management.

Notes

1. One of the authors experienced this first hand when he joined LaSalle in London (then CIN LaSalle) in June 1997 as European Research Director and was immediately asked to report on the prospects for the Paris office market. The result was an early example of a global property fund with an American manager attracting capital from a Far Eastern sovereign wealth fund, a Dutch pension fund, a German bank and an American endowment, to invest in Parisian offices.
2. In China, tenure comprises new leases/land use rights from the local government, not freeholds, with a term of up to 70 years for residential properties, 50 years for industrial usage and 40 years for commercial development.
3. Transactions should be interpreted widely in this context to include not just sales and purchases but also leasing, valuations, planning/zoning decisions, development activity, taxes and legal structures; in fact, all the ways in which real estate market participants interact.
4. See Thompson (1968).
5. See also Wellner *et al.* (2015), where different models for social housing are reviewed.
6. The survey is distributed to the global network of business leaders and researchers across JLL and LaSalle, who work together to provide the data for their respective countries. Regional coordinators act as point persons to ensure objectivity and rigour. A global benchmarking process is overlaid to ensure that the questions are interpreted consistently by all participants. Accounting, finance and legal experts are consulted on some technical questions to supplement the collective real estate knowledge.
7. See Thompson *op. cit.*
8. See, for example, Key and Marcato (2007).
9. See Transparency International, Corruption Perceptions Index 2017: www.transparency.org/news/feature/corruption_perceptions_index_2017?gclid=CjwKCAjw8O7bBRB0EiwAfbrTh9mAuXu9ILjclIhv13TUsqOXvLuvP2PyZHdbGP5Bkgs__Uh6XskPRoC8lIQAvD_BwE.
10. This also applies to sale and purchase agreements where a notary has to be involved. Usually the state reserves a right of pre-emption in case it wishes to take over the transaction, although this is very rarely exercised. It does, however, extend the transaction process.
11. See chapter on the United States by Peiser and Hamilton in Squires and Heurkens (2015).
12. This is an acronym for 'not in my back yard'. In the United States, the acronym 'BANANA' has come into use – 'build absolutely nothing anywhere near anybody' – which shows that anti-development sentiments are not confined to the UK.
13. Based on JLL prime capital values for offices in Q4 2015: the UK provincial average was £6,260/square metre, compared with £5,353/square metre in Amsterdam and £2,634/square metre average for the smaller centres of the Randstad.
14. See, generally, Denman and Prodano (1972) on different attitudes to land ownership.
15. Ball (2013), p. 201.
16. A notable exception is the US firm Hines, which has developed office buildings around the world. Its approach is to hire the best local talent in each market. That talent is attracted by the ability of Hines to finance its projects through its deep network of investors.
17. Institutional investors generally do not commit to finance development projects until all ownership rights and the main regulatory approvals, notably planning, have been secured, which is the general presumption in this section.
18. These differences in market practice between the UK and France provide multiple opportunities for empirical research; for example, their effect on construction costs and elasticity of supply.

References

Archer, W. and Ling, D. (1997) The three dimensions of real estate markets: linking space, capital and property markets, *Real Estate Finance*, 14, 7–14.

Arthur, W. (1994) *Increasing returns and path dependence in the economy*, University of Michigan Press, Ann Arbor, MI.

Ball, M. (2013) Spatial regulation and international differences in the housebuilding industries, *Journal of Property Research*, 30(3), 189–204.

Bao, H. and Feng, L. (2014) Land market in Beijing: goldmine or landmine? *Journal of Real Estate Practice and Education*, 17(1), 79–86.

Casson, M. (1990) *Enterprise and competitiveness: a systems view of international business*, Clarendon Press, Oxford.

Casson, M. (1995) *Information and economic organisation*, Department of Economics, Discussion Papers in Economics Series A, No. 317, University of Reading, Reading.

Cheshire, P. and Hilber, C. (2008) Office space supply restrictions in Britain: the political economy of market revenge, *Economic Journal*, 118(529), F185–F221.

Cheshire, P., Hilber, C. and Kaplanis, I. (2014) Land use productivity – land matters: evidence from a UK supermarket chain, *Journal of Economic Geography*, 15(1), 43–73.

Coase, R. H. (1972) Industrial organization: a proposal for research, pp. 59–73 in Fuchs, V.R., *Policy issues and research opportunities in industrial organization*, National Bureau of Economic Research; distributed by Columbia University Press, New York, NY.

Coase, R. H. (1984) The new institutional economics, *Journal of Institutional and Theoretical Economics* 140, 229–31.

D'Arcy, E. (2009) The evolution of institutional arrangements to support the internationalisation of real estate involvements: some evidence from Europe, *Journal of European Real Estate Research*, 2(3), 280–93.

David, P.A. (2000) Path dependence, its critics and the quest for historical economics, pp. 15–40 in Garroute, P. and Ioannides, S., *Evolution and path dependence in economics ideas: past and present*, Edward Elgar, Cheltenham.

Denman, D. and Prodano, S. (1972) *An introduction to proprietary land use analysis*, George Allen & Unwin, London.

Eggertsson, T. (1990) *Economic behaviour and institutions*, Cambridge University Press, Cambridge.

Ely, R. and Wehrwein, G. (1940) *Land economics*, Macmillan Company, New York, NY.

Gordon, J. N. (2000) Real estate transparency, Working Paper no. 605, Wharton School, University of Pennsylvania, Philadelphia, PA, available at: http://realestate.wharton.upenn.edu/working-papers/real-estate-transparency.

Hilber, C. and Vermeulen, W. (2015) The impact of supply constraints on house prices in England, *Economic Journal*, 126(591), 358–405.

Hodgson, G. M. (1994) The return of institutional economics', pp. 58–76 in Smelser, N. J. and Swedberg, R., *The handbook of economic sociology*, Russell Sage Foundation, Princeton, NJ.

House of Lords (2016) *Building more homes*, Select Committee on Economic Affairs, 1st Report of Session 2016–17, HL Paper 20, Stationery Office, London.

Keogh, G and D'Arcy, E (1994) Market maturity and property market behaviour: a European comparison of mature and emergent markets, *Journal of Property Research*, 11(3), 215–35.

Keogh, G. and D'Arcy, E. (1999) Property market efficiency: an institutional economics perspective, *Urban Studies* 36(13), 2401–14.

Key, T. and Marcato, G. (2007) *Index smoothing and the volatility of UK commercial property*, Investment Property Forum, London.

Lizieri, C. Reinert, J. and Baum, A. (2011) *Who owns the City 2011: change and global ownership of City of London Offices*, Research Report, Department of Land Economy, University of Cambridge, Cambridge.

McAllister, P. and Nanda, A. (2016) Do foreign buyers compress office real estate cap rates? *Journal of Real Estate Research*, 38(4), 569–94.

Mahoney, J. (2000) Path dependence in historical sociology, *Theory and Society*, 29, 507–48.

Needham, B. (2007) *Dutch land use planning: planning and managing land-use in the Netherlands, the principles and the practice*, Sdu Uitegevers, The Hague.

North, D. (1990) *Institutions, institutional change and economic performance*, Cambridge University Press, Cambridge.

Samuels, W. (1995) The present state of institutional economics, *Cambridge Journal of Economics* 19, 569–90.

Sanderson, B., Farrelly, K. and Thoday C. (2006) Natural vacancy rates in global office markets, *Journal of Property Investment and Finance*, 24, 490–520.

Squires, G. and Heurkens, E. (Eds.) (2015) *International approaches to real estate development*, Routledge, Abingdon.

Thompson, F. (1968) *Chartered surveyors*, Routledge and Kegan Paul, London.

Turvey, R. (1957) *The economics of real property*, Geo. Allen & Unwin, London.

Wellner, K., van Gool, R. and Geurts, T. (2015) Lessons learned from thirteen years of international real estate study abroad hosted by universities in the US, the Netherlands and Germany, *Journal of Real Estate Practice and& Education*, 18, 117–40.

3 Regulation of managers and investment vehicles

Bertram I. Steininger, Carolin Pommeranz, Ong Seow Eng and Richard K. Green

Introduction

This chapter focusses on selected tools for the regulation and supervision of managers and investment vehicles in Europe's real estate market. It also considers Asian markets and makes some limited comparisons with Australian and US markets.

Structured as a debt or equity product and traded on a private or public market, real estate investments can be carried out in all four quadrants of the real estate investment universe. Owing to their higher trading volume, historical experience and the fact that they are open to all investors, public and equity products have been in the focus of regulators for some time. In the aftermath of the sub-prime mortgage crisis of 2007–2009, however, supervisory authorities have increased their attention to private and debt products.

In general, regulators and supervisory authorities are continually working on: 1) a sounder, more stable and secure financial system; 2) a harmonised and stringent regulatory and supervisory framework in Europe and; 3) a higher level of consumer service and protection. These regulations, however, also incur higher costs for the real estate holding or managing entities.[1] According to the real estate industry, the process of harmonisation and thus the establishment of more and more regulations within the European Union (EU) could lead to an imbalance among the profits of a low-risk asset class, such as property. In this context, interest groups have expressed their concerns regarding the efficiency of fulfilling the original aim of various regulations as well as the short time frame as prescribed for implementation in their business process.

Rather than listing all the regulations connected with the real estate industry or all the concerns of the investment and managing industry, this chapter gives the reader a brief overview of the most recent and most relevant regulative and supervisory changes for the real estate industry in Europe.

The context of the European Union

Owing to the partial transfer of legislation to the EU, most European countries are obligated to comply with various EU regulations and directives. The European Parliament, the European Commission and the Council of the European Union[2] aim to set a common framework for certain aspects of laws, regulations and administrative provision for the EU member states. Even if not all European countries are members of the EU, most of them at least partly follow its legal requirements to maintain access to the European single market.[3] European politicians and economic researchers are assuming a similar course of action by the EU and the UK after the Brexit referendum on 23 June 2016 and continuing negations until the UK is due to leave the EU on 29 March 2019 (European Union, 2016). The real property market itself is naturally local but sources of investment and financing are as international as other financial submarkets. Therefore, a purely national regulation would not permit a country to reap the benefits of the European single market or the current situation on the integrated global financial market. Since the first version of the Basel Accord, international regulators have been cooperating and coordinating their prudential policies. Thus, the third version of the Basel Accord (Basel III) and the Solvency II Directive – the latter being the analogue concept for insurance companies – are the cores of the initial part of this chapter. The Mortgage Credit Directive (MCD) illustrates the direct link between the real estate industry and home owners, and the Alternative Investment Fund Managers Directive (AIFMD) and national real estate investment trust (REIT) regulations define the playing field of the important real estate investment vehicles in Europe. The following regulations therefore provide the framework for the main part of this chapter:

- Basel III (banking regulation)
- Solvency II (insurance regulation)
- MCD
- AIFMD (open- and closed-end funds)
- REIT regulation (listed investment vehicle).

The Undertakings for Collective Investment in Transferable Securities (UCITS) directive was established around 30 years ago, aiming at coordinating the differing laws of the EU member states with regard to collective investment undertakings while at the same time protecting unit-holders more effectively and in a more unified way. This was to make it easier for a collective investment undertaking to market its units in other member states of the EU and help to remove the restrictions on the units' free circulation, thus supporting the establishment of a single capital market (European Union, 1985). Today, it represents the investment fund framework of reference in Europe. Since the UCITS directive was updated in 2014, it can be compared with the AIFMD as a parallel framework for alternative investment funds (European Union, 2014b). However, most real estate and infrastructure funds are classified as alternative investment funds and thus fall within the scope of the AIFMD. In this chapter, we focus on a detailed introduction of that directive.

Basel III in Europe

Since the late 1980s, the evolution of banking regulations has shown how different countries[4] have cooperated in setting up rules for the financial supervision and minimum capital requirements of their banks. Since then, all Basel Accords (Basel I–III) have had a large influence on the financing decisions of private and institutional investors. Even if these regulations are not solely targeting the real estate industry, the industry does play a dominant role in the financing sector with its high investment and debt volume – on both the lending and the borrowing sides.

General objectives

The proposals of the Basel Committee on Banking Supervision (BCBS) with regard to Basel III and its implementing provision in the European Union – the Capital Requirements Regulation/Directive IV – were motivated by the shortcomings of the banking system's stability, which had become evident in the recent financial crisis triggered by the sub-prime mortgage crisis between 2007 and 2009 (see Basel Committee on Banking Supervision, 2011; European Union, 2013a; European Union, 2013b). To ensure more financial stability in future, financial institutions will have to adjust to a full set of new regulatory requirements.

To achieve the goal of increasing the stability of the financial sector, Basel III uses a 'three pillars' concept that was introduced in Basel II. The first pillar deals with the quantitative requirements that the minimum capital should vary with credit risk or market risk on the bank's balance sheet. The second pillar adds qualitative aspects, such as risk strategies, supervisory processes or frameworks for dealing with different types of risk. The third pillar is concerned with market disclosure, enabling market participants to obtain sufficient data about the company. The capital requirement is grouped into various capital brackets, which are differentiated depending on the type of (equity) capital necessary. The major components are tier 1 capital (going-concern capital) and tier 2 capital (gone-concern capital). Tier 1 capital consists of common equity tier 1 capital and additional tier 1 capital. To be classified for the different tiers, various criteria must be fulfilled (Basel Committee on Banking Supervision, 2011, 13–19). However, in general, it can be stated that tier 1 capital is used by a bank to absorb losses so that it is not compelled to quit its operations. Tier 1 capital comprises, for example, common shares issued by the bank, stock surplus and retained earnings. In contrast, a bank absorbs its losses with tier 2 capital in the event of its winding up or liquidation. Unaudited retained earnings, unaudited reserves and general loss reserves are examples of tier 2 capital. Basel III has also introduced two new buffers: the capital conservation and the counter-cyclical buffer. The aim of the capital conservation buffer is to establish a capital reserve outside periods of stress, which can then be used if losses occur. Now, banks have a buffer before reaching the binding minimum capital requirements that would automatically lead to supervisory consequences. The counter-cyclical buffer is used during periods of excess aggregate credit growth, mostly associated with the beginning of systemic risk in an economy, such as a real estate bubble. Both buffers have to consist entirely of common equity tier 1 capital. To counteract the moral hazard of 'too big to fail', the European Banking Authority defines global systemically important institutions as well as other systemically important institutions, which are obliged to maintain an extra buffer.[5] Furthermore, each member state can implement a systemic risk buffer for the financial sector or one or more subsets of that sector. Also, these buffers have to consist of and be supplementary to common equity tier 1 capital (European Union, 2013a, Art. 131–133). The exact numbers are shown in Table 3.1.

A further important aspect emphasised by Basel III is concerned with the leverage ratio of financial institutions in general. The minimum capital requirements allow a risk weighting of a bank's different assets – residential real estate is consequently underweighted. The leverage ratio, a simple non-risk-based measurement, monitors a bank's capital structure independently from the risk-based requirements. This ratio divides tier 1 capital by the total exposure of the bank. Currently, there is a minimum capital ratio of three per cent planned. The aim of this method is to restrict the build-up of excessive leverage based upon a highly relevant ratio for real estate financing institutions with their large debt volumes (Basel Committee on Banking Supervision, 2014). Another important ratio is connected to the available liquidity of the banks. This liquidity ratio was introduced to force banks to hold sufficient high-liquidity assets to meet their total net cash demands for 30 days (see Basel Committee on Banking Supervision, 2013).

Table 3.1 Phase-in arrangements of Basel III requirements into European Union law

	2011	*2012*	*2013*[a]	*2014*	*2015*	*2016*	*2017*	*2018*	*2019*
Leverage ratio	Supervisory monitoring		Parallel run: 1 January 2013–1 January 2017 Disclosure starts 1 January 2015					Migration to pillar 1	
Minimum common equity capital ratio			3.50%	4.00%	4.50%	4.50%	4.50%	4.50%	4.50%
Capital conversation buffer						0.625%	1.25%	1.875%	2.50%
Minimum common equity plus capital conservation buffer			3.50%	4.00%	4.50%	5.125%	5.75%	6.375%	7.00%
Phase-in of deductions from CET1 (including amounts exceeding the limit for DTAs, MSRs and financials)				20%	40%	60%	80%	100%	100%
Minimum tier 1 capital			4.50%	5.50%	6.00%	6.00%	6.00%	6.00%	6.00%
Minimum total capital			8.00%	8.00%	8.00%	8.00%	8.00%	8.00%	8.00%
Minimum total capital plus conservation buffer			8.00%	8.00%	8.00%	8.625%	9.25%	9.875%	10.50%
Capital instruments that no longer qualify as non-core tier 1 or tier 2 capital			Phased out over 10-year horizon beginning 2013						
Counter-cyclical capital buffers (determined through national regulatory authority)						0.000–0.625%	0.000–1.250%	0.000–1.875%	0.000–2.500%
Liquidity coverage ratio	Observation period begins				Introduce minimum standard				
Net stable funding ratio	Observation period begins							Introduce minimum standard	
Systemic risk buffer				0.00–3.00%	0.00–5.00%	0.00–5.00%	0.00–5.00%	0.00–5.00%	0.00–5.00%

Note: Shading indicates transition periods; all dates are as of 1 January.

a Omitted in the European Union. CET1, common equity tier 1 capital; DTA, deferred tax asset; MSR, mortgage servicing rights.

Source: Basel Committee on Banking Supervision (2011, 69).

Relevance for the real estate market

Although real estate financing is not the main target of these regulations, the amendments will also be binding for all financial institutions that are active in the real estate financing sector. The more stringent equity capital adequacy requirements as well as the implementation of a minimum leverage ratio and liquidity standards for banks are likely to have a negative impact on the financing possibilities for all real estate investments and their risk-weighted assets (Kröncke *et al.*, 2014, 64–66).

To analyse the effects of Basel III on real estate financing, it is necessary to differentiate between non-residential and residential as well as between private and commercial real estate sectors. Furthermore, the current quantitative easing policy in the euro zone is keeping the interest rate at a low level.[6] The effects on the residential market – particularly in the private sector – are estimated to be marginal. Although financing conditions can become more tightened (such as with regards to capital adequacy requirements or to the activation of a counter-cyclical capital buffer), borrowers of residential housing loans will still be able to find favourable conditions, even for long-term loans. Compared with the US and the situation after the sub-prime mortgage crisis, some real estate refinancing markets in Europe were first functioning well, due to their covered bond markets, a second refinancing source for a bank besides mortgage-backed securities. Twelve countries had already introduced covered bond legislation prior to the year 2000. Table 3.2 gives a full list of covered bond legislation in Europe. This advantage has been lost over the past few years because of a more intense public debt crisis and a slower recapitalisation of the European banks in general. Consequently, conditions (risk surcharges, maturity and so on) for financing non-residential properties will presumably deteriorate over the next years, reflecting the higher risks that this type of property actually brings with it. But all risk surcharges (for example 50–100 basis points) are on an absolute level low in the continuing period of low-level interest.

One of the aims of Basel III is the establishment of an enhanced risk-assessment provision and the backing of risk with equity capital. Having fully exploited the increased efficiency, the financial institutions will attempt to pass these higher equity capital costs on to the borrower in the form of higher interest rates, thus limiting access to loans. Irrespective of Basel III, loan providers are already taking a closer look at the quality of any property with regard to its adaptability for potential use by third parties. Any loss of quality will result in higher interest rates. However, there is no evidence of a general credit crunch at the moment, especially with the interest rates of the central banks being at historically low levels. Loans with solid loan-to-value ratios together with good-quality properties will bring few problems when it comes to a loan extension or a new loan. However, for more poorly rated properties and higher loan-to-value ratios, interest premiums will be higher to cover the high risk for the financing institution in the case of a default. This is a lesson learnt from the 2008 financial crisis.

To limit the ability to minimise the capital requirements with risk-weighted assets or an off-balance structure, the simple leverage ratio will be introduced as a publicly available measure.[7] Financial institutions that have focussed so far on the financing of high-volume projects, such as real estate or the public sector, will have greater difficulties reaching the minimum leverage ratio. The real estate industry emphasises this regulatory imbalance between the lower risk of these projects compared with corporate finance projects, neglecting however the cluster risk of such banks. It is assumed that the importance of such banks for the public sector and the public sector's own financing will put special attention on the final adjustments to the size of minimum leverage ratio in 2018.

Most capital requirements are the same for all member states. However, counter-cyclical capital buffers can be independently determined by national regulatory authorities. This type

Table 3.2 European covered bond market legislation, by year of introduction, as of December 2017

Country	*Year of introduction/most recent amendment*
Denmark	1851/2007
Austria	1899, 1905, 1927/2005
Germany	1900/2005
Switzerland	1931
Spain	1981/2007
Czech Republic	1995
Slovakia	1996
Hungary	1997
Luxembourg	1997
Poland	1998
Latvia	1998
France	1999/2010
Bulgaria	2000
Finland	2000/2010
Ireland	2002/2007
Lithuania	2003
Russia	2003
Sweden	2004
Norway	2006
Portugal	2006
Slovenia	2006
Ukraine	2006
Greece	2007
Italy	2005
Turkey	2007
Armenia	2008
Iceland	2008
The Netherlands	2008
United Kingdom	2008
Cyprus	2010
Belgium	2012
Romania	2015

Source: European Covered Bond Council (2018, 131).

of buffer should reflect the macro-financial environment of a specific country and can add up to 2.5 per cent of the required equity capital. As of yet, most countries have still not used this buffer even though their central banks have issued warnings about real estate bubbles in their respective markets. Only Switzerland already set a 'sectoral real estate' buffer at one per cent on 30 September 2013 and increased it to two per cent on 30 June 2014, aiming to prevent an overheating of the residential real estate market (Swiss National Bank, 2016). Norway set this buffer at one per cent on 1 July 2015. In this case, the supervision authority is not specifically targeting the real estate sector but is trying to make its banks more resilient against current financial imbalances across its whole economy (Norwegian Ministry of Finance, 2013). Neither country is a member state of the EU.

The current macro-economic environment in Europe and the expansive monetary policy and low base rate of the European Central Bank (ECB) imply that the impacts of the new regulatory framework conditions are only having a limited effect on real estate financing. However, this might change once the base rates of the ECB pick up again. Theoretically, alternative forms of financing – debt funds or crowd funding – can reduce a funding gap in real estate financing, particularly in the riskier sectors. Recently, and similarly to other industries, real estate financing has been attempting to finance directly via the capital market, thus avoiding the intermediary role of banks. Several debt funds and bonds have been issued this way. On account of the lack of trust in these alternative instruments with their too-short histories and expected low values, it is likely that alternative financing will continue to be implemented only hesitantly and only for those projects that cannot be financed in a traditional way or only at high cost. As long as this new shadow banking promotion is not the aim of Basel III, further monitoring of the risks outsourced by the credit institutions will be necessary. To avoid this risk shift to less supervised financial institutions, the risk monitoring idea targeted by Basel III and Capital Requirements Regulation/Directive IV should be transferred to all larger financial institutions and a level playing field – that is, a uniform framework – should be created. Furthermore, a harmonised application of the evaluation process of the different national supervisory authorities for internal risk models used by financial institutions is required, at least at the European level. Otherwise, the same risk, such as for real estate loans, might be assessed differently.

Solvency II

Further consequences for the real estate market could be initiated by Solvency II. This directive for the business of insurance and reinsurance companies aims at facilitating the taking-up and pursuit of the activities of insurance and reinsurance through aligning the differing rules of the EU member states, providing a common legal framework and making it easier for insurance and reinsurance undertakings to cover risks and commitments situated within the European Union. The increased supervision of insurance groups and protection of creditors should contribute to the proper functioning of the internal market in Europe (European Union, 2009, 1–2).

General objectives

Solvency II – which had already been proposed by the European Commission prior to the sub-prime mortgage crisis – is a fundamental reform of the insurance regulatory regime within the EU (European Union, 2009). At first glance, it follows a similar operational approach to that of Basel III with the 'three pillars'. Solvency II addresses quantitative, governance and risk management as well as disclosure and transparency requirements. The quantitative aspect includes the various risks that affect the required minimum capital for insurance companies. To calculate the solvency capital requirement, insurance companies may either use a standard model, which uses external calculated risk factors, or a (partially) internal model, which uses their own simulated risk data. These internal models are specifically designed for the respective insurance company, essentially reducing the required capital compared with the external model while still fulfilling the risk requirements (Munich Reinsurance Company, 2015). The different national European supervisory authorities have to review, approve and monitor such models.

Relevance for the real estate market

The Committee of European Insurance and Occupational Pensions Supervisors conducted five quantitative impact studies and a long-term guarantees assessment between 2005 and

2013. These studies aimed to test and calibrate the requirements for the risk management, the reports to supervisory authorities and the public, and the calculation of the implementing measures for the Solvency II framework. The results were then integrated into the final version of Solvency II. However, the European real estate industry deems the final standard decrease value of 25 per cent for all kind of properties (regions and types) to be too high and to differentiate insufficiently among regions and types. This value is mostly motivated by the real estate market in the UK, where the volatility is higher than in continental Europe and regulators are able to look back over a longer time when calculating the risk factor. The real estate industry argues that the Swiss Solvency Test, which became binding on 1 January 2011, assessed more realistically the risk of residential and commercial real estate: the former has a mean default risk of 10 per cent, and the latter 17 per cent.

Most European insurance companies, however, have announced that they will increase their real estate investment in their asset portfolios to guarantee the necessary return for their contracts during the low interest period. Until now, they have only hesitantly implemented their intention – and only in prime locations. However, as Solvency II will create the same rates for the risk covering of all properties in the standard model, it theoretically provides an incentive for investing in properties that have a higher return – and are thus, on average, riskier. The standard external risk model of Solvency II fails to adequately assess the real risk. Only a few European insurance companies will be able to use an internal model that would alleviate this problem, since the administrative resources needed are too high in relation to the percentage of real estate in the portfolio or the necessary data basis is not available. A partial internal model, which can be used by smaller insurance companies, could cover the real risks more effectively and could also prevent a distortion risk to the detriment of such companies. Even if the use of the standard model could theoretically lead to a higher risk shift in the real estate portfolio of European insurance companies, the real estate proportion in the total portfolio is, at around 10 per cent, small. The majority of assets consist of sovereign bonds with a currently low yield. Since the yield environment remains low with the current quantitative easing policy in the euro zone, stress tests on European insurance companies showed, for some of them, issues with fulfilling their long-term liabilities. During this time of low yields, we observe higher investment activities in infrastructure projects and insurance companies as real estate financers. So far, a systematic shift to higher direct real estate investments has not taken place. However, the focus on prime locations for company real estate investments is forcing property prices up and has increased the danger of regional property bubbles.

Mortgage credit directive

In the aftermath of the consequences of the US sub-prime mortgage crisis of 2007–2009 and the huge over-indebtedness or even homeless situation of some mortgage borrowers, the EU has tried to implement a directive to protect European borrowers from a similar situation and to avoid irresponsible lending and borrowing conditions for the home loan market in the future. In 2014, the EU published a directive which applies to secured credit and home loans and is supposed to increase the transparency, efficiency and competitiveness of the internal European market and to promote sustainable lending and borrowing. All credit intermediaries had to comply with the MCD by March 2016[8] for their retail customers. Its aim is to ensure, via better information on and for borrowers, responsible lending with a reduced risk of over-indebtedness; furthermore, better protection in the case of default.

Documentation and precontractual information requirements

The two requirements of providing standard precontractual information for borrowers through a European standardised information sheet and applying a consistent EU standard for the calculation of the annual percentage rate of charge are provisions requiring maximum harmonisation. For any other requirements of the MCD, such as the statutory permission requirement for mortgage credit intermediation, each member state may maintain or introduce more stringent provisions (see in particular: Art. 14(2)/17 and Annex I–II in European Union, 2014a).

Conduct and procedural requirements

At a glance, nine major conduct and procedural requirements are stipulated by this directive (European Union, 2014a, Art. 11, 12, 14, 18, 19, 23, 25 and Annex III):

1. Binding offer: lenders must make a binding offer or a conditional offer if a binding offer is made at a later stage of the lending process.
2. Advertising: the national law of a member state should involve disclosure requirements to protect the customer from misleading, poor and delusive advertising.
3. Tying and bundling: to protect mortgage customers from product tying that affects them negatively, certain rules for product tying should apply. These rules should allow the customer to take part in beneficial product tying while negative effects are restricted.
4. Seven-day reflection period: customers have the right of a seven-day reflection period; depending on the member state, this right will be granted in the pre- or post-sale period or as a combination of the two.
5. Assessment of customer creditworthiness: the possible increase in the value of residential properties cannot be the only condition of the customer creditworthiness, as there are various personal qualities that may influence a customer's ability to repay a credit. To ensure that a customer is creditworthy, member states should give additional lead on criteria and methods to approve an individual's creditworthiness.
6. Property valuations: proper and reliable valuation standards should be applied in the member states. Internationally renowned standards should be included.
7. Early repayment: to offer a higher level of competition and to ensure that the customer can react to specific life events (such as disability, divorce or unemployment), member states should guarantee the right of an early repayment to the customer. The customer's exercise rights may include restrictions such as time limitations, different treatment with respect to the type of borrowing rate (fixed or variable) or life circumstances. In return, the lender may be entitled to an objectively justified amount to compensate the directly linked costs of an early repayment.
8. Foreign currency mortgages: to reduce the customer's risk attached to credit agreements in a foreign currency, the directive recommends certain protection measures; the customer should be able to convert the currency of the credit agreement into an alternative currency.
9. Knowledge and competency: member states should support programmes that educate mortgage customers and thus lead them to better decisions. A monitoring system that verifies the knowledge and competency of creditors should be applied to ensure a high-level standard of professionalism.

Overall, the MCD aims to reach a high level of consumer protection by introducing minimum standards and by creating a common mortgage credit market in Europe. Mortgage credit granting institutions – in Europe traditional private, savings and cooperative banks as well as insurance companies – and their independent credit intermediaries will have to meet these requirements to stay in the market. Scholars assume that the higher requirements will not only have the desired effect of avoiding credit offers to customers who are in the long-term unable to repay their loans but will also avoid, for example, loans to low-income retirees who want to borrow small amounts for an age-based conversion of their homes. The new requirements will put a higher focus on their lower income, compared with that of their working lifetime, and a lower weight on the property value, even after the conversion. On the supply side, a harmonised European mortgage market will allow financial institutions, especially in online marketplaces, to offer their products easily in different countries. This higher competition could lower the spread over the central interest rate for mortgage customers, an advantage that is almost irrelevant during the current low-interest period. In the long run, it will foster a pan-European mortgage market with lower costs and more information for customers.

Alternative investment fund managers directive

As a consequence of the financial and economic crisis of 2008, various EU-wide regulations were introduced to handle systemic risk. Beside the banking system, the alternative investment fund industry has come into the focus of policy makers, since alternative investment funds have so far only been lightly or even not regulated (including hedge funds, private equity, and real estate and infrastructure funds). Even if markets and investors do mostly benefit from activities of operating alternative investment fund managers (AIFMs), those recent trends in financial markets (over-indebtedness, off-balance risk securitisations, fund frauds and funds' suspensions of redemption) have shown that negative developments of AIFMs can create additional risks that are transferred to the whole financial system. Furthermore, a proper risk management becomes more complex because of uncoordinated national operations within the EU single market (European Union, 2011, 1).

Thus, EU Directive 2011/61/EU (AIFMD) came into force on 21 July 2011, aiming to provide common requirements for the authorisation, supervision and marketing of AIFMs within the EU region. EU member states were required to transpose the provisions of the AIFMD into national law by 22 July 2013.[9] The directive targets those investment funds not regulated under the UCITS Directive at EU level that account for around 75 percent of all collective investments by small investors in Europe (European Union, 2014b). In contrast to the UCITS directive, the AIFMD regulates the managers themselves rather than the fund product, since the EU identifies the manager as the driving force behind the legal structure of the fund.

General objectives

AIFMs are subject to an authorisation process and a harmonised and stringent regulatory framework for management or marketing activities within the EU (European Union, 2011, 1). Besides the implementation of an internal market for alternative investment funds (AIFs), common requirements for the authorisation, supervision and marketing of AIFMs are being introduced to increase investor protection and to provide detailed information of operating AIFMs to regulators so that they can identify and prevent related systemic risk trends that may have a negative impact on investors and financial markets in the EU. More precisely, investor protection is being increased significantly and the market is being reinforced by increased competition and options for investors' choices under high and consistent regulation. This is mainly being achieved by a greater transparency towards investors, supervisors and employees of the companies that the fund invests in.

EU funds managed by an EU manager are marketed across the EU under an AIFMD passport if all requirements of the directive are complied with. Non-EU managers are not able to obtain such a passport. Thus, their EU or non-EU funds are only marketed under national private placement regimes. However, most of the AIFMD requirements also apply to non-EU managers of non-EU AIFs if the AIF is raising equity capital within the EU. After 2015, non-EU funds may also be allowed to obtain an AIFMD passport for distributing their funds within the EU. The European Securities and Markets Authority recommended in 2016 that Switzerland is granted an authorisation for using the passport and a further extension including especially Singapore and the US is conceivable.[10]

Authorisation process and main features

The first step within the authorisation process for AIFMs is the submission of a registration application to the competent authorities of the respective member state. The application identifies the management and the shareholders, information on remuneration policies and practices, as well as information on delegated services and tasks (European Union, 2011, 20). To receive authorisation, the AIFM also needs to own a minimum of capital and funds based on capital requirements listed below, to provide an activity programme including a description of the organisational structure and contemplated delegation, and to implement remuneration policies and arrangements for a depositary appointment. The directive also includes behavioural principles for managers to 'act honestly, with due skill, care and diligence, fairly in conducting their activities [and] in the best interests of the fund, the investors [...] and the integrity of the market' (European Union, 2011, 23).

The supervisory authorities of the member state in which the office of the fund is registered (or the member state of reference for non-EU AIFMs) only grant authorisation if they consider the AIFM to meet all requirements of the AIFMD, but authorisation is then also valid in all other member states of the EU. If authorisation is successful, the AIFM is able to execute investment management activities, especially portfolio and risk management, administration, marketing and other activities directly linked to the fund. The main features of the directive are displayed in Figure 3.1. These are capital requirements, delegation, conflicts of interest, risk/liquidity management, remuneration, valuation, transparency and depositary.

Capital requirements

To ensure the continuous and stable administration and management of an AIF, the fund manager is required to hold a minimum capital of €125,000 for an externally managed AIF. If the fund is internally managed, however, the minimum capital requirement is extended to €300,000. Furthermore, two basis points of the fund's portfolio value that exceeds €250 million must be held as additional funds, but the total sum of the capital requirement plus the additional amount is capped at €10 million. Member states can also authorise the AIFM to obtain up to 50 per cent of the additional funds held either by a guarantee provided from a credit institution, an insurance company registered in a member state, or – in a country with regulations deemed to be equivalent – by the competent authorities (European Union, 2011, 22).

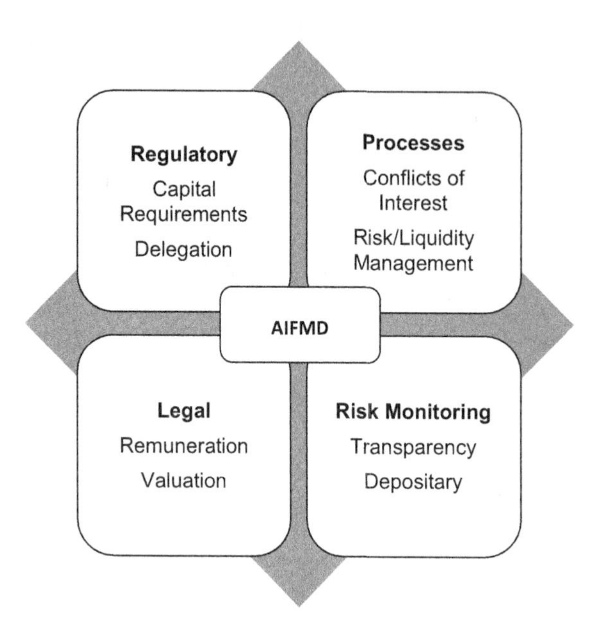

Figure 3.1 Conditions for a successful implementation of the Alternative Investment Fund Managers Directive

Delegation

The AIFM is responsible for performing investment management functions of one or several AIFs and for ensuring compliance with the AIFMD, but it can also delegate functions to external institutions. The AIFMD provides an adequate and highly restrictive framework for an external delegation of functions. The overall aim of this delegation framework is to ensure that the fund is still managed in the best interests of investors and that the delegation does not have any negative effects in terms of supervision and monitoring standards. A delegation of portfolio or risk management that exceeds the remaining internally managed functions to a significant extent results in the AIFM becoming a letterbox entity, which is strictly prohibited by the directive. A proper due diligence process provides the basis for the choice of an adequate delegate, who must be sufficiently experienced in undertaking delegated functions (Muller and Dogniez, 2013, 17).

Conflicts of interest

Conflicts of interest may occur between stakeholders linked to the AIF, resulting in negative effects for the fund and the investors. Stakeholders linked to the fund include the AIFM and operating managers, employees or persons directly or indirectly linked to the AIFM, the managed fund and the investors. According to the directive, the AIFM is required to implement organisational and administrative structures for conflict identification and to run sufficient monitoring, management and prevention measures. However, requirements to identify such conflicts between the fund manager and the investor, or even between one investor and another, can be complex and difficult to realise in practice.

If conflicts of interest still occur, the AIFM is required to make general disclosures regarding the nature of the conflict before undertaking business on an investor's behalf (Williams *et al.*, 2012).

Risk and liquidity management

The AIFM is responsible for the implementation of an adequate risk management system for a proper identification, management and monitoring of all risks to which the managed fund is exposed. Furthermore, the AIFMD requires a functional and hierarchical separation of the fund's risk management and operations, as well as the implementation of an efficient liquidity management system based on stress-testing procedures. It is important to note that the AIFMD does not limit the employed investments or strategies of an AIF. However, investment strategies, the liquidity profile and the redemption policy have to remain consistent at all times (European Union, 2011, 25).

The AIFMD requires fund managers to determine an individual maximum leverage limit for each fund managed. Relevant determinants for setting the leverage limit include the investment strategy, the sources of leverage, the asset–liability ratio, the need to limit the exposure to a single counterparty and the extent of collateral. Competent authorities, however, may lower imposed leverage limits again when raising concerns about systemic risk and disorderly markets (European Union, 2011, 25). Investors are informed about the employed total leverage level by the AIFM on a regular basis to ensure transparency.

Remuneration

The AIFMD also contains requirements for remuneration policies and practices of senior management, risk takers, control functions and any other employee whose professional activities have a significant effect on the risk profile of the managed fund (European Union, 2011, 4). The implemented remuneration policy is required to encourage only risk taking that complies with the risk profile, incorporation rules or instruments of the managed fund. Performance-based parts of remunerations are spread over time, taking redemption policy and investment risks of the fund into consideration. The relevant performance of employees is measured using a multi-year framework following the lifecycle of the fund. Furthermore, variable and fixed remuneration parts need to be well balanced, so that at least 50 per cent of the variable remuneration consists of shares or units and 40 per cent is deferred for a minimum of three or five years (Muller and Dogniez, 2013, 15).

Valuation

Adequate and consistent valuation methods for a proper and independent valuation of the AIF's assets provide the basis for a transparent and consistently regulated AIF sector. AIFMs can either perform the valuation themselves when they are functionally independent of the AIF's portfolio management and implemented policies ensure the mitigation of any conflict of interest, or they can engage an external, completely independent appraiser. The engagement of an external appraiser requires a professional registration recognised by national law or regulatory provisions as well as personal guarantees indicating the qualification for appropriately performing the valuation process. The independent calculation and valuation of assets is required at least once a year. However, this is controversially discussed, since it might increase operation and management costs significantly.

Transparency

To ensure investor protection, the AIFMD also includes certain transparency and disclosure requirements. These disclosures to investors include the investment strategy and objectives, all assets the fund can invest in, as well as employed techniques, details of all related risks, investment restrictions, and the kind and source of leverage used. Furthermore, information on investment strategy and policy changing procedures, risk management and valuation methods, fees and charges, costs and expenses, and preferential treatment given to particular investors must be provided by the AIFM. Investors also have to be immediately notified about significant changes concerning these fields. Moreover, an annual report must be provided to investors upon request no later than six months subsequent to the end of the financial year. The AIFM is also required to meet various other periodical reporting obligations, including informing the competent authorities of their domicile, such as information on liquidity, risk management and results of stress tests (European Union, 2011, 33).

Depositary

The asset supervision of each managed AIF is done by an external depositary who is assigned to the managed fund via a written contract. EU AIFMs of non-EU funds that are marketed to professional investors within the EU according to national private placement regimes are not entirely subject to these depositary conditions. However, they are also required to engage one or more external institutions for operating their fund's cash monitoring, safe-keeping and oversight duties (Muller and Dogniez, 2013, 19).

Relevance for the real estate market

Real estate fund managers who fall under the AIFMD have to meet regulations that are transposed into national law of the member state of the fund's origin or the referring member state when located outside the EU. For the real estate sector, AIFs capture many open-ended and closed-ended listed and unlisted real estate funds, but appeal especially to non-listed funds (European Union, 2011, 2).

The implementation of the AIFMD may result in notably increased operating costs, especially because of the capital requirements, the designation of external depositaries, external appraisers and the internal reorganisation needed to meet compliance and reporting requirements (Martougin, 2011). Consequently, higher operating costs could be reflected in a higher annual management fee rate. However, the management fee rate – measured by the total expense ratio on gross asset value – does not show significantly higher rates for the past few years (INREV, 2011, 19; INREV, 2016).

The directive is assumed to encourage consolidations within the real estate fund industry, since large funds benefit from European passporting by consolidating their entities throughout Europe (Martougin, 2011). For the UK and Ireland, many fund managers believed that the directive would reduce the competitiveness of the EU's alternative investment funds industry due to fewer non-EU managers operating in Europe before the AIFMD was introduced.[11] The regulatory environment is thus a significant factor for the choice of a fund domicile, resulting in a reduced choice for investors. Fund managers also expected that redemption terms would be affected and leverage figures, which are conditional on many different factors, potentially confuse investors.

REITs remain a special case in the context of the AIFMD. According to the criteria for AIF determination by the European Securities and Markets Authority, REITs may have a general commercial or industrial purpose due to property development or property retail. Thus, REITs are generally not classified as collective investment undertakings and, if they fall within the scope of the AIFMD, are based on an individual assessment (European Securities and Markets Authority, 2012, 16 and 36).

REIT regulation

In total, there are around 104 REITs listed in Europe, with the majority of them based in the UK. Numerous European countries have already introduced national acts to attract (foreign) equity capital, especially due to the increase in usage of that investment vehicle. In general, there are different reasons for this surge in capital invested in REITs. They offer a good chance for international investors to invest in foreign real estate without detailed knowledge of that particular market. Another reason can be seen in the tax exemption rules, which increase the attractiveness for investments in REITs. Apart from that, the real estate bubble negatively affected several European countries in the late 2000s. After the bubble burst, numerous developments were either unfinished or could be acquired at low prices. In particular, REITs allowed the Spanish and Greek governments to liquidate their assets (Pirolo and Whelan, 2014).

General aspects in Europe

So far, there is no uniform REIT Act in the EU, so that every European country can decide whether this investment vehicle should be available or not. Worldwide, a total of 37 countries have REIT legislations in place, of which 13 are European countries (European Public Real Estate Association, 2015, 2). By 2015, the worldwide market capitalisation for REITs was roughly €883 billion.[12] In 2014, the European market capitalisation amounted to only around €172 billion.[13] The common identifiers for REITs are the tax exemption rules excluding them from corporate taxation and the investment focus on real estate. To guarantee the tax payment on the investor level, REITs are also strictly regulated in Europe regarding their dividend payout ratio. In most cases, REITs have to distribute roughly 90 per cent of their taxable income. These rules are the reason why REITs are used as an income-generating asset rather than for accretion. In Europe, in 1969, the Netherlands was the first country to introduce national laws concerning REITs. Most other European countries introduced their legislations much later, generally between 2003 and 2007. The latest country to adopt REIT rules was Ireland in 2013.

Different REIT requirements in Europe

Because numerous countries have introduced their own national regimes since the beginning of this millennium, the privately organised European Public Real Estate Association (EPRA) has tried to introduce some guidelines regarding minimum REIT recognition requirements. These requirements are: the legal form has to be a corporate; they have to be listed; and the minimum mandatory distribution of income has to be at least 80 percent of after-tax income (European Public Real Estate Association, 2009, 4). However, there is no legally binding EU law in place, and every country has its own REIT recognition guidelines, so the different REIT requirements vary greatly. Table 3.3 provides the most important characteristics for the seven major European economic countries.

Table 3.3 Real estate investment trust market characteristics of seven major European economic countries

Country	*Market value (€ million)*	*REITs (n)*	*Regulation start (year)*	*Payout ratio*		*Leverage*	*Tax treatment on REIT level*
				Operative income (%)	*Income type*		
Belgium	5,640	8	1995	80	Net profit	Loans max. 65% of TA. Interest expenses max. 80% of total income	Rental income excluded. Capital gains tax-exempt
France	18,975	20	2003	95	Tax exempt profit	No specific leverage restriction but French thin capitalisation rule has to be applied	Tax exempt
Germany	1,837	3	2007	90	Net income	Min. 45% of TA of RE must be equity	Tax exempt
Greece	293	3	1999	50	Net profit	Max. leverage 75% of TA	Income taxed at 10% of ECB fund rate plus 100 basis points. Capital gains exempt
Italy	925	2	2007	70	Tax exempt profit	As stated in company bylaws	Income and capital gains from real estate related activities are tax exempt. Other income subject to ordinary taxation
The Netherlands	28,963	5	1969	100	Taxable profit	60% of fiscal book value of real estate	Tax exempt
UK	69,399	33	2007	90%	Tax property rental profits	Property profit: Property cost with a ratio of 1.25	Tax exempt residual business 20%

ECB, European Central Bank; max., maximum; min., minimum; REIT, real estate investment trust; TA, total assets.
Source: European Public Real Estate Association (2015).

Apart from these seven countries, another six European countries have REIT legislation in place that differs significantly from that in Table 3.3. The most distinct differences are as follows:

- With regard to the minimum share capital required to create a REIT, only €40,000 is needed in Lithuania, whereas it takes €40 million in Italy.
- The required payout ratio ranges from no obligations in Lithuania to up to 100 per cent of the operative incomes taxable profit in the Netherlands.[14]
- Asset level restrictions range from rather relaxed guidelines in France, which state that 'principal activities must be in renting out properties', to strict laws in Spain, stating that 80 per cent of income and 80 per cent of assets have to be directly linked to real estate, requiring a minimum holding period of 3 years.
- Some countries are very restrictive in terms of leverage, such as Lithuania, where a maximum of 50 per cent of real estate value can be debt financed. However, in Spain, no restrictions on leverage apply at all.[15]

Differences can also be found in taxation obligations. In general, the income component on the REIT level is tax exempted; in Greece however, the tax rate accounts for 10 per cent of the current ECB central interest rate plus 100 basis points, which in fact is almost zero per cent currently.[16] Whereas on the individual shareholder level, the personal tax rate is usually applied, this income is tax exempt in Greece, essentially subjecting profits from REITs in Greece to nearly zero per cent tax in total.

Concerning the tax treatment of foreign investors or of foreign REITs, the individual laws also vary. Generally, it can be stated that foreign investors are charged at a similar rate to local shareholders, although foreign investors may benefit from tax treaties between countries. The most notable difference can be found in Greece, where foreign shareholders do not have to pay any tax at all. However, foreign REITs often do not experience the same benefit: in fact, in most European countries, foreign REITs are not eligible for tax deductions, and therefore the normal corporate tax rate applies. This is due to the fact that most foreign REITs are not recognised as such under the local tax regimes. The Netherlands are an exception to this rule, though. Foreign REITs are tax exempt if they are comparable 'in nature, form and behaviour' to their qualifying Dutch counterparts (European Public Real Estate Association, 2015, 142).

Summing up, despite the tax benefit of REITs, the general dominance of real estate funds in Europe, their strongest argument of being decoupled from the stock market and the generally lower (continental) European ratio of stockholders has left REITs only little room for an expansion in Europe over the last years.

Regulation of fund managers and investment vehicles in Asia

While real estate is a significant asset class for investors in Asia, the vehicles by which real estate is managed vary substantially across countries. Country-specific legislative laws and policies dictate the way real estate is managed. The landscape is varied from family-oriented businesses with a traditional value attached to holding real estate to global fund management organisations. Investment vehicles also range from private and publicly listed development companies, equity and debt funds, and REITs.

This section focusses only on REITs in Asia and examines the differences in legislative framework for selected Asian countries. By way of overview, we will better understand why REITs emerged as a strong investment vehicle in Asia.

Basel III in Asia

The general description of Basel III is set forth above, but its implications for Asia are different than for Europe. The most important difference between Europe and Asia is the relative difference in economic integration: Europe is quite integrated, while Asia is not. Within Asia, banking systems vary dramatically across countries. Some countries (such as China) have banks that are state-owned enterprises, others have private enterprises, and still others have private enterprises with substantial government intervention. In some countries, banking is quite sophisticated, meaning, among other things, that capitalisation levels are based on models of risk, whereas in others, capitalisation levels are based on simple risk-weighting heuristics.

Ironically, one of the outcomes of this is that more sophisticated banking systems, such as Japan's, are more likely to fail to meet the capital requirements of Basel.

Solvency II in Asia

Although Solvency II is a European regulatory framework for capitalising insurance companies, it affects Asian multinational insurance companies that wish to do business in the EU. Specifically, if insurance companies external to Europe do not meet Solvency II standards, they may need to carry higher levels of capital to do business in Europe.

Cox *et al.* (2017) note that 'Japan and Australia attained provisional third-country equivalence status for group solvency (Article 227). This status is valid for ten years and reduces the administrative burden for the Solvency II calculation of subsidiaries in the European Economic Area (EEA).' Ernst & Young (2015) developed a table (Table 3.4) laying out the sophistication of insurance regulation in Asia and the appetite for meeting the requirements of the Solvency II framework, by country.

Mortgage regulation in Asia

Table 3.5 provides a summary of differences in mortgage supervision across Asia. Perhaps the most noteworthy thing about this table is that there is much variation in what is regulated

Table 3.4 Sophistication levels of solvency regulations in Asia

Market	*Ernst & Young Sophistication Score (1–3)*	*Ernst & Young Solvency II Appetite Score (1–4)*
Singapore	3	2
Malaysia	3	2
Indonesia	2	1
Thailand	2	1
Vietnam	1	1
Hong Kong	1	1
Mainland China	1	2
South Korea	3	3
Taiwan	2	1
Japan	3	4

Note: Most of Asia, regardless of regulatory sophistication, does not consider complying with Solvency II to be a priority (Ernst & Young, 2015, 6).

Table 3.5 Differences in mortgage supervision across Asia

Regulatory tool	*Countries/regions using tool*
Counter-cyclical provisioning	People's Republic of China (PRC), India
Loan-to-value ratio maximums	PRC, Hong Kong, Indonesia, Japan, South Korea, Malaysia, Philippines, Singapore, Thailand
Debt service ratio maximums	PRC, Hong Kong, South Korea
Counter-cyclical tightening	PRC, Hong Kong, South Korea, Malaysia, Philippines, Singapore, Thailand
Credit limits	PRC, Hong Kong, India
Counter-cyclical supervision	PRC, Hong Kong, India, South Korea, Malaysia, Singapore
Capital requirements	India, Malaysia
Sector exposure limits	South Korea, Malaysia, Philippines, Singapore
Capital surcharges for 'too big to fail' banks	PRC, India, Philippines, Singapore
Liquidity and funding requirements	PRC, India, South Korea, Malaysia, Philippines, Singapore, Thailand
Loan-to-deposit requirements	PRC, South Korea
Foreign exchange exposure limits	South Korea, Philippines
Limits on currency mismatches	India, Malaysia, Philippines

Source: Morgan, Regis and Salike (2015).

across Asia. China uses nearly every potential regulatory tool, while Thailand appears to be lightly regulated. It is particularly surprising that, given its historical vulnerability to currency shocks, Thailand does not regulate mortgage currency exposure.

Even when a regulation appears to be ubiquitous, such as loan-to-value ratio limits, its implementation can vary across countries, such as loan-to-value maximums that can range from 70 to 80 per cent across Asia. Perhaps more important, loan terms vary considerably, meaning that amortisation speeds vary and, therefore, implied loan-to-value maximums once loans have seasoned are quite different across countries.

REIT regulation in Asia

REITs did not exist in Asia prior to 2001. The investment community gained exposure to real estate market through either the ownership of direct property or listed property company shares, property funds and, to some extent, through mortgage-backed securities in market, such as Singapore and Korea.

The main impetus behind the creation of REIT in Asia was the 1997 Asia financial crisis, which left many corporations in Asia saddled with huge debts and undervalued real estate. Financial institutions in countries such as Japan, Taiwan and South Korea were loaded with foreclosed properties. Regulators viewed REITs as a feasible route to recapitalise the corporate balance sheet and as a means of revitalising the real estate market. Korea launched its corporate restructuring REIT (CR-REIT) in 2002 to take over assets from distressed firms.[17] Japanese developers considered REITs as an alternative source of raising funds as lenders shunned commercial mortgage loans following the collapse of Japanese real estate market in the 1990s. In Taiwan, Fubon REIT was backed by properties from Fubon Financial, a financial institution.

Corporations in Singapore, Hong Kong and Malaysia, in contrast, viewed REITs as a potential route to recycle capital through the divestment of their non-core real estate.

CapitaLand, a major property developer in Singapore, spun-off their real estate into two REITs, CapitalMall Trust and Capital Commercial Trust, to release capital for them to pursue more profitable property development projects in China, India and Vietnam. The same strategy was adopted by property developers in Malaysia. The largest Malaysia REIT, Starhill REIT, was created through the injection of commercial properties by property developer YTL Land Bhd. Besides releasing the capital from assets injected into REITs, such property companies still earn fees for managing the properties under the REITs.

Factors that worked in favour are:

1. Ample investible assets: the amount of investible assets in Asia ex-Japan was estimated at US$500 billion by UBS in 2005. A large chunk of these properties is owned by non-real estate corporation such as financial institutions, transport and retail companies, as well as government agencies. Non-real estate corporations own an estimated US$81 billion of investible real estate in the Asia region ex-Japan. These non-real estate companies have a financial incentive to divest their assets holdings to release capital and operate under a lighter balance sheet.
2. Favourable risk-return characteristics: from an investment perspective, the risk-return characteristics of REITs bode well for individual and institutional investors looking to diversify and to earn stable income returns.[18] In low interest regime countries, such as Japan, REITs provide larger yield spread between REIT dividend yield and deposit rates, which made an attractive investment instrument in Japan.[19]
3. Demographics: an ageing population and high saving rate in Asian countries, such as Singapore, Hong Kong, Korea and Taiwan, creates a ready demand for high income yielding investment products such as REITs. Pension funds in these countries are continually looking for stable income stream to match their near future liabilities commitment. Wealth and property fund management firms have been venturing into the untapped funds in Asia. REITs have become one of the best candidates for these fund managers to gain exposure to real estate market for liquidity and diversification benefits purposes.

The acceptance of REIT as a class of legitimate investment products in Asia and increasing REIT product knowledge among retail investors contributed to the development of REITs. The setting up of the Asian Public Real Estate Association in June 2005 further provided a platform for Asian REITs to lobby for conducive and competitive REIT legislation from the regulators. Similar lobby groups are seen in the developed markets, such as the National Association of Real Estate Investment Trusts in the US and the European Public Real Estate Association in Europe.

Ooi, Newell and Sing (2006) identify key factors that impeded the growth of REIT in Asia:

1. Restrictive legislation: the REIT legislative regimes in many countries in regard to gearing and foreign ownership of local real estate are more restrictive compared with that in the US (see the next section for comparison of REIT legislation between Asia, US and Australia REIT).
2. Tax transparency: the REIT tax transparency status, which shelter shareholders from double taxation, may not be that attractive in countries that practise an imputed tax system.
3. Low property yield: the low property yield by prime properties in Asia made it difficult to replicate and sustained the high dividend payout of US REITs.

4. High concentration risk: Asia REITs tend to have limited holdings of properties in their portfolios. US and Australia REITs have an average of 150 and 40 in their portfolios, respectively (Eldik, 2005). Most Asia REITs hold fewer than 30 properties, the prescribed number of properties needed to enjoy the diversification benefits according to conventional portfolio investment theory. This inevitably translates into higher volatility in returns.
5. Size: a related issue is the REIT size, which could enable them to enjoy economies of scale. Asia REITs are generally small capitalised firms, which could impede their efforts to improve yields over the long-term through cost saving strategy. Ambrose and Linneman (2001) find that an increase of a market capitalisation of US$1billion could reduce capital costs by about 2.2 per cent for US REITs. In addition, they also find that large REITs tend to be more profitable, have higher rental revenue ratio and incur lower implied capitalisation rates.

Notwithstanding the obstacles cited above, Asia witnessed a REIT initial public offering (IPO) boom during 2005–2006 with 66 IPOs come to the market during these two years. In comparison, the IPO boom in the US during 1993–1994 saw some 89 IPOs.

Comparison of Asian REIT legislative frameworks

The legislative framework for REITs in Asia is generally adapted from the US and Australian REIT markets, albeit with different country-specific variations. Table 3.5 provides a cross-comparison between Asia REIT regulatory regimes. For ease of reference, Japan REITs are referred to as J-REITs, Singapore REITs as S-REITs, and so on.

Some key difference should be highlighted:

1. External management structure: many REITs in Asia subscribe to an externally managed structure where a separate fund management company is set up to manage the REIT. This is contrary to the US REIT structure, which favours internal management.[20] Externally managed REITs tend to create agency problems, since the REIT management fees are often pegged to the size of the portfolio under their management. This provides an incentive to enlarge the portfolio size even to the detrimental of shareholders. In addition, most Asia REITs are structured as captive REITs, where the fund management company is a wholly owned subsidiary of the REIT sponsor, normally a property developer that injected the properties into the REIT during IPO.[21] The fund management company of Starhill REIT – the biggest Malaysia REIT – is 70 per cent owned by its sponsor, YTL Corporation Bhd. In Singapore, CapitaCommercial Trust is managed by CapitaCommerical Trust Limited, a wholly owned subsidiary of its sponsor, CapitaLand limited.
2. Geographic coverage: all Asia REITs are allowed to hold properties outside their home countries, with provisions in the case of Taiwan and the Philippines. Regulators in Singapore and Hong Kong have been proactive in promoting the cross-border listing of REITs.[22] Hong Kong cross-border REITs capitalise on acquiring investment grade properties in mainland China.
3. Property development: Japan, Taiwan, Thailand, Malaysia and Philippines REITs are prohibited from undertaking property development activities. For the other countries, the degree of property development activities allowed to REITs varies from 10 to 30 per cent.

Table 3.6 Comparison of Asian real estate investment trust legislative frameworks

	Japan	*Singapore*	*Hong Kong*	*Taiwan*	*Thailand*	*Malaysia*	*South Korea*	*Philippines*
Management structure	External	External	External/ internal	External/ internal	External	External	Internal/ external	External
Invested in real estate or real estate related assets (%)	75	75	100	75	75	75	70	75
Foreign assets	OK	OK	OK	OK (with central bank approval)	OK	OK	OK	Up to 40% (with approval)
Property development	Prohibited	Up to 25% of deposited property	Up to 10% of deposited property	Prohibited	Prohibited	Prohibited (unless approved by securities commission)	Up to 30% of total assets	Prohibited[b]
Gearing limit	No	45% of total asset value	45% of total asset value	35% of total assets[c]	35% of total assets[c]	50% of total asset value	No gearing for investment purpose	35% of total assets[c]
Minimum distribution requirement	90% of taxable income (post depreciation)	90% of taxable income (no depreciation)	90% of net income after tax	90% of taxable income (post depreciation)	90% of net profit	90%; undistributed income is tax-exempted	90% of net income	90% of net profit
Tax transparency	Yes	Yes	No	Yes	Yes	Yes	Yes	Yes
Tax concession for investors[d]	No	10% withholding tax for non-resident companies until March 2020	No	Final withholding tax of 6%	Non-resident individuals and companies are exempt from Thai tax	Yes, final withholding tax of 10% for individuals and non-corporate investors, up to 31 December 2016	No	Residents exempt from 10% withholding tax for 7 years, 10% withholding tax for foreign corporates

a K-REITs.
b Unless the REIT intends to hold such property post completion and provided that contract value/ investment in such property development does not exceed 10% of property deposited.
c May exceed gearing cap if the REIT obtains and discloses a credit rating from a major rating agency.
d Tax exemption at REIT level only applicable for distributed income to resident unit-holders.

Source: UBS Singapore property SREIT valuation guide, 11 April 2016.

4. Gearing: Japan does not put a limit on gearing, while South Korea does not permit gearing for investment purposes. Other countries permit gearing subject to caps ranging from 35 to 50 per cent. Taiwan, Thailand and the Philippines have a 35 per cent limit, but REITs may borrow more if the REIT obtains and discloses a credit rating from a major rating agency. Singapore REITs had a similar framework prior to 2015, but now have a fixed 45 per cent cap.
5. Distribution: most REIT legislations in Asia maintain a minimum distribution of 90 per cent of net income. However, the basis for deriving the net income available for distribution differs from country to country.
6. Tax transparency and tax concessions for investors: most countries allow for tax transparency. Singapore, Malaysia, Thailand and Philippines provide tax concessions for investors.

In earlier years, some countries gradually relaxed restrictions to make their REIT markets competitive with aspirations of becoming a regional hub. Hong Kong, for example, has revised its REIT guidelines to incorporate the tax transparency provision to boost investor demand for REITs. Singapore and Malaysia have increased the gearing limit to 60 per cent (for rated REITs) and 50 per cent, respectively, from 35 per cent in earlier guidelines. Since the Global Financial Crisis, many countries have refined their legislations and guidelines better to protect investor interests.

Summary and conclusion

Despite the attempts of international authorities to harmonise it, regulation varies around the world. Regulation also applies differently to different entities: publicly traded companies are treated differently from private entities, REITs receive differential tax treatment (and therefore different regulatory treatment) from other entities, debt is treated differently from equity, banks are treated differently from insurance companies. These issues are important to businesses trying to determine how to finance real estate investments, as differences in regulatory treatment create opportunities for regulatory arbitrage. As this chapter shows, there is more uniform regulation in Europe than in Asia, in large part because of the existence of the EU (even with Brexit, the UK may wish largely to conform to European regulations so as to continue to participate in that market). Asia, on the other hand, has wide variation in regulatory regimes, at least in part because of differences in levels of financial market sophistication in various countries.

Acknowledgements

The authors would like to thank Celina Becher, Eric Sachsenhausen and Christine Stibbe for their support on this chapter. The usual disclaimer applies.

Notes

1 Higher costs in terms of a monetary valuation of direct and indirect expenses, such effort, resources, time, material and external services to fulfil the requirements.
2 As the institution representing the interests of the European Union, the Commission has the right of initiative to propose new legislation within the legislative process of the EU. The European Parliament, which is directly elected by all European citizens and bears responsibilities for

legislation, supervision and budgeting, then proposes amendments, and finally approves or rejects the legislative proposal. The Council of the EU, representing the member states' governments and consisting of national ministers who meet according to the topic at hand, also has to approve new legislation and to coordinate policies. The Council of the EU has to take the Parliament's opinion into account before taking a decision. After new legislation has been implemented, the European Commission ensures that EU law is being correctly applied by the EU member states.

3 For example, Norway and Switzerland are among these countries. The Swiss financial industry is Europe's most important sector and follows international regulations such as the Basel Accords. However, it also diverges in some regulatory aspects to attract foreign investors and investment vehicles.

4 In 1992, Basel I started within the Group of Ten (G10) and was expanded to the Group of Twenty (G20) for Basel III.

5 Financial institutions that have a leverage ratio exposure measure above €200 billion and are potentially systemically relevant.

6 On 16 March 2016, the European Central Bank set the interest rate on the main refinancing operations (central rate) at 0 per cent; its rate on the deposit facility, which banks may use to make overnight deposits with the Euro system, has even been at a negative level since 11 June 2014.

7 So far, the leverage ratio has been only reported to supervisory authorities.

8 As of March 2018, all member states except Spain had already implemented the MCD (Directive 2014/17/EU). All had to transpose the regulations into their national law by 21 March 2016. This means that even if the EU directive is originally from 2014, national implementation of the binding rules for credit intermediaries had often not been finalised, giving them only a short period within which they can integrate the rules into their business model and business process.

9 Several of the EU member states had required a longer period to transpose the AIFMD into national legislation.

10 For a more detailed description of potential extension of the AIFMD passport to non-EU countries, see European Securities and Markets Authority (2016).

11 Statements are based on survey data and analysis by Deloitte in 2012; see Opp and Hartwell (2012, 4).

12 See Nareit (2016); US$960 billion; exchange rate from 1 January 2016 of €1 to US$1.0866.

13 See Pirolo and Whelan (2014): US$187 billion; exchange rate from 1 January 2016 of €1 to US$1.0866.

14 According to the Netherlands tax law, a REIT is required to distribute all of its taxable profit to its shareholders. The possibility of depreciation on passively held real estate to calculate the taxable profit was abolished in 2008. The net balance of unrealised capital gains on securities and realised capital gains on all other investments is excluded from the taxable profit and is, therefore, not subject to the distribution obligation (allocation of a tax-free reserve); see European Public Real Estate Association (2009, 5).

15 The average leverage ratio of Spanish REITs currently amounts to roughly 50 per cent. This is a further indication that even without a legal defined cap, most REITs keep their leverage ratio at common ratios to avoid a poor assessment by analysts or by the stock market in general.

16 $10\% \times (0\% + 1\%) = 0.1\%$

17 CR-REIT has a finite life. As of June 2008, three CR-REITs have been liquidated and delisted from the stock exchange: Kyobo-Meritz 1 CR-REIT, KOCREF 1 and Realty Korea 1 CR-REIT. Subsequent to CR-REITs, South Korea developed regular REITs known as K-REITs.

18 Academic studies generally support the diversification benefits gain from the inclusion of equity REIT into a mixed assets portfolio comprising of stocks and bonds (Geltner *et al.*, 2014).

19 Yield plays in Japan's REIT (J-REIT) market were eroded recently when compared with countries like South Korea and Malaysia, which offering higher yield spread than J-REIT in 2007 (Ernst & Young, 2007). One of the reasons is the increase in competitive among J-REIT for a limited supply of quality properties. While J-REIT is allowed to make their investment overseas, no acquisition has been made so far, owing to the ambiguity of overseas acquisition requirement (CBRE, 2008).

20 Academic research on US REIT documented that the internally managed stock and operating performance of REITs is better than that of externally managed REITs (Capozza and Seguin, 1998; Ambrose and Linneman, 2001).
21 Hsieh and Sirman (1991) argue that captive REITs tend to invite sponsor–shareholder conflict with the sponsor capitalizing on the REIT vehicle to support their financing needs.
22 There are six cross-border Singapore REITs backed by foreign assets: Allco Commercial REIT, Ascott Residence Trust, CDL Hospitality Trusts, CapitalRetail China Trust, Fortune REIT and First REIT.

References

Ambrose, B. and Linneman, P. (2001) REIT organization structure and operating characteristics, *Journal of Real Estate Research*, 21, 145–62.

Basel Committee on Banking Supervision (2011) *Basel III: A global regulatory framework for more resilient banks and banking systems*, Basel, Bank for International Settlements, available at: www.bis.org/publ/bcbs189.pdf, last viewed: 7 August 2018.

Basel Committee on Banking Supervision (2013) *Basel III: the liquidity coverage ratio and liquidity risk monitoring tools*, Basel, Bank for International Settlements, available at: www.bis.org/publ/bcbs238.pdf, last viewed: 7 August 2018.

Basel Committee on Banking Supervision (2014) *Basel III leverage ratio framework and disclosure requirements*, Basel, Bank for International Settlements, available at: www.bis.org/publ/bcbs270.pdf, last viewed: 7 August 2018.

Capozza, D. R. and Seguin, P. J. (1998) Managerial style and firm value, *Real Estate Economics*, 26, 131–50.

CBRE (2008) Asia Pacific ViewPoint Investment Activity.

Cox, A., Jones, G., Lobel, M. E., Van Beneden, E. and Sumner E. (2017) Solvency II equivalence in the international (re)insurance landscape: Part IV: Asia Pacific Solvency II equivalence, CG Capital Ideas.com, 20 February, available at: www.gccapitalideas.com/2017/02/22/solvency-ii-equivalence-in-the-international-reinsurance-landscape-part-iv-asia-pacific-solvency-ii-equivalence, last viewed: 7 August 2018.

Eldik, M. V. (2005) The emergence of REIT in Asia: is Asia heading the right direction? Master's dissertation, Amsterdam School of Real Estate.

Ernst & Young (2007) Global REIT Report 2007.

Ernst & Young (2015) *Solvency II. Implications for Asian life insurers*, available at: www.ey.com/Publication/vwLUAssets/Solvency_II_implications_for_Asian_Life_Insurers/$FILE/Solvency_II_implications_for_Asian_Life_Insurers.pdf, last viewed: 7 August 2018.

European Covered Bond Council (2018) *European covered bond fact book 2018*, Brussels.

European Public Real Estate Association (2009) European REITs and cross-border investments: summary paper, September 2009, Brussels, available at: http://prodapp.epra.com/media/EU_REIT_Summary_Paper_110909_1371717199321.pdf, last viewed: 7 August 2018.

European Public Real Estate Association (2015) *Global REIT survey 2015: a comparison of the major REIT regimes around the world*, EPRA Reporting, Brussels.

European Securities and Markets Authority (2012) *Final report:* Guidelines on key concepts of the AIFMD, Paris, available at: www.esma.europa.eu/document/guidelines-key-concepts-aifmd-0, last viewed: 7 August 2018.

European Securities and Markets Authority (2016) ESMA's advice to the European Parliament, the Council and the Commission on the application of the AIDMD passport to non-EU AIFMs and AIFs, Paris, available at: www.esma.europa.eu/system/files_force/library/2016-1140_aifmd_passport.pdf, last viewed: 7 August 2018.

European Union (1985) *Directive of 20 December 1985 on the coordination of laws, regulations and administrative provisions relating to undertakings for collective investment in transferable securities (UCITS) (85/611/EEC)*, available at http://eur-lex.europa.eu/legal-content/EN/TXT/PDF/?uri=CELEX:31985L0611&from=en, last viewed: 7 August 2018.

European Union (2009) *Directive 2009/138/EC of the European Parliament and of the Council of 25 November 2009 on the taking-up and pursuit of the business of Insurance and Reinsurance (Solvency II)*, available at http://eur-lex.europa.eu/legal-content/EN/TXT/HTML/?uri=CELEX:32009L0138&from=EN, last viewed: 7 August 2018.

European Union (2011) *Directive 2011/61/EU of the European Parliament and of the Council of 8 June 2011 on Alternative Investment Fund Managers and amending Directives 2003/41/EC and 2009/65/EC and Regulations (EC) No 1060/2009 and (EU) No 1095/2010*, available at: http://eur-lex.europa.eu/legal-content/EN/TXT/PDF/?uri=CELEX:32011L0061&from=EN, last viewed: 7 August 2018.

European Union (2013a) *Directive 2013/36/EU of the European Parliament and of the Council of 26 June 2013 on access to the activity of credit institutions and the prudential supervision of credit institutions and investment firms, amending Directive 2002/87/EC and repealing Directives 2006/48/EC and 2006/49/EC*, available at: http://eur-lex.europa.eu/legal-content/EN/TXT/HTML/?uri=CELEX:32013L0036&from=EN, last viewed: 7 August 2018.

European Union (2013b) *Regulation (EU) No 575/2013 of the European Parliament and of the Council of 26 June 2013 on prudential requirements for credit institutions and investment firms and amending Regulation (EU) No 648/2012*, available at: http://eur-lex.europa.eu/legal-content/EN/TXT/PDF/?uri=CELEX:32013R0575&from=EN, last viewed: 7 August 2018.

European Union (2014a) *Directive 2014/17/EU of the European Parliament and of the Council of 4 February 2014 on credit agreements for consumers relating to residential immovable property and amending Directives 2008/48/EC and 2013/36/EU and Regulation (EU) No 1093/2010*, available at: http://eur-lex.europa.eu/legal-content/EN/TXT/PDF/?uri=CELEX:32014L0017&from=EN, last viewed: 7 August 2018.

European Union (2014b) *Directive 2014/91/EU of the European Parliament and of the Council of 23 July 2014 amending Directive 2009/65/EC on the coordination of laws, regulations and administrative provisions relating to undertakings for collective investment in transferable securities (UCITS) as regards depositary functions, remuneration policies and sanctions*, available at: http://eur-lex.europa.eu/legal-content/EN/TXT/PDF/?uri=CELEX:32014L0091&from=EN, last viewed: 7 August 2018.

European Union (2016) *2016/C 202/01 Consolidated versions of the Treaty on European Union and the Treaty on the Functioning of the European Union*, available at: http://eur-lex.europa.eu/legal-content/EN/TXT/PDF/?uri=OJ:C:2016:202:FULL&from=EN, last viewed: 7 August 2018.

Geltner, D. M., Miller, N. G., Clayton, J. and Eichholtz, P. (2014) *Commercial Real Estate Analysis and Investments*, 3rd edition, OnCourse Learning, Mason, OH.

Hsieh, C.-H. and Sirmans, C. F. (1991) REITs as captive-financing affiliates: impact on financial performance, *Journal of Real Estate Research*, 6, 179–89.

INREV (2011) *Management Fees and Terms Study 2011*, Amsterdam, INREV Research and Market Information, available at: www.inrev.org/research/management-fees-and-terms-study, last viewed: 7 August 2018.

INREV (2016) *Management Fees and Terms Study 2016*, Amsterdam, INREV Research and Market Information, available at: www.inrev.org/research/management-fees-and-terms-study, last viewed: 7 August 2018.

Kröncke, T.-A., Schindler, F., Westerheide, P. and Steininger, B. (2014) *Effects of Basel III on real estate financing in Germany*, BBSR Publication 09/2014, Federal Institute for Research on Building, Urban Affairs and Spatial Development (BBSR), available at: www.bbsr.bund.de/BBSR/DE/Veroeffentlichungen/BBSROnline/2014/ON092014.html?nn=395966, last viewed: 7 August 2018.

Martougin, C. (2011) *The European alternative investment fund managers directive: how will it affect managers of real estate funds?* London, International Bar Association, available at: www.ibanet.org/Publications/Real_Estate_Newsletter/Real_Estate_Sept_2011_Luxembourg.aspx, last viewed: 7 August 2018.

Morgan, P., Regis, P. J. and Salike N. (2015) *Loan-to-value policy as a macroprudential tool: the case of residential mortgage loans in Asia*, ADBI Working Paper 528. Tokyo, Asian Development Bank Institute, available: www.adb.org/publications/loan-value-policy-macroprudential-tool-case-residential-mortgage-loans-asia, last viewed: 7 August 2018.

Muller, C. and Dogniez, N. (2013) *AIFMD: re-shaping for the future*, 6th ed., KPMG, Luxembourg, available at: https://home.kpmg.com/lu/en/home/insights/2012/10/alternative-investmentfundmanagers directive.html, last viewed: 7 August 2018.

Munich Reinsurance Company (2015) *Partial internal models – techniques for integration into the standard formula*, Münchener Rückversicherungs-Gesellschaft, Munich, available at: www.munichre.com/site/corporate/get/documents_E33771658/mr/assetpool.shared/Documents/5_Touch/_Publications/302-08531_en.pdf, last viewed: 13 April 2016.

Nareit (2016) *Global real estate investment: how is the global listed property market configured?* available at: www.reit.com/investing/reit-basics/global-real-estate-investment, last viewed: 7 August 2018.

Norwegian Ministry of Finance (2013) *Countercyclical buffer at 1 pct.*, Press Release No: 62/2013, available at: www.regjeringen.no/en/aktuelt/countercyclical-buffer-at-1-pct/id747825, last viewed: 7 August 2018.

Ooi, T. L. J., Newell, G. and Sing, T. F. (2006) The growth of REIT markets in Asia, *Journal of Real Estate Literature*, 14, 203–22.

Opp, S. and Hartwell, M. (2012) Alternative investment fund managers directive survey, Deloitte, available at: www2.deloitte.com/content/dam/Deloitte/ie/Documents/FinancialServices/investment management/2013_aifmd_survey_deloitte_ireland.pdf, last viewed: 7 August 2018.

Pirolo, A. and Whelan, R. (2014) European REITs are on a tear: record surge in fundraising boosts commercial property market, Wall Street Journal, 09 September, available at: www.wsj.com/articles/european-reits-are-on-a-tear-1410288158, last viewed: 7 August 2018.

Swiss National Bank (2016) *Basel III countercyclical capital buffer: stance of the Basel III countercyclical capital buffer in Switzerland*, available at: www.snb.ch/n/mmr/reference/CCB_communication_2016/source/CCB_communication_2016.n.pdf, last viewed: 7 August 2018.

Williams, M. L., Newell, M., Moss, J. and McKellar, S. (2012) *AIFM Directive – impact on real estate fund managers*, Norton Rose Fulbright, available at: www.nortonrosefulbright.com/knowledge/publications/64785/aifm-directive-impact-on-real-estate-fund-managers, last viewed: 7 August 2018.

4 Banking and real estate

Richard K. Green

Introduction

This chapter reviews the various roles that banks play as part of the real estate lending process. Real estate loans are important assets on bank balance sheets; for example, in the third quarter of 2017, 45 per cent of US chartered depository assets were in mortgages or mortgage-backed securities (Figure 4.1). But banks also participate in the real estate lending process even when they do not keep loans on the balance sheet. Banks might originate loans and then distribute them to capital markets and they might service the loans (that is, make sure that investors in loans receive the principal and interest due to them) that they have distributed to others. Subsequent sections review the role of banks in real estate construction lending, mortgage origination, mortgage funding and mortgage servicing.

Construction lending

Commercial banks have traditionally been sources of residential real estate construction lending. Residential construction lending aligns well with the expertise and structure of commercial banks. Such banks are supposed to have 'soft underwriting' skills, such as judgement about the expertise of builders and knowledge about local market conditions. These skills should give them an informational advantage over, for example, capital markets, when making decisions about whether or not to approve construction loans to privately held home builders.

Construction loans also align well with commercial bank balance sheets, which are heavily funded with short-term deposits (deposits make up 75.8 per cent of US bank funding; other debt, including corporate debt, contributes 12.9 per cent; and equity funds 11.3 per cent).[1] Residential construction loans have short duration – their maturities are the length of time it takes to build and then to sell a house. This means that banks need to focus on only one kind of risk – credit/default risk – when underwriting these loans. Balance sheet mismatch risk on construction loans is much smaller than it is for permanent loans, which have much longer durations.

Banks advance construction loans to developers and to individuals. Loans made to developers are usually called acquisition and development loans, and are used by developers to acquire land and build infrastructure (such as sewers and water) that turns land into finished lots. The developers may then either sell the land to a homebuilder, or may build homes on the land themselves. If a homebuilder wishes to build out a speculative subdivision, they will get funding from the bank to do so; it is common for banks to advance funds equal to 100 per cent of construction costs. Funds are drawn as needed and interest is paid on the outstanding loan balance. The principal is repaid as houses are sold. When houses are

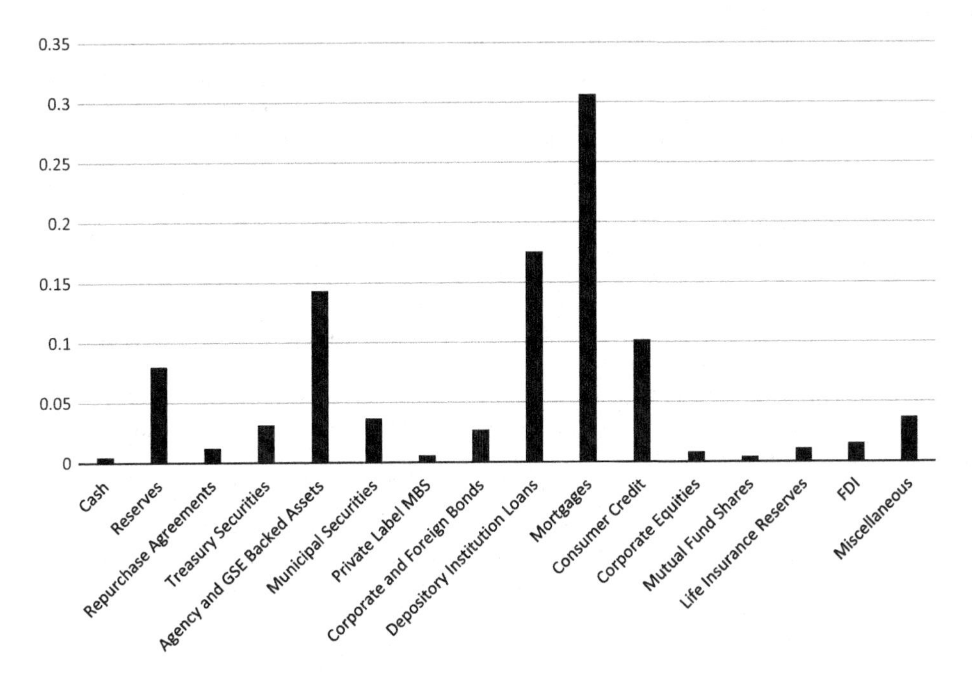

Figure 4.1 US chartered commercial bank asset shares
Source: Federal Reserve Board of Governors Flow of Funds Accounts (2017).

sold, banks typically require the homebuilder to remit all the revenue from the sales (not just the construction cost associated with the sales) until the all construction funds are repaid. The fact that developers get paid last is one of many contributors to the risks embodied in real estate development.

Construction loans to individuals seeking to pay to build houses for themselves to live in are far less risky than speculative homebuilding loans. Usually, homebuyers looking to get such a loan arrange for a permanent mortgage to take out the construction loan at the time the new house is ready for occupancy. So, while lenders take on substantial credit risk when making speculative loans (if houses built speculatively sell slowly or at lower than anticipated prices, the disappointing performance can make it difficult for the developer/borrower to repay the loan), they take on relatively little risk when making construction loans to individuals. The permanent lender underwrites the homebuyer, determines whether he is creditworthy, and once satisfied he is so, essentially removes credit risk from the construction lender by promising to make a loan once the house is completed.

Interest rates on construction loans are usually determined by adding a margin to a short-term interest rate, such as the prime rate, short-term Treasury rate or London inter-bank offered rate. The size of the margin is based on the bank's judgement of risk and the cost of capital for the loan product. Later in the chapter, we discuss how banks perceive that Basel capital standards have an impact on their cost of capital.

Permanent residential lending

Throughout the world, banks are important institutions for originating residential mortgages. Whether or not they keep them on balance sheet, however, varies dramatically by country.

Countries that rely heavily on fixed-rate mortgages tend to use capital markets to fund them, while countries that rely heavily on variable rate mortgages use banks to fund them.

Banks do, however, underwrite residential mortgages nearly everywhere. Lenders that sell loans into capital markets have a responsibility to do due diligence on loans before selling them to those markets. The due diligence process has changed dramatically over the past 30 years. Until the early 1990s, residential mortgage underwriting was based on a series of heuristics. Borrowers generally had to have loan to value (LTV) ratios as well as debt to income (DTI) ratios below some threshold level to qualify for a loan. For example, borrowers usually needed to have a debt payment to income ratio for all long-term debts of less than 36 per cent if they wished to receive the mortgage. The components of this DTI were the mortgage payment, property taxes paid, casualty insurance and other long-term debt divided by documented income.

Now, however, most financial institutions have automated underwriting systems, the foundations of which are various types of regression models. For example, a lender might use historical data to estimate a hazard model of default.[2] Default is usually defined as whether a mortgage is ever more than 90 days late, but there are other definitions. Typical right-hand side variables in an underwriting model would include some sort of credit score or components of credit history, debt payment to income ratio, LTV ratio, whether a loan is well documented or not, months of reserves banked for mortgage and property tax payments, and length of time in a particular job. This list is not exhaustive, and there is a wide variety of specifications that lenders use to develop automated underwriting models.

In the United States, the three most important automated underwriting systems are Fannie Mae's Desktop Underwriter, Freddie Mac's Loan Prospector and Federal Housing Administration's (FHA) Technology Open To Approved Lenders (or TOTAL) scorecard. These systems do two things: they rate borrowers by credit worthiness, based on findings from regressions, and they determine which borrowers essentially automatically get a loan and which need to be reviewed beyond the underwriting model, or require 'manual underwriting'. Borrowers not approved by models are said to have been 'referred'.

Since the global financial crisis, borrowers referred by models have generally been rejected by lenders. This contrasts with the pre-crisis period, when many borrowers were approved despite having been referred. In a well-functioning mortgage system, manual underwriting can reveal to lenders good risk borrowers even when they do not receive a good score from an automated underwriting model. But during the period 2004–2007, it seemed that many lenders ignored underwriting altogether.[3]

But suppose, for the sake of argument, that the automated underwriting models by themselves do a good job of determining borrower risk. Lenders using these models still have an important responsibility in the residential mortgage process. Specifically, they have a responsibility to make sure that loans are well documented. Corrupt data run through even the best underwriting model would produce corrupt outcomes. In the time since the global financial crisis, lenders have taken much greater care to make sure that loans are underwritten based on accurate information. It is possible that lenders are now *too* concerned with the accuracy of the information provided. They currently require potential borrowers to provide information multiple times. This may simply be redundant. There is no evidence that requiring borrowers to document assets multiple times leads to lower default risk. Having assets well documented once might well be sufficient to make good underwriting decisions and could produce a more efficient mortgage underwriting process.

There is an analytically incoherent aspect of mortgage underwriting. Suppose the regressions underlying default prediction are well specified. It is then the case that any use of explanatory variable beyond that implied by the regression will worsen predicted outcomes. Yet many lenders impose overlays on top of automated underwriting models. For example, a borrower may be deemed a good credit risk by an automated underwriting model and may yet be referred because they fail an overlay such as debt payment to income. This leads to an unattractive outcome: a marginal borrower with a DTI slightly below an arbitrary cut-off might be approved for a mortgage while a strong borrower with a DTI slightly above the cut-off will not get a loan. This means the use of heuristic overlays *worsens* the ability of lenders to manage the risk.

Mortgage product types

There are several types of mortgage products. The key components to a mortgage are how fixed is the interest rate, the amortisation, the term, upfront costs and prepayment penalties. The typical American mortgage has a fixed interest rate, has an amortisation period equal to the term, has some upfront cost, but no prepayment penalty. By contrast, the typical Canadian mortgage has a variable rate, has an amortisation period longer than the term – and therefore has a balloon payment – has some upfront costs and a prepayment penalty. Other countries have mixes and matches of features of Canadian and American mortgage terms (see Lea, 2010, for a good description).

We may describe the Canadian and American mortgages as 'vanilla' products for their countries. There are also more exotic mortgages. For example, some mortgages have a negative amortisation feature: for some periods, borrowers pay less than the interest due on the loan. Others have a teaser rate at the beginning of the mortgage that rises sharply later in life of the mortgage. This type of loan often features prepayment penalties. These mortgages have largely disappeared from the American market. In times of great inflation, such as in Latin America in the 1970s, some mortgages have a price level adjustment feature. These mortgages pay a real rate of interest, but have their balances adjusted by the rate of inflation each year. Andrew Caplin and others have advocated for the development of shared appreciation mortgages (Caplin *et al.*, 1997). These products would have low monthly payments in exchange for the lender receiving part of any house price appreciation the borrower might get at time of home sale. A few banks in the UK funded shared appreciation mortgages, but withdrew them from the market because of the public relations problems they created.

Finally, home equity conversion mortgages are mortgages that allow homeowners to extract equity from their house in exchange for repayment of principal and accrued interest at the time of house sale or death. In the event that the value of the mortgage balance exceeds the value of the house at the time the borrower dies, the sale price of the house, less selling expenses, still satisfies the lien.

Balance sheet issues

Mortgage type heavily influences the source of mortgage funding. Variable rate mortgages are attractive products for banks. These mortgages have little in the way of duration risk, so are assets that line up well with banks liabilities (deposits), which also have short duration. Fixed-rate mortgages that have heavy prepayment penalties or, in extreme cases, lock-out clauses,[4] are attractive to pension funds and insurance companies whose liabilities have long duration. The American mortgage, with its long duration and free prepayment feature, creates difficulties for any type of financial institution that is managing duration risk. Perhaps this is why agency-backed and government-backed mortgage-backed securities are frequently purchased by central banks. For example, more than one-third of Ginnie Mae securities outstanding are owned by central banks. Conversely, commercial banks hold only a small share of outstanding fixed-rate American mortgages.

Nevertheless, if the bank originates a loan, it remains on its balance sheet implicitly until the loan is paid off. For banks to sell loans to investors, they generally must represent and warrant to securities holders that the loans sold to the securities holders are accurately represented in the securities offerings. If a mortgage inside a mortgage-backed pool goes into default and foreclosure, and an investor in that pool finds that the mortgage has characteristics that differ from those represented by the originator, the investor can force the originator to buy the mortgage back at its face value. The originator thus bears the losses arising from the foreclosure. Only when a loan is completely paid off is a bank completely free of responsibility from the consequences of that loan.[5]

Credit risk issues

The credit risk embedded in mortgages of course varies from loan to loan. Some mortgages simply carry higher risk than others. For example, some housing markets are more volatile than others: loans made in more volatile markets will be riskier. Loans with higher LTV ratios are riskier than loans with lower LTV ratios. Loans made to borrowers with strong credit histories are less risky than loans made to borrowers with weaker credit histories.

Beyond the characteristics of the housing market and the borrower, the jurisdiction in which a loan is made has an influence on the riskiness of the mortgage. While a number of aspects of mortgage laws vary from state to state and from country to country, we focus on two things here. First, some states and countries are known as nonrecourse jurisdictions. This means that, when a borrower forfeits his house to a bank or other lender, he is absolved of all responsibility for the loan, even if the value of the house is less than the outstanding loan balance. In a recourse jurisdiction, however, a lender has recourse to collect the difference between the value of a house received as the result of the foreclosure and the outstanding balance of the loan, including accrued interest and fees associated with foreclosing on the house. Some scholars have argued that default rates in Spain, for example, were lower than might be expected in light of the economic crash because Spain is a recourse country. On the other hand, the global financial crisis made the recourse–nonrecourse issue moot for many borrowers, because they had no assets or income to attach to repay differences between foreclosed house values and mortgage balances.

The other distinction across jurisdictions with respect to mortgage default involves whether default is a nonjudicial or judicial process. Because lenders do not have to go through a court process to acquire a home which is backing a loan in default in a nonjudicial state, they can complete foreclosure proceedings in such states more rapidly. Some scholars have argued that the reason the mortgage crisis, and by extension the housing crisis, was shorter in California and Arizona than in Florida and New Jersey is because the western states had nonjudicial foreclosure processes while the eastern states had judicial processes (Ghent and Kudlyak, 2011).

Servicing

We have already emphasised that banks tend to sell long-term mortgages off their balance sheets. This is actually not a new phenomenon: if we returned to the nineteenth century, we would observe that most mortgages at the time were owned by investors other than banks.

But while banks sell mortgages, they often retain *the servicing* of those mortgages. When mortgages perform well, this simply means that the bank collects principal and interest and passes them along to an investor while collecting a small fee. The value of these fees is modelled and booked as an asset on the balance sheet of banks.

Valuing servicing is challenging. Servicing is very much like an interest-only strip, a security based solely on the interest payments from a pool of mortgages, Treasury bonds or other bonds. Once the principal on the mortgages or bonds has been repaid, interest payments stop and the value of the interest-only strip falls to zero.[6]

This means that, if interest rates fall rapidly, the value of the servicing can fall rapidly. This is because once a loan is refinanced, cash flows arising from servicing the loan disappear and the value of the servicing goes to zero. As of 2016, the market for servicing has become quite weak because of fears that the cost of loans will continue to fall and hence stimulate refinances. Worries about regulatory issues have also caused the mortgage servicing rights market to weaken.[7]

Things become more complicated when a mortgage goes into default. It is then the responsibility of the banker/servicer first to notify the borrower that he is in arrears and to attempt to restore the mortgage to a current status. Failing that, the service has the responsibility to foreclose on the property and dispose of it in a manner that is most beneficial to the investor. To some extent, there is a conflict of interest in this arrangement. The longer it takes the servicer to dispose of the property, the greater is the length of time over which the servicer collects fees. But a long drawn-out process is more costly to the mortgage investor than a shorter process.

The regulatory environment for servicing has changed markedly in the wake of the Dodd-Frank law.[8] Servicers now have a responsibility to make sure that they are only foreclosing on loans that are in arrears and to do their best to modify loans such that modifications produce better outcomes for investors as well as borrowers. If servicers do not fulfil these responsibilities, they can be fined or otherwise sanctioned. The value of servicing fell in 2016, in part because of uncertainty about the future direction of interest rates and in part because of concerns about possible sanctions.

A phenomenon arising from changing servicing conditions has been a movement away from banks toward other types of financial institutions for serving. The share of servicing performed by banks in the United States dropped from in excess of 81 per cent in 2011 to 51 per cent in 2014.[9]

The United States compared with other countries

In the United States, banks are important institutions in terms of the origination and servicing of home mortgages. However, banks only hold a small share of mortgage debt outstanding in the United States; more than 80 per cent of mortgages held in the United States are securitised (that is, in Fannie Mae, Freddie Mac, Ginnie Mae or private label securities), although the private label securities market has shrunk dramatically in the wake of the global financial crisis. The reasons that the US mortgage market relies so heavily on capital market funding are: 1) pre-payable fixed-rate mortgages do not match well with bank balance sheets; and 2) because there are not sufficient deposits in the United States to fund the appetite for mortgages.

Other countries are very different. For example, in the United Kingdom, Singapore and Canada, the vast majority of mortgage debt is funded by deposits. This works well for these countries, because mortgages in these places typically have variable rates and, hence, short duration. That is, the value of the mortgage assets changes little with changes in interest rates. As we have already noted, the mortgage term in Canada is also short, meaning that banks can easily recycle their deposits.

The problem with using deposits to fund fixed-rate mortgages was illustrated by the problems encountered by savings loans in the United States in the 1970s. Short-term interest rates over that time rose rapidly. This meant that for savings and loans to maintain deposits, they needed to pay higher rates of interest to depositors. But under the regulatory regime of that time, they were not permitted to raise the interest they paid to deposits and so their source of mortgage funding (that is deposits) disappeared. The regulatory environment for savings and loans produced illiquidity for the mortgage market.

But even had savings loans been able to match market interest rates, they still would have become insolvent. That is because fixed-rate mortgages have long duration, so when interest rates rise, the value of the mortgages falls. Typical mortgage duration at that time was seven years, meaning that a one percentage point rise in interest rates would lead to a seven percentage point decline in the value of mortgages on the savings and loans balance sheet. At the same time, deposit rates do move with market rates, making their duration nearly zero. Rising interest rates had thus had little effect on the value of savings and loan liabilities, while substantially diminishing the value of their assets (mortgages). The rapid increase in interest rates in the 1970s from five to six percentage points at the beginning of the decade to double digit rates the end of the decade meant that the savings and loans became fundamentally insolvent, as the value of their assets fell below the value of their liabilities.

Basel

Among the most important determinants of the behaviour of banks with respect to mortgages over the past 25 years has been a series of bank capital regulations that have been known as the Basel Accords. In particular, Basel II made mortgage-backed securities more appealing assets for banks than mortgages themselves. The reason for this is that, while mortgages had 50 per cent risk weights attached to them, mortgage-backed securities had 20 per cent risk weights. To understand what this means, consider that assets with 100 per cent risk weights need to have 8 per cent capital behind them. Mortgages thus had to have 4 per cent capital behind them, while mortgage-backed securities needed only to have 1.6 per cent capital behind them. As banks maintain that capital is more expensive than other funding sources, they viewed mortgage-backed securities as more profitable investments than whole mortgages.

Basel's reasoning was straightforward. Because mortgage-backed securities contained many mortgages, they diversified idiosyncratic risk. Individual mortgages did not do that. At the same time, Fannie Mae and Freddie Mac mortgages were grated AAA status by Moody's and Standard & Poor's, as were senior tranches of private label security mortgages. Before considering whether this was a reasonable regulatory setup, let us consider the claim of banks that capital is more expensive than other forms of funding.

The idea that capital is more expensive flies in the face of one of the most well-known theorems in economics: the Modigliani–Miller theorem, which maintains that a firm's total cost of capital is independent of capital structure. If a firm uses that cash to finance itself, its equity is less risky and, therefore, the return to equity necessary for investors should fall. The author has had conversations with bankers that suggest that at least some bankers at large institutions do not believe this. And small bankers are almost certainly correct that Modigliani–Miller does not apply to them. The reason is that these banks are funded almost entirely with deposits, so their marginal cost of debt is (1) subsidised and (2) independent of their leverage. This is because deposits are guaranteed by the Federal Deposit Insurance Corporation (FDIC) and therefore expose depositors to virtually zero risk. Hence, regardless of the capital position of a small bank, the cost of debt remains the same, and remains at below-market cost. The fact that the federal government subsidises bank debt through FDIC nullifies the predictions of Modigliani–Miller: deposit funded banks should use subsidised debt as much as possible.

Large banks are a different matter, however. Large banks issue bonds that are not guaranteed by the US government. The marginal cost of debt to large banks is thereby set by the market. Well-capitalised banks are seen as less risky, so get higher credit ratings and lower cost of debt. At the same time, reducing leverage reduces the cost of equity, so large banks should be largely indifferent to the capital structure imposed upon them by the Basel regulations. In any event, for many banks, Basel II made it unattractive to hold whole mortgages as assets on the balance sheet. If it is true that risk-based capital influences banking behaviour, Basel III will have an even larger influence on bank real estate lending than Basel II. In particular, construction lending is deemed by Basel III to be highly risky, and therefore carries a risk rate of 150 per cent, meaning that banks need to hold capital of 12 per cent against construction loans on their balance sheets. Since Basel III was implemented, we have seen a reduction in residential construction lending.

Let us turn to the issue of whether mortgage-backed securities should be rated AAA, and so need less capital behind them than other assets. With respect to Fannie Mae and Freddie Mac, we now know that, while in the absence of a federal guarantee, they issued securities that were manifestly not AAA worthy, they were, in fact, guaranteed. During the financial crisis of 2008, Fannie Mae and Freddie Mac were deemed to be institutions which were 'too big to fail', so they received injections from the Troubled Asset Relief Program[10] and were placed into receivership. Whether future Fannie, Freddie or their successors' securities will be guaranteed remains an open question.

As for private label MBS – those not backed by Fannie Mae and Freddie Mac – they clearly did not perform to AAA standards during the financial crisis. According to Ospina and Uhlig (2016), losses on AAA rated private label MBS were six percent. While this is not as catastrophic as rhetoric around PLS might imply, it is still 12 times Moody's expected 10 year losses for AAA rated securities.

Moving forward, the performance of MBS during the global financial crisis has important implications for bank regulation. In particular, if MBS are not at a capital advantage relative to whole mortgages, banks might take more mortgages back on their balance sheets. But that would mean either (1) variable rate mortgages will become more important in the US, or, (2) bank supervisors will require banks to hedge their interest rate risk using forward contracts or swaps. Because such contracts involve costs, they would likely raise the cost of borrowing on long-term, prepayable loans.

Non-bank lending

When it comes to real estate lending, the word bank is often used colloquially: borrowers will speak of going to the bank for a loan. But, in fact, about half of the residential loans in the United States are originated by non-depository financial institutions. During the sub-prime period, the best known of these was Countrywide Financial. In 2016, Quicken Financial was among the leading residential lenders in the country. Neither Countrywide Financial nor Quicken was/is a bank, because neither holds deposits.

These institutions originate mortgages that are, in turn, funded by other types of institutions, including secondary mortgage market agencies such as Fannie Mae, Freddie Mac, Ginnie Mae and banks. They collect fees for originating loans and then very often they retain servicing of loans. Approximately 300 of these types of institutions originate loans, certify they are eligible for FHA, Veterans Affairs or Rural Housing insurance and place the loans into Ginnie Mae securities that they issue. They then service the loans for Ginnie Mae. Once a loan goes into default, these non-bank institutions must either buy the defaulted loan out of the pool or, if they want to keep the loan in the pool, continue to pay investors the principal and interest due from the loan. Properly underwritten loans that fail will ultimately receive reimbursements from various government insurance programmes, but non-bank lenders who issue securities funding these loans must pay cash flows to investors for a period of time during which they are not receiving cash flows from mortgages. Very often, non-bank financial institutions have lines of credit from banks that allow them to remain liquid while awaiting their insurance payments. Hence, while non-banks are involved in the origination and servicing of loans, they rely on banks for liquidity.

It is worth noting that Ginnie Mae does not guarantee loans (FHA, Veterans Affairs and Rural Housing do that), but rather guarantees issuers. Non-bank lenders generally have very small levels of capital relative to the size of the mortgages outstanding that they have originated. This is why any interruption in bank liquidity could make these institutions quite vulnerable. If non-banks fail to meet their obligation on government insured loans, Ginnie Mae takes them over and assigns their assets and liabilities to other issuers. Servicers taking over loans from failed issuers receive sufficient funds from Ginnie Mae to assure that the acquisition does not produce losses.

Commercial lending

The role of banks in commercial lending markets has some similarities to the residential market and some differences. The most important similarity in the United States is that banks generally make construction loans but avoid having too many permanent loans on their balance sheets. While commercial loans are generally of shorter duration than residential loans (commercial loans in the United States typically have terms between five and ten years), such loans still have a longer duration than the liabilities of banks and are therefore not well suited to sit on bank balance sheets.

The construction lending process for commercial real estate has much in common with the construction lending process for residential real estate. First, banks are more comfortable making commercial construction loans to developers who have permanent loan commitments for when properties are ready for occupancy. Second, construction loans typically pay out the full amount of construction costs and have a term that is equal length to the construction period. Third, banks look at the strength and track record of the sponsor's developed properties in evaluating whether to advance a construction loan. Finally, the risk weight assigned by Basil III to commercial construction loans is the same as that assigned for residential construction loans: 150 per cent.

But commercial underwriting is quite different from residential underwriting when it comes to making loans on existing properties. On the residential side of the business, underwriting focusses more on the borrower than on the collateral (although the collateral surely matters). That is to say, on the residential side, banks use household income and credit history of the borrower as key determinants of whether to make a mortgage or not.

On the commercial side of the market, by contrast, lenders focus more on the collateral than on the borrower, although borrowers with poor track records will find it difficult to get a commercial loan.

Banks look at a minimum of three underwriting standards when making commercial loans. The first is LTV. LTVs for commercial loans are generally lower than for residential loans. In the United States, one can get an FHA loan with a LTV ratio of slightly under 97 per cent. One can also get very well-priced loans in the residential market for LTVs of 80 per cent. But in the commercial market, 80 per cent LTVs are rare. Office buildings, shopping centres and, to a lesser extent, apartment buildings, require equity contributions of at least 25 per cent. Hotels require even more equity than that.

The second underwriting standard commonly used for commercial mortgages is the DCR. This ratio is simply stabilised net operating income divided by mortgage debt service. Typical debt cover ratios range from 125 per cent to 150 per cent. In a low interest rate environment, it is usually the LTV constraint that is binding. For example, in 2016, when commercial mortgage rates could be found at less than four per cent, the LTV ratio, rather than the debt coverage ratio, generally determined maximum mortgage size. Suppose an office building with a net operating income of US$5 million sells at a capitalisation rate of 5 per cent; in financing the purchase, the buyer is constrained by a maximum LTV of 0.7 and a maximum debt coverage ratio of 1.3. Also, assume a 40-year amortisation schedule and a mortgage rate of 4 per cent. So the property sells for US$100 million and can, under the LTV rule, get a loan of US$70 million. The annual payments on the loan are US$3.51 million. So the debt cover ratio is 5/3.51, or 1.42, which is well above the minimum.

An underwriting standard that arose in the aftermath of the global financial crisis is debt yield ratio. This ratio is the return to the property divided by mortgage debt outstanding. The rationale for the standard is that many loans that came due between 2008 and 2010 could not be refinanced.

An important difference between residential loans and commercial loans in the United States is that residential loans are almost always self-amortising, whereas commercial loans are not. A typical commercial loan might have a 30-year amortisation period and a 5-year term. As a result, these loans have balloon payments that somehow need to be financed. Borrowers rarely have sufficient cash to pay off these balloon payments. Instead, they expect to refinance their loans at the time they come due.

A large publicly-traded shopping centre real estate investment trust that went bankrupt during the global financial crisis illustrates the point. The company operated shopping malls that performed well and had sufficient cash flows to make mortgage payments. Unfortunately, much of its debt matured during the middle of the liquidity crisis. As spreads widened, values on all assets, including shopping centres, fell. The value of the company's particular malls fell by 30 per cent. Hence, a mall once worth US$200 million backing a US$140 million loan became a US$140 million mall backing that same loan, even though the mall's cash flows remained largely unchanged. Because no lender would make 100 per cent LTV loans, the mall owner could not find a lender who would refinance the full balance of its mortgages. The mall valuation underlying the mortgage that needed to be refinanced at the time of the global financial crises came at a time when capitalisation rates were high. The change in cap rates put the business into bankruptcy.

Lenders believe that using debt yield as an underwriting tool mitigates against the sort of refinance risk that manifested itself between 2008 and 2010. By focussing on debt yield, lenders believe that properties will be able to obtain refinancing when loans come due, even in difficult times.

Banks and other entities

The United States has roughly US$10 trillion dollars of residential mortgage debt outstanding. Depository institutions fund roughly 25 per cent of these mortgages. Credit unions hold another four per cent. Two-thirds of the market is funded by Fannie Mae, Freddie Mac, Ginnie Mae and private label securities. The United States has also developed a fairly large commercial mortgage-backed securities market: Fannie Mae and Freddie Mac back apartment loans, but many mortgages for apartments, together with all securitised loans for office, retail, industrial and hotel real estate, are sold into securities with no government backing, either explicit or implicit.

Outside the United States, many countries used covered bonds to fund mortgages. According to the European Covered Bond Council, about €2.5 trillion in mortgages outstanding in countries outside the United States were financed by covered bonds. While in the United States, mortgage-backed securities are guaranteed by trusts (or special purpose vehicles), in countries such as Germany and Denmark, covered bonds are guaranteed by banks. The distinction is important, in that when a bank in the United States sells loans into a mortgage-backed security, the loan disappears from its balance sheet; when a bank in Germany funds a mortgage with a covered bond, the mortgage remains on its balance sheet, as it is the asset covering the liability of the obligation to the investor in the bond.

Investors in real estate face trade-offs when determining whether to obtain debt financing directly through banks, insurance companies or pension funds, or through real estate capital markets. The advantage of capital market funding is, in theory, liquidity. Mortgage-backed securities are commodities, can be traded in public markets and therefore might trade at a premium, reducing the costs to borrowers. This makes capital market funding appealing.

But should a problem arise with a property (say a mall anchor declares bankruptcy), capital markets work less well than a direct lender, because of governance issues. When there is a relationship between a borrower and a direct lender and the borrower faces difficulties because of an exogenous economic shock, the borrower and the lender can negotiate a work-out. But when a troubled borrower is dealing with a loan funded through capital markets, that borrower is dealing with a special servicer, whose ability to negotiate work-outs is limited by documents government the trust that holds the MBS.

In other words, when borrowers are deciding whether to get their funding from a direct lender or from capital markets, they are making a perceived trade-off between price and flexibility. Because different borrowers have different objectives, it is possible that debt-financed real estate will be provided through a variety of vehicles for many years to come.

Conclusion and summary

This chapter has reviewed the relationship between real estate and banking. In particular, it has discussed how banking finance is crucial for short-term real estate loans, such as construction loans, and how such loans match well to the duration of bank liabilities. It has also considered the regulation of banks, particularly with respect to capital, and how capital standards might or might not change the cost of lending. Finally, it has discussed how banks interact with non-bank financial institutions.

Notes

1 See Federal Deposit Insurance Corporation Quarterly Banking Profile.

2 A hazard model seeks to estimate the probability that the hazard of something will happen at a particular point in time. It usually contains two components: a baseline hazard function and a shift function. The former can be thought of as a function that relates time to the probability of a hazard happening under neutral conditions. This baseline is then shifted by a function, usually exponential, which contains coefficients that map certain characteristics into whether a hazard becomes more or less likely to happen. For example, a higher LTV ratio at loan origination will lead a hazard function to shift 'up' because the probability of a default will increase at all times. For an excellent treatment of hazard functions, see Kiefer (1988).
3 See Green (2013) for a discussion.
4 Clauses that forbid prepayment.
5 Representation and warranty issues were among the most important leading to the collapse of Countrywide Financial.
6 See Nasdaq, Interest-only strip (IO), www.nasdaq.com/investing/glossary/i/interest-only-strip.
7 See Sinnock (2016).
8 The Dodd-Frank Wall Street Reform And Consumer Protection Act is a law that was passed in the aftermath of the global financial crisis. The law substantially changed the regulation of banks (and other financial institutions) in the United States. See www.gpo.gov/fdsys/pkg/PLAW-111publ203/html/PLAW-111publ203.htm.
9 Schwartz, F. (2015) Loan servicing: the rise of the non-bank servicer, adapting to the changing marketplace. CoreLogic Insights Blog, 16 March. www.corelogic.com/blog/2015/03/loan-servicing-the-rise-of-the-non-bank-servicer.aspx.
10 For a description of the Troubled Asset Relief Program (TARP), see Kiel and Nguyen (2018). The TARP program advanced Fannie Mae and Freddie Mac US$187 billion in exchange for preferred shares to the US Treasury that pay a dividend of 10 per cent. While the institutions have nearly repaid the injection along with the ten per cent dividend, Fannie and Freddie were insolvent in 2008.

References

Caplin, A., Chan, S., Freeman, C. and Tracy, J. (1997) *Housing partnerships: a new approach to a market at a crossroads*, MIT Press, Cambridge, MA.

Ghent, A. C. and Kudlyak, M. (2011) Recourse and residential mortgage default: evidence from US states, *Review of Financial Studies*, 24(9), 3139–86.

Green, R. K. (2013) *Introduction to mortgages and mortgage backed securities*, Academic Press, San Diego, CA.

Kiefer, N. M. (1988) Economic duration data and hazard functions, *Journal of Economic Literature*, 26(2), 646–79.

Kiel, P. and Nguyen, D. (2018) The state of the bailout, *Pro Publica*, 20 July, https://projects.propublica.org/bailout.

Lea, M. (2010) *International comparison of mortgage product offerings*, Research Institute for Housing America, Washington, DC.

Sinnock, B. (2016) Can Fintech Fix Mortgage Servicing? *National Mortgage News*, 12 October, www.nationalmortgagenews.com/news/servicing/can-fintech-fix-mortgage-servicing-1088692-1.html.

5 The supply of investable buildings

Colin Jones

Introduction

The supply of investable buildings is at the heart of real estate markets as it affects their nature and scale. However, the supply of investable buildings is not confined to the private sector and many are built by the state or are financially supported from public funds or through taxation incentives. This is particularly true of housing. Housing can be differentiated by various types of tenure that are very important to the understanding of supply. The commercial property market is also segmented between owner occupation and leased.

This chapter examines the different facets of the supply process. It begins with a macro-economic perspective that provides an overview of the short and long-term factors driving the supply of real estate and highlights the role of net additions to the supply of buildings. The next section examines the importance of tenure. This is followed by sections covering the structure of the development industry, the mechanics of development finance and the influence of investors. The last two sections cover some potential public policy issues that are raised by the operation and outcomes of real estate development.

A macro-economic perspective

A macro-economic view of real estate sees it as an element of the fixed capital stock of a nation. Property development, whether it is residential, commercial or industrial construction, is then deemed to be increasing the capital stock of the country (that is, capital investment) and is referred to by statisticians as 'gross domestic capital formation'. Besides buildings, it also includes government expenditure on public infrastructure, such as new hospitals, schools and roads, business investment which can be divided into new plant and machinery, vehicles including new cars, trains, ships and aircraft. The proportion of capital investment accounted for by real estate development will vary from country to country and from year to year. In the UK, residential development is in the order of 15–20% of capital investment in any one year. Similarly, other buildings and structures can amount to one-third of all investment.

A nation's changing capital stock is not just the result of additions but is also a function of the depreciation of the existing stock, so it is important to assess additions in terms of their net impact. A new machine increases the investment stock but if it simply replaced an old one that is scrapped there may be no net overall addition. However, the new machine will probably be more advanced and have greater efficiency, so there will be a net addition. In the context of real estate, new buildings may simply replace obsolete ones that are demolished but may be larger or smaller or better quality, or redevelopment may involve a change of use.

Seen from this macro-economic perspective, we can view the changing supply of real estate as part of the business cycle, whereby net investment grows and contracts. In particular, Keynesian economic theory sees the variability in investment as driven by an 'accelerator', with increasing demand leading to increased net investment and vice versa. To take an individual example, a factory owner faced with rising demand can choose to meet this by building a new factory. Increased investment represents an increase in national output which, in turn, could stimulate further investment and, hence, the term 'accelerator' and, of course, it works in the reverse direction when the downturn comes.

Another major influence on investment is changes in interest rates, which influence the cost of borrowing. A key debate in economics between Keynesians and Monetarists is the responsiveness of investment to interest rates: the former emphasise the accelerator while, in contrast, the latter see interest rates as the major influence on investment. A further important short-term influence on the private sector investment decision is confidence in the future. This will be reflected in the expected future income flows fed into a discounted cash flow analysis. In turn, business confidence is fuelled by the attainment of recent high profits that are also a cheaper source of investment funds than bank borrowing.

Besides cyclical influences, there are also long-term influences on investment. One long-term driver is technological change. This is primarily seen in terms of labour being replaced by machines or computers but it has implications for real estate, for example, in terms of office space requirements. It is also seen in cash machines replacing banks and online sales challenging high street shops. Other long-term influences are changes to the structure of economic activity in cities. An increased population requires additional housing while rising real incomes lead to the demand for more shops. The switch to a services-based economy in many developed countries was reflected in a growth of offices and a decline in factories.

It is difficult to be precise about how much the stock of real estate changes every year. It is possible to identify the additional aggregate total of houses in many countries in any one year by simply taking government statistics on new housebuilding completions and subtracting demolitions. In the UK, this is of the order of 1%. However, this calculation would ignore improvements and depreciation of the existing stock and the whole dimension of its value, before and after. An assessment in other real estate sectors is even more complex as 'new' development is often redevelopment, involving change of use and mixed use. Real estate net additions are also highly cyclical, with substantial growth focussed primarily in booms. Such booms are global phenomena. Barras (2009) has identified three global office cycles since the 1980s, beginning with the speculative boom of the late 1980s, followed by a more subdued upturn in the late 1990s and another speculative driven boom in the mid-noughties.

The anatomy of net real estate stock changes can only be based on local case studies. New York and London provide two office examples from major cities. The period 1960–75 saw the total office space in the New York increase by 84% from 124 to 227 million square feet. Many of these offices were built during a development boom between 1967 and 1973 (Schwartz, 1979). In London, it is estimated that new development during a 1980s boom contributed a net addition of nearly 30% to the office stock of the central area (including the new docklands office area) (Fainstein, 1994). The increase in stock in the City of London alone was around 10%, but here there was significant redevelopment, with much larger new office suites reflecting the new shape of demand brought about by improvements in information technology (City of London, 2001). To a degree then, the development boom of the 1980s was stimulated by replacing offices in the City of London, unable to cope with the heavy cabling demands of information and communication technologies at that time (Ball, 2003).

Tenure

Real estate is a complex good, and ownership and use or occupation can be separated. In fact, there is a range of potential legal interests in property but the focus here is only on the distinction between renting and owning. The legal rights entailed in owning or renting vary across countries and there is often a distinction between the frameworks that govern residential and commercial/industrial sectors. There can also be differences between types of landlords. In the UK, for example, there are different security of tenure rights for tenants living in the private sector and public/charitable (social housing) sector. Broadly, the rights of tenants (and landlords/investors) relate primarily to the nature of leases, security of tenure and regulation of rent (increases). Owner occupation offers more rights to adapt a property and greater security of tenure but provides less flexibility to move to adapt to changing needs, as selling and moving involves time-consuming and expensive processes. Households that expect to move in the near future will tend to opt for renting from a private landlord, but some households rent as they cannot afford owner occupation. Broadly, most occupiers of housing are owner occupiers while the reverse is true in the commercial sector.

Focussing first on housing, Table 5.1 illustrates residential tenure patterns of selected countries. With the exception of Germany, the majority tenure is owner occupation, but there are differences in the split between the proportions of social housing and private rented sectors. Social housing is important in many northern European countries, although its role is in decline. In many countries, such as the USA, social housing has been seen simply as welfare housing and is available on a very limited scale (Harloe, 1995). Instead, these countries have a long-established private rented sector that represents a substantial proportion of the stock.

Housing finance systems and subsidies/taxation have a crucial influence on these national patterns of home ownership and renting. Wolswijk (2010) gives a summary of the diverse taxing of housing in the European Union, including taxes on imputed rent and capital gains, the deduction of mortgage interest against tax and value added tax on new housing. Home ownership is treated distinctively in different cultures with implications for how housing

Table 5.1 Distribution of households by tenure in selected countries

Country	*Owner Occupation (%)*	*Social Housing (%)*	*Private Rented (%)*	*Other (%)*	*Year*
Greece	80	0	20	0	2001
Iceland	78	2	5	16	2003
Portugal	76	7	15	2	1999
Belgium	74	7	16	3	1999
Australia	70	5	20	5	1999
UK	70	20	10	0	2001/02
USA	68	3	30	0	2002
Finland	64	17	15	4	2001
France	56	17	21	6	2002
Sweden	55	21	24	0	1997
Denmark	53	19	18	9	1999
Netherlands	53	35	12	0	1998
Germany	41	6	49	5	2001

Source: Scanlon and Whitehead (2004).

markets work and houses are supplied. For example, in southern European countries, households rarely move from their home, which is often purchased with the help of the family. Often several generations live together under the same roof. In contrast, in many Anglo-Saxon countries, owner occupiers have sought to purchase at an early age and move to adjust their housing requirements through the family life cycle, so there is a much more active housing market. In these latter countries, housing is seen more as an investment and is primarily built by builders on a speculative basis in advance of finding purchasers. Elsewhere, where there are inactive markets, housing is usually built on a bespoke basis and, in many under-resourced countries, on an incremental basis as funds become available.

In the commercial property sector, there is a predominance of firms as tenants rather than owner occupiers. For example, Mitchell (2014) quotes 3% of the UK's value of shopping centres and 14% of retail warehouses occupied by their owners. Landlords or investors benefit from rental payments for the duration of a lease, potentially subject to periodic rent reviews to market levels and ultimately a residual capital value that is likely to keep pace with inflation. The tenants pay rent but benefit from the economies of scale from the specialist expertise of investors, lower transactions costs, potential local agglomeration economies and lower risks (Benjamin *et al.*, 1998). In addition, tenants can use capital more efficiently and effectively in their own area of expertise rather than tied up in their property.

Development industry

Development is undertaken to meet the real estate needs or demands of the community. It is often undertaken on a speculative basis, anticipating what is required, although it can be bespoke. It can also be incremental as owners adapt their properties or through the redevelopment or refurbishment of buildings. The development industry is broadly split by different types of product with a fundamental division between residential and commercial/industrial sectors. Large residential developers tend to construct the houses themselves while other developers will employ a specialist construction company.

Commercial real estate property companies can build on a speculative basis with a view to finding a long-term investor to purchase and occupiers to let to. Ideally, the property would be pre-let or pre-sold before, or at an early stage during, the development period. If an investor has already agreed a pre-sale, they may have an input into the design (see finance section later). The whole project could also have been initiated by an investor who would then choose a developer with the desired expertise. In this case, there would usually be a partnership funding agreement drawn up as discussed later. For large projects, a special partnership may be drawn up for a range of parties/investors and the developer.

Some commercial property companies develop normally only with a view to adding to their own investment portfolios. These tend to be large companies, listed on the stock exchange and designated as real estate investment trusts (REITs), but could include smaller private companies that tend to operate at a regional rather than a national level. This latter group would range across a continuum of specialist developer to developer/investor. Often, developers/investors specialise in one sector of the real estate market. Of 165 members of the National Association of Real Estate Investment Trusts in the USA, just five are diversified REITs and the rest are specialists, investing, for example, only in shopping centres/regional malls or apartments (Nareit, 2016). Similar pictures are seen around the world.

Private development is dependent on the profit motive and is also risky, especially on a speculative basis. Potential viability is assessed by reference to existing land values and market trends. Where projected viability is not positive (given the risks) or there is no market evidence at all, private development will not normally occur. In these circumstances, the state may intervene to provide subsidies or through direct development to address the needs of the community. Examples in the UK include new town development corporations that were set up by the government during the 1950s and 1960s to build new settlements from scratch on greenfield sites to rehouse people from overcrowded cities. These public corporations effectively built whole towns, including the housing, industrial units and shopping centres (Alexander, 2009). In the interests of the local economy, public policy may also fill 'market gaps' left by private development (Jones, 1996). Cook (1989), for example, notes that UK local authorities in the late 1970s built small industrial units to fill gaps in market provision that private developers deemed unviable.

Social housing can be provided by the state or by publicly funded agencies for households who cannot afford market rents. The public sector was a direct provider of social rented housing for most of the twentieth century (in some countries there was also accommodation linked to employment). With rising real incomes, there has been a trend toward reducing subsidy and more indirect provision (Whitehead 2012). Since the early 1980s in the UK, most new social rented housing has been provided by independent specialist developer/landlords, notably housing associations. These landlords are provided with a capital grant from the government to build new housing but receive no other subsidies directly (although tenants may be eligible for income related housing benefit). There are similar policies around the world in modified forms. In China, for example, affordable housing (originally for sale and now rent) is provided by the private sector but with land given by the local authority. There are constraints on the profits made by developers and the subsequent sale by occupiers (Wang and Murie, 2011).

Construction and development finance

A key factor in the private development process is the provision of development finance; often the availability of finance is the catalyst to development. A distinction can be drawn between short-term finance for private development and long-term/investment finance once the building is complete, but the two are interrelated. This section examines the various forms and the principles governing their provision. There is a particular focus on the dynamics of development finance and partnership models between property companies and financial institutions. This leads to a discussion of partnership models with the public sector.

Short-term finance is broadly the financing of construction or, more precisely, the development process, including potentially the purchase of land until the disposal of the property, whether sold or retained as a long-term investment. Long-term finance, sometimes known as funding, is necessary to pay off the costs of development, including the short-term finance. It is not required if the property is sold on completion. Long-term finance, such as in the form of a mortgage, will usually be necessary if an equity interest in the real estate is to be retained in the property. In practice, this distinction can be blurred. It is also less straightforward with incremental self-build development in under-resourced countries, where there is often a dependence on informal loans and savings.

Forms of short-term finance

Short-term finance covers the acquisition of land and construction costs. Commercial real estate companies can raise these funds through banks, the stock exchange and partnership arrangements with financial institutions. The latter two are discussed in the next sub-section on long-term finance. The focus of this section is banking finance and individual projects.

A classic form is roll-up finance whereby the developer receives incremental funds, usually from a bank, to cover outlays at the different stages of the development period. On completion, the developer repays all these outlays with the built-up interest.

Usually the loan period is less than 5 years but can be up to 10 years (see below). Banks typically lend a maximum loan of 75% of the development cost, although the percentage available varies with the state of the real estate market. Capital for development is, therefore, usually a combination of debt and equity provided by the developer. During cyclical downturns, debt finance may not be available or may only be available under strict conditions; for example, only funding developments that are pre-let with tenants waiting, and even then banks may offer a lower loan to cost ratio requirement, in the order of 60%. Such a short-term development finance 'famine' occurred in the years following the global financial crisis after 2008. Development finance also varies over the cycle by type of real estate – during a strong upturn, debt funders are less risk averse and may be prepared to finance projects in less established areas or properties/uses that are not a central part of the 'investment' market. At other times, such developments will be extremely difficult to finance because of concerns about the future viability of sale or let.

Short-term finance can be provided on a fixed rate basis but, in the UK for example, finance is normally on a variable rate basis linked to a set number of base points above the bank base rates set by the Bank of England (since 1997). The precise rate will, therefore, depend on the level of interest rates. An unfinished building is of limited worth and is thus a poor security. Finance terms are, therefore, dependent on the financial standing of the borrower; for example, a property company's other assets and existing borrowing. Despite this, repayment of a short-term loan is at least partially dependent on the 'success' of the finished development in generating profit.

While banks have had a normal ceiling of 75% of development costs, specialist lenders can top this up with 'mezzanine finance'. This type of finance can enable developers to borrow normally up to 90% of their costs, but it is not widely available. This top slice is more risky and financiers require a higher rate of return and a share in any profit. Mezzanine finance, in this instance, is the *junior* debt and the owners of the mezzanine finance will only receive the interest and so on that they are owed once the *senior* debt has received its repayment including interest in full.

The following example gives a numerical illustration. The developer is able to finance 67% of the development value from traditional banking sources and supplements this debt by mezzanine finance equivalent to 13% of total development value. As Figure 5.1 shows, this leaves the development company to find the remaining costs from its own equity base. Total costs amount to 87% of the development's value. In this example, total external finance is 80% of final value and 92% of total costs. Mezzanine finance has allowed the developer to reduce its capital contribution from 20% to 7% of development value.

The development company is now more heavily geared so that there is the potential for achieving a high rate of return (even after any agreed clawback of profit share by mezzanine funders). However, the company's profits are now riskier: the company's returns are more risky than those of its financiers because it will need to pay these creditors before it makes any profits. Mezzanine finance incorporates interest charges and sometimes an equity share of the final value of the development. Such finance, supporting development in this way, applies primarily in a property boom, and even then is probably exceptional. Just like mezzanine finance funders, banks may also require not just interest payments on the senior debt but also an equity return from the completed development. This takes the form of 'exit' charges in the UK.

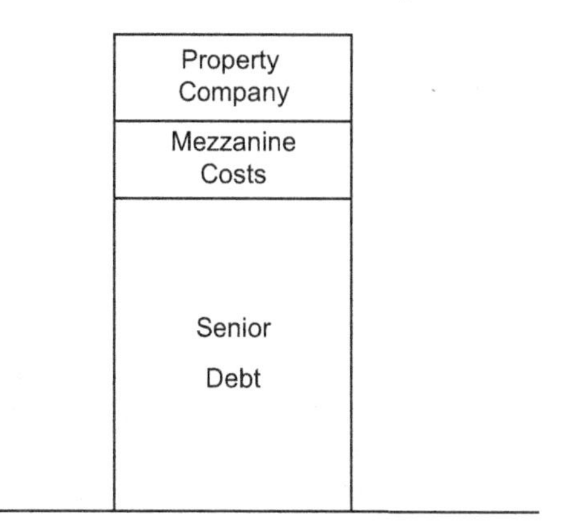

Figure 5.1 Breakdown of development capital between property company equity, senior debt provided by a bank and mezzanine finance

Ideally, as noted above, a real estate company that wished to hold a development as a long-term investment would seek out a mortgage to pay off the short-term debt, with the rental income used to pay the mortgage repayments. However, market conditions may be such that the rents on completion are not high enough to pay the repayments on a mortgage. In these circumstances, traditional short-term development finance can be extended to ten years to allow rents to rise with inflation (recouped at the first rent review). This funding is cheaper than mortgage finance as there is no repayment of capital even though the interest rates charged will be higher.

A wider alternative to roll-up bank finance is a general credit facility that covers all a company's development activities, not just an individual project. These facilities are often made available with options to take out loans at prior negotiated rates. This facility is often syndicated among a number of banks. These credit facilities extend up to 35 years, making it short and long-term finance. Credit facilities with variable interest charges may be subject to a 'cap' or a 'floor', limiting the upward and downward movement of the interest rate to be charged. To negotiate a cap may require an additional payment. These credit facilities can also incorporate complex arrangements for the interest rates, including swaps.

'Limited recourse' or 'non-recourse' finance loan arrangements were also introduced in the 1980s (considered by Fraser, 1993). In these arrangements, the bank lends only to the development project, which is set up as a subsidiary company of, say, one or two companies. Today, the terms have changed and the equivalents are now special purpose vehicles and limited legal partnerships (LLPs). The former is a general term for these partnerships. LLPs set legal limits to the liabilities of the partners, although the law varies across countries.

Forms of long-term finance

Long-term finance is usually required to acquire an equity interest in a property. In the 'traditional' roll-up finance model, a developer will pay off the development costs by taking out a mortgage aligned to the completed property's value. To be 'self-financing', the interest payments on mortgage finance have to be less than the initial rent received. This is arguably the perfect model for a developer/owner because it offers the potential benefit of a rise in rents/capital values, while mortgage debt/repayments are linked to the original costs/value that are falling in real terms. However, this model is not always available. This section examines two alternative forms of finance – raising capital on a stock market and equity sharing partnership schemes between property developers and other parties, notably non-banking financial institutions.

Property companies and REITs can finance development and purchase by raising capital on a stock market, which is undertaken in two ways:

1. A company may issue more shares through a 'rights issue', usually to expand the company. The company publishes a prospectus explaining what it plans to use the additional funds for, to justify the issue and to persuade investors to purchase. The incidence of funds raised in this way is a function of the state of the stock market and development activity. For example, 1987 was a record year for share issues in the UK when share prices were soaring. These rights issues can also be issued to support a company in difficult times when external funding is not available. In this case, the company's shareholders are called upon to safeguard their existing investment by providing more capital.
2. A company may issue debentures or loan stock on a stock market. The real estate portfolios of companies provide ideal backing for debentures and represent a securitisation of assets. Figure 5.2 gives a picture of debenture issues over the period 1983–98 in the UK. There was a marked fall-off in the late 1990s with the significant decline in stock values.

Both of the above means can be cheaper than borrowing debt capital from a bank, especially when share values are high.

An evolution from debentures is asset securitisation of properties set within a single-purpose property vehicle. Essentially, they are bonds secured against rental income but, rather than being issued on the stock exchange, they are placed by a bank with investors supported by a risk grading from rating agencies. These bonds can raise up to 90% or even 100% of the real estate value compared with a bank loan of up to 75% (Lizieri *et al.*, 2001). However, securitisation may bring constraints on restructuring a company's real estate portfolio or its management, such as subsequent lease terms. An extreme example of this approach was Olympia and York, a private Canadian property company that, just before it filed for bankruptcy in 1992, owned trophy buildings in Toronto and London, together

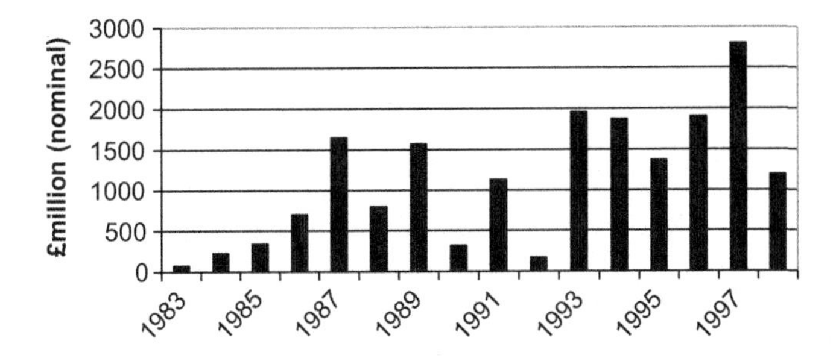

Figure 5.2 Capital issues (net of redemption) by UK property companies
Source: ONS (1999).

with 75% of Manhattan's office space. The bankruptcy files revealed that the company had taken out non-recourse loans with 91 creditors from across the globe secured against individual real estate and public stockholdings of the company. Over US$1 billion alone was securitised against Canary Wharf in London, its main underperforming asset and the primary instigator of its downfall (Ghosh *et al.*, 1994).

Equity sharing partnerships with non-banking financial institutions, such as life assurance companies, offer another way of forward funding development. These institutions own extensive real estate portfolios and participation in a partnership with a developer enables them to extend their investments directly in new property of their choice. These equity sharing schemes were originally a simple sale and lease back arrangement, whereby a property company sells a share in a completed development to a financial institution on condition that it leases it back to it on a long-term basis. The structure of these deals varies but the developer would retain a proportion, say 20%, of the equity, selling, say, just sufficient to pay back the rolled up development costs. The developer then sublets and manages the property, with the financial institution receiving an agreed (share of the initial market) rent, a guaranteed income. In this way, the property company could raise sufficient capital to pay off the development costs, and retain an equity interest in the property. The property company is then responsible for finding tenants, collecting rents, managing the property and paying the institution a rent. In such a scheme, the financial institution has the 'bottom' or secure equity in the property while the company has the top slice or the riskiest share of the equity (Fraser, 1993).

These funding agreements have become more complex. The institution is now normally involved from the outset of a development providing the finance for the project including land purchase and construction costs. On completion, the developer gets a long lease and acts as manager. There are a number of variations of these arrangements, often collectively referred to as 'side by side schemes'. In a priority yield arrangement, the development company prioritises the return to the financial institution by offering a set yield on its investment, with the next say 1% going to the developer, and the rest (if any) split equally. These schemes are popular where a development is difficult to plan. The breakdown of returns is shown in Figure 5.3.

In difficult market conditions during a property market downturn, the prioritised or guaranteed income proved an illusion. This led to the evolution of a 'profit erosion' model whereby, if the 'guaranteed' return on completion is not forthcoming, the developer is

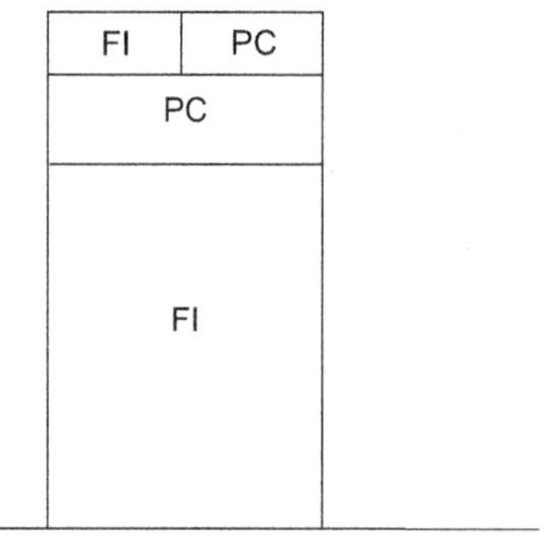

Figure 5.3 Breakdown of returns in a priority yield arrangement
(FI = financial institution, PC = property company)

subject to penalties (Darlow, 1988). If the profit erodes to a certain point, the developer's role disappears and, while the fund has a financial cushion, the developer has to find tenants for the property. A common feature of these partnerships is that they provide incentives to the property company in the development stage and its ultimate returns are based on its performance in completing the project on time and within budget. The funding institution shoulders most of the risk as it provides the capital, but the developer risks losing the right to profit in the development process (Fraser, 1993). Generally, these arrangements include a buyout by the institution at an agreed yield on an agreed base rent, and a higher yield on surplus rents ('overage'). The ultimate step in the changing forms of partnership between developers and financial institutions is the appointment of the property company as a project manager to the development. Payment then takes the form of a basic fee plus a performance incentive.

Public–private partnerships

There are many different forms of public–private partnership around the world. In recent years, affordable housing provision has been a particular focus of public–private partnership and, earlier in this chapter, the case of China is discussed in this context. Very often, large-scale city-centre commercial development projects depend on the role of the local authority. Local authorities contribute through planning support, the compulsory purchase of land and so on. A local authority may already own land central to the project or may acquire it compulsorily. It thus makes a crucial contribution to unlocking the development potential of the land. As a result, the local authority also has an equity interest in the development. Sometimes, a public authority or agency may seek a joint venture with a private-sector partner to provide finance for a project that is not commercially viable. In these cases, the financial return models may be formulated with up to three partners to reflect the different roles and risks (Fraser, 1993). Alternatively, the local authority may provide a long lease to a property company as part of a development agreement that requires the company to meet a set of conditions or standards for the finished development (Heurkins, 2012).

Investors and the real estate stock

The previous section examined development finance to expand or adapt the real estate stock. This section considers the role and attitudes of investors toward segments of real estate as long-term influences on the nature of the stock. In particular, financial institutions, REITs and other large investors own much of the 'top quality' commercial real estate stock of cities, so the focus is on these investors, using the UK again as an example. In a study of the real estate stock, Mitchell (2014) found that retail and industrial assets valued less than £1.5 million and offices of less than £2.5 million are generally excluded from most institutional investors' portfolios. The industrial sector, in particular, has a small percentage of stock that is attractive to financial institutions and other investors. As a consequence, almost half the value of the UK's commercial property stock by value does not meet the requirements of large investors.

Mitchell (2014) estimated that in 2013 the investment sector was 56% of the total commercial property stock and that the contributors to the Investment Property Databank (IPD) and its UK database represent around two-fifths of this investment stock. IPD members are more biased toward retail than other investors, owning more than half of the retail investment stock. The biggest of the other investors are unlisted property companies or overseas investors, the latter of which strongly favour offices. The structure of the ownership of the

Table 5.2 Breakdown of investment stock by financial institutions and overseas investors (£ billion)

Property segment	*Financial institutions*[a]	*Overseas*	*Total*
Standard retail:			
Central London shops[b]	6	2	15
South-East	14	3	29
Rest of UK	14	1	24
Shopping centres	32	7	51
Retail warehouses	32	3	43
Offices:			
City	9	24	38
West End and mid-town	22	13	53
Rest of London[c]	5	11	23
Rest of South East	14	14	39
Rest of UK	7	4	16
Industrials:			
South-East	16	2	22
Rest of UK	12	1	18
Other commercial	14	11	32
Total	182	88	364

a Includes insurance companies, pension funds, collective investment schemes and listed property. The balance is made up of private property companies, traditional estates and charities, private and other investors.
b Included in standard retail South-East.
c Included in rest of South-East.

Source: Derived from Table D7 of Mitchell (2014, p. 61).

investment stock, broken down by segments, is given in Table 5.2, which reveals a range of variations by type of investor. Central London offices are predominantly owned by overseas investors. Three-quarters of 'investment quality' retail warehouses and three-fifths of shopping centres by value are owned by financial institutions. Similarly seven out of ten industrial investment properties are owned by financial institutions.

There are clear sectoral differences in investor attitudes, but these have changed over time. Investment directly in real estate began effectively during the 1950s in the UK when high street shops were the most popular form of investment. As Table 5.3 indicates, following successive office development booms from the 1960s, offices proved a more attractive investment, only for shops to return to popularity in the 1980s, regaining their position as the largest component of institutional portfolios in the 1990s. There are a range of reasons for this, which are now reviewed.

The traditional attractiveness of the high street shop as an investment stemmed from two important pillars. First, rental income (growth) was supported by the long-term rise in real incomes and consumer expenditure from the Second World War onwards. Second, limited development opportunities in town and city centres constrained the supply elasticity of high street shops (Fraser, 1993). Furthermore, the prime urban shopping pitch at the heart of the high street represented the apex of the local retail hierarchy. As usually the most accessible point within the shopping area, there would always be excess demand for this location. If a tenant vacated a shop, there would be another in line to replace it. If a retail sector declined in profitability, there would be other shops selling different goods waiting in the wings to occupy the premises. The implication was that the specific risk of the investment was low and systematic risk was limited (Jones, 2010).

Table 5.3 Percentage structure of UK institutional property portfolios 1950–2010

	Offices	*Retail*	*Industrial*	*Residential*	*Other*
1950	36	40	4	13	6
1960	41	47	6	6	–
1970	64	30	6	–	1
1981	54	27	15	–	4
1985	51	34	12	–	3
1990	52	35	12	–	2
1995	39	46	13	1	3
2000	35	47	14	1	3
2005	31	50	15	–	3
2010	31	50	15	1	1

Sources: Table 10.7 of Scott (1996); Investment Property Databank (2010).

The expansion of office supply, supported by the growth in services and demand for office space, underpinned its rise in attractiveness as an investment class. The 1970s had been a decade of rampant inflation, so property in general, and office property in particular, was viewed as a long-term real investment with good growth. However, this perspective was severely dented by the emergence of obsolescence problems in the 1980s, with the beginnings of the ICT revolution. With obsolescence leading to the depreciation of rental and capital values, there were major challenges to the basis of investing in offices. In contrast, high street shops were immune to obsolescence fears, except to changing pedestrian flows where town centres were subject to reconfiguration (primarily a risk for secondary rather than prime locations). The periodic refitting of high street shops and revamping of shop fronts was the responsibility of the tenant.

Factories and industrial units have seen only limited institutional investment, partly because many industrial units were built on a bespoke basis to meet specialist requirements, but also because they were viewed as subject to a relatively short life and rapid obsolescence (Fraser, 1993). The market in the UK was also historically dominated by public sector provision based on low rents aimed at promoting local economic development, especially in peripheral regions. In the 1980s, the state retreated from this role, selling off its stock to property companies (Jones, 2005), which partly explains the subsequent rise of industrial units in institutional portfolios. Other factors include the rise of the ubiquitous industrial shed. These modern buildings are suitable for a range of alternative users and are often built in 'parks' close to motorway junctions, with good regional accessibility (Dunse and Jones, 2005). There has also been a significant transformation in the role of distribution in the economy wrought, at least in part, by ICT and road network improvements with implications for the demand for warehousing. Distribution warehouses have developed over the last 30 years to become a distinct investment class.

The changes in industrial real estate are part of a wider vista that has been driven by information and transport technologies. These changes can be seen as the latest in a series of urban development cycles, lasting approximately 30 years and caused by technological progress, as identified by Barras (1987) and discussed in detail by (Jones *et al.*, 2017). They have led to fundamental changes in urban real estate markets through decentralisation and new property forms, such as office parks and retail warehouses (Jones, 2009). Office parks were first established during the 1980s, and rose to around 10% of office investment in 2010. However, change has been most dramatic in the retail sector with the advent of out-of-town shopping. Retail warehouses emerged in the 1980s as a new retail format and, while comprising less than 3% of the institutional portfolio in 1981, by 2010 represented almost one-fifth of total investment. Overall investment in decentralised retail formats increased from a nominal proportion to 46% of all retail investments in 2006, and these are now on a par with town centre developments (50%, if department stores are included; Jones, 2010). In contrast, the high street shop, the backbone of retail investment in the 1980s, fell from 18.7% of the institutional portfolio in 1985 to 10.3% in 2010. In fact, there was a more than 50% fall in the number of shops owned by financial institutions between the mid-1990s and 2006 alone, many probably through redevelopment (Jones, 2010).

These changes have occurred despite a planning system wedded to maintaining the retail hierarchy status quo (Jackson and Watkins, 2005). The reasons are that (out-of-town) shopping has many advantages over many existing high streets from both an investment and consumer perspective. The consumer is offered accessibility and a comfortable shopping experience. For the investor, a shopping centre can be designed and built to precise specifications, enabling full control of the retail offering and the opportunity to be a perfectly discriminating monopolist in the sense that it can charge differential rents to tenants. In this way, rents can be maximised by controlling retailer locations and space allocations.

The consequences of this out-of-town revolution are that the long-standing constraints on the supply of retail units no longer hold. This has contributed to an oversupply of shops with high levels of vacancies across all but the most successful 'high street' shopping centres, since the global financial crisis and the subsequent recession led to falling real incomes. Many of the empty shops are too small for current demand and are now obsolescent. In addition, there has also been the rise of online shopping, which has exacerbated these impacts (Jones and Livingstone, 2015). This restructuring of retail property has favoured shopping centre investment but even here there are concerns. Consumer spending is less dependent on location and more on the quality and attractiveness of the shopping centre. This means that spending in a centre is susceptible to displacement if a more attractive centre is built in an urban area. In other words, depreciation is now a part of retail investment and owners have continually to upgrade to maintain their custom.

The preceding paragraphs in this section demonstrate the recent pace of change in all sectors of the real estate market and the consequences for supply and commercial real estate investment. This has represented a major challenge for large institutional investors as prime property is replaced by new prime when new decentralised locations and property forms have emerged. Much of this new supply was originally built by specialist property companies prepared to take greater risks. To a degree, the conservative approach of institutional investors has lagged these changes and even slowed these supply changes but, ultimately, they have embraced them as shown in Table 5.2 (Jones, 2009). The next section also looks at the initial slow response of investors to the green agenda.

Large-scale private investment in residential accommodation to let is limited to a few countries. The most significant occurrence is in the USA, where REITs own around 8% of the stock (Ball, 2012). They generally own and manage large, standardised multi-apartment blocks for young, middle-low income households (Jones, 2007). Most private rented accommodation around the world is owned by landlords with a small number of properties. In general, residential investment is seen as being less favourable than commercial property by large investors because of several characteristics of the asset class. These include the high transaction costs relative to the value of individual properties; the fact that returns encompass a significant capital element which can only be realised by selling; intensive management and maintenance with poor scale economies; high tenant turnover and vacancy rates. There are also potential reputational issues from evictions and concerns about illiquidity caused by thin markets that make it difficult to sell blocks relatively quickly. Many governments have been trying to reverse this position to persuade institutions to invest in the residential market to address their countries' housing shortages, but there are doubts about the success of this policy (Ball, 2012).

Selected policy issues

The aim of private developers is fundamentally to make a profit by meeting the needs and demands of individuals and communities. But speculative development is essentially a very risky business and one way to minimise risk and costs is to replicate a 'winning' formula. This could, for example, take the form of transplanting a successful shopping centre format from one location to another, leading to a loss of local identity and sense of place. It can be also be seen in standardised new housing designs which create monotony. This criticism applies not only to speculative privately built housing but also to modular high and medium-rise social housing units designed to minimise costs.

Institutional investors in developed countries own much of the modern large commercial real estate stock and thus have a major role in setting construction standards. For example, Guy (1998) refers to offices in the 1990s being required to be built to an 'institutional standard' as this was seen by such investors as essential to ensuring that their investments had a long-term attractiveness. These air-conditioned buildings clearly also met the demands of the information age and occupiers seeking prestige office space. But, in the process, argues Guy, this standard, although beyond the demands of many occupiers, became universal because of the power of financial institutions.

With global concerns about the carbon foot print of cities and buildings, these offices have been criticised for the heavy energy consumption required by air conditioning (Roaf *et al.*, 2003). The initial adoption of the green agenda by the real estate sector has been slow. A major constraint was an apparent unwillingness to move from the long-standing prime office specification with air conditioning and the perceived lack of market interest in green buildings. However, Oyedokun *et al.* (2015) report that there was a sudden green transformation in office development in the UK in the noughties. Indeed, in 2009, over eight million square feet of green stock was completed, expanding the green (BREEAM certification) market office stock by 54%. A parallel pattern of green office development occurred in the USA where, at the end of 2005, only 0.1% of commercial offices in the top 30 centres was certified as green (Leadership in Energy and Environmental Design rated). However, by the end of 2013, the figure had risen to 5.1% (Kok and Holtermans, 2014). The driving forces include the fear of future obsolescence by large investors.

The failure to produce the right product is not necessarily a problem for investors or developers where there is excess demand. Indeed, constraining production and taking a conservative approach to building is a means of reducing risk and maintaining sale values and profits. This has been a long-term criticism of housebuilding in the UK, although the industry blames a restrictive planning system (Jones and Watkins, 2009). The consequence has been rising prices and unaffordability and falling home ownership rates among young adults. This picture of the interaction of rising demand, fuelled by the readily available mortgage finance from the 1990s until the credit crunch combined with inelastic supply, was seen in many countries including Denmark and the Netherlands in Europe, the USA and Australia (Jones, 2012).

Conservative approaches to the supply of investable buildings can also be seen in a risk averse approach to where properties are built. Houses, for example, may not be built in inner parts of cities on brownfield sites because builders are unconvinced of the subsequent marketability of such properties or believe there are excessive site condition risks. On the other hand, they prefer greenfield sites at the edge of cities with resultant unnecessary sprawl. A further example is in the regional pattern of offices in the UK, caused by London-centric investment strategies of financial institutions. It is arguably driven by a risk averse benchmarking culture that reinforces traditional investment decisions. Henneberry *et al.* (2008) found that London benefits substantially more from new developments than from its share of office employment, thereby enhancing the quality and the attractiveness of its office stock relative to provincial cities. As a result, the economic development and competitiveness of provincial cities is being hindered by this London bias, which has contributed to the long-term imbalances in regional development in the UK. This issue is not unique to the UK. Other countries have sought to restrict development activity in major centres as part of regional dispersal policies. Examples include policies framed to disperse offices from Paris and New York (Alexander, 1979; Schwartz, 1979).

Where land lies unused or properties are vacant or derelict for some time (or are likely to be so) there can be a strong argument for state intervention to increase the supply of real estate. The reasons for the market leaving offices vacant may lie in a combination of a lack of private sector confidence to invest and doubts about the viability of regeneration. There is a range of solutions that encompass state subsidies and tax incentives, and a variety of types of area strategies in which the state focusses and coordinates resources to set a direction and vision for the future. Enterprise zones are one model that has been applied around the world, including France, Italy, USA, Dubai and China, offering tax incentives for development (Jones, 2006, 2013). Another approach is the use of development corporations for defined areas that buy up extensive land tracts, provide modern infrastructure, including new access roads, and provide subsidies for development and market land parcels (Jones, 2013). These are pump-priming strategies in which initial public sector expenditure/tax incentives are provided for a limited period to stimulate private real estate investment.

Summary and conclusions

The real estate stock is constantly changing as properties are added, modified, refurbished and even demolished in response to the cycle of the macro-economy, the state of local markets, demographic trends and technological developments. Much of the new supply of commercial and private housing real estate in developed countries is provided on a speculative basis. However, social housing is usually built by the state or by specialist landlords supported by public funds. In under-resourced countries, housing is constructed in an incremental way as finance permits.

Development finance is crucial to the new supply of real estate and can usefully be distinguished as short or long term, although the distinction is increasingly arbitrary. The traditional model of short-term private finance is a property company receiving incremental funding from a bank to pay outlays through the development period. Once the development is complete, these debts are paid from the sale of the property or by taking out a mortgage. Property market conditions rarely enable this simple model to work, with the repayment of development funding having to stretch into the medium term until rents or capital values rise. This has led to the use of general credit facilities from banks. Developers generally seek to maximise their level of debt gearing, and mezzanine finance can extend gearing beyond the finance available from banks. This is normally only available in a property boom, and this top slice is more risky, so financiers require a higher rate of return and a share in any profit. More generally, the availability and terms of debt finance from banks is very cyclical, with droughts in downturns.

Alternative forms of finance include raising capital through rights issues or debentures on a stock market and equity sharing partnership schemes between property developers and other parties, notably non-banking financial institutions. Rights issues are attractive when share prices and development activities are high but can also be used to support a company in difficult times when external funding is not available. In equity sharing partnerships, a financial institution provides the funds for all the stages of the development project and ultimately owns the property. These partnerships give efficiency incentives to the property company which, as a result, is subject to significant risk in the development process.

Investors' attitudes have a long-term influence on the nature of the commercial and industrial stock and have changed over time; for example, in the UK, with shops and offices vying to be the most popular sector since the 1950s. These trends partly reflect responses to the underlying economics and to technological change, and the expansion of the motor age. This has resulted in not only urban decentralisation but also new property forms, together with obsolescence of the existing real estate stock. The pace of change has represented challenges for the portfolios of institutional investors owning the prime stock. Adjustments to portfolios have tended to lag change, with investors waiting for new types of developments to have clear market acceptability. In contrast to the commercial sector, large-scale institutional investment in housing is only found in a small number of countries. There are many other potential conflicts between public 'need' and real estate supply, primarily led by private profit motives as, for example, demonstrated by the international problems across the developed world of insufficient new housing and the reluctance to enjoin the green agenda.

References

Alexander, A. (2009) *Britain's new towns: garden cities to sustainable communities*, Routledge, Abingdon.

Alexander, I. (1979) *Office location and public policy*, Longman, London.

Ball, M. (2003) Is there an office replacement cycle? *Journal of Property Research*, 20(2), 173–89.

Ball, M. (2012) The private rented sector as a source of affordable housing, pp. 255–81 in Jones, C., White, M. and Dunse, N. (eds.) *Challenges of the housing economy: an international perspective*, Wiley-Blackwell, Chichester.

Barras, R. (1987) Technical change and the urban development cycle, *Urban Studies*, 24(1), 5–30.

Barras, R. (2009) *Building cycles: growth and instability*, Wiley-Blackwell, Oxford.

Benjamin, J. D., de la Torre C. and Musumeci J. (1998) Rationales for real estate leasing versus owning, *Journal of Real Estate Research*, 15(3), 223–37.

City of London Corporation (2001) *Office stock in the City of London*, City of London Corporation, London.

Cook, G. (1989) Local authorities and industrial property markets, *Property Management*, 7(1), 3–12.

Darlow, C. (ed.) (1988) *Valuation and development appraisal,* 2nd ed., Estates Gazette, London.

Dunse, N. and Jones, C. (2005) UK roads policy, accessibility and industrial property rents, pp. 128–47 in Adams, D. Watkins, C. and White, M. (eds.) *Planning, public policy and property markets,* Oxford: Blackwell.

Fainstein, S. (1994) *The city builder: property, politics and planning in London and New York*, Blackwell, Oxford.

Fraser, W. D. (1993) *Principles of property investment and pricing,* 2nd ed., Macmillan, London.

Guy, S. (1998) Developing alternatives: energy, offices and the environment, *International Journal of Urban and Regional Research*, 22(2), 264–82.

Harloe, M. (1995) *The people's home? social rented housing in Europe and America*, Blackwell, Oxford.

Henneberry, J., Roberts, C. and Rowley, S. (2008) *Regional inequalities in office property development and investment in the UK*, Paper presented to Regional Studies Association Annual International Conference University of Economics Prague, Czech Republic, 27–29 May 2008.

Heurkins, E. (2012) *Private sector-led urban developments*, CreateSpace Independent Publishing Platform, Colorado Springs, CO.

Investment Property Databank (2010) *IPD digest*, Investment Property Databank, London.

Jackson, C. and Watkins, C. (2005) Planning policy and retail property markets: measuring the dimensions of planning intervention, *Urban Studies*, 42(8), 1453–69.

Jones, C. (1996) Theory of property led local economic development, *Regional Studies*, 30(8), 797–801.

Jones, C. (2005) A regional perspective on the impact of the privatisation of the UK public industrial property stock, *Environment and Planning C*, 23, 123–39.

Jones, C. (2006) Verdict on the British enterprise zone experiment, *International Planning Studies*, 11(2), 109–23.

Jones, C. (2007) Private investment in rented housing and the role of REITS, *European Journal of Housing Policy*, 7(4), 383–400.

Jones, C. (2009) Remaking the monopoly board: spatial economic change and property investment, *Urban Studies*, 46(11), 2363–80.

Jones, C. (2010) The rise and fall of the high street shop as an investment class, *Journal of Property Investment Finance*, 28(4), 275–84.

Jones, C. (2012) Conclusions: the challenges ahead, pp. 282–93 in Jones, C., White M. and Dunse N. (eds.) *Challenges of the housing economy: an international perspective*, Wiley-Blackwell, Chichester.

Jones, C. (2013) *Office markets and public policy*, Wiley-Blackwell, Chichester.

Jones, C. and Livingstone, N. (2015) Emerging implications of online retailing for real estate: twenty-first century clicks and bricks, *Journal of Corporate Real Estate*, 17(3), 226–39.

Jones, C. and Watkins, C. (2009) *Housing markets and planning policy*, Wiley-Blackwell, Oxford.

Jones, C., Dunse, N., Livingstone, N. and Cutsforth, K. (2017) The restructuring of the institutional real estate portfolio in the UK, *Journal of Property Research*, 34(2), 129–46.

Kok, N. and Holtermans, R. (2014) *National building adoption index*, CBRE, New York.

Lizieri, C., Ward, C. and Lee, S. (2001) *Financial innovation in property markets: implications for the City of London,* City of London Corporation, London.

Mitchell, P. (2014) *The size and structure of the UK property market 2013: A decade of change*, Investment Property Forum, London.

Nareit (2016) REIT sectors. Available at: www.reit.com/investing/reit-basics/reit-sectors [accessed 11 August 2018].

Office for National Statistics (1999) *Financial statistics*, HMSO, London.

Oyedokun, T., Jones, C. and Dunse, N. (2015) The growth of the green office market in the United Kingdom, *Journal of European Real Estate Research*, 6(3), 267–84.

Roaf, S., Crichton, D. and Nicol, F. (2009) *Adapting buildings and cities for climate change: a 21st century survival guide,* 2nd ed., Architectural Press, Oxford.

Scanlon, K. and Whitehead, C. (2004) *International trends in housing tenure and mortgage finance*, Council of Mortgage Lenders, London.

Schwartz, G. G. (1979) The office pattern in New York City, 1960–75, in Daniels, P. W. (ed.) *Spatial pattern of office growth and location*, John Wiley, Chichester.

Scott, P. (1996) *The property masters*, E&F Spon, London.

Wang, Y. P. and Murie, A. (2011) The new affordable and social housing provision system in China: implications for comparative housing studies, *International Journal of Housing Policy*, 11(3), 237–54.

Whitehead, C. (2012) Developments in the role of social housing in Europe, pp. 216–34 in Jones, C., White, M. and Dunse, N. (eds.) *Challenges of the housing economy: an international perspective*, Wiley-Blackwell, Chichester.

Wolswijk, G. (2010) Fiscal aspects of housing in Europe, pp. 158–75 in Arestis, P., Mooslechner, P. and Wagner K. (eds.) *Housing market challenges in Europe and the United States*, Palgrave Macmillan, Basingstoke.

Part II

The players

6 Fund managers

David Parker, Alex Moss, Paul McNamara and Robin Goodchild

Introduction

Property fund managers are intermediaries who raise third party equity and debt capital and pool it to form collective investment vehicles that can invest in direct property and property securities. The main sources of equity capital range from government-owned sovereign wealth funds (such as the Abu Dhabi Investment Authority, the Government Investment Corporation of Singapore and the government pension fund of Norway), pension or superannuation funds and insurance companies through to private investors whether 'high net worth' or otherwise. The main sources of debt capital range from global capital markets and investment banks through to high street banks.

Direct property can be defined as an investment in physical properties such as high rise office towers, industrial units or shopping malls occupied by tenants who pay rent to the owner for the right to occupy the property. Property securities comprise an investment in shares or units in a listed or unlisted company or trust which, in turn, holds an investment in physical property. Maintaining this twofold classification for property investment (direct property and property securities), this chapter begins with a description of the direct property and property securities funds management industries. This is followed by a review of property funds management business models and a discussion of future directions in the property funds management industry.

The management of third party funds investing in property probably developed over centuries from more rudimentary forms into the specialist land agents appointed to run the landed estates of the British aristocracy from the eighteenth century. The current funds management industry emerged after the Second World War when UK and US insurance companies and pension funds started to build property investment portfolios in partnership with developers and/or through their own in-house estates departments. Contemporaneously, property companies started to emerge as a significant investment sector on the London Stock Exchange when Harold Samuel took control of Land Securities and repositioned the portfolio away from residential towards commercial property (see Marriott, 1967, for more information concerning the evolution of UK commercial property companies in the immediate post-war period).

The growth of the listed property sector in the UK was halted when capital gains tax was first introduced by the British government in 1965. This made investing directly in property more attractive for tax exempt entities like pension funds, which were not affected in the same way as property companies. Thus, the late 1960s saw the emergence of the first private collective property investment funds in the UK. One example was the Schroder Exempt Property Unit Trust. This enabled pension funds to gain an exposure to the direct property asset class without having to develop the capacity to manage the properties themselves. Very high inflation in the 1970s, when the UK the Retail Price Index averaged 13.8% per annum, further encouraged pension fund investment in property, with property unit trusts (PUTs) increasing their holdings as a result.

This trend peaked in the early 1980s, as the stock market surged and pension funds switched investment from property to equities. When this happened, many investors found their units in PUTs to be much less liquid than they expected. This further contributed to a loss in market share by PUTs and pension fund property allocations reduced sharply from 20% to 5% over the course of the decade. Pension funds slowly began to return during the 1990s and PUTs have prospered since.

Similar forces drove fund manager growth in other markets. In the US, pension funds started investing in real estate from the mid-1970s. The Trumbull Property Fund, managed by UBS Real Estate Advisors, started in 1978 and is now an open ended fund with assets of over US$23.5 billion (March 2018). It is one of 33 open ended 'comingled' funds that comprise the National Council of Real Estate Investment Fiduciaries Fund Index – Open End Diversified Core Equity (ODCE) Index,[1] which is a key component of the National Council of Real Estate Investment Fiduciaries (NCREIF) Property Index, both dating from 1978. However, the ODCE Index members comprise only a part of the property funds market. There is also a large number of closed private vehicles pursuing a range of investment 'styles', ranging across the risk spectrum from low risk core through value-add to opportunistic. These date mainly from the mid-1990s and, in particular the higher risk strategies, were opened up to investors outside the US from around 2000, which, until then had focussed principally on low risk, low return strategies.

In Germany, the funds management industry can trace its history to the 1950s and regulations to ensure liquidity for investors investing in open ended funds date from 1969. The German open ended funds were important domestically but, after 1991 when they were first permitted to invest outside Germany, they became a powerful market force globally and by 2003 were the largest single owners of European commercial real estate with assets approaching €100 billion. Liquidity issues and the market downturn following the global financial crisis of 2007/08 have hit some individual German open ended funds hard but, collectively, they remain important private fund players (Bannier *et al.*, 2008).

Real estate investment trusts (REITs) were invented in the US in 1960 as a vehicle to allow every individual to be a property owner through holding a share of a property asset by being a unitholder in a trust listed and traded on a stock exchange. However, US REITs did not become significant until the early 1990s when tax rules were adjusted to make their structure tax efficient. In the meantime, similarly tax efficient listed vehicles had become established in Australia in the early 1970s and the Netherlands in the 1980s. More countries, such as Belgium and Canada, permitted REITs in the 1990s but it was not until the twenty-first century that REITs truly became a global means to invest in property securities when Japan, France and, finally, the UK, in 2007, developed similar tax efficient structures. Today, close on 40 countries have a tax-transparent REIT structure (European Real Estate Association, 2014). In the UK at least, many existing property companies converted to REIT status.

Sovereign wealth funds are state owned investment funds. They have become increasingly important since the 1970s and have been central to the development of globally mobile capital for property investment. Alongside a number of UK pension funds, these funds created a substantial demand for funds management whether through comingled vehicles or 'separate accounts' especially created and managed for them.

A further burst of cross-border investment and fund management activity occurred in the 1980s, led by Japanese investors with the Dutch and Swedes close behind. This

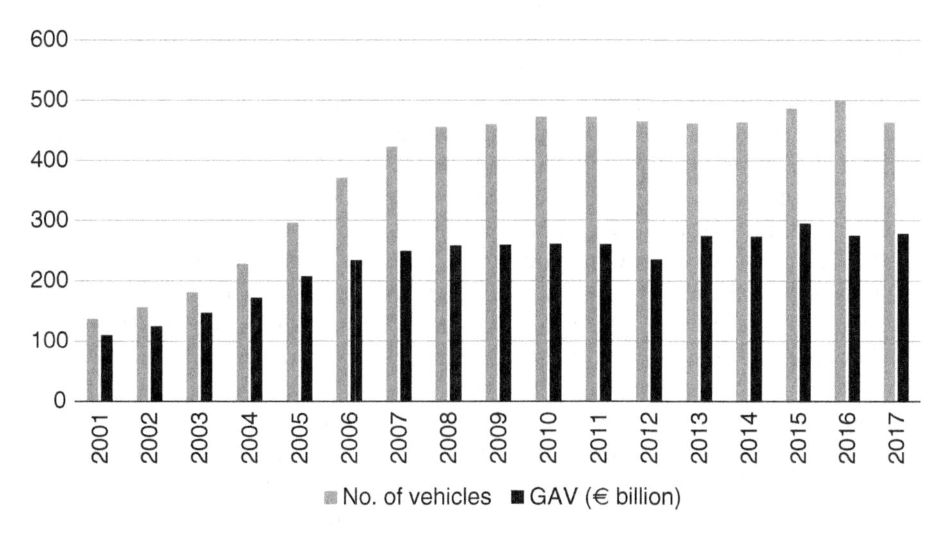

Figure 6.1 The growth of private funds in Europe, 2001–2017
GAV = gross asset value.

trend increased significantly in the 1990s when US managers expanded internationally and started offering global investment funds, often with a higher risk, higher return opportunistic focus.

The private funds industry continued to grow very significantly across all investment styles, after the Millennium, at least until the global financial crisis of late 2007 (Figure 6.1).

While the property funds management industry globally has suffered periodic significant downturns after major property market reversals in the late 1980s and early 1990s and the global financial crisis of 2007/08, the property funds management business model has proved remarkably resilient and continues to be popular with investors seeking access to investment property locally, nationally and globally.

Structure of the industry

The funds management industry was responsible for managing almost €3 trillion of real estate assets around the globe in 2014. The industry is highly disaggregated with the largest manager, Brookfield Asset Management, responsible for only 3% of the total.[2]

The fund managers discussed in this chapter comprise two groups – property fund managers and publicly listed entities (including both REITs and real estate operating companies, REOCs). The former offer a mix of investment products to clients. These range from separate accounts (where the ownership of the underlying assets is held by the client but managed by the fund) to private funds (where ownership is held and managed by the fund and investors buy a right to an income plus any change in capital value), funds invested in entities listed on stock markets (like REITs, REOCS or property companies) or 'funds of private funds'.

We should note that in much the same way that private funds can invest in REITs, REITs can sometimes invest in private funds. For example, in the UK, British Land plc is involved with the Hercules Retail Warehouse Fund. It also undertakes joint ventures with institutional investors in respect of specific projects or portfolios.

The main motivation of fund managers and REITs and REOCs differs. First and foremost, REITs and REOCs look to optimise the return on assets to create shareholder value. In contrast, fund managers are service companies who prosper through retaining and winning new investor clients and growing their total assets under management. While producing good investment performance is a key requirement for doing that, developing new products to grow the asset base is important to fund managers too.

In this chapter, the analysis of the funds management industry reflects the distinction between these two main groups. The initial focus is on fund managers operating mainly in private (unlisted) direct property investment markets. The public market managers are discussed separately with an analysis of the different types of REITs and REOCs. This is followed by a review of the managers who invest in publicly listed entities as a means to deliver real estate-like returns in a more liquid form than is achievable from private direct property markets.

Some mainstream fund managers, as opposed to REIT managers, invest in both the public and private markets. Given this, the remainder of this section reviews the nature of that group.

The current leading fund managers are listed in Table 6.1. This is measured by assets under management (AUM), the conventional measure for determining size in investment management. Size could also be measured by the number of employees or profitability, but data on those metrics are less readily available. There can be issues with all metrics but, for simplicity, AUM is used here. Generally, AUM is measured at the gross assets level rather than as net assets following the deduction of any debt secured on those assets.

Table 6.1 2014 Ranking of real estate fund managers

	Company	*Location of headquarters*	*Total real estate assets under management at 30 June 2014 (€ million)*
1	Brookfield Asset Management	Canada	€ 92,106
2	CBRE Global Investors	USA	€ 67,800
3	Blackstone	USA	€ 58,897
4	TIAA Henderson Real Estate	USA	€ 56,594
5	AXA Real Estate	France	€ 52,983
6	UBS Global Asset Management	Switzerland	€ 49,008
7	Prudential/Pramerica Real Estate Investors	USA	€ 47,287
8	Invesco	USA	€ 44,909
9	JP Morgan Asset Management	USA	€ 42,541
10	LaSalle Investment Management	USA	€ 38,650
11	Principal Real Estate Investors	USA	€ 38,428
12	Credit Suisse	Switzerland	€ 37,737
13	Hines[a]	USA	€ 36,489
14	Deutsche Asset & Wealth Management	Germany	€ 35,217
15	Cornerstone Real Estate Advisers	USA	€ 33,201
16	M&G Investments	UK	€ 32,640
17	APG Asset Management	Netherlands	€ 30,402
18	Aviva Investors	UK	€ 28,764
19	Cohen & Steers Capital Management	USA	€ 28,046
20	Aberdeen Asset Management	UK	€ 27,810

a Assets under management as at 31 December 2013.

Source: *IPE Real Estate* November/December 2014.

This list of top managers is dominated by North American businesses. Brookfield Asset Management, headquartered in Toronto, Canada, is the largest by AUM. They are followed by CBRE Global Investors and Blackstone, both US based. All three have experienced significant change during recent times through restructuring, expansion or merger, and all manage assets globally in Europe, the Americas and Asia Pacific.

The origins of the firms in the top 20 fall broadly into three categories:

- real estate teams within insurance companies or pension funds;
- real estate teams within investment banks or multi-asset management businesses; and
- specialist real estate operations.

No individual model has proved the most successful although the top three all have more specialist characteristics.

The vast majority of these top 20 fund managers currently invest in Europe, the Americas and Asia Pacific even if their AUM typically has a domestic bias. Moreover, most offer a range of investment products ranging from segregated accounts, usually focussing on core assets, through to closed end funds with a value-add or opportunistic profile. A number also offer portfolios that invest in public listed real estate and some, especially the Europeans, act as multi-managers investing in the private funds of other managers.

Cohen and Steers merits a special mention, as it is the only manager in the top 20 that invests in real estate solely through publicly listed entities. APG Asset Management has 60% of its AUM in public markets, reflecting the particular approach of Dutch investors to real estate investment. All the other managers listed in Table 6.1 have a distinctly private market bias. Fund managers outside the top 20 are generally less likely to invest globally and more likely to specialise in a particular investment product, for example, closed end value-add or opportunistic funds.

The property fund management industry remains widely dispersed. The above IPE real estate survey shows that the top 20 managers represent only 50% of the total AUM of the top 100 managers with the largest entity, Brookfield, holding a market share of just 5.5%.

This level of dispersion suggests substantial scope for future industry consolidation. CBRE Global Investors' acquisition of ING Real Estate from its Dutch insurance company parent in 2011 was the most significant merger and acquisition activity since the global financial crisis. However, growth through mergers and acquisitions has not proved to be an especially successful long-term strategy to AUM growth in the past. Table 6.2 shows AUM league tables from 1990 and 2011 from two US sources – Pensions and Investments and Institutional Real Estate Newsline. The names have changed significantly in the intervening 21 years, with only three managers appearing on both lists, and one name in the 2011 list absent from Table 6.1. The easiest time to increase AUM is when demand for real estate investments is strong. However, it can prove hard to retain that capital once the market cools in what is a highly cyclical asset class. Thus, we might expect the names in Tables 6.1 and 6.2 to change significantly over the next 10 years and beyond.

Following the classification of property investment as either direct property or property securities, the following section outlines the private direct property funds management industry. This is followed by sections outlining the public direct property funds management industry and the property securities fund management industry, before a review of property funds management business models and a final discussion of future directions in the property funds management industry.

Table 6.2 Leading property fund managers in 1990 and 2011 by assets under management (AUM)

Rank	*Top 10 real estate equity providers in 1990*[a]	*AUM (US$ billion)*	*Rank*	*Top 10 real estate equity providers in 2011*[b]	*AUM (US$ billion)*
1	Equitable Real Estate	11.6	1	Brookfield Asset Management	107.1
2	JMB Institutional Realty	11.3	2	CBRE Global Investors	94.1
3	Copley Real Estate Advisors	9.1	3	RREEF Real Estate Investors	58.5
4	Heitman Advisory	6.5	4	JP Morgan Asset Management	49.1
5	Prudential Real Estate	5.5	5	Prudential Real Estate	48.6
6	LaSalle Advisors	5.1	6	LaSalle Investment Managers	47.7
7	Aetna Life	5.1	7	AEW Capital Management	45.2
8	Aldrich, Eastman and Walch	4.3	8	Invesco Real Estate	43.7
9	Yarmouth Group	4.3	9	Blackstone Real Estate	42.8
10	RREEF	4.0	10	Principal Real Estate Investors	38.5

AUM = assets under management.

a Source: Pensions and Investments.

b Source: Institutional Real Estate Newsline 3Q 2011 total gross real estate assets including real estate securities, mortgage debt and other real estate related strategies.

Private direct property fund managers

Private direct property funds are unlisted investment products open to investors that shares common investment goals. They comprise shares or units that may be traded off market between investors but which are not listed on a stock exchange. Such funds are thus governed by their own articles of formation and generally exhibit lower liquidity than public funds and often comprise higher units of denomination.

Being 'direct property' funds, the fund manager invests in physical property, such as office blocks or shopping malls, occupied by income producing tenants. The fund manager will generally not only invest in the physical property asset but will also then manage it in an attempt to maximise the rental potential of that asset. This may include asset management activities (such as undertaking refurbishment or major lettings and lease renewals) as well as property management activities (such as rent collection and operational management).

The private direct property funds management industry comprises a wide range of managers offering a diverse range of products. These include geographically focussed funds, diversified and land use sector-specific funds and specialist funds which may be distinguished in terms of their investment style and risk–return profile. These funds can be marketed to both professional investors (wholesale) and to individuals (retail), albeit with differing requirements in terms of the information to be provided.

Geographic private direct property fund managers

Geographically focussed direct property funds may range from holding one or more individual assets in a specific city through to a regional portfolio of property assets, a nationwide portfolio of property assets or even a global portfolio of property assets.

Most funds declare a defined geographic scope unless they are genuinely global and can invest anywhere in the world. The geographic scope will correspond with the expressed expertise of the manager, for example, within a single national market. However, managers with global reach may still choose to also offer national market funds where these fit better with investor demand.

Investors have become increasingly wary of funds with a wide geographic scope. This trend began as long ago as 1990 when the global fund Rodamco, then managed from the Netherlands by Robeco, could no longer provide liquidity for unitholders at appraised net asset value, following a worldwide collapse in real estate values. This was followed by some influential research by Eichholtz (1997), which showed that geographically focussed funds had materially outperformed those with a wider market exposure.

In the run up to the global financial crisis, when the number of private funds increased rapidly, increasing numbers of multi-country 'regional' fund products were offered to investors seeking intercontinental exposures, for example, US pension funds wanting investment exposure in Europe and Asia Pacific. Such regional funds appeal to investors whose scale limits the number of direct real estate investments they can make in any particular international market or do not have the internal resources to identify specific market opportunities.

Thus, the range of geographically based fund products is wide. Fund managers, such as Centuria in Australia, offer a range of direct property funds which invest in single assets. Take, for example, the Centuria 10 Spring Street Property Fund, which invests in a single commercial property in central Sydney. Other managers similarly finance transactions through clubs of investors, often high net worth individuals, on a deal by deal basis.

Most funds operate, however, within a single national market. This group of funds comprises US ODCE funds, UK PUTs, and Australian unlisted trusts. Such funds can also combine a focus on specific submarkets within a regional or national market believed to have particular attractions. One such example would be the AEW South East Office Fund in the UK.

The creation of the Eurozone encouraged pan-European fund entities where properties could be acquired in a number of countries without introducing currency risk. The small size of many national markets in Europe (20 of the current 28 European Union countries have populations of fewer than 11 million) has further encouraged sub-regional funds; for example, the CBRE Property Fund Central Europe LP. Indeed, the European Association for Investors in Non-Listed Real Estate Vehicles (INREV) database for Europe comprises almost an equal number of single country and multi-country funds. Perhaps unsurprisingly, the multi-country funds prove slightly larger by value and comprise 54% of the gross assets on the database.

The world's largest institutional investors, including the sovereign wealth funds, are increasingly building global real estate portfolios. However, these generally comprise a mix of direct holdings held individually or through joint ventures, private funds and publicly listed securities rather than just making use of a number of global direct property funds. The investment banks' global opportunistic fund series, with names like MSREF (Morgan Stanley) and Whitehall (Goldman Sachs) are now a shadow of their former selves following the global financial crisis. Blackstone, though, continues to be able raise significant sums for both its global and regional real estate vehicles.

Diversified versus sector-specific private direct property fund managers

Diversified and sector-specific direct property funds can be identified by their target assets for investment. Diversified or 'multi-sector' direct property funds invest across a range of property market sectors (such as office, industrial and retail properties) while, as the name suggests, sector-specific direct property funds invest only in one specific property market sector.

In Europe, the bulk of the funds in the INREV database are 'diversified' investing in a range of property sectors (Figure 6.2). Most core and many opportunity funds are diversified, but for different reasons. Core funds are generally designed to provide a risk-reducing diversified exposure to the property asset class. Such funds often seek to match or outperform a market index that itself comprises properties from multiple sectors. By contrast, managers of opportunity funds feel free to invest wherever they perceive the best deals can be found, regardless of property sector.

The managers of funds that specialise by property type tend to offer core or value-added investment products. As can be seen from Figure 6.3, in Europe one can find specialist vehicles for all the main property sectors as well as funds specialising in 'alternative' property types such as hotels and parking. The reasoning behind creating a specialist property type fund varies from offering investors the specific expertise required in, say, managing

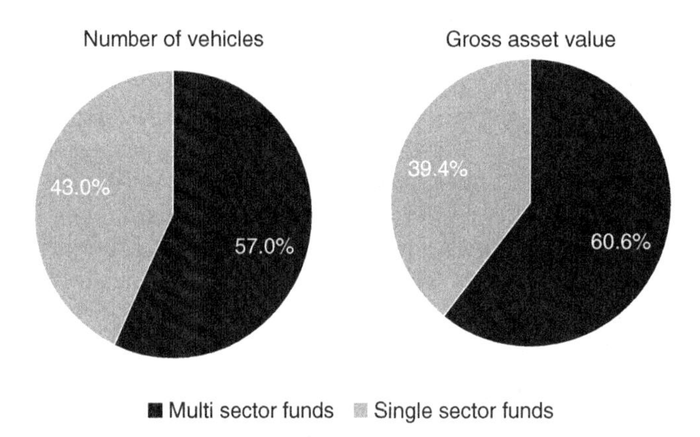

Figure 6.2 Private funds by single versus multi-sector in Europe
Source: INREV Vehicles Universe, 31 May 2017.

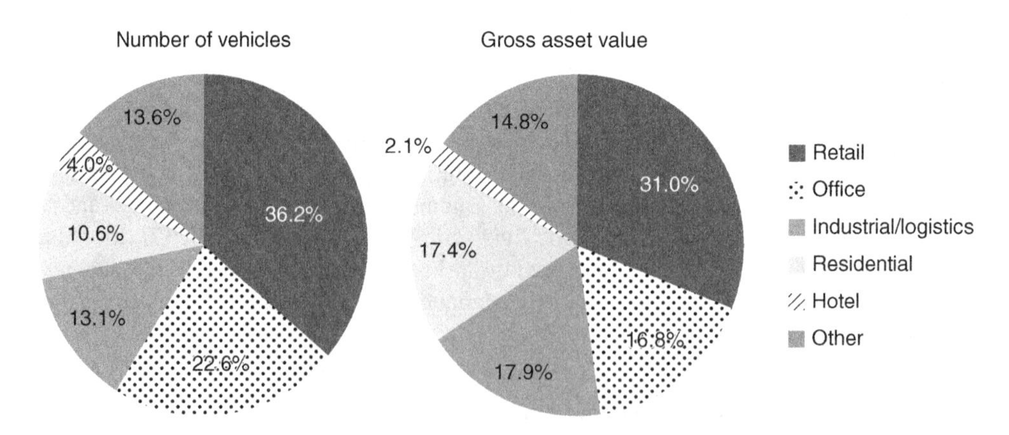

Figure 6.3 Private funds in Europe: composition of funds with a single property sector focus
Source: INREV Vehicles Universe, 31 May 2017.

shopping centres to creating funds to exploit a specific market timing opportunities in a specific sector market.

Generally, specific property type funds are designed for institutional investors who either want to maintain overall control of their real estate asset allocation strategy themselves or who recognise the benefit of using a specialist for assets that require specific management skills that they themselves do not possess. The current growth of residential funds in the UK is a good example of the latter.

Funds designed for private individual 'retail' investors tend to be diversified offerings. This is because most such investors do not have the skills or simply do not want to construct their own diversified property exposure through investing across a range of specialist products.

Specialist managers

Specialist private direct property funds include geographically focussed funds and diversified or sector-specific funds. They can be open or close ended funds and they may be directed at wholesale or retail investors (see below). However, they are generally distinguishable by their investment 'style' or return focus.

Style-based specialist managers

There are many existing nomenclatures and definitions of investment style – the following has been derived from Parker (2011).

ACTIVE OR PASSIVE STYLE

A passive investment style is where, through what is bought and sold, a manager deliberately sets out to replicate or follow a benchmark or index and so approximate the risk-return of that benchmark or index over time. In contrast, an active investment style is where the manager sets out to add value and enhance returns above those achieved by a benchmark or index within a stated risk tolerance through the active management of either or both the overall portfolio and the properties within it.

Very few managers in private real estate offer passive funds because it is virtually impossible to replicate an index comprising thousands of unique properties. The uniqueness of property assets is such that, even when two properties are adjoining, the investment returns they deliver can vary markedly because of differing tenants, lease terms and building condition. Callender *et al.* (2007) estimate that, in the UK, a portfolio with 350 properties is required to ensure a performance that exhibits a standard deviation of differential performance (or tracking error) of 1% or less with the biggest UK national commercial property market index.[3] This implies that an investor would need to own a portfolio of £4.3 billion if the average asset size within the index is replicated. Clearly, this is only possible for the very largest investors.

Just because passive investment is difficult,[4] however, and most managers are 'active', does *not* imply that consistent outperformance is simple to achieve. Notwithstanding that most managers set strategies in the belief they can beat their benchmark, a different UK study (Mitchell and Bond, 2008) established that the generation of systematic outperformance was limited to only a small elite of top managers. Winners have to be averaged out by losers.

TOP DOWN OR BOTTOM UP STYLE

A top down style is an investment management style where a manager sequentially considers the global economy, national economy, regional economies and local economies and then considers the global real estate market, regional real estate markets, national real estate markets and local real estate markets to identify the best geographic areas and/or real estate sectors for investment. By contrast, a bottom up investment management style is one where the manager specifically considers the investment attributes of identified individual assets and their acceptability for acquisition, potentially disregarding other than local economic and real estate market conditions.

Bottom up strategies are more common in opportunity funds where the main focus is on specific, high returning, deals. However, even there, the individual investments made can be themed, for example, Blackstone's creation of a global portfolio of modern logistics warehouses.

Most managers now employ property researchers to advise on strategy so nearly all combine 'top down' and 'bottom up' approaches because they are not mutually exclusive.

Value or growth style: A value style is an investment management style where the manager focusses on identifying assets believed to be significantly mis-priced and thus offer the potential for abnormal income, capital and/or total returns over a defined future timeframe. A growth style is one style where the manager focusses on constructing a portfolio comprising assets that each offer the potential for growing income, capital and/or total returns over an undefined but usually longer future timeframe.

In the UK, the Threadneedle team (now part of Zurich Assurance) have a long track record as a value investor focussing on income return much more than capital growth. This style often involves purchasing older assets, let on short leases, at a high yield. Other insurers, for example the investment arm of insurer Legal and General, concentrate much more on growth, overtly seeking assets where rents can be expected to increase in line with the economy.

CORE, VALUE ADDED OR OPPORTUNISTIC STYLE

A core style seeks to provide a risk adjusted return that is approximately equal to the market but through the holding of only a small portfolio of high quality properties. The value added style seeks to achieve outperformance by identifying opportunities to add value using mixed quality real estate assets, such as through undertaking development in an undersupplied market. The opportunistic style seeks to generate outperformance through a wide spectrum of multiplicative risk approaches, usually including higher risk real estate assets, such as through a contrarian approach of acquiring empty buildings in a temporarily over-supplied market where confident of long term economic growth. Moreover, the levels of leverage employed increase in line with the risk profile. This magnifies not only the expected return but also the increased losses if the unlevered returns are below the cost of the debt.

One can find other style adjectives referred to such as 'core plus' (generally regarded as between core and value-add). However, these descriptions tend not to have a formal definition. By contrast, funds industry bodies, notably INREV, provide quite precise definitions for the three main styles in terms of leverage used, return from income producing assets and return from development activities (INREV, 2012).

The German open ended funds are classic core funds, for example, Union Investment Real Estate GmbH of Hamburg's UniImmo: Europa Fund. Europa Capital and Tristan Capital

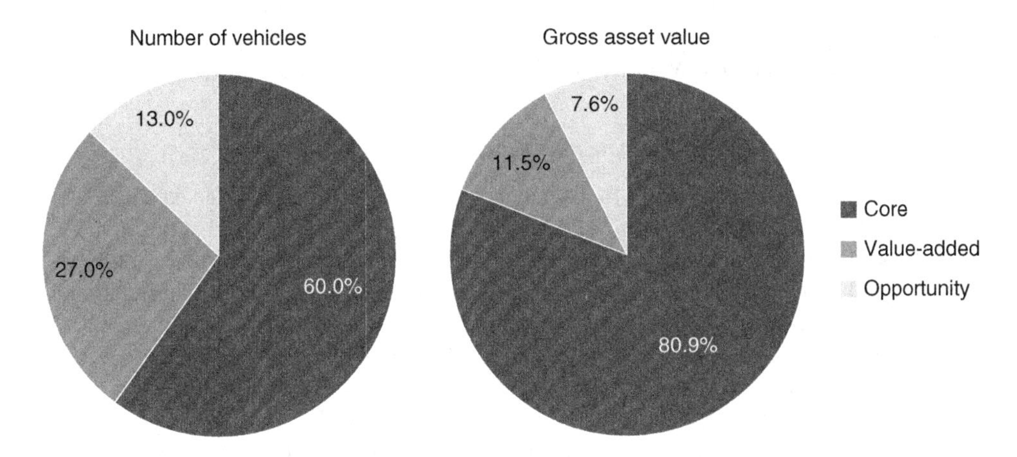

Figure 6.4 Private funds by style in Europe
Source: INREV Vehicles Universe, 31 May 2017.

Partners are two London based managers who offer Europe wide value-add funds. Patron Capital is an example of a manager that specialises in providing investors with opportunity fund products.

Some managers offer funds across the style spectrum. Examples include CBRE Global Investors and LaSalle Investment Management. This trend is increasing with Blackstone, with its longstanding reputation as an opportunistic investor, now offering core and value-add products.

In Europe, core funds predominate, both by number and especially by value (Figure 6.4) comprising a mix of single and multi-country funds. Value-add funds show a similar pattern of geographical exposures but opportunity funds tend to follow a multi-country strategy.

Return focus based specialist managers

Specialist private direct property fund managers may be distinguished either by investment style, as considered above, or by their return focus which is generally either an income return focus, a capital return focus or a total return focus.

Fund managers focussing on income return will prioritise investment in properties that provide higher levels of prospective net income yield over those offering capital growth. Conversely, fund managers focussing on capital return will seek to invest in properties offering higher prospective capital growth rather than on prevailing income yields. Fund managers offering a total return focus fund will seek to balance a risk adjusted income return with prospective capital growth to provide an optimal prospective total return.

Value-add and opportunistic funds generally produce most of their returns through capital gains rather than through income. As such, they are capital return focussed. More of the return from a core fund is from income and this is reflected in how INREV classifies investment styles, with the proportion of returns from income a key criteria.

Real estate funds offering inflation linked income have become popular in recent times, with pension funds adopting investment strategies that closely match their ongoing liabilities. Such an approach minimises the risk to the plan sponsor that they will have to meet a shortfall because of underfunding at some time in the future. The existence of long leases with rent reviews linked to the Consumer Price Index or Retail Price Index on some UK properties (for example, supermarkets) has enabled low risk property funds to be created that provide inflation-proof dividends. The M&G Secured Property Income Fund is one such example.

Wholesale compared with retail private direct property fund managers

Wholesale and retail direct property funds may be distinguished by their targeted sources of equity, with wholesale direct property funds generally targeting sophisticated or professional investors (such as pension funds or high net worth individuals) and retail direct property funds generally targeting 'mom and pop' or private investors. While both wholesale and retail direct property funds may be closed ended (operating for a fixed term) or open ended (no fixed end date for the fund), wholesale funds will generally have a much higher level of minimum investment per investor (typically ranging from €0.5–25 million) than retail funds (which might be as low as €100).

Some funds impose a maximum limit on how much an investor can place in a fund. However, this can sometimes be circumvented through a 'feeder fund', which enables investors' contributions to be combined. In such circumstances, investors' voting and control rights are more limited than those holding units directly within the main fund.

Generally, since the global financial crisis, institutions investing in wholesale funds have become more wary of who they invest alongside in such vehicles. They much prefer to invest alongside investors with a similar perspective on risk, such as other similar institutions. They perceive retail investors and 'fund of funds' managers (a fund that invests in other funds) to have a more short-term focus and potentially less liquidity to meet any capital calls that may be needed to prevent the vehicle becoming a distressed seller at times of market stress.

Seventy-five per cent of the funds in the European INREV database are open to institutional investors only. The remainder include a mix of retail investors and institutions among their unit-holders. The main mixed investor vehicles are large funds with an average size of €4 billion,[5] where retail investors own over 50% of the entity. These are principally German open ended funds.

As already noted, wholesale and retail investor funds can be either 'open' or 'closed.' An open fund offers a formal redemption process whereby investors can sell their units through the manager at a price at or close to that reflecting the net asset value of the fund. Closed funds have a defined lifespan, at the end of which the manager must return the investors' cash to them. The initial investment is used to buy specific assets and/or assets to be identified that meet the fund's strategy.[6] These assets have to be sold by the end of the fund's life and the proceeds returned to investors. This said, extensions to the fund's lifespan may be negotiated or permitted, depending on the wording of the investment contract. There is no mechanism offered by the manager to redeem units during the life of a closed fund, although secondary markets can emerge for units in the largest funds, such as the Hercules Retail Warehouse Fund in the UK (see also Schneider, 2014).

Retail funds, designed for 'mom and pop' investors, are open ended because it has become unrealistic to expect individuals to tie up their capital for long periods with no capacity for early redemption. Many institutional funds are also 'open' as the funds are designed to perform like direct property for those without either the desire to be a direct owner or sufficient assets to build their own diversified direct portfolio.

Open ended funds in Europe have a higher total value than closed-end funds, although there are more by number for the latter (Figure 6.5).

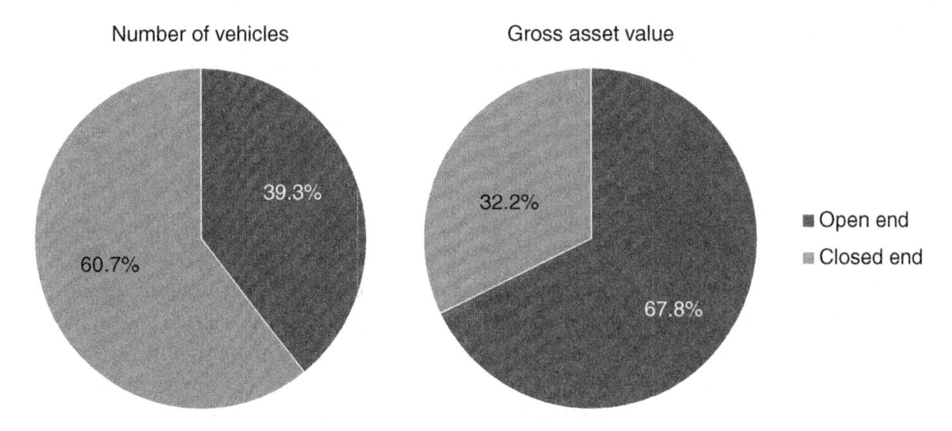

Figure 6.5 Private funds by structure in Europe
Source: INREV Vehicles Universe, 31 May 2017.

The redemption process can take a number of forms but tends to exhibit two common features. First, each fund has a predetermined procedure by which unit-holders can redeem units. This is usually designed to coincide with a date when the assets are formally appraised so that unit-holders receive a fair price. Second, the manager can suspend the redemption process if the fund does not have the liquid assets available to pay out redemption requests.

Three basic models may be identified for redemption requests used by open ended funds around the world. The simplest, but most fragile, has been adopted by the UK PUTs. These trusts generally provide for a redemption window quarterly (sometimes monthly), with a date by which requests must be received; cash payments are normally made a month after the relevant quarter day so that the valuation is as current as possible.

The German model is similar except that open ended funds must hold a buffer of liquid assets to meet redemptions. This buffer was set by law in 1969 (Bannier *et al.*, 2008) and must be between 5% and 50% of the fund's net asset value. There is, therefore, a need to have readily saleable or 'liquid' assets (not direct real estate) available to meet redemptions at all times. UK PUTs have no comparable requirement.

US open ended funds, the world's largest group of such funds, have a different approach. These funds do not have a full obligation to meet redemption requests, merely a duty to use 'reasonable endeavours'. The funds publish quarterly, or annually, the volume of units they are prepared to redeem and unit-holders can apply for a portion of the allocation. This approach is the only one that sensibly recognises the illiquid nature of real estate and avoids a fund becoming a 'forced seller' simply to meet redemptions.

The US approach also recognises that redemption requests are likely to be at their highest when markets are at their least liquid and property values are falling. This is at the expense of making the 'redemption promise' a heavily constrained one, or so it appears to Europeans, for whom such funds may be regarded as only 'semi-open'.[7] However, this approach makes them much more robust, ensuring managers are not forced to sell the fund's best assets at the worst possible times to the detriment of those longer-term unit-holders intent on holding through the downturn.

The above is well reflected in how the various open ended funds fared during the GFC. UK PUTs saw significant redemption requests in 2007/08 with many forced to suspend their usual payment schedule. Some also managed unit pricing so that redeeming investors received less than the last published net asset value/unit price in an attempt to be fair to all unit-holders at a time when market prices were declining sharply, and appraised values struggled to keep up.

The German open ended funds also suffered severely as, despite their liquidity buffers, some were overwhelmed with redemption requests. This was exacerbated by some investors being offered weekly or even daily redemption rights in the buoyant market immediately prior to the global financial crisis. The situation was further compounded by a long standing requirement that German open ended funds are not permitted to sell assets at a price lower than their last independently appraised level. As most assets are valued only annually this restricted the ability of funds to sell assets to boost liquidity. Funds may 'close' if they are unable to meet redemptions. If they cannot meet all redemptions within a 24-month period of closing, they must liquidate their assets. Fourteen German open ended funds went into liquidation during 2011–13, with a further four funds closed and selling assets to generate cash to meet redemptions.

By contrast, US open ended funds weathered the 2008/09 property market slowdown relatively well despite values dropping by 30% in 2008/09 (per NCREIF). They did not have to change their redemption promises which damage the bond of trust with unit-holders. They merely reduced the volume of units offered for redemption. These funds are currently as popular as they have ever been and the leading vehicles have significant queues of investors waiting to have their capital drawn down.[8]

Public direct property fund managers

Following the classification of property investment as either direct property or property securities, the previous section outlined the private direct property funds management industry. This section outlines the public direct property funds management industry, after which we provide an outline of the property securities funds management industry, a review of property funds management business models and a discussion of future directions in the property funds management industry.

'Public funds' are products listed on a stock exchange and open to any and all investors (subject to any specific jurisdictional controls). They comprise shares or units that can be traded on that stock exchange. As such, public funds are governed by their articles of formation together with the securities legislation and regulation relevant to the jurisdiction they operate in. Generally, they exhibit higher levels of tradability or liquidity than private funds and often comprise lower monetary units of denomination.

Being direct property funds, the fund manager invests in physical property, such as high rise office towers or regional shopping centres, occupied by income producing tenants. The fund manager will generally undertake the process of investment in the physical property asset but may either undertake or outsource the management of the physical property asset, including asset management (such as undertaking refurbishment or effecting major lettings and lease renewals) and property management (such as rent collection and operational management).

The public direct property funds management industry comprises two principal forms – the first being investment through trust structures (such as REITs) and, second, investment through company structures (such as REOCs, non-traded REITs[9] and property companies).

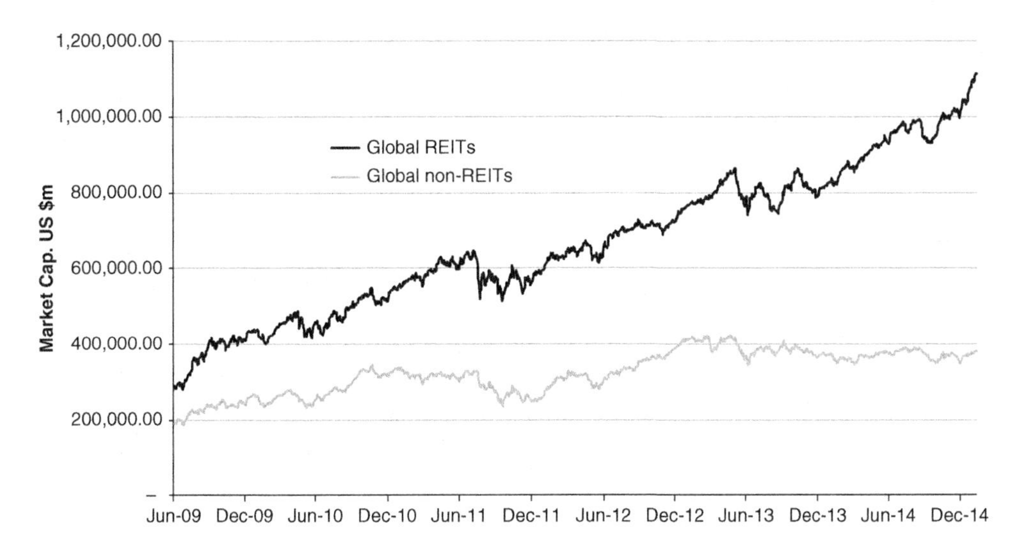

Figure 6.6 Relative growth in market capitalisation of real estate investment trusts (REITs) and non-REITs since the global financial crisis

Source: Consilia Capital, European Real Estate Association.

Since the global financial crisis, REITs have managed to recapitalise far quicker than non-REITs, primarily due to two factors; namely:

- the US concentration of REITs; and
- the tax efficient mechanism, whereby rental income is effectively passed through to investors as dividends which, from an income viewpoint, makes the vehicle similar to an investment in direct property.

Figure 6.6 shows the relative growth in market capitalisation of REITs and non-REITs since the global financial crisis. However, the percentage of REITs relative to the total listed universe varies dramatically. As can be seen from Table 6.3, which looks at the largest listed markets globally, the percentage varies from 100% REITs in Australia, the Netherlands and France and 99% in the US to 18% in Hong Kong and only 3% in Germany. Table 6.3 also illustrates the significant income advantage of REITs over non-REITs where direct comparisons can be made.

Real estate investment trusts

The principal distinctions between REITs and REOCs, non-REITs and property companies relate to the way tax is paid, the minimum dividend distribution requirements and the balance between income producing investment and development. In most jurisdictions, REITs are generally not taxed at the entity level provided that they distribute the required proportion of their taxable income to unit-holders (typically 90%), who then bear the liability for paying tax.

Specific REIT legislation varies globally but, despite minor regional variations, it should be noted that in a number of the major developed markets (including US, UK, France,

Table 6.3 Global market composition

	REIT market capitalisation (US$ million)	*Non-REIT market capitalisation (US$ million)*	*REITs as a percentage*	*REIT yield (%)*	*Non-REIT yield (%)*	*REIT premium (%)*
US	658	6	99.1	3.56	0.00	3.56
Japan	67	79	45.9	2.94	0.60	2.34
Hong Kong	17	76	18.3	3.86	3.04	0.82
Australia	74	0	100.0	4.11	0.00	4.11
UK	62	14	81.6	3.01	1.99	1.02
Canada	38	3	92.7	5.77	5.43	0.34
Singapore	20	20	50.0	5.64	1.98	3.66
Netherlands	34	0	100.0	4.40	0.00	4.40
Germany	1	28	3.4	4.88	1.33	3.55
France	16	0	100.0	4.95	0.00	4.95
Europe	**121**	**73**	**62.4**	**3.75**	**2.33**	**1.42**
Asia	**179**	**175**	**50.6**	**3.83**	**1.83**	**2.00**
Global	**997**	**257**	**79.5**	**3.71**	**1.96**	**1.75**

REIT = real estate investment trust.

Source: Consilia Capital, EPRA, 2014.

Australia and Canada) the REIT structure is now the dominant form of listed vehicle. In Asia, however, the composition is different, with development based companies being dominant (as measured by market capitalisation) in Japan and Hong Kong, where REITs are typically formed as a separate investment vehicle by their sponsors (typically listed developers such as Mitsubishi Estate or Mitsui Fudosan).

The sponsor plays a pivotal role as it is the originator of the REIT and the entity placing most of the properties into the REIT at the time of its listing. When the REIT is offered to the market at its initial public offering, the sponsor often establishes a subsidiary company to serve as the manager of the REIT while retaining substantial unit holdings in the REIT. This close interrelationship established between sponsor and manager can potentially lead to conflicts of interest between them and other unit-holders.

Globally, REITs account for around 70% of the public direct property sector by market capitalisation. Mimicking elements of the private direct property sector, they too can be categorised into two principal groups, namely, those pursuing diversified or sector-specific investment strategies and those that pursue geographically focussed investment strategies.

Diversified compared with sector-specific REITs

Diversified and sector-specific REITs may be distinguished by their target assets for investment. Diversified REITs seek to invest across a range of property market sectors (such as office, retail and industrial) while sector-specific REITs seek to invest in one specific property market sector (such as offices, shopping centres or industrial buildings.). The advantage of specialisation from an operational point of view is its economy of scale while from an investors' viewpoint it both reduces uncertainty by limiting the REITs operations to areas of expertise and allows investors to assemble their own portfolios of REITs to satisfy diversification needs and personal market preferences.

Table 6.4 summarises the largest REITs globally by market capitalisation (as at May 2014). It shows:

Table 6.4 Largest real estate investment trusts by market capitalisation

Company name	*Listing country*	*Main asset type*	*Dividend yield (%)*	*Market cap. (US$ million)*
Simon Property Group Inc.	USA	Regional malls	2.96	54,567
American Tower Corp.	USA	Wireless towers	1.44	35,083
Public Storage	USA	Storage	3.26	29,615
Unibail-Rodamco SE	France	Regional malls	1.99	26,267
Equity Residential	USA	Apartments	3.24	22,319
Westfield Group	Australia	Shopping centres	5.01	21,138
General Growth Properties Inc.	USA	Regional malls	2.54	20,883
Prologis Inc.	USA	Warehouse/industrial	3.20	20,587
Ventas Inc.	USA	Health care	4.28	19,944
Vornado Realty Trust	USA	Diversified	2.77	19,768
HCP Inc.	USA	Health care	5.18	19,295
Health Care REIT Inc.	USA	Health care	4.94	18,767
Boston Properties Inc.	USA	Office property	2.18	18,278
Avalon Bay Communities Inc.	USA	Apartments	3.33	18,058
Weyerhauser Co.	USA	Timberlands	2.90	17,726
Host Hotels & Resorts Inc.	USA	Hotels	2.61	16,221
Land Securities Group plc	UK	Diversified	2.78	14,585
British Land plc	UK	Diversified	3.75	12,210
Link REIT	Hong Kong	Shopping centres	3.99	11,627
Essex Property Trust	USA	Apartments	2.68	11,217

REIT = real estate investment trust.

Source: Consilia Capital, Bloomberg, September 2014.

- the current dominance of the US, which accounts for almost 50% of the global listed sector market capitalisation. This was not always the case. Before the 'modern REIT' era, which started in 1992, the UK listed real estate sector was larger than that of the US;
- the largest REITs globally tend to be sector specific. In general terms, assets of more than two-thirds by value of a portfolio indicate a level of specialisation. An exception to this can be seen in the UK, where the two largest REIT portfolios are broadly split between offices and shopping centres; and
- in general terms, that the level of REIT specialisation is greatest in the US.

REOCs, non-REITs and property companies

As stated earlier, the principal distinctions between REOCs, non-REITs and property companies, compared with REITs, relate to the way in which tax is paid, the minimum dividend distribution requirements and the balance between income producing investment and development. In most jurisdictions, unlike REITs, REOCs, non-REITS and property companies are typically taxed at the entity level, providing post tax dividends to shareholders who may then receive some form of personal tax relief (such as the franking credits system in Australia).

Generally, in most jurisdictions, REOCs, non-REITs and property companies will comprise a company structure rather than the trust and/or management company structure

Table 6.5 Largest real estate operating companies, non-real estate investment trusts or property companies by market capitalisation

Company name	*Listing country*	*Dividend yield (%)*	*Market cap. (US$ million)*
Cheung Kong Holdings Ltd	Hong Kong	2.66	39,143
Sun Hung Kai Properties Ltd	Hong Kong	3.39	34,759
Mitsubishi Estate Co. Ltd	Japan	0.50	32,583
Mitsui Fudosan Co. Ltd	Japan	0.70	27,128
Wharf Holdings Ltd	Hong Kong	3.23	20,601
China Overseas Land and Investment Ltd	Hong Kong	2.56	19,403
Emaar Properties PJSC	UAE	1.52	19,200
Sumitomo Realty and Development Co. Ltd	Japan	0.50	18,700
Ezdan Holding group QSC	Qatar	1.23	18,360
Swire Properties Ltd	Hong Kong	2.56	17,735
Henderson Land Development Co.	Hong Kong	2.22	16,609
Hong Kong Land Holdings Ltd	Singapore	2.60	16,258
Hang Lung Properties Ltd	Hong Kong	3.24	13,395
China Vanke Co. Ltd	China	4.42	13,371
Jabal Omar Development Co.	Saudi Arabia	n/a	11,950
China Resources Land Ltd	Hong Kong	3.02	10,877
SM Prime Holdings Inc.	Philippines	1.12	10,785
Global Logistic Properties Ltd	Singapore	1.44	10,552
CapitaLand Ltd	Singapore	2.64	10,326
Ayala Land Inc.	Philippines	1.30	10,299

Source: Consilia Capital, Bloomberg, September 2014.

adopted by REITs. Furthermore, REOCs, non-REITS and property companies will generally focus on investment in a greater proportion of higher risk income producing property assets and a greater proportion of development activity. This gives them a more equity market or share like characteristic.

Table 6.5 shows the largest REOCs, non-REITs or property companies by market capitalisation (as at May 2014). We can see that:

- whereas the largest REITs had a US bias, the largest property companies have a strong Asian bias;
- not only are the property investment activities of these companies more diversified by asset type, but there is also a higher level of development activity (particularly residential) as well as other non-property investment activities; and
- the yield on these companies is significantly lower than that for REITs, reflecting the non–investment activities.

Property securities fund managers

Following the classification of property investment as either direct property or property securities, the previous sections outlined the private direct property funds management industry and the public direct property funds management industry. This section outlines the property securities funds management industry. It is followed by a general review of property funds management business models and a concluding discussion about the future of the property funds management industry.

Being property securities funds, the fund manager invests in property securities, comprising an investment in shares or units in listed or unlisted companies or trusts which, in turn, hold direct investments in physical properties. In this type of fund, fund managers will make the decision on which specific property securities funds to invest in but, unlike fund managers in direct property funds, they will not be involved in the management of the underlying physical property asset. This is undertaken by the relevant personnel in the company in which the property securities fund manager is investing.

Property securities funds may be open or closed ended, with generally lower liquidity and higher denominations of investment for the former than the latter. They may even be listed on a stock exchange themselves. Property securities funds are generally open to any and all investors (subject to any specific jurisdictional controls), offering investors shares or units governed by their articles of formation together with, for closed ended and listed funds, the securities legislation and regulation prevailing in the jurisdiction.

Typically, for an open ended fund, different investor groups, such as institutional and retail investors, would have different share classes in the same fund as well as different fee structures for the same collective pool of assets. A range of fund structures may be used around the world. For example, a number of European funds use the Luxembourg-based *Société d'Investissement à Capital Variable*[10] structure; elsewhere, other structures are used.

There are at least three distinct types of fund manager operating property securities funds, these include:

- real estate asset managers, such as CBRE Clarion and LaSalle Investment Management, which have securities research and investment teams in addition to their significant direct real estate asset management departments;
- dedicated real estate securities managers, such as Cohen and Steers in the US and B&I Capital in Asia, that do not have a significant direct property asset management team; and
- general fund managers, such as Fidelity, Blackrock and Morgan Stanley, that possess specialist global real estate teams and funds in addition to other regional and global equity and bond products.

At the end of September 2014, the EPRA Global Developed Index[11] was valued at US$1.147 billion. The AUM of the property securities funds in the Consilia Capital database represent around 26% of this figure. This suggests, therefore, that specialist investors account for around one-quarter of the shareholdings of listed real estate companies. However, this may be an underestimate since, with the exception of Japan, the Consilia Capital database does not include individual country funds, comprises only funds or collective investment vehicles and does not include separate account mandates where two of the largest specialist managers, CBRE Clarion and LaSalle Investment Management, predominantly operate. Taking these omissions into account, dedicated real estate securities fund managers may own up to 30% of the shareholdings of listed real estate companies. By definition, this figure rises when there is little interest in the sector from generalist investors and falls when there are significant inflows from non-specialists (as in 2009–12).

Figure 6.7 shows the number of global listed real estate funds in the Consilia Capital database, grouped by year of inception. As can be seen, prior to 2005/06, they were relatively insignificant. However, the bull property market of 2006/07 and the subsequent search by investors for secure income after the global financial crisis has led to a significant increase in their number and significance in recent times.

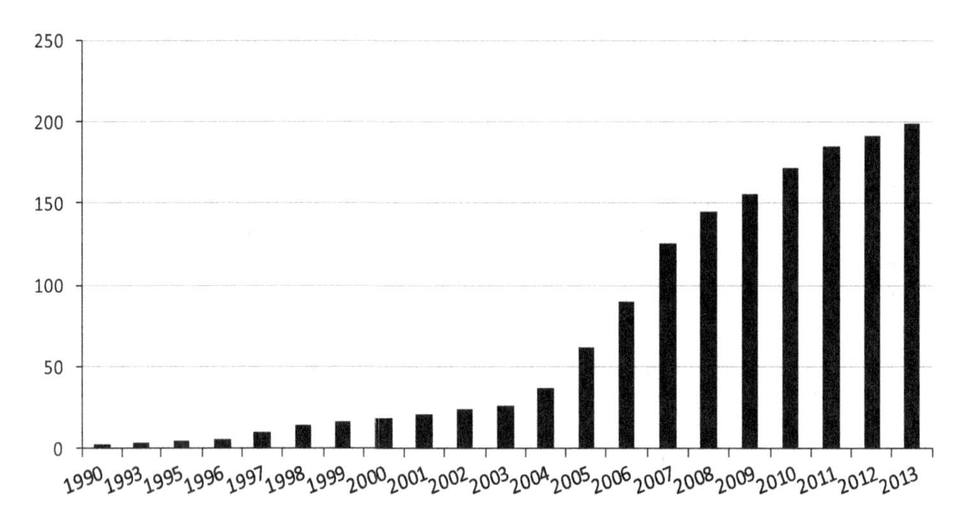

Figure 6.7 Number of global listed real estate funds in the Consilia Capital Database, 1990–2013
Source: Consilia Capital, December 2014.

The two principal investment styles for property securities funds are actively managed versus passive vehicles (such as exchange traded funds).[12] They can also exhibit global or region-specific mandates.

Table 6.6 shows the size and shape of the major types of fund available as at 30 September 2014. Table 6.6 splits the funds by type (structure), then geographic mandate and, finally, by aggregate AUM and number of funds. In this context, Global REIT funds are a structure designed particularly for the Japanese retail market, where income is seen as all-important, and have seen significant growth in recent years. Global real estate funds will typically include both REITs and property companies.

Active compared with passive property securities fund managers

A passive property securities fund is typically managed to replicate or follow a benchmark or index and so approximate the risk-return of that benchmark or index. These can either be exchange traded funds or index tracking funds. By contrast, an active property securities fund is managed to add value and enhance returns above those achieved by a benchmark or index within a stated risk tolerance.

The most commonly used benchmark is the Financial Times Stock Exchange/EPRA/Nareit series of benchmarks. Other index benchmark providers include GPR (Geopolitical Risk), MSCI and Standard & Poor's. In Asia, Thomson Reuters has combined with APREA (the Asian Public Real Estate Association, Singapore) and GPR to produce an Asian Index, which reflects the largest companies in the sector (as a number are excluded from other indices owing to their non-property activities).

With respect to active property securities fund strategies, there are a number of different methodologies employed to generate outperformance against a nominated benchmark or 'alpha'. These include, but are not limited to:

Table 6.6 Major types of property securities fund available as at 30 September 2014

Type	*Mandate*	*AUM (US$ million)*	*No. of funds*
Closed end fund	US real estate	4,053	8
	European real estate	1,096	1
	Global real estate	1,845	3
Exchange traded funds	US real estate	39,551	29
	European real estate	3,016	7
	Global real estate investment trust	994	3
	Global real estate	11,468	11
	Asian real estate	969	10
	Japan	2,437	7
FCP	European real estate	1,262	13
	Global real estate	420	2
Fund of Funds	US real estate	32,646	15
	European real estate	14	1
	Global real estate investment trust	24,942	35
	Global real estate	3,194	10
	Asian real estate	16	5
	Japan	15,524	20
Hedge fund	European real estate	94	1
Investment trust	US real estate	17	1
	European real estate	2,782	2
	Global real estate	67	1
Open ended investment company	European real estate	343	1
	Global real estate	1,385	6
	Asian real estate	12	1
Open ended fund	US real estate	87,526	82
	European real estate	1,899	21
	Global real estate investment trust	2,769	21
	Global real estate	34,519	110
	Asian real estate	2,134	27
	Japan	3,906	14
Open end pension	Global real estate investment trust	64	4
	Global real estate	169	9
	Japan	160	6
Société d'Investissement à Capital Variable	US real estate	424	2
	European real estate	4,578	26
	Global real estate investment trust	237	2
	Global real estate	4,718	23
	Asian real estate	586	4
Unit investment trust	Japan	27	1
Unit trust	European real estate	18	1
	Global real estate investment trust	395	6
	Global real estate	7,234	27
	Asian real estate	270	7
Variable annuity	US real estate	2,258	8
	Global real estate	335	1
TOTAL		**302,375**	**595**

AUM = assets under management; FCP = *Fonds commun de placement*, a common investment fund.

Source: Consilia Capital, Bloomberg, September 2014.

- bottom up company analysis to produce an in-house proprietary assessment of net asset value, which is then compared with the prevailing share price for individual stock selection. This approach is used by organisations like Cohen and Steers, JP Morgan, LaSalle and Morgan Stanley;
- taking long and short positions against benchmark weightings based on macro and top down trends;
- adopting benchmark regional weightings but taking long and short positions with respect to countries within those regional benchmarks;
- a form of 'smart beta' strategy where stock exposures are weighted not by reference to free float market capitalisation but by reference fundamental performance drivers such as rental income, gross assets, and so on, as used by the Kempen Fundamental Index Fund;
- a focus on more liquid stocks leading to a more concentrated portfolio. Heitman and Forum Partners have recently focussed strategies in this area; and
- a focus on stocks that are not included in any benchmarks (for example, investing in emerging markets rather than a developed markets benchmark). Alpine Woods' funds tend to have an emerging market bias.

Some investors adopt a passive index replication strategy but seek to enhance returns (and potentially increase losses) by using a 'leveraged exchange traded fund' strategy. One US example of this is the Direxion Daily Real Estate Bull 3x Shares exchange traded fund. In simple terms, through leverage, this exchange traded fund seeks to deliver three times the return of the underlying index (that is, if the index rises by 2%, the exchange traded fund should rise by 6%).

Similarly, it is also possible to purchase an exchange traded fund that seeks to return the inverse of the underlying index, known as a mirror or reverse exchange traded fund. This is usually done by using derivative instruments on the relevant index. An example in the US, using the Dow Jones US Real Estate Index, would be the ProShares Short Real Estate Fund where, if the index declines 2%, this fund would seek to return +2% to investors.

Geographical property securities fund managers

Geographically focussed property securities funds may hold a portfolio of national property securities, a portfolio of regional property securities or a portfolio of international property securities. Typically, the international classifications are global real estate, global REIT and international (defined as global less a specified country) with the most popular regional funds being US, Asia, Asia Pacific, Japanese and European. In terms of countries, the most popular single country funds (after excluding the two largest – US and Japan) are Australian and South African.

Table 6.7 shows that global funds dominate by number while US oriented funds dominate by total AUM.

Fund manager business models

Following the classification of property investment as either direct property or property securities, the previous sections outlined the private direct property funds management industry, the public direct property funds management industry and the property securities funds management industry. This section reviews typical property funds management business models and is followed by a final section that discusses future directions in the property funds management industry.

Table 6.7 Geographic property securities fund managers

Region	*AUM (US$ million)*	*No. of funds*
US	166,476	145
Global	65,355	203
Global REIT	29,401	71
Japan	22,054	48
European	15,102	74
Asian	3,987	54
TOTAL	302,375	595

AUM = assets under management; REIT = real estate investment trust.

Source: Consilia Capital, Bloomberg.

Across the property funds management industry generally, there are two main business models; namely, those that manage various asset management functions in-house and those that outsource those functions. Following discussion of the relevant issues for a fund manager when considering in-house management or outsourced management, the in-house management and the outsourced business model are reviewed.

In-house compared with outsourced service provision

In common with other major business enterprises, some activities carried out by fund managers lend themselves to being outsourced where the laws, regulations and rules in that jurisdiction permit. The decision whether to use outsourced service providers is usually based on a broad range of considerations. These include:

- cost – while outsourced service provider costs may be substantial in terms of fees, the remuneration and on-costs for in-house staff in terms of human resources, information technology, workspace and staff turnover may also be substantial;
- control – the use of outsourced service providers may result in an actual or perceived loss of control by a fund manager compared with using in-house staff;
- management – securing the same level management and motivation of outsourced service providers can be a challenge, given the intermediated nature of the relationship;
- communication – there is a need to ensure that the amount, quality and timeliness of information provision to decision makers within the fund manager from an outsourced service provider is at least as good as that possible from in-house staff;
- expertise – the ability to provide the necessary skills and expertise for all services on an ongoing basis solely through a small in-house team can be challenging;
- flexibility – the cost and time needed to address underperformance and replace poorly performing staff may vary between outsourced service providers and in-house staff; and
- conflicts of interest – outsourced service providers may be, or be perceived to be, pursuing a strategy servicing their own business interests which, by definition, does not occur with in-house staff.

As individual situations differ, there is no simple guide to the decision whether to use outsourced service providers or in-house staff. Often, some combination of the two models is adopted by fund managers.

In-house business model

A pure in-house business model would see all functions within the funds management process managed by in-house staff. These would include:

- all aspects of fund management including strategic direction, overview of operational management, treasury and finance, accounting and so forth;
- all aspects of portfolio management including analysis of property markets, analysis of property assets or property securities for acquisition or disposal, measurement of property and/or portfolio performance and so forth;
- all aspects of asset management including the trading and documentation process involved in the acquisition or disposal of property assets or property securities;
- all aspects of property and facilities management for a direct property portfolio; and
- all aspects of unit-holder or shareholder reporting and communication.

While adoption of a wholly in-house business model by a fund manager is now effectively non-existent, Westfield Group continues to provide most of the functions listed above through its own in-house staff.

Outsourced business model

The use of outsourced service providers by fund managers is now increasingly common, reflecting the relative costs and benefits of the considerations referred to above. Generally, fund managers will seek to maintain those functions in-house that add greatest value and competitive advantage while outsourcing those which simply comprise cost.

Among the direct property fund managers, LaSalle Investment Management adopts a widely used approach where fund management, portfolio management and asset management functions are undertaken by in-house staff while property and facilities management functions are outsourced to a variety of service providers, including its sister company JLL.

Within the property securities funds management industry where, as we have seen, property and facilities management functions do not exist, outsourcing may be less common. While fund management and portfolio management functions may be undertaken by in-house staff, asset management functions such as trading securities may be outsourced to a service provider.

Future directions

Having now completed our review of the current property fund management industry, this final section discusses trends and potential future directions in the industry.

As might be expected, the property funds management industry is constantly changing under the influence of a variety of forces. Pressures towards growth and consolidation among large firms, which occurs across many industries, may be expected to continue in the property fund management industry. At the other end of the size range, there will be ample scope for new boutique investment managers to prosper through offering new specialist services.

In the last five years, among the largest firms, the businesses focussing primarily on real estate have grown faster than generalist fund managers. This trend is likely to wax and wane. Blackrock, with over €3 trillion of AUM across all asset classes, is a relatively new entrant to the global property funds industry, having €17.5 billion of real estate AUM (as at mid-2014) ranking it as 33rd in IPE real estate management survey. However, if it were to move to holding just 3% of its AUM in real estate, it would rise to the top of the league table to challenge current leaders.

A further influence on the future of the industry is how the wider investment world views real estate. While property should be regarded as an asset class distinct from stocks and bonds, some asset allocators have been reluctant to give it that status, variously including it within their 'alternatives' category, which also includes hedge funds and private equity, or as part of a wider 'real asset' grouping alongside infrastructure, commodities, timber and agricultural land. This labelling could affect the structure of the property industry. This is particularly so should the 'real asset' grouping gather traction. This is because there is more similarity in the skills required for managing the other investments in this category along with real estate than with, say, hedge funds.

The long-established drift from pension schemes being defined benefit to defined contribution in nature has already and will continue to affect property funds managers, as it favours greater investment in daily priced liquid assets over those in private markets. As such, it may be expected that the public listed market could grow in relative importance compared with the private market. This will benefit the property securities fund managers as well as offering scope for a greater variety of investment products.

The trend towards more liquid holdings for a defined contribution pension scheme world is also likely to encourage more use of synthetic investment instruments. Managers have been seeking to create more liquid structures for real estate investing for a long time but with limited success. However, we should note that any attempts to improve the liquidity of the real estate market are likely to increase its price volatility as well. It may be expected that the industry will continue innovating in terms of new ways to invest in property but radical change is not expected in the foreseeable future.

While most property securities funds today are managed actively, we can expect the continuing growth of passive funds together with the following trends:

- increased use of 'smart beta' strategies – although free float market capitalisation indices are widely used by fund managers, there is increasing interest in alternative methods of weighting securities, such as smart beta;
- combining active and passive strategies – with increased pressure on fees, a lot of work is currently being undertaken in the area of combining active and passive strategies to generate outperformance at lower cost. Such strategies range from 'active exchange traded funds' to variations on the smart beta strategies outlined above; and
- using listed funds as part of multi-asset strategies – real estate securities are increasingly seen as an attractive asset class, not just in isolation, but also within both a multi-asset (equities and bonds) portfolio as well as a direct real estate portfolio. The best example of the latter is the 70% direct property, 30% global listed real estate securities adopted by the new National Employment Savings Trust in the UK, for its intended allocation to property in its defined contribution scheme.

The property funds management industry is a dynamic and evolving business employing many well-educated and internationally trained experts who are easily capable of adapting to changing trends in continuously growing product demand worldwide. This presages a bright future for both their businesses and the industry.

Acknowledgements

We are grateful to Henri Vuong (Director of Research and Market Information) and Edgar Orlovskis (Research Analyst) from INREV for their help with the data. The usual disclaimer applies.

Notes

1 Constituent funds must comply with a number of criteria relating to leverage (less than 40% loan to value), non-core holding (maximum 20%) and other metrics – see NCREIF Data and Product Guide).
2 The data on which this section is based come from a survey of real estate managers by Investment Pensions Europe and published in IPE Real Estate, November/December 2014.
3 As represented by the Investment Property Databank annual index.
4 The most reliable way to invest passively in direct real estate is through holding a basket of diversified core funds. Ideas for investing passively through property index-based derivatives have typically floundered on the limited liquidity in such markets.
5 The average fund size within the INREV database is €610 million.
6 Funds where there are no assets at the outset are referred to as 'blind pools.'
7 However, this mechanism still complies with the INREV definition of an open ended vehicle (INREV, 2014).
8 IPE Real Estate reported that two US pension funds decided to invest into specific open ended funds despite an expected wait of over 12 months before their capital is invested (April 2015).
9 A non-traded REIT does not trade on a securities exchange and, as such, is relatively illiquid for long periods.
10 A type of open-ended investment fund in which the amount of capital in the fund varies according to the number of investors. Shares in the fund are bought and sold based on the fund's current net asset value.
11 Now the FTSE EPRA/Nareit Global Developed Index.
12 An exchange traded fund is a marketable security that attempts to replicate or 'track' a given index.

References

Bannier, C. E., Fecht, F. and Tyrell, M. (2008) Open-end real estate funds in Germany – genesis and crisis, *Kredit und Kapital*, 41, 9–36.

Callender, M., Devaney, S., Sheahan, A. and Key, T. (2007) Risk reduction and diversification in UK commercial property portfolios, *Journal of Property Research*, 24, 355–75.

Eichholtz, P. (1997) How to invest internationally? Region and property type on a global scale, *Real Estate Finance*, Fall, 51–6.

European Real Estate Association (2015) *EPRA global REIT survey 2014*, EPRA, Brussels.

INREV (2012) *INREV style classification: revised version*, INREV, Amsterdam.

INREV (2014) *INREV guidelines – definitions*, INREV, Amsterdam.

Marriott, O. (1967) *The property boom*, Hamish Hamilton, London.

Mitchell, P. and Bond, S. (2008) *Alpha and persistence in UK property fund management*, IPF Research Report, Investment Property Databank, London.

Parker, D. (2011) *Global real estate investment trusts*, Wiley Blackwell, Chichester.

Schneider, P. (2014) Is there a relationship between REIT prices and pricing in the growing market for secondary trading in unlisted funds? IPE Real Estate, November/December. Available at: https://realassets.ipe.com/investment-/portfolio/comparing-prices/10004241.article (accessed 12 August 2018).

7 Real estate agents and brokerage

Robert Edelstein and Richard K. Green

Introduction

The buying and selling of real estate is complicated. Unlike commodities, real estate transactions involve heterogeneous products, asymmetric information, and search costs. As a result of these complexities, real estate is generally transacted through agents and/or brokers. Because owners typically do not sell their own properties and buyers do not buy their own properties, the real estate market is also filled with principal–agent problems. This chapter briefly reviews the industrial organisation of the real estate brokerage industry and discusses the literature on brokerage and contracting.

Some basics

Some aspects of real estate brokerage are common across a number of countries. Generally, the seller of a house will engage the real estate agent to sell that house. The agent represents the seller. In most countries, it is the seller who compensates the agent on the completion of a sale. Buyers will also engage agents to assist them looking for a house. At the time the house sells, the agents receive a commission. While the seller of the house pays the commission to the listing agent, the listing agent will split the commission with the buyer's agent. This clearly means that the buyer's agent cannot unambiguously represent the best interests of the buyer, because their commission depends in part on the price of the house when it sells. It is in the best interest of the buyer to obtain a house for as little money as possible, while it is in the best interest of the agent for the house to be sold for as much money as possible. This is one of many conflicts within the principal–agent relationship. Needless to say, while the seller of the house pays the direct compensation to the agent, if the agent is doing the job properly (that is, maximising value for the client), some of the incidence of the commission falls on the agent.

While the commission structure for compensating agents is common across the world, commission sizes vary significantly from place to place. Tranio.com produced a comprehensive study of commission rates around the world. These rates range from a low of 50 basis points in the UK to 8% in France and Cyprus. The modal rates seem to range from 3% to 5%.[1]

Leasing agents for office buildings, retail space and industrial space are also compensated through commissions. The payment they receive is generally a percentage of the total net income generated by a lease. For example, if a leasing agent brokers a five-year, 25,000 square foot property at a triple-net lease rate of US$50 per square foot, and the commission rate is 5%, the broker will be paid 5 years multiplied by 25,000 square feet multiplied by US$50/square foot/year multiplied by 0.05, or US$312,500.

Generally speaking, owners of apartment buildings do not use agents to find tenants; they have in-house property managers do that. If they hire a property management company, the company charges a fee that is a percentage of the gross rental, so in that way, the company behaves like a broker. But the individual property managers who work for these companies are often salaried employees.

Why brokerage

When users of real estate shop (in principle, for rental as well as owner-occupied property), they cannot walk into a store and buy real estate off the shelf. They must search for real estate that meets their particular needs with respect to location, physical characteristics, neighbourhood amenities and so on. Buyers have heterogeneous tastes, which is why there is a heterogeneous housing market. When selling a house, sellers are searching for the buyer to whom the house is most valuable. This creates thin markets and a matching problem. Rosen (1974) wrote the classic paper on how heterogeneous products get allocated through price mechanisms in a competitive economy.

Real estate agents are intermediaries who are compensated to solve these at problems. Interestingly, in the US, there are far more agents than necessary to solve these problems. We know this because there are, according to the National Association of Realtors, around one million agents in the US. This means that in a typical year, in which around six million houses transact in the US, there are about six housing transactions per agent. If the average transaction is US$250,000 and the average commission is six per cent, this means the gross commission per deal per agent is US$15,000.[2] The typical commission split between an agent and his broker (the person who runs the agency) is 50–50, meaning that an average agent grosses about US$45,000/year (agents generally pay the expenses associated with selling the house). But, of course, there are very strong producers among brokers, leading to skewness in the distribution of sales per agent. Median gross income must thus be lower than US$45,000, meaning that many agents receive subsistence income, or less, from the business.

Moral hazard and the principal–agent problem

Levitt and Syverson (2008) created a stir when they wrote a paper about the incentives of real estate agents under standard commission-based contracts. They argued that agents had an incentive to sell houses quickly at prices that are less than the maximum price they would command if exposed to the market for the optimal length of time.

Let us defer for a moment the question of how one would compute the optimal length of time for a house to remain on the market. Levitt's argument is simple. Suppose a house has a market value US$250,000 and would command this value if left on the market for 60 days. The agent knows that if this house is offered at US$225,000, it will sell rapidly. Real estate agents generally bear high fixed costs for selling a house. Once they have borne these costs, they want to keep their marginal cost as low as possible. Selling a house quickly reduces the marginal cost of sale. It is thus in the interest of agents to list houses at low prices and then to sell them as quickly as possible, perhaps by encouraging owners to accept the first offer they receive from a potential buyer.

To test the hypothesis that real estate agents sell houses and at a faster pace and a lower price than is optimal for sellers of houses, Levitt and Syverson compared the outcomes of sales when agents sold houses of others and when agents sold real estate that they themselves owned.

They found that agents sold their own homes more slowly than they sold the homes of others. Levitt and Syverson also found that agents were far less likely to take a first offer when selling their own homes compared with selling the houses of others. Agents also tended to sell their own houses for more money (after adjusting for housing quality).

The problem with the study is that it did not take into account unobservables that might explain differences in optimal sales strategy between non-agents, who want to sell their houses, and agents. Given the nature of real estate compensation (it is commission based), we may say that people who choose to be real estate agents have greater tolerance for risk than, say, salaried employees. We cannot observe whether agents advise their clients to take early offers or offer their house at a quality adjusted low price; we can only observe the characteristics of deals that transact. If agents have greater risk tolerance than their clients, they may be willing to risk awaiting second and third offers before agreeing to sell their houses.

One study that attempts to control for this omitted variables problem is by Hendel *et al.* (2009), who compare the characteristics of sales from limited-service brokers with those of full-service brokers. The subject of their study was the Madison, Wisconsin, real estate market, where a company founded by nurses gave sellers, in exchange for a fixed fee, access to the multiple listing services. The paper found that houses handled by brokers sold at the same price as those sold by homeowners, and over a shorter length of time. While this gives evidence that brokers do not leave sellers with a price premium, it also undermines the evidence that they sell for less. At the same time, they are unambiguously providing services: they take the time to find buyers, stage houses, develop a listing strategy and take care of contractual arrangements. Whether their marginal productivity is equal to their compensation is another issue altogether. The literature on wasteful competition suggests that the compensation structure in real estate brokerage is not Pareto efficient.

Wasteful competition in residential brokerage

One stylised fact about residential brokerage in the US is the uniformity of real estate commissions. While the National Association of Realtors argues that there is no price fixing in real estate, local realtor boards, by virtue of their ownership of multiple listing services, create natural monopolies. Before discussing this further, it is worth discussing the nature of multiple listing services.

When real estate agents represent sellers, they contract with the seller to have an 'exclusive' listing. This means that the seller agrees that, no matter who sells their house, the agent with whom they contract for the listing will be compensated when the house is sold. This exclusive listing arrangement allowed for the development of multiple listing services.

A multiple listing service is a cooperative service, where the real estate agents in a region agree to post their listings on a common platform. The benefit to an agent is obvious: it allows them to expose houses to an entire market. The cost is that it allows all agents to observe the availability of a house for sale. In the absence of listing exclusiveness, it could allow any agent to step in with a buyer, hence snatching away compensation from the listing agent.

Participants in multiple listing services generally have a co-brokerage arrangement. The listing agent markets the house through a multiple listing service. A buyer agent may match a buyer to the house and bring about the consummation of a sale. Under such circumstances, the buyer and seller agent usually split the real estate commission. In the absence of exclusive listing contracts, the incentive not to market through a multiple listing service would be very powerful.

The multiple listing services, by virtue of collecting and making available information about a large number of houses for sale in a market at a particular time, has obvious efficiency benefits. A paper by Ben-Shahar (2004) shows that the publication of house price information in Israel led to a substantial reduction in price dispersion in that country's housing market. Until the advent of the internet, however, the information in multiple listing services tended to be closely held by local boards of realtors and their members. Indeed, multiple listing service information was published in books (usually monthly) and these books were not to be shared with the general public. This gave real estate agents and brokers an informational advantage over consumers. Companies born of the internet, such as Zillow, Redfin and Trulia, have changed all that, a phenomenon to which we return later in this chapter. In any event, the existence of the structure of the multiple listing service implies that agents cooperate, as well as compete, with each other and may help to explain the uniformity of commissions within markets.

A little more mysterious is the uniformity of commissions across markets. As Hsieh and Moretti (2003) show, while house prices vary a lot across regions, commission rates do not. For example, while house prices in Los Angeles are roughly 2.5 times higher than house prices in Minneapolis, commissions in Los Angeles are not 40 per cent of the commission rate in Minneapolis. It is, therefore, the case that a Los Angeles agent selling 40 per cent the number of houses as a Minneapolis agent will be paid the same amount. And yet unless it is the case that a home sale in Los Angeles requires 2.5 times the effort of a home sale in Minneapolis (an implausible possibility), the productivity of the Los Angeles agents will be considerably lower than the Minneapolis agent.

Thus, there arose the possibility of wasteful competition. In markets with high house prices, agents enter the labour market until the number of houses sold per agent produces income that equals the reservation wage for being a real estate agent. And so it is that Hsieh and Moretti (2003) found another regularity – the ratio of sales per agent is inversely related to the price of a house. This suggests that competition in the real estate agent market was 'wasteful'; that too many agents chase too few deals. The statistics about total number of agents cited above supports this view. But the introduction of the internet to the real estate market may have changed this. In particular, while multiple listing services remain cooperatives, and while at the regional level there is no competition between them (in fact, multiple listing services have become more consolidated over the years), the internet has changed the ability of agents to withhold information about the market from their clients. Zillow was a pioneer in consolidating information about listings; it became a platform through which agents could showcase their listings. Whereas 20 years ago, potential homebuyers were forced to go to an agent to find out the range of houses available on the market, now all homebuyers (and even those that are simply curious about the housing market), have easy access to information on the vast majority of houses listed for sale.

An indicator of how the market has changed can be derived by viewing location quotients for agents and brokers by states against median sales price. A location quotient computes the share of local employment in a sector divided by the share of national employment in a sector. A location quotient of one implies that a local economy has a disproportionately large amount of employment in a sector; a location quotient of less than one implies a disproportionately small amount.

Figure 7.1 plots median house sales price against location quotients for real estate agents and brokers by state. Note that there seems to be little relationship between the two: the computed correlation is 0.2, which implies that differences in house prices explain about four per cent of the variation in employment share in real estate brokerage. Part of this is driven by an extreme outlier, however (North Carolina). When it is dropped, the correlation

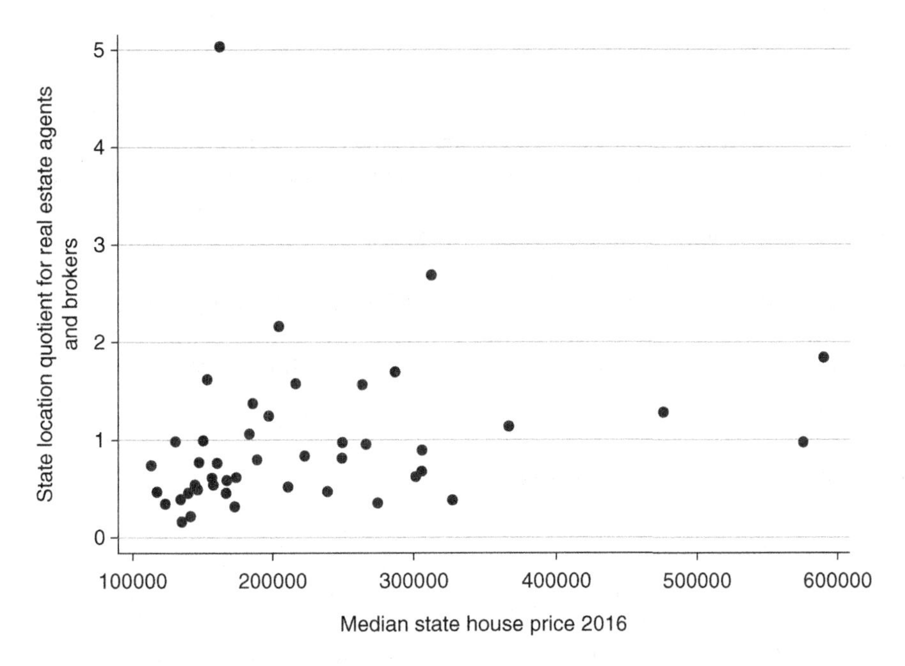

Figure 7.1 Location quotients for real estate agents and brokers and median house prices by state
Source: Bureau of Labor Statistics and American Community Survey, and author calculations.

rises to 0.4. We hold open the possibility that technological change has reduced the wasteful entry problem discussed in Hsieh and Moretti (2003), but the evidence is muted.

Nevertheless, commissions remain frustratingly constant and seem impervious to much downward pressure. In a paper that is largely sympathetic to real estate brokers, Schnare and Kulick (2009) showed that, when house prices go up, commission rates do fall, but by a much smaller amount. Put another way, the amount that real estate agents get compensated per transaction rises and falls with house prices. This would be sensible, if it takes more effort to sell a house in a high priced market than a low priced market but, if anything, the opposite seems to be the case with strong housing markets tending to exhibit both: they not only have price increases and but also shorter times on the market.

Brokerage and strategy

Listing price and bid acceptance are likely the two most important aspects of the real estate marketing process.[3] Consider what the seller's agent is trying to do. She is trying to list a property such that it attracts the 'correct' distribution of buyers to view a property. She does not want buyers who ultimately are not willing or capable of offering the seller's reservation price for a house, and so wants to avoid a listing price that is 'too low'. At the same time, she does not want to chase away potential, *bona fide*, buyers by advertising a listing price that is 'too high'. The purpose of a listing price is to maximise the number of buyers that might consider competing for a house. In hot markets, however, some agents purposefully list a house at a price that is below its fair market value, to start a bidding war. The idea is to create an auction environment: theoretical models of auctions show that they are a mechanism by which sellers of assets receive the greatest proceeds (Krishna, 2009).

This gets at the second aspect of strategy: when to accept an offer. Suppose a house is listed and an offer is made within a week. While it is possible that the person who most values the house visits it immediately, and therefore makes the best offer that the seller would see, it is not likely. Allowing a house to remain on the market for a while allows it to be exposed to a fuller distribution of potential bidders, and therefore to the bidder who values the house most. This suggests that a key element of strategy arises from having a strong understanding of the market value of a particular house. If an initial, fast, bid is well above market value, the best strategy may be to accept that bid. But if the bid is just equal to, or slightly below, market value, the best strategy may be to expose the house longer.

Of course, as already noted, the broker's strategy should depend on client preferences. If a seller is highly risk averse and highly values getting a house sold quickly, he may be willing to accept the discount associated with accepting an early, fast bid. But a good broker makes the seller aware of what he may be giving up as a result.

The role of negotiating in the brokerage process

Negotiations are an essential and omnipresent element in real estate market transactions. Almost every real estate transaction and interaction, such as buying or selling real estate, leasing real estate, financing real estate, managing real estate and engaging service providers for real estate (that is, brokers, lawyers, asset managers, property managers, contractors, subcontractors, architects, maintenance services and so forth) require various forms of negotiations. Successful negotiations typically require a strategy and plan that delineate goals and objectives. For example, in purchasing a specific piece of real estate, the investor is seeking to achieve certain goals such as maximising their rate of return. Negotiations should be seen as a cooperative enterprise between the competing parties, where common interests must be sought to consummate negotiations with a successful transaction.

Negotiations can be seen as a useful tool of human behaviour and, as such, can be improved if not mastered with study and experience. Negotiations for the acquisition of real estate investments involve the exchange of ideas. For example, a very heterogeneous group of individuals with varying educational backgrounds, personalities and levels of experience might be gathered for negotiations at a conference table. Each party is influenced by his or her own subconscious emotional drivers. The success or failure of the real estate negotiation depends on following the strategic plan, knowing all the underlying assumptions, being fully prepared, spotting the effects of human behaviour on the process, and finally recognising that negotiation is the process of need fulfilment.

If one were to buy a 12-pack carton of Cherry Coke Zero in a supermarket, one would not haggle over the price at the checkout counter. As another example, one would not negotiate with one's stockbroker over the price of a share of Tesla common stock purchased on the stock exchange. Real estate transactions are different. The value (price) and many of the other specific terms for the sale of a real estate parcel in an open market transaction with many potential buyers and attendant service providers, such as brokers, mortgage lenders, and property inspectors can *a priori* only be estimated. Why is this so? The uncertainty over price is the result of the unique features and attributes of real estate as an economic good. The buyer is contemplating purchasing the real estate in order to receive a flow of benefits over a relatively long time horizon. The seller is relinquishing ownership, and seeks to maximise his overall gains from the transaction. Both parties are operating in a market in which the quality of information is less than perfect. Real estate markets are highly stratified and, even in a seller's market, the buyers may be relatively few and not easily identified.

The buyer may be concerned with many elements of the transaction, such as the sale price, the down-payment (cash) requirements, required escrows, financing, closing costs, personal liability, the timing of the closing and other terms that affect the nature, substance and the costs of the transaction. Of course, the nature of real estate markets is such that the buyer must also be concerned with the location and marketability of the property. Since it takes time to uncover such information, the seller, if he is in a hurry to sell, must be willing to provide written representations and warranties about zoning, existence of adequate utilities, ownership, absence of condemnation or other adverse proceedings and other critical matters that affect the value. The seller is concerned about the ability of the buyer to perform according to the deal terms. The seller's willingness to negotiate and close the sale would necessarily be a combination of the price he receives for the sale of the property and the amount of time it may take to close the transaction. Put somewhat differently, the seller and his representatives need assurance that once the terms of the contract have been agreed upon, it will be fully executed and binding on the buyer. The seller usually prefers to limit exposure to contracted contingencies subsequent to the closing.

In effect, although negotiations for the purchase and sale of the parcel of real estate are fundamentally an adversarial relationship, both buyer and seller should realise that there are mutual benefits to be derived from minimising conflict and seeking mutual accommodation to achieve a successful acquisition sale.

Many real estate transactions, and especially buying and selling (as opposed to leasing), are in the form of offer–counter offer. The initial listing for sale offer typically has a crucial impact on the ultimate price and the amount of time for the property to be sold (that is, time on market). In essence, since the seller wishes to achieve the highest price possible, everything else being the same, the longer time duration the seller is willing to wait to receive additional offers the more likely they are to achieve a higher price. However, holding the property for a longer period of time before a sale occurs will incur holding costs, such as property taxes and interest payments on existing loans, maintenance, wear and tear repairs and so forth. Put somewhat differently, there is an optimal trade-off between the transaction sale price and the time on market for the property.

Once a listing offer is generated by the seller and made available to potential market buyers, the seller waits for offers to buy to appear. In turn, once a buyer offer is made, the seller can accept the offer or create a counter offer, or reject the offer. The offer–counter offer process may have multiple stages. One might ask how to estimate the range of offers and counter offers. If you are the buyer, it is strongly urged that before entering into negotiations you devise a range of potential offers based upon financial capability, including financing terms, price, and tax planning. One should also estimate the effect of non-price concessions on the viability of an offer. The possibilities to consider in the offer –counter offer may include the following:

1. The seller agrees to defer the date of settlement without changing the price, therefore absorbing some interest costs and other cash outlays.
2. The seller agrees to finance all or part of the debt at terms better than those obtainable in the marketplace.
3. The seller provides warranties that are better than normal expectations.
4. The seller agrees to assume more than a *pro rata* share of transaction costs and fees.

In addition, negotiations may require dealing with more than one interested and/or competitive parties simultaneously. For example, if there are multiple buyer offers, the prospective seller may issue counter – offers simultaneously to some or all of the prospective buyers. In such circumstances, some or all of the potential buyers are competing with one another quite directly. Another example with multiple negotiations proceeding simultaneously could happen when the buyer is in the process of trading offers and counter offers with the seller and, simultaneously, is negotiating with one or more lenders for financing. Finally, negotiations frequently are done through agents serving as intermediaries and surrogates for the buyer and seller. In such situations, the incentives of the agents may not be perfectly aligned with those of either the buyer or seller. As a simple example of this issue in a property sale, the agent typically earns a percentage of the final selling price, so has the incentive to seek a higher rather than lower price to increase their compensation. From the perspective of the buyer, this creates a principal–agent problem.

In the sale of real estate, some of the conditions that the negotiating parties normally expect to be embodied in the real estate contract include:

1. Seller requirements: the seller typically has less need for conditions in the sales contract than the buyer. His or her primary objective is to seek a firm price with a clearly specified time and method of receipt of the net proceeds from the sale. The closing documents can provide the remedies for any default. Usually the seller seeks to avoid any further obligation after the date of the final settlement. It is appropriate for the seller to seek assurances that the buyer has the legal power to close the transaction and that the person acting on behalf of the buyer has been duly authorised to do so. The seller may also insist that the buyer confirms the availability of financing before a certain date.
2. Buyer requirements: objective standards should be set forth to define the purchaser's right to terminate the prospective sale. For a buyer to use non-occurrence of a condition as a reason for not closing the contract, he or she must prove due diligence in attempting to make the condition come about. For example, if the purchaser wishes to retain the right to withdraw from the transaction because of an unsatisfactory inspection report, the buyer must make a 'best effort' to investigate the conditions of the property. Of course, if possible, the buyer should obtain seller's representations and warranties for conditions that must be fulfilled prior to, or at the time of, the closing of the transaction. Some of the typical representations and warranties might be:
   a. The property will not be threatened or adversely affected as a result of acts of God or municipal authorities, disaster, condemnation and so forth on the closing date.
   b. The seller shall provide at the time of closing a final list of personal property, furniture, fixtures and equipment that are not attached and affixed to the realty.
   c. The seller should warrant the adequacy and availability of all utility services as well as that the structure is sound and in good operating condition.
   d. The seller should provide an affirmative covenant to assure the buyer's right to use the property for the intended purpose. This may include occupancy permits that are required by local law.
   e. The seller should acknowledge that he bears the risk of loss because of damage to the property through acts of God, casualty, or acts of government or private parties during the period prior to the closing of the transaction or, more simply, the seller should warrant that all special assessments and existing liens and taxes will have been paid prior to the closing.
   f. The buyer should have protection against any defects in the title to the property.

3. Joint buyer/seller requirements: both parties should provide for a specific fixing of liability for all closing costs, rather than depending on vague customs and traditions that vary from one local area to another. The purchase contract should specify who is to pay brokerage commissions and any other fees, including proration of real estate taxes and so forth. Both parties should be willing to agree to specify the nature of the seller's duty to deliver a good and marketable title. Both parties should agree who is responsible for payment of title insurance.

In summary, real estate transactions are complex because each parcel is unique, and negotiation priorities vary from one transaction to the next. A successful negotiator needs to be able to find and define the issues salient to the transaction, evaluate the opponent's position to determine strengths and weaknesses, engage in mutual accommodation where needed and justify her own position in reasonable terms. The successful negotiator also should be thoroughly prepared so that he or she is in control of the compromise and the concessions that may be necessary to produce the final agreement as well as ultimately generate a closing of the transaction.

Brokerage and expertise

Gilbukh and Goldsmith-Pinkham (2017) show how expertise (or rather lack thereof) in the brokerage market can intensify the real estate cycle. The argument looks like this: when the real estate market is very strong, it attracts agent into it. As already noted, the barriers to entry for real estate agents are very low. This means that, at the top of real estate cycles, the brokerage business has a large number of inexperienced agents. Gilbukh and Goldsmith-Pinkham (2017) show that inexperienced agents get different outcomes for their clients. Specifically, houses sold by inexperienced agents have longer times on market and are less likely to sell at all; this is not compensated by higher sales prices.

This makes for a fascinating case in regulating the industrial organisation of the real estate brokerage business. Gilbukh and Goldsmith-Pinkham (2017) create a model where they test counterfactuals on the impact of raising barriers to entry in the real estate agent market. They find that barriers to entry improve consumer outcomes.

Brokerage and local knowledge

A place where brokers potentially add value to their clients is through local knowledge. Suppose a buyer wants to purchase a property in a city where she does not reside (or for that matter, a city which she has never visited). While one can use data to infer property values with some accuracy, such models are rarely precise. More specifically, the R^2 on hedonic model regressions rarely exceeds 0.8, which means that about 20 per cent of values, at minimum, are explained by characteristics that are unobservable from afar. Moreover, one could argue that those with local knowledge have a greater sense of which characteristics not easily depicted in data (say design) are valuable.

Under these circumstances, buyers of real estate may wish to engage a broker with local knowledge of a real estate market. While there has yet to be specific work of the impact of brokers on when outsider buyers enter a local market, a paper by Eichholtz *et al.* (2015) shows the impact local property managers have on the returns of investors.

One can think of property managers as providing at least one brokerage function – they are responsible for keeping properties occupied. The Eichholtz work shows that, in general, investors of lower quality income property who do not live where the property is located receive worse performance than local investors, but that this difference is reduced by the use of local property management.

Brokerage and new technology

One of the most important issues facing brokerage firms is the impact of two types of technology: aggregator web sites and automated valuation.

Aggregator web sites in one area – travel – have had an enormous impact on the travel agent business. In the year 2000, about 100,000 people were employed as travel agents; that number has dropped to 60,000, as travellers use aggregator sites such as Kayak, Priceline and others to make reservations for airline trips, hotels and car rentals.

The three largest aggregator web sites in residential sales, Zillow, Trulia and Redfin, have changed the relationship between buyers of real estate and agents, but not in the same way that travel sites have changes the demand for travel agents. While travel agency employment has fallen by 40 per cent since 2000, real estate agent and brokerage employment has *increased* by more than 50 per cent since then. Clearly, the method by which people search for houses has changed. Before the advent of the aggregator web sites, buyers of houses had to go through brokers just to find out which houses were available for sale in a particular market. It is now the case that buyers can find out the availability of the large majority of houses available for sale from their own homes. Buyers can, moreover, get information about comparable sales quite easily now, whereas in years past collecting comparables would have entailed a trip to a local registrar of deeds and assessor office to find out sales prices and house characteristics,[4] meaning that buyers (and sellers) are well informed about house prices within neighbourhoods. By simply using the heuristic of price per square foot, they can have a reasonably good idea about what any particular house might be worth.

The aggregators also have algorithms that produce value estimates of large numbers of houses. The algorithms, or automated valuation models, are designed by data scientists, and are not particularly popular with the real estate brokerage community, who see them as a threat to their perceived expertise. Zillow is actually quite forthcoming about the limitations of its models; it provides users not just its Zestimate of value, but also a range, which represents estimated value plus or minus one standard deviation. The tightness of the estimates varies with characteristics of housing markets. In homogeneous markets with large numbers of transactions, automated valuation models work very well and can be quite precise. In heterogeneous markets, with small numbers of transactions, the automated valuation models are not particularly informative.

One would think that the upshot of all this would be that broker commissions in thick, homogenous markets would be shrinking, while commissions in thin, heterogeneous markets would remain strong, as the effort required by a broker (or anyone else) to get price discovery might still be considerable. Yet to this point, there is no evidence that this is true.

So why has the explosion of information in the market not done much to change its basic attributes? Perhaps it is that sellers of real estate value the service they perceive they receive from agents; that they need advice on staging property, making sure a buyer is qualified and insuring against risks that might arise from inappropriately drawn contracts – even though contracts used for selling houses are generally forms that need blanks filled in.

Conclusion

Real estate markets are lumpy, heterogeneous and prone to asymmetric information. For these, and other reasons, they rely heavily on brokers to negotiate and consummate both sales and rental transactions. While Rosen (1974) posited that real estate markets could rely on Walrasian auctioneers efficiently to match buyers and sellers, the continuing existence of brokers, even in the simplest of transactions (say the sale of a typical home in markets with thick transactions) suggests that this is not true.

The fact of brokerage not only suggests that the market has some inefficiencies, but also adds some inefficiencies. The principal–agent problem alone suggests that it is difficult, if not impossible, to write perfect, incentive compatible contracts for the sale and lease of real estate. Many commentators, knowing the inefficient nature of the market for real estate transactions, suggested that technology could begin 'disrupting' brokerage. There is little to suggest that this has happened yet, but we are eager to see whether or not changes take place in the years to come.

Notes

1 See Tranio, Real estate agency commission rates in different countries. Available at: https://tranio.com/traniopedia/tips/real_estate_agents_commissions_in_various_countries (accessed 12 August 2018).
2 Transactions have two 'sides', so one could argue that there are two sides per agent, but the commission is split in two between them.
3 See Genesove and Han (2012) for a good discussion of the problems with attempting separately to identify the impacts of listing price and time on market on ultimate sales price.
4 One of the authors of this chapter, at the beginning of his teaching career, begged his local multiple listing service for copies of their books that contained information on recent sales, so that he could teach his students how to get sales data to estimate hedonic regressions.

References

Ben-Shahar, D. (2004) Productive signaling equilibria and over-maintenance: an application to real estate markets, *Journal of Real Estate Finance and Economics*, 28(2), 255–71.

Eichholtz, P., Holtermans, R. and Yönder, E. (2015) The economic effects of owner distance and local property management in US office markets, *Journal of Economic Geography*, 16(4), 781–803.

Genesove, D. and Han, L. (2012) Search and matching in the housing market, *Journal of Urban Economics*, 72(1), 31–45.

Gilbukh, S. and Goldsmith-Pinkham, P. (2017) Heterogeneous real estate agents and the housing cycle. Job Market Paper. https://docs.google.com/viewer?a=v&pid=sites&srcid=ZGVmYXVsdGRvbWFpbnxnaWxidWtofGd4OjMyMTFkZmQwYjBkZjdiYWY (accessed 29 August 2018).

Hendel, I., Nevo, A. and Ortalo-Magné, F. (2009) The relative performance of real estate marketing platforms: MLS versus FSBOMadison.com, *American Economic Review*, 99(5), 1878–98.

Hsieh, C.-T. and Moretti, E. (2003) Can free entry be inefficient? Fixed commissions and social waste in the real estate industry, *Journal of Political Economy*, 111(5), 1076–122.

Krishna, V. (2009) *Auction theory*, Academic Press, San Diego.

Levitt, S. D. and Syverson, C. (2008) Market distortions when agents are better informed: the value of information in real estate transactions, *Review of Economics and Statistics*, 90(4), 599–611.

Rosen, S. (1974) Hedonic prices and implicit markets: product differentiation in pure competition, *Journal of Political Economy*, 82(1), 34–55.

Schnare, A. and Kulick, R. (2009) Do real estate agents compete on price? Evidence from seven metropolitan areas, in Glaeser, E. L. and Quigley, J. M. (eds.) *Housing markets and the economy: risk, regulation and policy*, Lincoln Institute of Land Policy, Cambridge, MA.

Part III

Real estate appraisal and performance measurement

8 Valuations and their importance for real estate investments

Neil Crosby, Norman Hutchison, Kenneth Lusht and Shi Ming Yu

Introduction

This chapter considers the need for valuations and outlines the growth of the valuation profession over the past 150 years across the world. Background market information is provided on selected markets and valuation standards are discussed and definitions provided. Valuation methodologies are then explained, together with reporting requirements, and the chapter concludes with an overview of market practice. Throughout, the terms 'valuation' and 'appraisal' are used interchangeably. For consistency, valuation will be used unless the term appraisal forms part of the official name of an organisation, standards or qualifications, which is particularly the case in the US and China.

In a single chapter, it is not possible to give an in-depth analysis of the real estate market in each country, but Appendix 8A provides a brief description of the different legal and real estate market systems and covers, property rights, title, units of measurement and typical lease structures.

Why we need valuations

Valuations are required for a number of purposes, including the buying and selling of property, development appraisal, monitoring the level of property performance, loan security, tax matters, company accounts and insurance reinstatement. The lack of a central trading market and the opaqueness of the market mean that investors in real estate are not able immediately to obtain a valuation of their asset. Instead, investors rely on independent valuers to provide this service. The purpose of the valuation and the type of property that is to be valued will determine the basis of the valuation and the techniques that should be employed. The basis of valuation, for example 'market value' or 'market rent', are discussed later in the chapter.

The main requirement of the major investors is for performance measurement and valuations provide the data for measurement to be carried out. Data on capital value, market rent and the components that have driven performance, such as yield shift and rental growth, provide the level of information needed to analyse the performance of real estate investments over different time periods.

The valuation profession

The United States

Although professional valuation associations in the US trace their beginnings to the late 1920s, the modern regulatory environment for real estate appraisers and valuations can be traced to the collapse of commercial property markets and the savings and loan industry (which had made a substantial percentage of construction loans) beginning in the late 1980s. Legislation and subsequent regulation beginning at that time established the Appraisal Foundation and effectively mandated state licensing and certification of appraisers. The Appraisal Foundation has established minimum appraisal standards (through its Appraisal Standards Board), minimum qualifications for appraisers (through its Appraisal Qualifications Board) and, more recently, has begun issuing guidelines for valuation practice (through its Appraisal Practices Board). These standards are the basis for state regulations with respect to education and experience requirements for licensing and certification. Though the details of those requirements vary across the states, they must pass the test of 'adequacy' with respect to standards and qualification. Appraisers typically progress from an appraisal training licence to either a certified residential appraiser (certified to appraise residential properties) and/or a certified general appraiser (certified to appraise all properties). Each licensing or certification level carries with it increasing education and experience requirements. In addition, those licensed or certified must periodically complete state-mandated continuing education.

There are approximately 95,000 real estate appraisers in the US, which is about 10% fewer than in the mid-2000s. The declining number of appraisers can be traced to the collapse of housing markets, which began in 2006, and the demographics of the valuation profession. More than 50% of appraisers are currently in the 51–65 years age group and only about 12% are under the age of 35 years. As a result, various industry observers forecast increasing demand for appraisers in the foreseeable future.

The industry is fragmented, with about 50% of firms being single-owner operators, with an average number of employees per firm of around 1.4. There are a few national and regional firms, but the market share of the top five is less than 15%, with the largest having about 6% of the market.

The largest demand for valuation services comes from mortgage lenders. As part of the increasing regulation of the industry, valuation assignments for lending purposes must now be administered through third-party appraisal management companies. The motivation for the mandate of appraisal management companies is an attempt to separate the valuer from direct contact with the mortgage lender; contact which some believe may compromise the independence of the valuer.

In addition to required state licensing and certification, some valuers choose to differentiate themselves by membership of professional valuation associations. These associations require additional education and experience in order to qualify for professional designations. The Appraisal Institute is the most visible and arguably most prestigious of these associations. The two designations offered through the Appraisal Institute are the SRA (a residential designation), and the MAI (a general designation). Unpublished surveys undertaken by the Appraisal Institute suggest those holding the MAI designation can expect higher earnings, controlling for other variables.

The United Kingdom

In the UK, the major professional institution for property valuers is the Royal Institution of Chartered Surveyors (RICS). The Institution can trace its history back to 1792 but more formally to 1868, albeit with a much wider remit than valuation.[1] The requirement for such an organisation was driven by rapid industrialisation: as infrastructure, housing and transport links grew, so did the need for more stringent checks and balances. The Royal Charter requires members to promote the usefulness of the profession for the public advantage in the

UK and in other parts of the world. Over the years, it has taken over or merged with many of the other professional organisations representing valuers, for example, the Chartered Land Agents' Society and the Chartered Auctioneers' and Estate Agents' Institute in 1970 and, most recently in 2000, the Incorporated Society of Valuers and Auctioneers.

Given the size and coverage of the RICS, it is split into 17 professional groups of which the valuation professional group is one. Professional groups focus on four main areas:

- standards
- professional statements
- market insights
- regulation.

The valuation professional group covers the following areas of practice:

- general valuation
- compensation bases
- assessment for compulsory acquisition
- investment appraisal
- performance measurement and analysis
- decision taking
- rating valuation and property taxation law and practice
- property funding and financing.

It is this group, therefore, that has responsibility for developing and maintaining the RICS Valuation Professional Standards and all the other valuation-related professional guidance (codes of practice, guidance notes and information papers).

The most common route to membership is by an accredited degree followed by two years' work experience culminating in an Assessment of Professional Competence. There are three grades of membership: FRICS (Fellow), MRICS (Member) and AssocRICS (Associate), with a global membership of around 125,000 organised around professional groups covering the full remit of land, property and construction. The valuation profession in the UK is run under a self-regulation model, with the members internally monitored and inspected. Since 2011, as a further layer of quality assurance, all valuers who wish to undertake valuations based on the *RICS Valuation – Professional Standards* (commonly referred to as the Red Book) must not only be a member of the RICS but are also required to be Registered Valuers with the Institution. RICS accredits individuals not firms. The Registered Valuers programme monitors all members undertaking valuations in accordance with the mandatory RICS valuation standards. As at February 2018, there are 16,000 Registered Valuers globally, of which 14,000 are based in the UK and Ireland.

Asia – overview

Given the size and complexities of Asia, only a few key countries are highlighted in this chapter. The countries chosen were selected based on their significance economically, as well as their role in real estate developments and activities in the region: Australia, China, Hong Kong, India, Japan and Singapore.

These six leading countries of Asia demonstrate a diverse set of regulatory environments and the current structure and state of the valuation industry. Nevertheless, two distinct groupings can be identified. First, the countries which are part of the British Commonwealth: Australia, Hong Kong, India and Singapore. These countries have laws and practices which can be traced to their colonial periods and the present regulatory environments and valuation practices are still very similar to those of the UK. RICS has been established in these countries and continues to play a significant role in the valuation profession. The second grouping includes Japan and China, countries with distinctive regulatory environments depending largely on their historical, political and economic developments over the years. Japan, as the third largest economy in the world (based on gross domestic product), is very well established both in terms of the regulatory framework as well as the valuation industry. China, the world's potentially largest economy, has witnessed the greatest pace of development, especially in the real estate sector and the attendant services including valuation. The structure of the profession in each country is considered in turn.

Australia

The Australian Property Institute (API) can trace its history back to the formation of the Commonwealth Institute of Valuers in 1926, and is the national professional body for property professionals, with about 8600 members,[2] some of whom have certified practising valuer (CPV) status. The criteria for membership include possessing an approved undergraduate degree, a minimum of two years' relevant professional experience, demonstrating a satisfactory record of continuing professional development, approval by an interview panel and continuing compliance with the API's code of ethics and rules of conduct.

Until recently, three states in Australia (New South Wales, Queensland and Western Australia) required valuations undertaken in their jurisdictions to be carried out by a registered valuer. In other states and territories, the general requirement for commercial property and security valuations was the API CPV qualification.

However, in 2017, the API formed a strategic alliance with RICS. This alliance has three strands. First, the two organisations have aligned their registration schemes. API members will adopt the RICS global assurance regime of valuer registration. Second, the alliance will lead to a common valuation standard with API adopting the Global Red Book with both parties developing aligned national standards for Australasia. Finally, the API aims to align its pathways to that of RICS. Once completed, both API members and RICS professionals will be mutually recognised by both organisations in Australia and there will be one process and membership (either API or RICS) rather than the two different processes.

China

The main professional valuation body in China is the China Appraisal Society (CAS) which was established in 1993 under the purview of the Ministry of Finance. As of 2005, it had approximately 29,000 members. One of the aims of the CAS is to assist members in improving their professional skills and to advance the credibility of the profession. Other professional bodies include the China Institute of Real Estate Appraisers and Agents and the China Real Estate Valuation Association.

To be a qualified real estate appraiser in China, a candidate must first pass the real estate appraiser licensing examination, which is conducted annually, to obtain a Real Estate Appraiser Qualification Certificate, whereupon a Real Estate Practicing Appraiser Qualification Certificate (REPAC) will be issued by the government. A qualified appraiser holding a REPAC must apply to the government to be registered within three months of issuance of the REPAC. Registration is valid for a term of three years.

For land valuations, a similar annual licensing examination is conducted. A candidate who passes the examination will be issued a Land Appraiser Qualification Certificate (LAQC). The holder of a LAQC must then pass a work experience assessment conducted by the Land Appraiser Association of China to become a practising appraiser.

Hong Kong

Members of the Hong Kong Institute of Surveyors (HKIS) and RICS are qualified to value real estate in Hong Kong. HKIS is Hong Kong's professional surveying institute. It is the only professional organisation representing surveying practitioners in Hong Kong. HKIS members numbered 10,147[3] in August 2018.

India

The main professional valuation body in India is the Practising Valuers Association of India. It was incorporated in 1999 and is a self-funded and independent organisation. However, there is no centralised oversight of the valuation profession in India. Members of the Institution of Valuers, the first national professional valuation society in India, established in 1968, may practise valuation as an approved valuer. Their backgrounds are mainly in architecture and civil engineering. The Institution of Surveyors also conducts valuation surveying examinations which are recognised by the government of India.[4] Other recognised bodies include the Institution for Government Approved Valuers, the RICS, India Chapter, and the Valuation Institute, USA.

Japan

Valuation practitioners in Japan are regulated and licensed by the Japanese Association of Real Estate Valuation, established in 1965, which falls under the purview of the Ministry of Land, Infrastructure and Transportation. To be a certified valuer, a person must pass the national examination to be a Licensed Real Property Appraiser and must undergo technical training.

Singapore

Singapore has a relatively small valuation profession that is regulated by the Inland Revenue Authority of Singapore. Licensed valuers are required to possess a relevant undergraduate degree such as a bachelor's degree in real estate from the National University of Singapore or a similar degree from an accredited overseas institution, or equivalent professional qualifications certified by the RICS and relevant practical professional valuation experience.

The Singapore Institute of Surveyors and Valuers (SISV), established in 1982, is the only professional body that represents land surveyors, quantity surveyors and valuers nationwide. The aims of the SISV are to advance and facilitate the acquisition of professional knowledge in the areas of land surveying, quantity surveying and valuation and general-practice surveying, to promote the general interests of the profession, to maintain and improve its usefulness for the benefit of the public, and to regulate and improve the standards and conduct of the profession.[5] With businesses in Singapore securing more overseas development opportunities, demand for international valuation consultancy services by Singapore-based clients has been rising. As a result, international valuation standards, such as those promulgated by RICS, have gained traction with Singapore consultancy firms. For example, in 2014, Colliers International, one of the leading property consultancies, announced that it would embark on a scheme to register all its valuers for RICS valuer registration across the region with the aim of raising standards and pursuing service excellence.

Valuation standards

A brief history

Over the last 40 years since the 1970s, there has been significant progress in first producing and then developing consistent real estate valuation standards across the world. At the beginning of the 1970s, there was no formal framework for the production of guidance and standards, although there were already well-established organisations of professional valuers set up to provide, among other things, education and guidance to their fellow valuers.

It was, arguably, the major property crash in the UK in the early 1970s that precipitated the drive to formal valuation standards. Before that period, guidance had been in the form of the production of rules for statutory valuations, and practitioner and academic textbook suggestions regarding methods of valuation, such as, in the UK, *Modern Methods of Valuation*, which had its first edition published in 1943 (Lawrence and May, 1943), and, in the US, *Valuation of Real Estate*, first published in 1951 by the Appraisal Institute (Appraisal Institute, 2014). An earlier UK text, *Curtis on the Valuation of Land and Houses*, had seven editions ranging from before 1900 to 1933 (for example, Davies, 1908). In response to criticism from users of valuations and observers of property markets following the 1970s property market crash, the RICS published the first set of national UK standards in 1976, followed by new editions in 1981 and 1990. At the time of writing, the latest edition is 2017 and this edition incorporates the international valuation standards of 2017. The official title is currently *RICS Valuation – Global Standards* but it is universally known as the RICS Red Book (RICS, 2017). The RICS now publishes the Global Red Book separately from the national UK supplement; at the time of writing the national UK Red Book was last revised in 2015 but a revised version is due in 2018.

The US Uniform Standards of Professional Appraisal Practice (USPAP) were also developed in the wake of a savings and loan crisis. These standards can be traced to the work of an ad hoc group established in 1987 by nine Canadian and US appraisal organisations. In 1989, USPAP was formally established by the Appraisal Foundation, a non-profit regulatory organisation (Appraisal Foundation, 2018). The Appraisal Foundation has the responsibility of establishing, improving and promoting minimum uniform appraisal standards, appraiser qualifications and guidelines with respect to appraisal practice. The USPAP are revised every two years.

The origins of the International Valuation Standards (IVS) lie in the International Assets Valuation Standards Committee, which was formed in 1981 in Melbourne, Australia, following initial discussion between, mainly, US and UK valuer organisations. Its objective was the development of consistent standards across national borders. The organisation is now known as the International Valuation Standards Council (IVSC). Commencing with cooperation among 20 organisations, it has nearly 100 organisations in membership from 57 countries.[6] IVSC first produced standards in 1985 and, at the time of writing, the latest edition is 2017 (International Valuation Standards Council, 2017a).

Alongside the development of national and international standards, there also have been some attempts to set up intermediary standards at a regional level, the most obvious case being within the European Union. At the time of writing, the current edition is the eighth set of European Valuation Standards (EVS), produced by the European Group of Valuers' Associations (TEGoVA) and published in 2016. The first edition was published in the early 1980s. In the past, there has been some tension between the objectives of the International and European standard setting bodies but this has now receded as TEGoVA has adopted most of the principles of IVS and concentrates on EU issues, as well as promoting the development of national standards within EU countries.

The content of valuation standards

The IVS 2017 contains the IVS Framework, the IVS General Standards and the IVS Asset Standards. The current edition was approved by the IVSC Standards Board for implementation on 1 July 2017. Current policy is to review the standards every two years. IVSC also produces free-standing Technical Information Papers available as separate booklets.

The IVS Framework identifies generally accepted principles and concepts including issues surrounding competency, objectivity, judgement and departures and does not include any procedural requirements. IVS General Standards sets out the requirements for the conduct of all valuation assignments such as engagement, bases, methods and reporting and is designed to be applicable to all types of assets and for any valuation purpose. The IVS Asset Standards has both requirements and commentaries, including illustrations of how the principles in the General Standards are generally applied to different types of asset such as real property, intangible property and business property.

Given that IVS are sponsored by a significant number of countries, it is not surprising that, in the most part, national (and regional) valuation standards such as the RICS Red Book or USPAP tend to repeat the principles set out in the IVS, but retain a national standard to cope with national variations. For example, the RICS Red Book (Royal Institution of Chartered Surveyors, 2017) uses the IVS Standards in its global practice statements, but then includes four mandatory UK practice statements with 14 supporting appendices and an additional seven UK guidance notes for the national market. It also encourages its international members to develop local statements and guidance notes for individual countries based around the global section of the Red Book.

Arguably, the most controversial issue is how far standards should go in identifying valuation methods for different purposes or situations. Over the years, while valuation standards have been developing, opinion within the valuation standards setting bodies, internationally, regionally and nationally, has tended to sway between being more or less prescriptive on method. Some of this relates to whether the regulation of the valuation industry in a particular country is by government or self-regulation by the industry. This has resulted in a variety of additional information papers and guidance notes that illustrate and illuminate the application of the standards and, in some cases, methods.

Valuation standards predominantly try and regulate and control the process by which valuations are produced, especially those that can impact on third-party decisions, such as information within financial statements concerning a company or fund or the behaviour of lenders and borrowers. To that end, valuation standards address issues of objectivity, including ethical standards and conflicts of interest and competence (that is, the correct knowledge and skills for any particular task). As far as the actual process is concerned, the IVS address the selection of the valuer, the format of instructions, concepts and definitions of value (often related to purpose of the valuation) and reporting of valuations (including the content of reports but also the process around reporting of draft valuations as well as final reports). These issues, as well as methods, are addressed in the following sections of this chapter.

Other codes of practice and guidance which impact on property valuations can be found – for example, in the UK, the RICS has produced a range of papers outside the remit of its valuation standards board. Over 30 are listed in the Red Book, around half of which have valuation in the title. In addition, the RICS has published guidance note on financial viability within UK planning (Royal Institution of Chartered Surveyors, 2012) and one on discounted cash flow for commercial property investments (Royal Institution of Chartered Surveyors, 2018).

As an example of standard setting in another jurisdiction, the HKIS stipulates mandatory valuation standards for real estate valuations in Hong Kong. The standards cover the criteria for qualification as a professional valuer, the matters which a professional valuer should consider in their terms of engagement, the basis of a professional valuation, assumptions and key considerations that should be addressed, minimum standard forms for a valuation report and required disclosures. IVSC standards are also adopted by the HKIS as supplementary to its own standards.

Another recent global initiative which affects valuation is the attempt to produce consistent global measuring practices through an internationally agreed code of measuring practice (International Property Measurement Standards).[7] This will ensure that units of value per unit of space are more comparable across countries. However, inconsistencies remain; for example, different terms of rent contracts mean that property incomes expressed as yields are not comparable across countries with major differences between the percentages of gross income retained by owners in different countries.[8]

Specific valuation issues, such as bases of valuation and conflicts of interest and their implications, are discussed in more detail at different points in this book, both in this and other chapters.

Definitions

The International Valuation Standards (International Valuation Standards Council, 2017a) identify the following bases of valuation.

- *Market value* is the estimated amount for which an asset or liability should exchange on the *valuation date* between a willing buyer and a willing seller in an arm's length transaction, after proper marketing and where the parties had each acted knowledgeably, prudently and without compulsion (Section 30).
- *Market rent* is the estimated amount for which an interest in real property should be leased on the valuation date between a willing lessor and a willing lessee on appropriate lease terms in an arm's length transaction, after proper marketing and where the parties had each acted knowledgeably, prudently and without compulsion.
- *Equitable value* is the estimated price for the transfer of an asset or liability between identified knowledgeable and willing parties that reflects the respective interests of those parties (50.2). Equitable value requires the assessment of the price that is fair between two specific, identified parties considering the respective advantages or disadvantages that each will gain from the transaction. In contrast, market value requires any advantages or disadvantages that would not be available to, or incurred by, market participants generally to be disregarded.

- *Investment value/worth* is the value of an asset to the owner or a prospective owner for individual investment or operational objectives (Section 60).
- *Synergistic value* is the result of a combination of two or more assets or interests where the combined value is more than the sum of the separate values. If the synergies are only available to one specific buyer then synergistic value will differ from market value, as the synergistic value will reflect particular attributes of an asset that are only of value to a specific purchaser. The added value above the aggregate of the respective interests is often referred to as 'marriage value'.
- *Liquidation value* is the amount that would be realised when an asset or group of assets are sold on a piecemeal basis. Liquidation value should take into account the costs of getting the assets into saleable condition as well as those of the disposal activity. Liquidation value can be determined under two different premises of value: (a) an orderly transaction with a typical marketing period, or (b) a forced transaction with a shortened marketing period.

The IVSC (International Valuation Standards Council, 2017a) also identifies a number of other bases of value which it does not define, the majority of these are tied to specific regulatory or legal issues and a number are country specific. The most important of these is fair value used within International Financial Reporting Standards (IFRS). IFRS 13 defines fair value as the price that would be received to sell an asset or paid to transfer a liability in an orderly transaction between market participants at the measurement date. For financial reporting purposes, over 130 countries require or permit the use of the International Accounting Standards. The Financial Accounting Standards Board in the United States uses the same definition of fair value (International Valuation Standards Council, 2017b).

Exchange value concepts

The market value basis dominates property valuation. It is an exchange price concept and is supposed to identify the price at which a property interest actually exchanges in a free market with all participants acting knowledgeably and without any compulsion. IVSC (International Valuation Standards Council, 2017b) distinguishes market value from fair value. As discussed above, IFRS define fair value as the 'price that would be received to sell an asset or paid to transfer a liability in an orderly transaction between market participants at the measurement date'. The RICS global standards suggest that:

> references within [Accounting Standards (IFRS 13)] to market participants and a sale make it clear that for most practical purposes the concept of fair value is consistent with that of market value, and so there would ordinarily be no difference between them in terms of the valuation figure reported.
>
> (Royal Institution of Chartered Surveyors, 2017, VPS4, para 7.3)

There are issues with market value, as it tries to define a single-point estimate of price of an asset that takes time to transact and has no centralised market place of identical assets. There is, therefore, variation around any estimate and this variation has been the subject of much research and comment (see, for example, MSCI, 2017). These issues are discussed in Chapter 9 on property valuation-based indices. The timing of the date of valuation is at the end of a normal marketing period. The valuer thus has to assume that the property has been placed on the market some time previously, to allow a proper marketing period before the date of valuation, but that the prevailing market conditions have been as they are at the date of valuation. Market value is, therefore, not the same price as would be expected if the property was put on the market at the valuation date and marketed properly from that date. The price would then be agreed at some point in the future in a market that might have changed.

A liquidation value is a new basis of value in IVS (International Valuation Standards Council, 2017b). It is linked to what has formally been called a forced sale value, which IVS does not recognise as a separate basis. The distinctions are set out in IVS (International Valuation Standards Council, 2017a, p25). A 'forced' sale has often been characterised as a market value under a restricted marketing period. The use of special assumptions can be adopted to enable clients to specify valuations which answer particular needs. A restricted marketing period could be a special assumption as would be an assumption that a particular permission was in place when it is not, or a lease in place when it is not (or vice versa), or even that the property is not quite the same physically as it actually is (age at the end of a loan period rather than at the beginning for example). IVS comments that all assumptions and special assumptions must be reasonable under the circumstances, be supported by evidence and be relevant having regard to the purpose for which the valuation is required (International Valuation Standards Council, 2017b, p28)

Market value assumes highest and best use (assuming both permissible and viable development/change of use) and a market consisting of 'numerous' buyers and sellers. Market value does not acknowledge any special advantages to an individual. Equitable value and synergistic value do acknowledge these issues. Equitable value accepts that one individual may get or have a special advantage over and above all others from ownership of a particular asset and synergistic value the advantage that may come from combining or restructuring interests.

Finally, rental values are just as important to property investors as capital values and IVS defines rental value as 'market rent'. Market rent is defined as 'the estimated amount for which an interest in real property should be leased on the valuation date between a willing lessor and a willing lessee on appropriate lease terms in an arm's length transaction, after proper marketing and where the parties had each acted knowledgeably, prudently and without compulsion'. It is virtually the same definition as market value, but has the added complication of rental value being affected by the terms of the lease contract. The definition identifies only 'appropriate lease terms', so each rental value assessment requires the valuer to report the assumed lease terms. Incentives to secure lettings such as rent free periods, stepped rents, landlord capital contributions to tenant fit out expenditure and other non-specific contributions all lead to some major adjustments to headline rents paid from the effective rental value that would have been paid for the premises from day one of the lease with no incentive package. In addition to any difficulties this creates in analysing comparable lettings, it distorts valuation-based rental value indices used to measure occupational markets, as the detail of all the terms of the deal may not be known or analysed consistently by all the market participants to get the effective rent. This issue is discussed further in Chapter 9 on appraisal-based indices.

Investment value

The other main basis of value identified in the IVS is investment value. It is a value in use concept tied to a particular purchaser or owner and is not an identification of the expected exchange price of the asset at the date of valuation. It had its genesis in the 1990s, in a period where there was evidence of systematic mis-pricing of property assets in the UK market after the second major property crash in that country, not additional value created by the individual circumstances of particular investors. Assessments of market value were primarily undertaken using comparable capitalisation rate techniques but major investors had invested heavily in research, enabling them to model property markets into the future using cash flow techniques. This modelling often identifies individual assets or locations or segments that are deemed to be mis-priced by the market. Early definitions of investment value introduced into the Red Book were called 'calculations of worth' by the RICS to distinguish them from a valuation. The definition contained reference to both individuals and groups of investors, acknowledging that an asset can have a different value than market value or price to a wider investing community, rather than just to an individual (Hutchison and Nanthakumaran, 2000). The current IVS definition is, therefore, a major step backwards as the reference to groups of investors has been removed (International Valuation Standards Council, 2017a).

Mortgage lending value

There is one other concept and definition of value that is not included in IVS but cannot be ignored, especially in the aftermath of the global financial crisis. Sustainable value, in the sense that it can be sustained through time, is the conceptual basis for mortgage lending value used by some mainland European banks as a risk management tool for their commercial loan books. It is part of the Basel Accords, together with market value, and is used in the determination of bank capital ratios. It is used in 'covered bond'[9] markets and within the German Pfandbrief bank loans for over one hundred years. The definition set out in the European Valuation Standards is:

> The value of the property as determined by a prudent assessment of the future marketability of the property taking into account long-term sustainable aspects of the property, the normal and local market conditions, the current use and alternative appropriate uses of the property. Speculative elements shall not be taken into account in the assessment of the Mortgage Lending Value.
>
> (European Group of Valuers' Associations, 2016, EVGN9, p162)

The EVS (European Group of Valuers' Associations, 2016, EVGN2) suggest that the 'intended purpose of mortgage lending value is to provide a long-term, sustainable value as a stable basis for judging the suitability of a property as a security for a mortgage which will continue through potential market fluctuations'.

The EVS (European Group of Valuers' Associations, 2016) provide further guidance which includes that the underlying time perspective goes beyond the short-term market and covers a long-term period. Longer-term sustainable aspects include the quality of the location, construction and layout, that the income stream of the property should be no more than the 'sustainable' net rental income of that type of property. EVS suggests that this means 'assessing the sustainable yield on the basis of a judgment of past and current market situation as well as future market trends and not taking any uncertain elements into account, e.g. possible future income growth' (European Group of Valuers' Associations, 2016, EVGN2).

Some jurisdictions stipulate that a mortgage lending valuation must be less than a market valuation. This suggests that it is not a long-term sustainable *trend* value that could, depending on cyclical movements in prices, be above market value in a recessionary market and below in a boom market. It suggests that it should be assessed to be no higher than any possible market value in a future or current trough in these jurisdictions (within the Pfandbrief Act regulations for example).

Not surprisingly, this approach has come under criticism, not for the objective of trying to introduce counter-cyclical constraints on bank lending through the valuation process, but for the lack of a conceptual and objective base to the valuations themselves (Crosby, French and Oughton, 2000; Crosby and Hughes, 2011). First, valuation has to have a valuation date and cannot provide a longer term value, but it could identify a future market value. However, forecasting is specifically excluded from the valuation. Second, the approach set out in texts and guidance (for example, Ruchardt, 2003) relies on rules rather than objective inputs. However, application does give one desired effect – a stable valuation that does not follow the cyclical movements of the market cycle. Nonetheless, the application of Investment Value using cash flow based on market data modelling gives exactly the same result in a more defensible manner, identifying under- as well as over-priced markets which MLV fails to do, and is a recognised basis of value with an established body of technique and analysis (Crosby and Hughes, 2011), especially in larger more mature markets with better data sources. The search for a better basis of valuation than using market value alone for lending is currently a major objective of stakeholders within property valuation and real estate finance.

Valuer selection and instruction

The genesis of valuation standards was industry concerns about the objectivity and accuracy of valuations in the wake of property market crashes. This was particularly apparent in valuations in the bank lending sector but also in the performance measurement and financial accounting roles. There are different issues for valuations which are performed regularly (performance measurement) against those that are one-off by nature (bank lending) but some of the major threats to objectivity come from a poor valuer selection process. In particular, client and other stakeholder influence on the outcome can be accomplished by having the 'right' valuer in place at the outset. Valuation standards have increasingly included statements on conflicts of interest, valuer selection and instructions. The IVSC has a separate paper on ethics (International Valuation Standards Council, 2011).

Valuation professional organisations that are members of the IVSC are required to have rules on ethical conduct by their members. A valuation professional organisation may adopt the IVSC code or maintain its own rules, providing such rules reflect the five fundamental principles of the IVSC code. These principles are:

- Integrity: to be straightforward and honest in professional and business relationships.
- Objectivity: not to allow conflict of interest, or undue influence or bias to override professional or business judgement.
- Competence: to maintain the professional knowledge and skill required to ensure that a client or employer receives a service that is based on current developments in practice, legislation and valuation techniques.
- Confidentiality: to respect the confidentiality of information acquired as a result of professional and business relationships and not to disclose such information to third parties without proper and specific authority (unless there is a legal or professional right or duty to disclose), nor to use information for the personal advantage of the professional valuer or third parties.

- Professional behaviour: to act diligently and to produce work in a timely manner in accordance with applicable legal requirements, technical and professional standards. To always act in the public interest and to avoid any action that discredits the profession.

IVSC (2011) sets out some of the potential threats to valuer objectivity and a number of them relate to client and other stakeholder influence and moral hazards for the valuer. There is a now a wealth of behavioural economics research aimed at client influence on valuations, including valuer selection processes, mainly from the US and UK but also from Asia Pacific and Africa. For the latest literature review, see Crosby, Lizieri and McAllister (2010) and, for an earlier review of this field, Diaz (2002) for the RICS Foundation.

Valuation methodologies: the users' perspective

Valuations add value to the investment decision-making process by providing a third-party, unbiased, and (hopefully) informed estimate of what the property would be likely to sell for in the open market. The topic in this section is how those value estimates are developed. The underlying concepts and application details of the main valuation methodologies are discussed, including the implications for investment decision making of their relative strengths and limitations. We begin with an overall perspective on what valuation estimates are intended to be, and what they are not.

Market value estimates: some caveats

A market value estimate is the valuer's opinion of the most probable selling price of the property. It is *not* the valuer's opinion of what the property may actually be worth. In other words, a valuation is an opinion of what *will* happen, not what *should* happen. This is a critical distinction, particularly during periods of market disequilibrium, when 'true' value and price may be significantly different. As a user of valuation estimates, it means that your valuation fee is not buying an opinion about whether a property is under- or overpriced. It is buying only an opinion about what the price will be, not the wisdom of that price. A judgement about the relationship between prices and values can of course be obtained, but that must come from an individual in a non-valuation (consultant) role. The fact that some individuals' practices include both valuation and consulting makes it important to understand the difference.

Market and investment values often differ. Suppose we ask, say, ten investors what they would be willing to pay for a particular property. It is likely that we would get ten different answers. Each would reflect the property's *investment value* to a specific investor. Those investment values could differ for many reasons; for example, differences in risk tolerance, portfolio composition, tax status, or simply because of different expectations with respect to future cash flows. It is not clear where, in any distribution of investment values for an individual asset, the market value lies. It might be the mid-point but is more likely to be near to the top of the distribution given that market value is likely to be closer to the best price rather than the average price. If an investment value exceeds an asking price that reflects the appraised value, it may represent a positive net present value opportunity. Conversely, if the investment value falls below an asking price some negotiation would be necessary to make it an acceptable investment.

Valuation estimates are opinions, not facts. The methodologies that valuers use are models of the price determining process. Like all models, they are intended to simplify something exceedingly complex (price determination in real estate markets) into something more manageable. Paraphrasing statistician George Box, this means while all models are to some extent incorrect or incomplete, some (like valuation methodologies) are useful. These useful, though imperfect, models make estimates of prices that have yet to occur in markets that are themselves imperfect. With this understanding, you arrive at the important conclusion that valuation *opinions* are just that – unbiased and informed, but without the benefit of crystal balls.

Valuation methodologies: overview

The valuation opinions are developed using one or more of three basic methodologies, or approaches. They are 1) sales comparison, 2) cost, and 3) income. It is unusual for a valuation to include all three approaches. The kind of property, the available data and, perhaps, regulatory or client requirements determine which approach(es) will be used in a particular situation. When two or more approaches are included, each will produce an estimate of value. Because valuers are modelling imperfect markets using imperfect models and often with imperfect data, only by extreme coincidence will the value estimates from different methodologies produce the same value estimate. Thus, the valuer's final 'number' will reflect their opinion as to which of the value estimates is most credible in that circumstance. Often, this will be a weighted average (including the possibility of a zero weight for some estimates) of the individual value estimates produced by the approaches used.

The sales comparison approach

Suppose someone were asked to provide a valuation of the current market value of a share of stock in a certain company. That would be an easy assignment, as a call to a broker or a glance at a tickertape would provide the answer, which would be the price at which the last share sold. Though we may not think of it this way, estimating the share's value in this way is rooted in two fundamental assumptions. The first is that past selling prices are a reliable estimator of current price, and second, that the next share will sell for the same (or a very similar price) to the previous share. And we would be quite confident in the value estimate because the next share of that stock that sells will be identical to the previous share (on which you based your value estimate) and because in most cases the last sale occurred very recently.

The sales comparison approach to estimating a value in real property markets is based on the same kinds of assumptions, that is, market prices are a reliable (though imperfect) indicator of value, and that identical properties should sell for identical prices, especially when the transactions occur within a short period of time. Therefore, the starting point in the sales comparison approach is the same as it is when 'valuing' a share of stock, that is, the selling prices of comparable properties. After this starting point, however, the application of the approach begins to differ for two reasons. First, unlike our homogenous shares of stock, no two properties are identical and, second, unlike shares of stock, they tend to sell infrequently. So we need to modify our underlying assumption to something like: 'comparable (similar) properties will sell for comparable (similar) prices'. For property valuation, then, the sales comparison approach is about getting from the observed prices of comparable (similar) properties to an estimated value of the subject property.

For single family houses, this is done by adjusting the prices of the comparable properties for differences between them and the subject. These adjustments will reflect the familiar list of those things that impact values; things like location, size, age, various amenities and, perhaps, externalities.

The valuation of investment properties also begins with the selling prices of comparables but, because commercial properties tend to be more heterogeneous than houses, finding comparable properties sufficiently similar to the subject property is often difficult. This is especially so for differences in size. As a result, while the basic 'unit of comparison' for houses is the whole property, for commercial properties it is common practice to work with a smaller, more homogenous unit, such as the price per square foot or square metre. Adjustment for quantum may need to be made to the price per square foot/metre, if units are particularly large or particularly small and thus direct comparison is not possible. The unit of comparison used for a particular valuation will reflect how that property type is typically sold or leased in the market place. For an office building, the price of the comparable may be divided into the price per square foot/metre. For an apartment, common units of comparison are price per square foot/metre or per individual apartment. For a theatre, perhaps price per seat. In any event, this kind of approach allows value to be estimated on a more comparable basis. For example, if three sales of comparable retail properties indicate a price of £50 per square foot, that number would be multiplied by the number of square feet in the subject property to arrive at one indication of value. Because valuers are always looking for as many indications of value as possible, it is common for value to be estimated in this way for more than one unit of comparison. For example, an office building might be valued using both price per gross square foot and price per rentable square foot.

Not surprisingly, some units of comparison for investment properties are income based. In a sense, these units are bottom line relationships between expected income and value. Suppose an industrial property sold for £10,000,000, and it had expected annual gross income of £500,000. That relationship can be expressed by saying the property sold at a multiple of 20 times gross income (a years' purchase of 20 in valuers' language), or that the initial yield or cap rate would be 5%. If two other comparable sales produced gross income multiples of, say 18 and 22, the valuer would probably multiply the subject property's gross income by about 20 to arrive at the indication of value using that unit of comparison. All of this may sound familiar – it is exactly analogous to the frequent reporting of price to earnings ratios for securities; for example, that company 'A' is selling at a price/earnings multiple of, say, 15.

Because for most valuations more than one unit of comparison is used, the valuer's final task within the sales comparison approach is to use his or her professional judgement to determine which of those units have produced the most credible estimate.

Strengths and limitations of the sales comparison approach

The main strength of the sales comparison approach is that it is firmly anchored in observed market prices, which are direct and relatively objective evidences of value. For that reason, valuers tend to rely heavily on the estimates produced by sales comparison.

A limitation of the sales comparison approach is that its application is often compromised by a lack of sufficient comparable sales. This becomes increasingly likely as properties become larger and more heterogeneous; for example, when valuing regional shopping centres or unique office properties. In those situations, valuers commonly rely on the income approach (discussed below) as the primary evidence of value.

Another potential weakness of the sales comparison approach is that because it relies on past prices as the starting point, it is somewhat 'rear-view mirror' oriented. While an adjustment can be made to reflect changing market conditions between the date of sale of the comparable and the date of the valuation, studies have consistently observed this adjustment tends to be inadequate. The result is 'valuation lag', meaning that values tend to fall below subsequent selling prices when markets are moving sharply upward, and vice versa.

For institutional investors, another potential problem is appraisal smoothing (Edelstein and Quan, 2006; Geltner *et al.*, 2003), which is discussed in more detail in Chapter 9. Smoothing sometimes occurs when properties in a portfolio are valued frequently for fiduciary and regulatory reasons, and the valuer is the same from valuation to valuation. The result may be value 'anchoring', where the estimate from one period tends to influence the estimate in the subsequent period. The result is a smoothing of value estimates, carrying with it the problem that those estimates are not picking up larger price changes occurring in the market.

The cost approach

The use of the cost approach to estimate the most probable selling price is rooted in the idea that the market value of a property should be the same as what it would cost to produce an identical property. Following that logic, the cost approach looks like this:

> Market value = Replacement (or reproduction) cost of the subject property's improvements as if new, minus accrued depreciation on the improvements, plus land value.

The cost model tells us that the valuer first estimates the value of the improvements as if they were to be built as of the date of the valuation. Unless the property is newly built, however, this 'cost new' will overstate the value of the improvements, as they will have lost some of their value over time. Thus, to get to the value of the improvements, depreciation must be subtracted from the cost as if new. Finally, the value of the underlying land is added to arrive at the estimate of property value.

It is helpful to think of the cost approach as a special case of sales comparison. Imagine two properties sitting side by side. They are identical as far as size, floor plan, building materials and other improvements to the site. However, one of the buildings is ten years old, while the other is brand new. Suppose the ten-year-old property is the subject property, and the identical (except new) property next door has recently sold. Using the identical property as a comparable in the sales comparison approach would require only a single adjustment – for the impact of ten years of age (depreciation) – to arrive at an estimate of the value of the subject. This is exactly what happens when using the cost approach, where the cost to 'duplicate' a 'new' subject is first estimated, and then any value effects associated with the difference in age between the new subject and the actual subject are subtracted. Conceptually then, the cost approach is similar to the sales comparison approach, with all the variables held constant except for the effects of depreciation. That is, the subject is compared with a 'new' duplicate of itself.

There is strong intuitive appeal to the cost approach. On the demand side, potential buyers of a property have the alternative of purchasing an equivalent site and constructing equivalent improvements. Thus, it can be argued a buyer will pay no more for an existing property than it would cost to reproduce the property. Cost also disciplines price on the supply side. While sellers would like to get the highest price possible, in competitive markets, the cost to produce – defined to include a normal profit and to reflect the costs and risks associated with the development process – will effectively limit prices. That said, in some countries, such as the UK, land supply is restricted and those seeking alternative sites may well find a scarcity of supply, thus forcing up prices.

Strengths and limitations of the cost approach

Despite the intuitive appeal of the cost approach, it has serious limitations that often relegate it to a secondary role in value estimation. The main problem with using cost as a proxy for market value is that cost equals market value only when markets are in equilibrium. Unfortunately for the cost approach, in real estate markets, equilibrium tends to be elusive. Typically, there is an over- or undersupply of certain property types, meaning that prices will fall below or above the cost to reproduce, which may be affected by local scarcity of land affecting the land price and cost inflation or deflation in the building cost component. While solutions to this difficulty are available, they involve adjusting the cost estimate to reflect any such disequilibrium. However, this process effectively transforms the cost approach into the sales comparison approach, making it somewhat redundant with respect to the value estimate.

A second limitation of the cost approach is that, as described above, it requires estimates of both physical depreciation as well as any functional obsolescence, and such estimates can be very difficult and imprecise, particularly when the subject's improvements are relatively old. Therefore, in practice, the cost approach tends to work better for newer rather than older properties.

Despite these conceptual and mechanical limitations, the cost approach is quite useful in certain situations. For investors and developers, the cost approach is valuable for analysing potential new development. Simply, when the market value at completion is expected to exceed the cost to produce, development is justified. When the reverse is true, development should not occur. Finally, a cost estimate may be mandated for some valuations, such as when estimating value for property insurance purposes.

The income approach

The rationale of the income approach is straightforward: the value of an income property, like the value of any investment, is a function of the income it is expected to produce and the certainty of receiving the expected income. There are a number of value models under the income approach umbrella. The two most commonly used are 1) direct capitalisation, and 2) discounted cash flow (DCF) models.

The direct capitalisation model estimates value by capitalising first-year expected net operating income by a capitalisation rate extracted from comparable sales. The capitalisation rate (cap rate) is calculated by dividing the first year of expected net operating income by the selling price. For example, if an industrial property sold for £1,000,000 and had expected first-year net operating income of £125,000, it sold at a capitalisation rate of £125,000/£1,000,000, which equals a capitalisation rate of 0.08 or 8%. The inverse of the cap rate is the price/earnings multiplier (or years' price), so we can also say our industrial property sold at a multiple of 1/0.08, which equals 12.5 times earnings. The valuer selects a cap rate for the subject property based on the rates calculated from comparable sales, and applies it to the subject property's expected first year net operating income to arrive at a value estimate. In analysing comparable evidence, it is important to be aware of whether or not the first year net operating income is at market rent. If the passing rent is below (or above) the market rent, the initial yield will be different from the yield at 'reversion', the point at which the rent payable will revert to the market rent, following a rent review or lease renewal. For a fuller explanation see Baum *et al.* (2015). This phenomenon is most likely to happen where the leasing regimen allows for rent to be fixed for long periods between rent revisions back to market rent or where there is a disconnect over a long period between the rent revision mechanism and real estate occupier markets (for example, index linking to financial rather than real estate indicators).

The second major category of income approach models is the DCF. DCF models differ from direct capitalisation in that they explicitly consider all expected cash flows in making the value estimate. The expected cash flows (including terminal value at the end of the forecast holding period), are then discounted to a present value using a discount rate (the required return) that reflects the risk level of the investment.

As an investor making use of valuation estimates, it is important to understand how the capitalisation rate used in direct capitalisation relates to the discount rate used in DCF models. The link between those rates is understood by keeping in mind that market prices reflect all future expectations. Because the direct cap model explicitly includes only first-year income, expectations about future income must be reflected in the capitalisation rate. Based on Gordon's growth model, which has its origins in the equity market, the following relationship is established:

Discount rate = Capitalisation rate + expected annual growth rate of income and value.

This discount rate–capitalisation rate relationship works perfectly only when the growth rates of income and value are the same and the rate is the same each year. Although that scenario is virtually impossible, it is a close enough approximation to make the relationship useful for decision making. Note also that the growth estimate reflects inflation and depreciation expectations (assuming the discount rate is also nominal). For example, if properties are selling at cap rates of 7% and the market expects annual growth of 3%, the appropriate discount rate will be 10%. (In reality, this equation is slightly more complex as the annual growth is not necessarily participated in annually, as rents sometimes cannot be raised until a future rent review date or lease expiry. Thus an adjustment has to be made for the rent participation pattern.)

This relationship between cap rates and discount rates has powerful implications for investment decision making, as it provides information about what must occur with respect to income and value over the holding period to achieve a target yield. For example, if a property is being considered for purchase at a cap rate of, say, 5%, and the yield requirement is 12%, that target yield will be achieved only if income and value increase at a rate of 7% annually.

Strengths and limitations of the income approach

Because direct capitalisation is effectively a sales comparison model, it benefits from the fact that cap rates are extracted from actual market transactions. Thus, like other units of comparison, cap rates reflect the pricing behaviour of the market, which is what the appraiser is attempting to replicate. For this reason, when there are sufficient comparable sales from which to extract a cap rate, most appraisers and investors consider the resulting number to be a relatively reliable estimate of value.

One limitation of direct capitalisation is the need for sales of sufficiently comparable properties. This is typically not an issue for single family properties, but is often an issue for commercial properties. In those cases, the value estimate must come from either the DCF model and /or the cost approach.

The DCF model is more transparent with its inputs than the direct capitalisation approach, in that it requires both explicit forecasts of future cash flows, and an estimate of the discount rate. Its strength is that it explicitly shows those forecasts and the rate, meaning that the investor not only has the 'number' (the single-point price estimate) but also the cash flow and rate assumptions on which the value estimate is based. Where the inputs are derived or implied from market evidence, the resulting valuation, using a DCF approach, should be similar to the value produced by the direct capitalisation approach, albeit with the underlying assumptions exposed to scrutiny. However, where investor specific inputs are used in the DCF model, then the investment value or worth to that particular investor is calculated. At this point the investor can compare the market valuation, perhaps calculated using the direct capitalisation approach, with what they *should* pay for the investment based on their own specific assumptions and requirements.

As discussed above, taken together, cap rates and discount rates provide a powerful tool for analysing the necessary performance to reach a yield objective, that is, given the cap rate at which a property has been purchased, or is being considered for purchase, the difference between that rate and the required yield is a measure of the annual change in income and value necessary to reach that objective.

Summary

Valuers use three kinds of methodologies to estimate value. They are the sales comparison, cost and income approaches. Conceptually, all three approaches may be used in a given valuation, but in practice data limitations, client requirements and regulations may favour (or preclude) the use of one or more approach. For market value estimates, the sales comparison approach is typically preferred, as it is firmly anchored in the results of market transactions. For investment value, DCF models become relatively more attractive as they are flexible enough to reflect individual investor assumptions and requirements. The cost approach is currently relied on less frequently than the other two approaches for market value estimates (except when data limitations or property type mandate its use), but it is a primary tool for development decision making.

Reporting

To avoid any ambiguity and confusion between the valuer and the client, key parts of the valuation process require to be confirmed in writing. Prior to any valuation being undertaken, the client and the valuer should agree in writing the terms of the engagement, including the timescale and the fee. IVS 103 Reporting (International Valuation Standards Council, 2017a) sets out a list of standards that require to be adhered to in the reporting of a valuation to a client. The requirements are:

- identification and status of the valuer;
- identification of the client and other intended users;
- purpose of the valuation;

- identification of the asset or liability to be valued;
- basis of value;
- valuation date;
- extent of investigation;
- nature and source of the information relied upon;
- assumptions and special assumptions;
- restrictions on use, distribution or publication;
- conformation that the assignment has been undertaken in accordance with the IVS;
- valuation approach and reasoning;
- amount of the valuation or valuations (stating clearly the currency in which it is expressed); and
- date of the valuation report.

The requirements are there to ensure that the client knows exactly what has been valued, at what time and on what basis, given a certain set of assumptions. Where a valuer makes additional assumptions, special instructions or departs from the expected norm, then these should be clearly stated. A negative value is possible where the costs of expenditure are greater than the revenue flow, perhaps due to the cost of contamination clean up, and the value should be clearly stated as a negative figure and not as zero.

Summary and conclusions

It is clear that valuations play a crucial role in real estate investment throughout the differing stages of the investment journey. This chapter has outlined the nature of the valuation profession across the main investment markets, provided an explanation of the varying valuation standards, explained the definitions and bases of valuations as well as illustrating the differing valuation methodologies. However, in a single chapter it is impossible to do full justice to the differences in valuation practice across the globe. Regional differences in practice do exist and users of valuations need to be aware of these differences between the various jurisdictions and how they may affect the valuation.

Across all the countries, the valuation profession is subject to a diverse set of regulatory environments reflecting to some extent their industrial heritage and past and present property market dynamics, which have prompted regulatory action. Nonetheless, all of the countries studied in this chapter share the same ambition to maintain a standard of competency for entry to the profession and continuing proficiency, although the exact levels of education and training required to achieve and maintain full membership differs across jurisdictions and so the minimum standard is not uniform. While government regulation may also exist, self-regulation of professional conduct and standards by the in-country professional associations is common in most of the jurisdictions.

With respect to valuation standards, the past 30 years have witnessed the growth of IAVSC the IVSC, which enjoys a wide membership and influence across 57 countries. The resulting IVS now sit alongside country-specific standards, introduced to reflect unique domestic market characteristics, such as those involving property rights, title, lease structures and perceived best practice. In many countries, notably in the UK and US, the updating of the valuation standards has often been precipitated by some form of property market crisis. While this dual level of standards does lead to the risk of potential contradiction, owing to the wide acceptance of the international standards much consistency exists on the key definitions of value and the bases of valuation. The introduction of International Property Measurement

Standards for offices (International Property Measurements Standards Coalition, 2014) is a good illustration of the collaborative work of IVSC to ensure the consistent measurement of a property asset, which attracts considerable amounts of global capital and which, prior to this new standard, had been subject to a variety of different measurement approaches, thus making consistent analysis of yields and total returns across markets difficult to undertake.

While there is broad consistency on definitions and bases of valuations, the valuation methodologies adopted tend to reflect local custom and practice albeit within the guidance provided by the in-country professional associations. That said, the principles underpinning the sales, income and cost approach to valuation are accepted across all markets, albeit the terminology used may differ and their application may be subject to the level of transparency in the local market and the volume of transaction evidence. Market transparency is different between London and Beijing and between Madrid and Mumbai and, thus, the techniques used to estimate value have to adapt to the availability of market evidence. In opaque and thin markets, uncertainty exists as to the correct level of value and this additional risk needs to be communicated properly to the client. The users of valuations tend to demand single-point estimates of value which may not be backed up by fully verifiable recent transaction evidence and this needs to be flagged.

Whether or not there are differences in market practice within different regions and between countries, it is essential that there is absolute clarity between the valuer and the client on the purpose and basis of value and the legal and market context within which the value of the property is estimated. Valuations are required at point of purchase and sale and throughout the holding period to assess performance and it is thus essential that users of the valuation understand the context and the approach adopted.

Appendix 8A: Market background

Australia

Land	Legal definition of land includes the ground and any building improvements on and everything attached to the land.
Property rights	All land is held under tenure from the Crown. The highest form of ownership is an estate in fee simple. Lesser forms of ownership include leasehold, joint tenancy, and tenancy in common.
Title[10]	Crown land: All land in Australia is Crown land unless alienated by grant, sale or resumption. The Crown manages Australia's land in a variety of ways such as free grant, freehold alienation, short-term leases and licenses. Old System title: Prior to the establishment of the Torrens system, land ownership was based on the English common law system known as 'Old System'. Unlike Torrens title, Old System title is good title only if a better claim cannot be established. A chain of evidence (known as a chain of title or chain of deeds) is needed to establish good title. Torrens title: This is a system that establishes title based on registration and certification, and not on deeds. Title held under the Torrens system is guaranteed by the Australian government. Native title: Australia has taken steps to recognise the native title of indigenous Aboriginal and Torres Straits Islander peoples who made up 3% of the Australian population as at 2011.[11] Native title is a property right that reflects a relationship to land which is the very foundation of indigenous religion, culture and well-being.[12]
Units of measurement	Metric system (SI): square metres, or cubic metres where cubic capacity is relevant say in industrial buildings. For residential property transactions, land prices may be referenced using traditional British imperial measures (price per acre or per perch).
Typical lease structure	Office: Three- to five-year leases, with annual or mid-term reviews for market or inflation pegged adjustments are the norm for office space leases. Larger tenants may be granted 7–10 year leases.[13] Rents are paid monthly in advance. Tenants bear all outgoings relating to the building based on their leased floor space and a share of outgoings of common areas based on the proportion of their leased floor space to the total leased area of the building. Such outgoings include repairs, maintenance, cleaning, utility costs, property management, building insurance, land tax etc. Retail: Speciality retail leases are generally for three to five years, with option to renew and rent reviews similar to that for an office space lease. Anchor tenants are given much longer leases, from 10–40 years on favourable terms to the tenant. Renewals are typically made on the same terms as the original lease save for rents which will be revised. Percentage or turnover rents are sometimes paid. Outgoings paid by the tenant are similar to that of office tenants, but there may be additional expenses such as promotional levies or merchants' association fees. Industrial: Lease of industrial space varies with the size of the property and range from three, five, or ten years, with market or inflation adjusted rent reviews. Smaller units of industrial space are often held under a strata-title[14] and may be leased on a gross or net basis. The tenant is responsible for all outgoings including management, but excluding structural repairs that involve capital expenditure.

China

Property rights	Pursuant to the People's Republic of China (PRC) Constitution adopted in 1982, there is no private ownership of land in China; land in urban areas is state owned, whereas land in rural and suburban areas is generally owned by collective economic organisations for the benefit of the people.[15] Economic dealings with collectively-owned land are highly restricted and typically cannot be used for non-agricultural purposes, unless approved by the government. Individuals and businesses may acquire 'use rights' in state-owned land by way of allocation or grant. Use rights give the holder the right to occupy, build and operate on the land. PRC law generally provides for 'granted' land use rights and 'allocated' land use rights.

Granted land use rights	Allocated land use rights
Granted by the state	Allocated by local government
Right to transfer, lease or mortgage	Right to transfer, lease or mortgage subject to government approval
Fixed term: Residential purpose – up to 70 years Industrial purpose – up to 50 years Commercial purpose – up to 40 years	No definite period of allocation, dependent on specific use and regulatory requirements
Payment of land grant premium and annual land use fee	No land premium payable. If land is occupied, user must bear resettlement costs
Granted by way of mutual agreement, invitation of tender or auction. In practice, it is often carried out by negotiated agreement	Involves negotiated agreement with local government and occupants of land, if any

Title	There is a registration and certification system in place, which requires land users and owners to apply for land use rights and property ownership certificates.[16]
Units of measurement	Square metres is the typical unit of measurement. For land, the traditional Chinese unit of measure, the mu (1 mu = 666.667 square metres) may be used.
Typical lease structure	Leases can be granted by the holder of the land use rights and are typically for a term of two years, with an option to renew for a further two to three years at prevailing market rental rates. Rent is payable monthly, and is usually reviewed as part of the renewal negotiations. As noted in the JLL Global Real Estate Transparency Index 2016, China's real estate practice is semi-transparent and there is room for greater transparency to enable investors to make more informed real estate decisions. However, in tier 1 cities, the situation is improving and China is coming closer to breaking into the transparent block of countries.

Hong Kong

Land	Under the Conveyancing and Property Ordinance, Chapter 219, 'land' includes (a) land covered by water; (b) any estate, right, interest or easement in or over any land; (b) the whole or part of an undivided share in land and any estate, right, interest or easement in or over the whole or part of an undivided share in land; and (c) things attached to land or permanently fastened to anything attached to land.
Property Rights	Today, all the land in Hong Kong is owned by the People's Republic of China (the Hong Kong special administrative region government), save for the land on which St John's Cathedral stands.[17] Land leases are sold by the government by public auction, tender or private treaty grant. Before July 1997, the term of leases granted by the Crown varied from 999 years, to 99 years, to 75 years. However, government leases granted after July 1997 are 50-year leases except those for special purposes.[18] In addition to a land premium, the acquirer is also required to pay land rent being an amount equivalent to 3% of the rateable value assessed by the rating and valuation department.[19]
Title	Hong Kong is in the process of transitioning from a deeds registration system to a title registration system. The deeds registration system provided a record of registration for all instruments which affect land or interests in land in Hong Kong, but involved a cumbersome and uncertain search process. The title system will make public searches more accessible and transparent, and will reduce the burden on potential purchasers in ascertaining the identity of legal and equitable owners.
Units of measurement	Square metres is the typical unit of measurement.
Typical lease structure	Residential space is generally leased for two-year terms with a break clause after the first year whereby the lease is terminable with two to three months' notice. Office and retail leases are typically three-year fixed-term leases. Rent is payable monthly; rental rates are subject to negotiations during renewal discussions. The landlord is responsible for internal repairs and repairs of the common areas, but these costs are sometimes passed on to the tenants in the form of a service charge.

India

Land	'Land' includes benefits to arise out of land and things attached to the earth or permanently fastened to anything attached to the earth.[20]
Property Rights	Most properties in India are freehold properties. Apartments are typically sold on a leasehold basis of 30, 60 or 99 years.
Title	India adopts a 'recording system' similar to that in the United States. This system involves registration of deeds in a system of 'presumptive' title. Land records are not conclusive evidence of title, but simply records of transactions and registration.[21] Owners typically purchase title insurance to insure against loss or damage sustained in connection with errors in title examination, defects, liens or encumbrances on the title.[22]
Units of measurement	There are numerous units of measurements used in India. In Delhi, Gurgaon and Noida, property and land measurements are made in square feet; in Mumbai and Goa, measurement is done in square metres. In other states like Uttarakhand and Himachal Pradesh, the Nalli (1 Nalli = 240 square yards) is used.

Typical lease structure	A typical commercial lease has a term of three years with an option to renew for a further two years. Rent is payable monthly in advance with rent reviews negotiated up front, with fixed increments of between 15–20% every three years or 5% annually. Tenants are responsible for internal fitting out, while landlords are responsible for structural and external repairs, repairs of common areas and insurance for the building. Subletting is usually prohibited save with the landlord's approval.

Japan

Land	Land and buildings are regarded as separate and independent real estate, and can have different owners.
Property rights	The two main categories of land ownership rights in Japan are similar to the concepts of freehold and leasehold. *Shoyuken* (freehold) is absolute ownership of land and building. *Chishakuken* is a leasehold interest that gives the holder a right to occupy and use the property. Other lesser property rights include *Chijoken*, a right to use the land of others to own structures on that land; *Chiekiken*, a right to use the land of others for certain specific purposes non-exclusively; and *Tanpoken*, a right to create a security.[23]
Title	There is no title system in Japan, but there is a system for registration of land and buildings (*fudosan tokibo*). Ownership is perfected via a time-consuming boundary confirmation process which involves the procurement of signatures of all adjoining property owners to evidence agreement of the site boundary.
Units of measurement	A combination of metric and traditional units of measure (*tsubo* or *jo*) is used in Japan. A *tsubo* is equal to 35.58 square feet (the area of two standard sized tatami mats); a *jo* is equal to half of a *tsubo*. Real estate areas may be quoted in *tsubo* or square metres, but rents and prices per unit are based on *tsubo*.
Typical lease structure	Office: A standard lease of office space in Japan usually has a two-year term, a statutory renewal right and a break clause exercisable by the tenant with six months' notice. Fixed-term leases are common in larger and newer office buildings. Rents are payable monthly. Landlords may require three types of deposits: *Shiki kin* (six to 12 months' rent) for unpaid rent and reinstatement; *Kenri kin* (two to six months' rent) for key money, which is non-refundable; and *Hosho kin*, a refundable deposit paid before lease commencement which is commonly used to help fund the construction of the building. Retail: Retail leases are similar in structure to office leases but may contain a percentage rent provision. Anchor tenants are granted longer terms with a rent review mechanism in the lease. Smaller tenants may have very short leases, even month-to-month. Residential: A lease for an apartment is usually for a term of two years. The tenant has to bear utility costs and the tenant's employer is usually required to co-sign the lease.

Singapore

Land	The legal definition of land includes the ground and any building improvements on and everything attached to the land.
Property rights	The highest form of ownership is an estate in fee simple. Other forms of ownership include an estate in perpetuity by way of a state land grant,[24] leasehold, joint tenancy and tenancy in common. Freehold or leasehold estates may be subject to legal restrictions, e.g. rights of way and easements.

Title	Land registered under the Land Titles Act (LTA; Torrens system) has indefeasible title. Land not registered under the LTA is regulated by the English common law system of deeds. Although there is a separate system of registration for deeds, registration of a deed does not guarantee good title.
Units of measurement	Square feet or square metres.
Typical lease structure	A lease of office or retail space in Singapore is typically for a term of one to three years. Owing to a highly competitive local retail space market, the retail landlord would typically require annual fixed upwards rent revisions and a redevelopment or 'break' clause. Turnover or percentage rent may be payable by a retail tenant in addition to a base monthly rent. The tenant is responsible for all outgoings relating to the property and would usually pay a service charge; and in the case of a tenant occupying premises owned by a retail real estate investment trust, an additional advertising and promotional fee is payable. Industrial leases acquired from the JTC Corporation, the main statutory board overseeing industrial land in Singapore, tend to be for longer terms. A recent change in policy has stipulated that the maximum tenure of industrial leases from JTC will be reduced from 60 years to 30 years.

United Kingdom

Land	The legal definition of land includes the ground and any building improvements on and everything attached to the land.
Property rights	The two principal rights in land are freehold and leasehold. Freeholders hold an estate from the Crown in perpetuity (fee simple) while leaseholders are granted the use of the land and buildings for a certain term of years.
Title	The Land Registry holds records about most property or land sold in England or Wales since 1993 while the Land Register in Scotland was introduced in 1981.
Units of measurement	Square feet or square metres.
Typical lease structure	Commercial and industrial property occupational leases in the UK have become much more diverse since the end of the 1980s when over 90% of the leases held by the major institutional investors and property companies were for 20–25 years, had five yearly upwards-only rent reviews and full repairing and insuring liabilities by the tenant. There is now a diversity of lease lengths, often 5, 10 or 15 years, tenant breaks are common but the 5-year upwards-only rent review to market rent has survived, supporting the use of incentives such as rent free periods and capital payments upon new lettings. Indexation and other rent revision types are sparsely used at present. The higher value properties let to corporate tenants attract the longest leases. Rents are normally paid in advance, quarterly or half yearly.

United States

Real estate and real property	Real estate and real property are terms often used interchangeably, but they have slightly different meanings. Real estate is land plus improvements on and to the land, whether natural or man-made. Real property is broader in meaning. It is real estate plus all legal rights, powers and privileges inherent in the ownership of property.

Property rights	Ownership of real property is by freehold estate. The highest form of freehold estate is an estate in fee simple absolute. Lesser forms of ownership include fee simple defeasible and life estates. Non-ownership estates are called non-freehold (or leasehold) estates. They are of limited duration and are created by a lease or rental agreement. Both freehold and non-freehold estates may be subject to legal or contractual restrictions such as easements or rights of way.
Title	Transfer of title is described in law as alienation. Alienation may be voluntary or involuntary. Voluntary title transfer is accomplished by the delivery of a valid deed by the grantor to the grantee. Involuntary title transfer may occur as a result of a lien foreclosure sale, adverse possession, filing a petition in bankruptcy or condemnation under the power of eminent domain.
Units of measurement	The most common unit of measurement is the square foot, whether referring to land or buildings. Land size is sometimes quoted in acres. The measurement of certain kinds of buildings, for example industrial buildings, may include height as well as floor space.
Typical lease structure	Market conditions largely drive commercial lease structures and terms, so there is not an industry standard. However, during 'normal' market conditions, three- to five-year leases are common for office space, with industrial and retail leases often five or more years. Rent may be fixed, but more often escalates periodically by an agreed upon percentage, or as a function of an inflation index or reappraisal. Commercial leases also vary widely with respect to the responsibility for operating expenses. Longer term industrial properties are often leased on a 'triple net' basis, meaning the tenant is responsible for all operating expenses. Quoted nominal rental rates must be carefully analysed, as they may differ significantly from the effective rate including expenses.

Notes

1 See RICS History: www.rics.org/uk/about-rics/who-and-what/history/ (accessed 13 August 2018).
2 See Australian Property Institute, Our History: www.api.org.au/our-history (accessed 13 August 2018).
3 Data from HKIS: www.hkis.org.hk/en/hkis_aboutus.php (accessed 13 August 2018).
4 The Institution of Surveyors, http://iosindia.co.in/sub-divison-3rd (accessed 13 August 2018).
5 Singapore Institute of Surveyors and Valuers Overview: www.sisv.org.sg/overview.aspx (accessed 13 August 2018).
6 IVSC, About Us: www.ivsc.org/about (accessed 13 August 2018).
7 See International Property Measurement Standards: http://ipmsc.org (accessed 13 August 2018).
8 In an analysis of retail cap rates within Europe by the Investment Property Databank in 2004, the UK retained 97% of gross to net income while Germany and the Scandinavian countries only retained around 80%.
9 A covered bond is a security created from public sector loans or mortgage loans where the security is backed by a separate group of loans; it typically carries a maturity rate of 2–10 years and enjoys relatively high credit ratings. Covered bonds provide an efficient, lower-cost way for lenders to expand their business rather than issuing unsecured debt instruments.
10 NSW Government Land and Property Information, *Old System Information and Search Guide*, March 2013.
11 Australian Bureau of Statistics, Estimates and Projections, Aboriginal and Torres Strait Islander Australians, 2001 to 2026, www.abs.gov.au/ausstats/abs@.nsf/Products/C19A0C6E4794A3FACA257CC900143A3D?opendocument (accessed 13 August 2018).

12 Australian Human Rights Commission, Native Title, www.humanrights.gov.au/native-title (accessed 13 August 2018).
13 Australian Real Estate investment Guide 2013, Savills.
14 Strata-title allows individual ownership of part of a property (such as a townhouse), combined with shared ownership in the remainder – the 'common property' (e.g. foyers, driveways, gardens).
15 Jones Day, *International Real Estate Briefing, Real Estate Practice in China*, September 2004, www.jonesday.com/files/Publication/ee7778f4-cc2a-466f-9276-8b12924a100f/Presentation/PublicationAttachment/b38781ad-cd63-4cd1-9883-59a097f2c687/IT%20RE%20Sept.pdf (accessed 13 August 2018).
16 *Ibid.*
17 Community Legal Information Centre, I. Basic knowledge of land ownership in Hong Kong, www.hkclic.org/en/topics/saleAndPurchaseOfProperty/basic_knowledge_of_land_ownership_in_hong_kong (accessed 13 August 2018).
18 Li, L.-H. (2006) *Development Appraisal of Land in Hong Kong*, rev. ed., Chinese University Press, Hong Kong, at pp. 19–20.
19 *Ibid.*, at p. 38.
20 Dictionary of Valuers, Practising Valuers Association India, www.pvai.info/dictionary_of_valuers.php. (accessed 29 October 2014).
21 At page 68.
22 At pp. 70–71.
23 Jones Lang LaSalle, *Japan Property Investment Guide 2016*, Adelaide, www.joneslanglasallesites.com/investmentguide/uploads/attachments/PIG2016-Japan-v5.pdf (accessed 13 August 2018).
24 The payment of nominal ground of SGD$12 per year has been waived since 1992.

References

Appraisal Institute (2014) Our history, www.appraisalinstitute.org/about/our-history.

Appraisal Foundation (2018) *Uniform standards of professional appraisal practice (USPAP)*, Appraisal Foundation, Washington, DC.

Baum, A., Mackmin, D. and Nunnington, N. (2015) *The income approach to property valuation*, Routledge, London.

Crosby, N. and Hughes, C. (2011) The basis of valuations for secured commercial property lending in the UK, *Journal of European Real Estate Research*, 4(3), 225–42.

Crosby, N., French, N. and Oughton, M. (2000) Bank lending valuations on commercial property: does the European mortgage lending value add anything to the process?, *Journal of Property Investment and Finance*, 18(1), 66–83.

Crosby, N., Lizieri, C. and McAllister, P. (2010) Means, motive and opportunity? disentangling client influence on performance measurement appraisals. *Journal of Property Research*, 27(2), 181–201.

Davies, T. D. (1908) *Curtis on the valuation of land and houses*, 3rd ed., Estates Gazette, London.

Diaz, J. (2002) Behavioural research in valuation and some perspectives on implications for practice, *RICS Research Review Series*, RICS, London.

Edelstein, R. H. and Quan, D. C. (2006) How does appraisal smoothing bias real estate returns measurement?, *Journal of Real Estate Finance and Economics*, 32(1), 41–60.

European Group of Valuers' Associations (2016) *European Valuation Standards*, 8th ed., TEGOVA, Brussels.

Geltner, D., MacGregor, B. D. and Schwann, G. M. (2003) Appraisal smoothing and price discovery in real estate markets, *Urban Studies*, 40(5–6), 1047–64.

Hutchison, N. and Nanthakumaran, N. (2000) The calculation of investment worth: issues of market efficiency, variable estimation and risk analysis, *Journal of Property Investment and Finance,* 18(1), 33–51.

International Property Measurements Standards Coalition (2014) *International property measurements standards: office buildings*, IPMSC, London.

International Valuation Standards Council (2011) *Code of ethical principles for professional valuers*, IVSC, London.

International Valuation Standards Council (2012) *Financial viability in planning*, RICS guidance note GN 94/2012, IVSC, London.

International Valuation Standards Council (2017a) *International Valuation Standards 2017*, IVSC, London.

International Valuation Standards Council (2017b) *International Valuation Standards Committee Annual Report 2015–16*, www.ivsc.org/about/annual-reports.

International Valuation Standards Council (2018) *Discounted cash flow for commercial property investments*, IVSC, London.

Lawrence, D. M. and May, H. G. (1943) *Modern methods of valuation*, Estates Gazette, London.Royal Institution of Chartered Surveyors (2012) *Financial viability in planning*, RICS guidance note, GN 94/2012, RICS, London.

Royal Institution of Chartered Surveyors (2017) *RICS valuation – global standards 2017, incorporating the IVSC international valuation standards*, RICS, London.

Royal Institution of Chartered Surveyors (2018) *Discounted cash flow for commercial property investments* (archived), RICS guidance note (August 2010–June 2018), RICS, London.

Ruchardt, K. (2003) *Mortgage lending value*, Fritz Knapp, Frankfurt am Main.

9 Appraisal-based indices

Neil Crosby and Steven Devaney

Introduction

The measuring of asset prices through time is well established in most asset markets. For example, the Dow Jones Industrial Average for the US equity market was established as early as 1896, the FT30 index for UK equities was started in 1935 and the Nikkei index was first published in Japan in 1950. These indices aggregate the price movements of individual equities as captured by a wealth of transaction evidence for identical shares being traded at any particular point in time. Such price movements are weighted either equally or with reference to the market capitalisation of the constituent firms to produce a market index. Individual equities may also be categorised into industrial sectors, including real estate companies, or in terms of other characteristics to enable sector indices to be produced. Similar price and performance indices are also published for bonds.

There are several major differences between direct real estate investment and exchange traded investments, such as equities and bonds, that make transaction price indices much more difficult to construct. First, there is a limited volume of transactions in real estate markets and they occur at irregular intervals. Second, there is no transparent central market place where details about real estate transactions can be observed, while public depositories of property ownership and transaction details are not easy to access in many countries. Third, the heterogeneity of each individual property creates difficulties. No single property is identical to any other, with a unique location and unique physical and legal characteristics. These characteristics create considerable variation in prices and the challenges of controlling for them in the construction of transaction-based indices are set out in Chapter 10.

On account of these difficulties, reliable indices of the performance of direct real estate investments were formulated later than in the case of equities and bonds. Their introduction was preceded by significant change and growth in real estate investment markets during the twentieth century in the major developed economies. In the post-Second World War period in the UK, ownership of commercial real estate began to move from the hands of owner-occupiers and local entrepreneurs to real estate companies operating at a national level.[1] This trend was followed in the 1960s and 1970s by a rise in the ownership of real estate by financial institutions, such as insurance companies and pension funds (Scott, 1996). In contrast, UK residential property markets became more dominated by owner-occupation whereas, in other mature economies, such as the US, investment in residential real estate was, and still is, significantly more important.

With increased ownership by financial institutions, commercial real estate became part of a multi-asset portfolio. As such, the requirement for measuring its performance and comparing it against other assets led to the introduction of real estate investment indices. According to Fisher (2005), the major objectives for introducing such indices are to monitor the risk and return of real estate investments and to understand how their performance compares with that of other asset classes such as equities and bonds. They also facilitate benchmarking of individual assets, funds, locations and types of property against one another and such comparisons are now fundamental in asset allocation and the selection of investments. Given the interest from, and requirements of, large-scale institutional investors, it was perhaps inevitable that real estate indices concentrated on the more significant ownerships with the largest and most modern portfolios comprising what came to be termed institutional grade assets. This categorisation tended to include the larger lot sizes in the more significant locations within large cities, built to high specifications and let to major occupiers on standard institutional lease contracts.

In the UK, attempts to construct real estate price and performance indices started in the 1960s and 1970s. In the absence of centralised records, the development of indices was initiated by a number of private organisations. These organisations were often managing agents that held a significant amount of data on individual properties and markets gathered during their agency and management activities. Some indices were based on actual properties or funds and some on appraisals of hypothetical properties in actual locations. Morrell (1991) lists early initiatives for the UK real estate market and Crosby (1988) gives further details on the composition and construction of early UK market measures. Arguably, a few early initiatives were driven by some organisations deciding that the production of 'market intelligence' supported business development and new client capture. Yet the gains to be made in market transparency and efficiency were not lost on the real estate industry which, in the most mature markets, was becoming more integrated with the financial sector and more international in outlook.

Right from the beginning, the real estate investment industry resorted to appraisals as a substitute for transaction prices, to overcome the problems with constructing transaction-based indices mentioned above. Appraisals were already a regular feature of real estate investment markets for all kinds of purposes including one-off appraisal for acquisition, sale and bank lending decisions and periodic appraisal for investor reporting and financial statements (as discussed in Chapter 10). In many cases, the latter could be employed for performance measurement purposes and in the construction of indices. This approach was formalised in the 1980s in the two highly mature real estate investment markets of the US and the UK. In the US, the National Council of Real Estate Investment Fiduciaries (NCREIF) was established in 1982 and collected data on individual properties to facilitate construction of an appraisal-based real estate return index (Diehl, 1993). This index was initially produced by the Frank Russell Company on behalf of NCREIF and was known as the FRC index and the RN index before becoming the NCREIF Property Index. Meanwhile, the Investment Property Databank (IPD) (now part of the MSCI group) started collecting data on properties from UK institutional investors in the early 1980s, and published its first index of investment returns for the UK real estate market in 1985.

As the pioneers of constructing indices that have both significant market coverage and depth in terms of individual property details, MSCI (through their predecessors, IPD) and NCREIF are the two best-known providers of real estate investment indices. NCREIF have remained focussed on the US real estate market, but IPD expanded its services internationally and is now part of MSCI. Both organisations share the same basis for their principal indices – appraisals rather than transactions. In both cases, the indices are based on actual property (rather than hypothetical or fund level) information, which is then aggregated to form real estate market measures. It is only in recent years that increasing availability of transaction data coupled with research into index construction using hedonic and repeat sales regression methods has led to the construction of several transaction-based indices for commercial real estate in both the UK and US. Although IPD was taken over by MSCI, many of the indices still carry the IPD name rather than that of MSCI. However, all IPD indices are now produced by MSCI.

The next section reviews the different types of appraisal-based indices and the key performance measures that are produced from them. Subsequent sections identify the international coverage of such indices and highlight the issues surrounding the use of appraisals to measure real estate performance.

Types of appraisal indices and key performance measures

Different types

Appraisal-based indices fall into three major categories:

- Whole-fund indices – constructed from fund performance data and using aggregated, portfolio-level cash flows and values rather than data on individual properties held by those funds. In the UK, a number of early real estate indices adopted this approach.[2]
- Individual properties – indicators constructed from cash flows and values of individual property investments that are aggregated into various sector, location and/or regional series and, ultimately, into a national 'all property' series. This is the approach adopted by MSCI and NCREIF.
- Individual locations – indicators constructed from the appraisal of hypothetical properties in selected locations rather than actual properties. Many market barometers released by real estate service providers are produced on this basis. The widest coverage comes from international consulting firms such as CBRE, Jones Lang LaSalle and Cushman & Wakefield, but indicators for national or local markets are also often produced by more local organisations in each country.

This chapter focusses on indices formed from individual property rather than from fund data, as the former now dominate real estate investment markets. However, market barometers for individual locations, as distinct from assets, are an important source of information for market participants. For example, where the objective is to compare the movement in values in one location against another, market barometers can be more useful indicators than the performance of actual buildings. The barometers are produced by real estate service firms based on knowledge gained from their agency and other activities. Changes in value are identified based on appraisals of either a hypothetical new property or the best property in that location. They are simple to construct and tend to focus on two measures: rental value and yield/capitalisation rate. They require some assumptions to be made concerning the location (often prime, but not always) and the building in that location (in regard to specification and lease terms) but, as occupier requirements change over time, the specific location and the assumed building specification may also change.

Measures

The three main performance measures are income return, capital return and total return. These can be measured in two basic ways: as money-weighted rates of return or time-weighted rates of return. Money-weighted rates of return are the internal rate of return of the cash flows. This rate takes account of the amount of money that is invested in each period. When calculated across several periods, the times at which money was invested or withdrawn will affect the outcome. In contrast, a time-weighted rate of return is based on a succession of return rates measured for individual periods that are then compounded to establish performance over multiple periods. By this compounding, the impact of any injections or withdrawals of capital between periods is neutralised. This is useful when trying to understand the performance of a market versus that of an individual investor.[3]

However, in real estate performance measurement, the shortest periods over which return rates are measured are often one month or one quarter. Therefore, assumptions must be made about the timing of receipts or payments such as rent or capital expenditure that occur within each period. For example, the standard measurement period for returns in the MSCI series is one month and the formulas used make assumptions as to when cash flows occur within each month and so are approximations of the internal rate of return over those intervals (Bacon, 2008). When annual or quarterly return rates are reported, though, they can be regarded as time-weighted returns, as each contributory monthly return rate is given equal importance in determining the outcome.

NCREIF adopts a similar approach whereby the measurement period is quarterly and the formulas make assumptions about the timing of cash flows within those quarters. The quarterly return rates are then chain linked to form indices that span longer periods.

The formulas used by MSCI to calculate income, capital and total return for real estate investments are presented here, as they produce performance indices in the most countries and these indices are compliant with Global Investment Performance Standards (GIPS; MSCI, 2018). MSCI provides contributors with definitions for the inputs so that investors are aware of what constitutes, say, net income or capital expenditure when they supply the data. Standardised approaches and definitions are necessary so that index results can be compared across markets. Starting with income return, this is calculated by MSCI as net income divided by capital employed over the period.[4] The formula is as follows:

$$IR_t = \left(\frac{NI_t}{CV_{t-1} + CX_t} \right) \times 100 \tag{9.1}$$

where IR_t is the income return in period t, NI_t is the rent receivable net of ground rent and other irrecoverable expenditure during period t, CV_{t-1} is the capital value at the end of the prior period, and CX_t is the capital expenditure in period t.

Capital return is calculated as the change in capital value, less any capital expenditure incurred, expressed as a percentage of capital employed over the period. The formula is:

$$CR_t = \left(\frac{CV_t - CV_{t-1} - CX_t + RC_t}{CV_{t-1} + CX_t} \right) \times 100 \tag{9.2}$$

where CR_t is the capital return in period t and RC_t equals any capital receipts in period t, while other terms are as previously defined.

Finally, total return is calculated as the change in capital value, less any capital expenditure incurred, plus net income and any capital receipts, expressed as a percentage of the capital employed over the period. The formula is:

$$TR_t = \left(\frac{CV_t - CV_{t-1} - CX_t + RC_t + NI_t}{CV_{t-1} + CX_t} \right) \times 100 \tag{9.3}$$

where TR_t is the total return in period t and other terms are as previously defined. Hence, in each month, total return is simply the addition of income return and capital return. Indices that span longer intervals can be computed by chain linking the monthly return rates; multiplying an arbitrary base value at t_0 by $(1 + r_1)$; that is, one plus the first period return rate, to produce an index value for t_1, and so on.

Although the calculation frequency is monthly, this does not mean that appraisals are available for each month or that index numbers and return rates are published at this frequency. In practice, the frequency of appraisals differs between investors and across markets. For example, open-ended funds may commission monthly appraisals to assist with unit pricing, but other types of investors may only obtain annual appraisals of their real estate assets. This means that to implement a standard calculation interval, MSCI and other index providers have adopted interpolation techniques to generate intermediate appraisal inputs. The techniques include linear interpolation between two genuine appraisals, shaped interpolation with reference to other performance data or holding over the previous appraisal value until a new appraisal is supplied, the latter approach having been used by NCREIF.

When measuring portfolio or market performance, the principle of value weighting is applied, such that the components of each formula become summations of income, values, expenditure and so on across the set of properties being examined. The outcome is that changes in income or value affecting the most valuable assets have the most influence on reported return rates. This is logical for reporting portfolio performance and it has become established practice for reporting market-level performance as well.

The sample of assets used to measure market or segment return rates is held constant in each month. Thus, return rates will relate to an ageing set of buildings. Between months, the sample is refreshed so that subsequent periods include newly purchased assets and exclude assets that have been sold. So the pool of properties on which the index is based should not age or decline in quality in the long run if sold assets are replaced by newer and better quality ones. The measures for each interval will relate to a depreciating portfolio, but the effects of depreciation will differ from those that a static portfolio would experience. Whether this means a higher or lower depreciation rate for the changing sample against a static one depends on the profile of depreciation. Research suggests that new properties have higher depreciation rates than older ones (Bokhari and Geltner, 2016; Crosby *et al.*, 2016). In that case, a refreshed sample could experience more depreciation than a static sample. This might seem counterintuitive, but an old asset getting one period older may lose less value in relative terms than a new asset getting one period older.

There are two issues relating to income and capital return. First, the linking of income return rates into an index seems to be a widespread practice for real estate, but not for tracking the performance of other assets. Both MSCI and NCREIF publish income return indices and this practice is now recognised in GIPS (CFA Institute, 2010). An income return index can be used to work out the relative contribution of income to total return over longer horizons. However, such indices might be construed as measures of income *change* by uninformed users, so MSCI and NCREIF also report indices of income change that do measure how much income rises or falls relative to the previous period.

The second issue is how capital expenditure is treated. There has been some debate as to whether it should be treated as a deduction from income rather than from value when measuring real estate investment performance (Young *et al.*, 1995; Young, 2005). Both MSCI and NCREIF deduct capital expenditure from capital value change in the numerator of the capital return formula.[5] This helps to isolate the element of capital return that is attributable to market movements rather than capital injections. Yet, arguably, it means that the full extent to which values rise over time is hidden while the income return from real estate investments appears more stable than it is in reality. The approach taken has no effect on total return, but it has a major impact on both capital and income return rates, so this issue concerns the reporting of how investment returns are delivered.

In addition to the measures presented above, some other measures are produced to quantify and explain real estate investment performance. These include rental value indices and measures of yield/capitalisation rate for the assets being monitored. Rental value indices, where published, use appraisal-based assessments of the market rent for each property rather than the actual income received by investors from period to period.[6] Meanwhile, some form of yield or capitalisation rate series is reported for all markets. Initial yield is the simplest measure and this is current income as a proportion of current capital value, analogous to the dividend yield reported in equity markets. However, given differing market conventions, it has proved difficult to obtain even a consistent initial yield measure across all national markets. Differences can arise from how income is defined and from how transaction costs are dealt with in different markets. Both rental value indices and yields can be affected by the rent determination process and whether a headline rent with rent-free periods or an effective rent is used as the input to its calculation.

Both MSCI and NCREIF adopt some further conventions when producing segment or market indices. First, the indices only use 'standing investments', that is, properties that have not been traded and are not undergoing development or major refurbishment over the measurement interval. In contrast, all properties are included when benchmarking fund performance so that the impact of trading or management decisions on returns can be monitored. Second, the indices do not reflect the effects of any leverage. Finally, fund-level management fees are not incorporated into the return calculations. However, some indices do incorporate the impact of leverage and fund management fees, such as the Association of Real Estate Funds/IPD UK Quarterly Property Fund Index. This is relevant to investors that use funds to access the real estate market rather than investing directly.

Further technical details relating to the different indices and measures are set out in the published technical guides released by each index provider (MSCI, 2018; National Council of Real Estate Investment Fiduciaries, 2016).

Global coverage

Real estate market indices and performance measurement now extend across many parts of the globe. The main provider of real estate investment indices is MSCI, which operated in 32 countries across five continents in 2016. In 25 of those countries, the data collected are deemed to be sufficiently developed to contribute to the construction of a global real estate index. These countries are listed in Table 9.1. MSCI also monitors real estate investment markets in several Asian countries, including China, for which indices were not published at the time of writing (Table 9.2). MSCI only releases one index for countries in Africa and none for countries in South America, reflecting historical patterns of economic development, investment activity and real estate market maturity. Not all of the national indices listed in Table 9.1 were initiated by either MSCI or their predecessors, IPD. For example, the Australia index was initially developed by the Property Council of Australia, while the index for Finland continues to be produced by KTI, but within the MSCI technical guidelines.

As can be seen from Tables 9.1 and 9.2, coverage of each national market varies widely. This coverage is assessed in relation to the estimated total value of real estate held in professionally managed investment portfolios (Teuben *et al.*, 2017) and not against the value of

Table 9.1 IPD Global Annual Property Index – constituent countries as at end 2016

Country	*No. of funds*	*No. of assets*	*Value of assets US$ billion*	*Market size US$ billion*	*Coverage to end 2016 (%)*
Australia	62	1,436	124.5	225.9	55.1
Austria	15	334	6.9	34.3	20.2
Belgium	23	238	6.3	51.9	12.1
Canada	44	2,454	105.7	287.7	36.7
Czech Republic	14	111	2.1	16.8	12.6
Denmark	16	534	12.5	49.8	25.1
Finland (KTI)	26	1,718	19.4	61.4	31.6
France	109	5,944	134.8	353.1	38.2
Germany	90	1,796	53.1	395.8	13.4
Hungary	9	57	0.8	8.2	9.4
Ireland	13	443	8.8	26.3	33.6
Italy	53	1,512	19.2	105.4	18.2
Japan	69	3,515	156.5	729.2	21.5
Netherlands	72	4,027	40.3	128.8	31.3
New Zealand	17	434	9.6	17.4	55.0
Norway	16	429	15.1	48.6	31.0
Poland	23	210	5.1	37.7	13.4
Portugal	30	572	7.6	23.3	32.8
South Africa	13	1,450	21.7	39.5	55.0
South Korea	90	178	22.0	60.7	36.3
Spain	40	509	21.6	73.0	29.6
Sweden	48	3,937	77.6	165.7	46.8
Switzerland	37	4,014	92.6	213.2	43.4
United Kingdom	272	22,530	249.8	604.6	41.3
United States	98	5,721	363.0	2,729.7	13.3

Source: Compiled from Teuben *et al.* (2017) and from individual index factsheets.

Table 9.2 MSCI-monitored Asian markets not included in Global Index as at end 2016

Country	*Value of assets US$ billion*	*Market size US$ billion*	*Coverage to end 2016 (%)*
China	15.5	415.6	3.7
Hong Kong	40.8	310.6	13.1
Indonesia	2.3	11.5	19.7
Malaysia	7.9	22.8	34.6
Singapore	52.6	139.8	37.6
Taiwan	2.6	36.3	7.2
Thailand	5.7	16.7	34.1

Source: Teuben *et al.* (2017).

the total property stock, estimates of which are often unavailable. In Australia, New Zealand and South Africa, MSCI estimates its coverage at over 50% of the professional investment market, but in Germany and the US, it estimates coverage to be below 20%, while in Japan it is just over 20%. Nonetheless, the MSCI US index comprised over 5700 properties worth over US$350 billion as at end 2016. However, the NCREIF Property Index had a greater coverage of the US market, measuring over 7500 assets worth more than US$550 billion at the end of 2017.

Coverage of each market varies because private indices rely on investors choosing to contribute data and participate in the index and any associated benchmarking service. This is more likely to occur in larger, more mature markets where large-scale professional investors are present. Within each national market, the coverage of individual property types and locations will also vary. With institutional investors typically being the main contributors, the makeup of any index will reflect their investment preferences, which are likely to be higher value assets in prime locations within major cities – often office buildings and large retail malls.[7] Secondary locations and assets or more unusual properties and property types are less likely to be included. Yet the MSCI indices are not simply prime property indices since the contributing investors typically have some older properties and some inferior locations in their portfolios. In some instances, these may have been the prime assets of an earlier period that have not yet been sold and have suffered depreciation over time.

The MSCI indices have varying histories, ranging from a start date of December 1980 for the main UK Annual Index to one in the mid-2000s for several markets, including Belgium, Poland and South Korea. In most cases, the index histories are unfrozen, which means that the addition of new investors to the MSCI services can cause revisions to results for earlier years. However, in some markets, such as France and the UK, the indices have been frozen to preserve historically published figures, even if new contributors can supply additional older data. There are also varying frequencies, with some markets, such as the UK and Ireland, able to support quarterly as well as annual indices (and even a monthly index in the UK case).

MSCI has combined data from different countries to produce a global index for annual real estate investment returns since 2006. This is despite a number of technical challenges, including varying start dates for different national indices, varying coverage within each market and the different currencies that are involved. A discussion of these challenges is provided by Cullen (2010). At the end of 2016, the Global Index was based on 61,800 properties worth over US$1,470 billion from the 25 countries listed in Table 9.1, and provided a time series stretching back to the end of 2000 (MSCI, 2017). Meanwhile, for the seven Asian countries not included in the Global Index, MSCI monitor properties worth US$127 billion as at the end of 2016. Together with South Korea and Japan, this gives a pan-Asia measurement portfolio of around US$300 billion of real estate at end 2016.

Latin America has no MSCI indices. JLL (2016, p 42) notes that 'very low transparency' in regard to performance measurement and data on market fundamentals is 'continuing to pose the greatest challenges for most countries throughout Latin America and the Caribbean'. Brazil is an exception, with the General Index for the Commercial Real Estate Market (IGMI-C) having been created by the Brazilian Institute of Economics and launched in 2011.[8] This index measures income, capital and total returns using the same basic approach as the MSCI indices discussed above. At its launch, the IGMI-C is reported to have consisted of 190 individual properties, of which 50% were offices. In the third quarter of 2017, it was based on 529 properties with a quarterly index history dating back to the first quarter of 2000. The quarterly publications do not reveal how the composition has developed; the sample of buildings initially increased, but, since 2014, it has declined from 580 to 529.

Finally, in addition to Japan being included in the MSCI Global Index, the Association for Real Estate Securitization in Japan publishes the Japan Property Index using income-producing office, retail and residential assets situated in several core markets: Tokyo, Nagoya, Osaka and Fukuoka.[9] The main index began in 2002, based on data for 24 properties owned by one fund, but had grown to 3880 properties within 94 funds by the middle of 2017. The indices are based on methods used by NCREIF and they provide income, capital and total returns at monthly, quarterly and annual frequency, while data such as occupancy rates, rents and capitalisation rates are also reported for the locations listed above.

Issues with appraisal-based indices

There are a number of issues with appraisal-based indices of real estate performance, many of which relate to the use of appraisals as a substitute for transaction prices. The reasons why appraisal-based indices dominate real estate performance measurement were discussed at the start of this chapter and their creation enabled more thorough investment analysis of real estate markets to take place. However, such analysis must be undertaken with full awareness of the limitations of these series and their inputs.

The appraisal process was discussed in a previous chapter. The basis of appraisal for performance measurement purposes is market value. Market value is defined as an exchange price concept and is an attempt to identify the price of the asset at the date of appraisal in the absence of an actual sale. Although there is little dispute concerning the definition, there can be subtle differences in its interpretation by appraisers across countries. These differences stem from the variations in market circumstances and professional practices in different parts of the world. Some real estate markets are highly liquid and transparent, but others are illiquid and opaque, and this contributes to the ease or otherwise of estimating values in those places. Nonetheless, appraisal theory, practice and legal precedent suggest a preferred method of market valuation: comparison with transaction prices for other, similar properties where a transaction of the actual property has not occurred (see Chapter 10).

Appraisers search for evidence of transaction prices and that evidence may be sparse and imperfect. This means that appraisers must exercise judgement about the relationship of those price signals to the property in question. In doing so, appraisers may make errors in their estimate of market value. Given the quality of the available evidence and the difficulty of the task, such errors are unsurprising and do not necessarily imply a lack of competence. However, academic research has highlighted the potential for bias in the estimation of values with the result that appraisals might systematically lag and/or understate market price movements. Explanations for such bias are reviewed below and fall into rational, behavioural and institutional explanations, the latter encompassing the legal and client context in which appraisals are provided. Such issues are not confined to performance measurement appraisals, but the sub-sections below review the production, accuracy and veracity of appraisals in this particular setting.

Appraisal accuracy, variation and bias

The uncertainty surrounding appraisals is now firmly recognised in appraisal standards.[10] There has never been an expectation of complete accuracy but there is an expectation that appraisers will produce a solution and that it will be within certain parameters. These parameters have been discussed by courts in appraisal negligence cases (Crosby, 2000) and have been tested in studies where sale prices of assets have been compared with prior appraisals (accuracy) or where estimates of value by one appraiser have been compared with appraisals of the same property by another appraiser (variation). Most empirical studies have examined the commercial real estate markets of the UK, US and Australia. Crosby (2000) reviews studies for these markets undertaken in the 1990s. Since then, fewer studies have explored these markets, but work on appraisal accuracy has been done for other parts of Europe (see, for example, Hordijk, 2005) and for Africa (Adegoke, 2016).

The most recent US study by Cannon and Cole (2011) analysed over 7000 apartment, retail, office and industrial real estate investments that were sold from portfolios in the US NCREIF database over the period 1984–2010. The study measured both the percentage difference and absolute percentage difference between prices and preceding appraisals, controlling for market movements and capital expenditure between the sale and prior appraisal date. The average absolute percentage difference across the period was 12.5%, while the average percentage difference, where positive and negative differences can cancel each other out, indicated that prices were 3.9% higher than appraisals. However, the latter figure, in particular, hides the impact of market state and the authors reported that differences were more positive when markets were appreciating, while in 2008–2009 (a declining market), the differences were negative, with appraisals above sale prices. Thus, they concluded that appraised values were biased estimates of sale prices and the direction of that bias changes in up and down markets.

IPD, in conjunction first with Drivers Jonas (now part of Deloitte) and then the Royal Institution of Chartered Surveyors, carried out a series of similar studies for the UK, starting in the 1990s. This exercise was subsequently extended to France, Germany and the Netherlands and, recently, extended again by MSCI to 12 countries where it has a long index history (Reid, 2017). These countries are Australia, Canada, France, Germany, Italy, Japan, Netherlands, South Africa, Sweden, Switzerland, UK and the US. Tables 9.3 and 9.4 set out the average absolute percentage difference and the average percentage difference between prices and prior appraisals for those countries over the 17 years from 2000 to 2016. As in the case of Cannon and Cole (2011), market movements between the sale date and appraisal date are controlled for, but the averages are weighted so that differences for more valuable assets have more influence on the results. Another difference is that in Cannon and Cole (2011) the denominator in the calculation of percentage difference is the preceding appraisal whereas in the IPD and MSCI studies, it is the price.[11]

The shape exhibited by the average percentage difference over time in most countries is similar to that suggested in Cannon and Cole (2011). Nine of eleven countries exhibit increasing absolute variation in the period 2004–2007, but, during the global downturn in 2008, only the US, UK and Sweden had a negative average difference (with appraisals higher than prices). Investors in the other nine countries still sold assets at more than appraised values, on average. However, by 2009, Germany, Japan, the Netherlands, Canada and Australia all exhibited negative differences as well.

There are issues with these studies as a test of appraisal accuracy. One issue is that observed prices may be noisy signals of any true market price given the private and decentralised markets in which real estate transactions take place. Another issue is that the sample of assets that is transacted may not be a representative sample. Finally, there is little work on the role of appraisals in selecting assets for sale and whether appraisals and sale prices are truly independent of one another. It may be that an appraisal figure is instrumental in the decision to market and sell a particular asset and crucial to the price that can be accepted for that asset. For example, in normal circumstances, German open-ended funds are prohibited from selling assets at amounts more than a few percentage points below the prior appraisal.[12] However, investment committees may consider the relationship of price to prior appraisal as a factor even where no formal rules exist.

Despite this, these results have potentially important implications for appraisal-based indices. Errors will affect the reliability of appraisal-based indices as measures of market conditions and investment performance. Yet the impact of individual errors should be diversified at index level provided that the index is based on a large sample of assets and that

Table 9.3 Weighted average absolute difference between sale prices and preceding appraisals, by country

Country	*2000*	*2001*	*2002*	*2003*	*2004*	*2005*	*2006*	*2007*	*2008*	*2009*	*2010*	*2011*	*2012*	*2013*	*2014*	*2015*	*2016*
Australia	3.8	3.9	4.3	4.8	4.8	–	–	13.7	10.1	8.2	5.6	6.8	3.5	5.8	9.3	12.7	10.1
Canada	7.4	6.4	9.7	8.1	9.3	11.6	15.7	13.5	8.8	9.8	8.2	10.4	16.7	7.2	9.5	15.6	12.0
Denmark	–	16.1	12.3	11.5	17.5	22.2	22.5	16.6	14.7	–	–	–	6.0	20.1	17.4	10.5	17.6
France	6.6	7.8	6.6	5.4	11.5	10.2	14.5	12.9	9.9	7.8	11.1	10.5	9.6	9.2	9.3	12.6	11.1
Germany	12.2	9.2	7.2	11.6	5.1	6.1	14.7	15.1	14.8	6.1	10.6	9.5	9.2	7.6	8.9	9.9	13.2
Italy	–	–	–	–	–	–	9.3	–	17.5	12.5	11.4	7.3	10.0	5.7	9.3	8.6	8.6
Japan	–	–	–	–	–	22.3	8.1	12.9	7.3	10.1	8.6	8.2	12.0	11.6	10.9	14.0	12.8
Netherlands	10.2	8.3	9.0	7.9	8.3	8.6	11.6	12.5	5.6	9.3	4.8	4.8	7.5	9.5	5.8	7.0	10.2
South Africa	11.8	9.3	9.3	9.5	7.6	11.5	9.2	21.7	9.6	9.4	6.7	10.5	10.5	9.2	9.0	3.7	5.2
Sweden	18.5	9.6	10.1	8.0	10.0	10.4	21.6	15.8	13.7	16.7	9.0	11.4	7.1	10.8	10.8	13.0	12.4
Switzerland	–	–	–	10.3	9.1	8.5	8.2	9.5	9.1	13.6	11.3	10.7	12.2	7.5	7.3	19.2	–
UK	7.8	7.0	7.6	7.5	7.9	7.8	8.9	9.9	9.4	11.2	9.7	9.6	8.7	10.3	10.9	10.1	8.7
USA	5.1	8.6	7.7	6.3	9.6	11.6	10.8	10.3	8.6	14.9	10.8	9.5	8.7	11.1	8.6	8.8	6.2
Other	–	16.1	6.8	8.9	13.3	12.6	15.5	12.6	9.0	12.7	10.4	8.9	8.5	9.8	8.9	10.7	13.6
Global	8.6	7.2	7.6	7.3	8.4	9.2	11.5	12.0	10.1	11.1	9.5	9.4	9.0	9.5	9.4	10.4	9.1

Note: Reid (2017) analysed 13 of the largest national markets included in MSCI's Investment Property Databank Global Annual Property Index. In addition, results for another 11 countries, with fewer recorded transactions, are grouped together in the 'Other' category. This includes Austria, Belgium, the Czech Republic, Hungary, Ireland, New Zealand, Norway, Poland, Portugal, South Korea and Spain.

Source: Reid (2017).

Table 9.4 Weighted average difference between sale prices and preceding appraisals, by country

	2000	*2001*	*2002*	*2003*	*2004*	*2005*	*2006*	*2007*	*2008*	*2009*	*2010*	*2011*	*2012*	*2013*	*2014*	*2015*	*2016*
Australia	0.4	–0.2	0.0	1.9	1.3	–	–	11.8	3.5	–4.6	1.4	3.6	–0.3	3.2	7.4	11.9	5.5
Canada	–1.4	0.7	2.0	2.5	6.5	5.5	15.4	10.5	5.8	–0.2	1.6	6.3	14.4	3.4	–0.4	11.8	7.9
Denmark	–	14.4	8.7	6.6	13.6	19.7	18.5	13.5	11.5	–	–	–	2.3	–1.7	12.1	8.4	13.1
France	2.6	–0.1	1.2	2.5	8.8	8.6	12.9	10.4	3.5	0.9	5.6	8.5	5.9	5.1	3.7	8.9	6.9
Germany	3.6	1.2	–3.3	–4.8	–1.0	0.8	0.5	12.3	9.7	–2.9	4.4	7.2	3.3	3.4	4.3	6.5	4.8
Italy	–	–	–	–	–	–	6.1	–	16.2	3.9	2.8	2.8	1.9	–3.0	0.1	2.4	0.3
Japan	–	–	–	–	–	21.0	7.1	11.5	4.8	–8.5	–3.6	–2.1	–3.4	2.3	9.1	10.1	8.8
Netherlands	7.6	2.2	6.2	2.5	4.7	5.2	4.6	10.6	2.9	–5.2	2.0	1.4	–0.2	–6.0	–1.4	–1.4	3.5
South Africa	0.1	–3.0	0.3	1.9	–0.6	6.3	0.4	18.1	1.6	6.6	0.9	5.4	6.7	7.6	–0.7	1.3	1.0
Sweden	–8.7	4.8	5.9	4.5	7.3	7.5	21.3	10.8	–7.7	12.9	1.0	10.2	3.2	5.9	1.2	7.2	4.0
Switzerland	–	–	–	6.2	4.5	0.7	5.8	6.6	7.3	13.1	9.7	8.9	9.8	5.8	5.1	15.4	–
UK	3.8	3.4	5.1	5.5	6.0	5.8	6.6	2.9	–2.9	3.8	5.2	6.2	2.7	7.3	8.6	6.1	3.0
USA	–1.5	1.0	4.2	4.4	5.5	7.4	7.5	4.8	–4.3	–10.3	5.3	4.8	4.1	2.3	4.2	5.7	0.7
Other	–	4.4	4.9	6.5	10.3	9.3	11.0	7.9	3.6	–0.8	0.9	5.7	2.3	–0.1	–0.6	6.5	11.6
Global	0.9	2.2	3.6	3.9	5.4	6.4	7.6	7.6	0.0	–0.1	2.6	5.5	4.0	3.6	4.4	6.6	3.9

Note: Reid (2017) analysed 13 of the largest national markets included in MSCI's Investment Property Databank Global Annual Property Index. In addition, results for another 11 countries, with fewer recorded transactions, are grouped together in the 'Other' category. This includes Austria, Belgium, the Czech Republic, Hungary, Ireland, New Zealand, Norway, Poland, Portugal, South Korea and Spain.

Source: Reid (2017).

any inaccuracy in appraisals is random rather than systematic. In this respect, it is of some concern that the average percentage difference is not zero and that the size and direction of this difference varies with market state. Possible explanations for these observed biases are explored in the next section.

Anchoring, smoothing and lagging

A large literature has emerged over the past three decades on the reliability of appraisal-based indices. While some of this literature refers to the appraisal accuracy debate, other research is founded on the statistical attributes of appraisal-based indices and their perceived smoothness relative to other indicators or practical experience of market conditions. It has been argued that movements in appraisal-based indices both understate and lag movements in prices.[13] If true, this creates problems when such indices are used to measure the volatility of real estate investment returns and the covariance of such returns with those of other asset classes. It also makes multi-asset portfolio managers more conservative towards real estate as an asset class owing to the uncertainty around the veracity of the performance measures (Fisher and Geltner, 2000).

Geltner (1993), among others, identifies two sets of factors that may explain the smoothness and lagging associated with appraisal-based indices. One set of factors surrounds the production of individual appraisals and how appraisers behave. The other set concerns how appraisals are then aggregated to form an index. Taking the production of individual appraisals first, it is argued that appraisers anchor on past appraisals or past price evidence rather than just using contemporaneous information to estimate values. In a context of uncertainty, where there is only a limited pool of recent price information, Quan and Quigley (1991) argue that such behaviour is rational as the appraiser seeks to minimise the amount of error in relation to each individual appraisal. They represent this behaviour using the following mathematical expression:

$$V_t = \alpha V^*_t + (1 - \alpha) V_{t-1} \tag{9.4}$$

where V equals the appraised value as at time t or $t - 1$, V^* equals the contemporary indicator of market value and α is a parameter that captures the degree of weight that the appraiser puts on contemporary information.

Although this may be rational behaviour in the production of an individual appraisal, it does cause problems when appraisals are used to form aggregate performance measures. A random error that is significant in the context of a single asset is not important at index level provided there is a large sample of other buildings across which the effects of individual errors can be reduced. In contrast, a small systematic bias may be less significant for an individual appraisal, but impossible to eradicate from an index because that same error occurs in other appraisals as well. Yet, while this is a widely accepted argument, some studies dispute whether this behaviour at a disaggregate level necessarily produces smoothing at an aggregate level.[14]

The Quan and Quigley model has been used and extended in subsequent research that has sought to reverse the effects of appraiser behaviour on aggregate level indices, a process that has been called unsmoothing or de-smoothing. A key issue is how to parametrise α accurately. Geltner *et al.* (2003) review early studies in this area, many of which assumed a value for α that would facilitate removal of all autocorrelation from the adjusted series. This is consistent with ideas on how prices behave in markets with full informational efficiency.

Later studies relax this assumption. They also note that results from research in the US and UK show the standard deviation of return rates from an adjusted series to be anything from 1.5–5 times higher than that exhibited by return rates from the original index. Such findings are contingent on time period and methods used, as well as the frequency of the appraisal-based index: those using monthly or quarterly appraisals appear to exhibit more smoothing than those based on annual appraisals.

One issue is that the degree of smoothing may depend on market conditions and the amount of transaction evidence available to appraisers.[15] Geltner *et al.* (2003) suggest that anchoring on past appraisals is greater in less liquid markets (where liquidity is defined as the amount of transaction activity), but the accuracy studies show that the gap between prices and appraisals increases in booms where transaction activity is often greatest. This suggests that the speed and scale of price changes might have an influence as well. In a boom, new information might not be incorporated into appraisals quickly enough for them to keep pace with rapidly rising prices. This would mean that, when prices start to fall, appraisals 'catch up' with price levels, with overvaluation only occurring if a downturn is particularly steep and prolonged. In a downturn, any propensity to anchor on prior appraisals might then increase owing to the lack of transactions taking place. This is consistent with the patterns shown in Tables 9.3 and 9.4.

However, there is surprisingly little empirical work on the existence and nature of smoothing that refers directly to individual appraisal data. One exception is provided by Clayton *et al.* (2001), who studied 202 individual appraisals for a sample of 33 real estate investments and tested how much weight was placed on previous appraisals versus price evidence for comparable assets. Another exception is Bond *et al.* (2012), who examined a larger sample of 2394 individual asset returns from the IPD UK Monthly Index. The findings of Bond *et al.* (2012), in particular, suggest that the smoothing in individual appraisals is not as great as has been implied from analysis of index-level data which they suggest could reflect that previous papers had too simple a model of the return generating process for real estate assets.

Another explanation for this may lie in how appraisals are aggregated to create indices. For instance, US research identified a 'stale appraisal' problem in relation to the NCREIF NPI.[16] Here, a quarterly index was developed based on a sample of properties where some were valued less frequently than quarterly. To retain these assets in the sample, values for the intervening quarters were populated with the figure from the last appraisal. This practice reduces the information content of the series, as movements in value are dampened by the group of assets whose values do not move. In the case of MSCI indices, this is why the reporting frequencies vary across countries, as these are tied to the frequency with which appraisals are conducted. Yet, even if all properties were revalued each period, some temporal aggregation can arise because it is not logistically practical to conduct all appraisals on a single date such as a calendar year-end; instead, they will be conducted over the days and weeks leading up to that date.[17]

Aside from rational concerns to minimise inaccuracy, appraisers may be influenced by behavioural and institutional factors. Diaz and Wolverton (1998) conduct experimental research in which results suggested a tendency by appraisers to anchor on their own previous assessments of value. Clayton *et al.* (2001) found that anchoring was greater when a property was appraised previously by the same appraiser and suggest that rotation of appraisers might be necessary to reduce this. More generally, appraisers may be influenced by criticisms, usually voiced in the aftermath of a property crash, of overvaluation. For example, in the UK, appraisers have been sued or threatened with court proceedings by banks for appraisals produced in previous boom markets. As undervaluation has rarely been contested, this is a further reason why appraisers might be expected to err towards under- rather than overvaluation (Crosby, 2000).

Client influence on appraisals

Appraisal accuracy can be also compromised by undue client or other stakeholder influence on the outcome. Principal–agent issues arise when the objectives of the principal and their agent are not aligned or when there are incentives for both principal and agent to act unprofessionally. Baum *et al.* (2000) identified opportunities for UK investors to compromise the objectivity of appraisals, such as in draft valuation meetings. For the client, motives to do this include a performance bonus culture, which prevails in the asset management business, links between portfolio values and banking covenants, or the impact of performance on company share prices or unit prices of open-ended funds. Appraisals can also be used by managers to support particular asset management decisions, such as disposals from the portfolio. For the appraiser, repeat business could be jeopardised by a reluctance to move appraisals in line with client motivations.

The client influence literature includes studies that relate directly to performance measurement and indices (for example, Levy and Schuck, 2005; Crosby *et al.*, 2018). Many appraisal-based indices are constructed from assets in very different types of ownership; for example, pension funds, insurance companies, real estate investment trusts (REITs), open-ended and closed-end funds. These different owner groups can have different motivations. For example, in many countries, property company and REIT appraisals are also used for financial statements and can have a direct impact on the share price. Thus, the firm may have an interest in keeping appraisals as high as possible to underpin the share price. However, other types of owner may want appraisals to fall. For example, open-ended funds may want appraisals to fall by as much as possible in a downturn to prevent a run on funds where unit-holders think that the appraisals overstate true values. Fund managers may also have reasons to influence appraisals. For example, a new fund manager may want a low starting value and then subsequently influence appraisals upwards to maximise performance (Baum *et al.*, 2000).

Crosby *et al.* (2018) examined individual property returns from the IPD UK Quarterly Index to see how values changed during the global financial crisis and to identify whether type of owner had an impact on that performance. After controlling for property type and other attributes, they found differences between the returns of properties held by open-ended and unit-linked funds and the returns of other types of owner such as REITs. However, such effects were temporary and did not persist throughout the downturn. Hence, although clients may influence appraisals in a particular direction in the short-term, there are limits to the process because the appraisal from one period becomes the starting point for calculating returns in the next period. Continued pressure in a given direction would eventually make performance and values unrealistic, even allowing for the inherent uncertainty around appraisals.

Basis of valuation interpretation

Over the past 50 years, there has been substantial movement towards consistent valuations across the world and definitions have been standardised through the work of the International Valuation Standards Council. However, how valuers interpret these standards and definitions is more difficult to standardise. For example, market value is an exchange price concept,

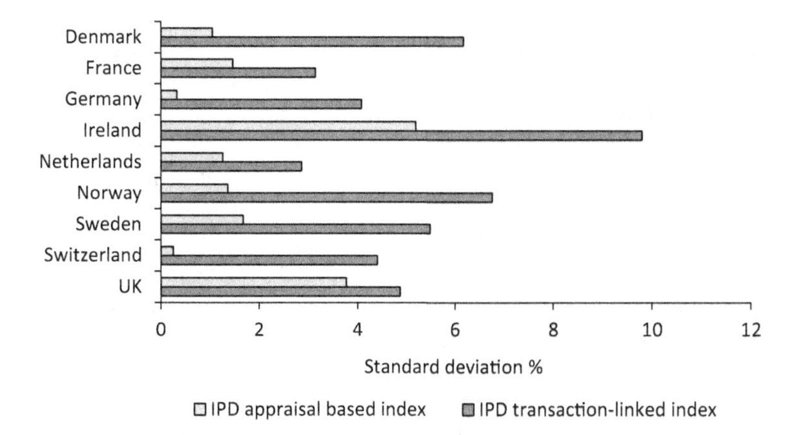

Figure 9.1 Standard deviations of quarterly capital return rates from different types of index (2002–2012)

Source: Adapted from MSCI (2013).

but appraisers in some parts of the world may seek to identify the 'best' price that could be achieved while others may attempt to identify an average price or, alternatively, a 'sustainable' price. Information on such interpretations is sparse and mainly confined to anecdotes from international investors. However, comparisons between appraisal-based and transaction price indices, where the latter are available, illustrate very different relationships in different countries and this, coupled with other evidence (for example, Crosby *et al.*, 2011), sustains such doubts. This reduces confidence when comparing returns for different national markets owing to uncertainty about the consistency of appraisals and whether they track market trends in similar ways.

To illustrate this further, transaction-linked indices produced by MSCI for a range of European markets can be compared with the corresponding appraisal-based indices for those countries.[18] Figure 9.1 compares the standard deviation in quarterly capital return rates produced by each type of index for several countries over the period 2002–2012. This comparison raises some interesting questions. Clearly, some real estate markets over this period were more volatile than others, such as Ireland. Of more concern here are discrepancies between the two types of index. At one extreme, the UK has similar figures for volatility regardless of index type, but, at the other extreme, Germany and Switzerland each has a transaction index volatility only just below the UK, but an appraisal index volatility below 0.5%. It is differences like this that have raised questions as to how an ostensibly similar basis of appraisal is interpreted in different countries and whether appraisal-based indices can identify differences in the performance characteristics of different international markets.

These differences in interpretation are becoming increasingly problematic as the ownership of real estate in major cities such as London, Frankfurt, Sydney and New York is changing and moving from national to international investors. To maintain coverage, properties in foreign ownership should be included in the index sample for these locations. At present, many national and sub-national indices are based on assets owned by domestic investors only. Index providers such as MSCI could include assets owned by foreign investors in their indices if interpretations of value were harmonised. At present, any amalgamation of international and domestically owned assets could distort the indices.

Summary and conclusions

This chapter has introduced and examined appraisal-based indices of real estate performance. In most cases, the performance of assets in other investment markets can be measured by reference to transactions of those assets.[19] In the case of real estate, the absence of a centralised market and a heterogeneous set of assets, coupled with a relatively low level of transaction activity, make the use of transaction-based indices difficult. This explains why appraisal-based indices still dominate real estate investment performance measurement, despite the conceptual superiority of transaction-based measures. Appraisal-based indices enable larger samples to be used, leading to possibilities of greater disaggregation than currently possible from transaction indices. Therefore, it is likely that they will continue to be the main basis for measuring real estate investment performance for the foreseeable future, despite their limitations.

The first appraisal-based indices emerged in the mature commercial real estate investment markets of the US and the UK. Such indices have now spread around the increasingly global real estate investment market. The development of indices has helped national real estate markets to become more transparent which, in turn, encourages the growth of foreign and domestic investment. This chapter has identified the different types of indices and the different measures produced by the index providers, which include income, capital and total returns, as well as various other measures useful in analysing real estate markets. Other types of appraisal index include those which measure movements in a location and are not based on actual properties.

Issues arise in the construction of appraisal-based indices. Some of these relate to coverage of the market, which varies widely between and within countries, but they also relate to problems that arise because the indices are based on appraisals, rather than actual transactions. Performance measurement appraisals are universally based on market value, which is an exchange price concept. The theory and practice of appraisal reinforces the use of transactions on similar real estate assets as the main evidence base for undertaking appraisals. However, transactions take time to complete and there is a substantial literature on appraisers' reliance on past information, which includes past valuations, versus contemporaneous market signals. This is thought to lead to some element of smoothing of real estate appraisals as compared to prices, with appraisals understating the peaks and troughs of market cycles. This has implications for comparing the performance and risk of real estate against other asset classes.

The usefulness of the performance measures generated from the appraisal-based indices has been improved by research into the limitations of these indices. Most of this research relates to the use of appraisals and their impact on the measures. Research into transaction-based indices has been important for identifying differences between their outcomes and those of appraisal-based indices at the more aggregated level. An aspect that has been identified for further research is the interpretation of the basis of appraisal used for appraisal-based indices in different countries. Although they all use the basis of market value, existing research coupled with anecdotal comment suggests that appraisers in different countries interpret it differently. This makes international comparisons based on appraisal-based indices and subsequent cross-border investment decisions more difficult. There is, therefore, a need to continue research into the impacts of appraisal methods and the appraisal process on the outputs from appraisal-based indices, with particular emphasis on less well-researched markets outside of the US and UK where the use of performance measurement indices is less established.

Notes

1 Commercial for the purposes of this chapter is used as a generic title for all non-residential real estate assets and includes retail, office and industrial properties.
2 Examples were the Morgan Grenfell Laurie/Corporate Intelligence Group Property Performance Index and The Property Index, neither of which is now published.
3 Numerical examples showing the difference between money- and time-weighted rates of return can be found in many real estate textbooks. For example, see Geltner *et al.* (2007) or Hoesli and MacGregor (2000).
4 Note that any capital expenditure during the period is assumed to occur at the start of the period.
5 In contrast, maintenance expenditure is deducted from rent to produce net operating income.
6 Market rent is the rent that could be agreed in a new rental transaction at that point in time and may differ from the actual rent being paid under the terms of an existing lease contract.
7 For critical comment on the role of benchmarking in reinforcing these preferences, see Henneberry and Roberts (2008).
8 Details are available at FGV/IBRE, [Real Estate Indicators] (site in Portuguese), http://portalibre.fgv.br/main.jsp?lumChannelId=402881 8B33F047B80133F5334C941336 (accessed 14 August 2018).
9 See Association for Real Estate Securitization, ARES Japan Property Index, http://index.ares.or.jp/en (accessed 14 August 2018).
10 See International Valuation Standards Council (2013) and Royal Institution of Chartered Surveyors (2017).
11 In both cases, the numerator is the difference between achieved sale price and preceding valuation.
12 See Freshfields Bruckhaus Deringer (2011) or Pylypchuk (2008).
13 See Geltner *et al.* (2003) for a review of the early literature in this area.
14 See Lai and Wang (1998), Edelstein and Quan (2006) and Cheng *et al.* (2011).
15 This has been recognised in some papers that attempt to adapt de-smoothing techniques as a result. For examples, see Chaplin (1997) and Lizieri *et al.* (2012).
16 See Geltner (1993), Fisher *et al.* (1994) or Geltner and Goetzmann (2000).
17 Note that transaction-based indices face similar problems when combining observations of prices across a period to create a single index value for the period in question (Geltner, 1993).
18 See Devaney (2014) for a more in-depth comparison of these series.
19 However, some asset classes such as private equity and infrastructure face similar issues in creating indices to those raised here.

References

Adegoke, O. J. (2016) Effects of valuation variance and inaccuracy on Nigerian commercial property market, *Journal of Property Investment and Finance*, 34(3), 276–92.

Bacon, C. R. (2008) *Practical portfolio performance measurement and attribution*, 2nd ed., John Wiley & Sons, Chichester.

Baum, A., Crosby, N., Gallimore, P., Gray, A. and McAllister, P. (2000) *The influence of valuers and valuations on the workings on the commercial property market: report for the Education Trusts of IPF*, RICS and Jones Lang LaSalle, London.

Bokhari, S. and Geltner, D. (2016) Characteristics of depreciation in commercial and multifamily property: an investment perspective, *Real Estate Economics*, DOI: 10.1111/1540-6229.12156.

Bond, S. A., Hwang, S. and Marcato, G. (2012) Commercial real estate returns: an anatomy of smoothing in asset and index returns, *Real Estate Economics*, 40(4), 637–61.

Cannon, S. E. and Cole, R. A. (2011) How accurate are commercial real estate appraisals? Evidence from 25 Years of NCREIF sales data, *Journal of Portfolio Management*, 35(5), 68–88.

CFA Institute (2010) *Global Investment Performance Standards (GIPS®)*, CFA Institute, Charlottesville, VA.

Chaplin, R. (1997) Unsmoothing valuation-based indices using multiple regimes, *Journal of Property Research*, 14(3), 189–210.

Cheng, P., Lin, Z. and Liu, Y. (2011) Heterogeneous information and appraisal smoothing, *Journal of Real Estate Research*, 33(4), 443–69.

Clayton, J., Geltner, D. and Hamilton, S. W. (2001) Smoothing in commercial property valuations: evidence from individual appraisals, *Real Estate Economics*, 29(3), 337–60.

Crosby, N. (1988) An analysis of property market indices with emphasis on shop rent change, *Land Development Studies*, 5(2), 145–77.

Crosby, N. (2000) Valuation accuracy, variation and bias in the context of standards and expectations, *Journal of Property Investment and Finance*, 18(2), 130–61.

Crosby, N., Devaney, S. and Law, V. (2011) Benchmarking and valuation issues in measuring depreciation for European office markets, *Journal of European Real Estate Research*, 4(1), 7–28.

Crosby, N., Devaney, S. and Nanda, A. (2016) Which factors drive rental depreciation rates for office and industrial properties?, *Journal of Real Estate Research*, 38(3), 359–92.

Crosby, N., Devaney, S., Lizieri, C. and McAllister, P. (2018) Can institutional investors bias real estate portfolio appraisals? Evidence from the market downturn, *Journal of Business Ethics*, 147(3), 651–67.

Cullen, I. (2010) Constructing a global real estate investment index, pp 100–13 in Newell, G. and Sieracki, K. (eds.), *Global trends in real estate finance,* Blackwell Publishing, Chichester.

Devaney, S. (2014) Measuring European property investment performance: comparing different approaches, *Journal of European Real Estate Research*, 7(1), 112–32.

Diaz, J. and Wolverton, M. L. (1998) A longitudinal examination of the appraisal smoothing hypothesis, *Real Estate Economics*, 26(2), 349–58.

Diehl, J. B. (1993) The Russell-NCREIF property indices: institutional real estate performance benchmarks, *Journal of Real Estate Literature*, 1(1), 95–103.

Edelstein, R. H. and Quan, D. (2006) How does appraisal smoothing bias real estate returns measurement?, *Journal of Real Estate Finance and Economics*, 32(1), 41–60.

Fisher, J. D. (2005) US commercial real estate indices: the NCREIF property index, pp 359–67 in *Real estate indicators and financial stability*, Vol. 21, Bank for International Settlements.

Fisher, J. D. and Geltner, D. (2000) De-lagging the NCREIF Index: transaction prices and reverse-engineering, *Real Estate Finance*, 17(1), 7–22.

Fisher, J. D., Geltner, D. M. and Webb, R. B. (1994) Value indices of commercial real estate: a comparison of index construction methods, *Journal of Real Estate Finance and Economics*, 9(2), 137–64.

Freshfields Bruckhaus Deringer (2011) *Possible sales in the German real estate market: survey on open-ended real estate funds,* Freshfields Bruckhaus Deringer LLP, Hamburg.

Geltner, D. (1993) Estimating market values from appraised values without assuming an efficient market, *Journal of Real Estate Research*, 8(3), 325–45.

Geltner, D. and Goetzmann, W. (2000) Two decades of commercial property returns: a repeated-measures regression-based version of the NCREIF index, *Journal of Real Estate Finance and Economics*, 21(1), 5–21.

Geltner, D., MacGregor, B. and Schwann, G. (2003) Appraisal smoothing and price discovery in real estate markets, *Urban Studies*, 40(5–6), 1047–64.

Geltner, D. M., Miller, N. G., Clayton, J. and Eichholtz, P. (2007) *Commercial real estate analysis and investments*, 2nd ed., South-Western Cengage Learning, Mason, OH.

Henneberry, J. and Roberts, C. (2008) Calculated inequality? portfolio benchmarking and regional office property investment in the UK, *Urban Studies*, 45(5–6), 1217–41.

Hoesli, M. and MacGregor, B. D. (2000) *Property investment: principles and practice of portfolio management*, Longman, Harlow.

Hordijk, A. (2005) Valuation accuracy in real estate indices: the case of the ROZ/IPD Netherlands Property Index compared to the IPD UK Index and the NCREIF USA Index, IVSC Information Paper, March 2005.

International Valuation Standards Council (2013) *Valuation uncertainty*, Technical Information Paper No 4, International Valuation Standards Council, London.

JLL (2016) *Taking real estate transparency to the next level: Global Real Estate Transparency Index, 2016*. Jones Lang LaSalle, London.

Lai, T. and Wang, K. (1998) Appraisal smoothing: the other side of the story, *Real Estate Economics*, 26(3), 511–35.

Levy, D. and Schuck, E. (2005) The influence of clients on valuations: the clients' perspective, *Journal of Property Investment and Finance*, 23(2), 182–201.

Lizieri, C., Satchell, S. and Wongwachara, W. (2012) Unsmoothing real estate returns: a regime-switching approach, *Real Estate Economics*, 40(4), 772–804.

MSCI (2013) *IPD Quarterly Property Price Indicators, December 2012*, MSCI, London.

MSCI (2017) *IPD Global Annual Property Index*. MSCI. www.msci.com/real-estate-fact-sheet-search (accessed 14 August 2018).

MSCI (2018) *MSCI global methodology standards for real estate investment*. MSCI, Chicago, IL. www.msci.com/real-estate (accessed 14 August 2018).

Morrell, G. D. (1991) Property performance analysis and performance indices: a review, *Journal of Property Research*, 8(1), 29–57.

National Council of Real Estate Investment Fiduciaries (2016) *NCREIF data, index and products guide 2016–17*, NCREIF, Chicago, IL. www.ncreif.org/public_files/NCREIF_Data_and_Products_Guide.pdf (accessed 14 August 2018).

Pylypchuk, I. (2008) *German open-ended funds: past, present and future*, EMEA Viewpoint, Autumn, CB Richard Ellis, London.

Quan, D. C. and Quigley, J. M. (1991) Price formation and the appraisal function in real estate markets, *Journal of Real Estate Finance and Economics*, 4(2), 127–46.

Reid, B. (2017) *Private real estate: valuation and sale price comparison*, MSCI, Chicago, IL. www.msci.com/www/research-paper/private-real-estate-valuations/0183964217 (accessed 14 August 2018).

Royal Institution of Chartered Surveyors (2017) *RICS valuation – global standards 2017*, RICS, London.

Scott, P. (1996) *The property masters*, E&FN Spon, London.

Teuben, B., Shah, S. and Hariharan, G. G. (2017) *Real estate market size 2016*, MSCI, London. www.msci.com/www/research-paper/real-estate-market-size-2016/0183961169 (accessed 14 August 2018).

Young, M. S. (2005), Making sense of the NCREIF Property Index: a new formulation revisited, *Journal of Real Estate Portfolio Management*, 11(3), 211–23.

Young, M. S., Geltner, D. M., McIntosh, W. and Poutasse, D. M. (1995) Defining commercial property income and appreciation returns for comparability to stock market-based measures, *Real Estate Finance*, 12(2), 19–30.

10 Transaction-based indices

Kwong Wing Chau, Siu Kei Wong, Jiancong Liang, William McCluskey and Ciara Cunningham

Introduction[1]

A transaction-based price index uses actual property transactions to calculate the general change in prices over time. This entails collection of data on the transacted properties. Such data typically come from the government if a central deed or title registration system exists. Alternatively, the data can come from property agencies that undertake transactions or banks which supply mortgage loans. In most cases, only transactions in the secondhand market will be used since first-hand transaction prices are usually very noisy due to the use of pre-sale arrangements. In addition, there are often different financial arrangements, terms of sales, discounts and rebates for different properties that are not properly recorded. Similar to an initial public offering of newly listed company shares, first-hand sale prices offered by a developer rarely coincide with the market clearing price. The developer's offer prices may sometimes be set, intentionally or unintentionally, below market price, resulting in non-price allocation (for example, by first come first served or random ballot). An active and transparent market is necessary for the construction of transaction-based property price indices that can reflect general changes in the price levels of properties.

Before discussing the statistical methods for index construction, it is useful to explain why they have to be used. As set out in Chapter 9, a key issue is heterogeneity – no two properties are exactly identical. Even if they share the same physical and property rights attributes, they always differ in location. This is not necessarily a problem if the same basket of goods is sold in every period, as in a consumer price index. However, properties are traded much less frequently. The property basket changes each time because the properties sold in one period differ from those in a previous period. For example, if the sample of sales in one period is disproportionately skewed towards low-quality properties, the price change observed could be underestimated. Statistical methods are needed to produce a price index that is free from any quality variations. Such an index is also known as a constant-quality price index. The key issue of constructing a transaction-based property price index is to keep quality constant (as measured by the observed attributes of the property) across time.

In this chapter, four different statistical methods that can be used to construct a transaction-based index are examined: (1) mean and median; (2) hedonic price; (2) repeat sales; and (4) a hybrid model. Each method deals with the problem of quality heterogeneity differently and has its own advantages and disadvantages. Case studies from Hong Kong and Northern Ireland are used for illustration.

Mean/median and modified mean/median

Mean/median is the simplest method, which only requires data on sale prices and dates. It takes the mean or median of the sale prices observed in each time period as the price index value. If data on property size (such as floor area) are also available, sale prices are preferably normalised first (such as price per square foot) to control for any difference in size. To control for other important quality attributes (such as property type and location), it is common to divide the property market into submarkets so as to reduce heterogeneity and to generate a mean or median for each submarket, provided that the sample is sufficiently large.[2] Otherwise, quality variations are generally ignored, on the assumption that they have little impact on the mean or median prices and that the quality distribution of the transacted properties is similar over time. Therefore, among the four statistical methods, the mean or median price index is deemed the most vulnerable to the problem of quality heterogeneity.

On the other hand, a mean or median price has an advantage over the other methods. Since the mean or median is expressed in monetary terms, it is possible to tell not just the percentage change in price levels over time but also a snapshot of the 'average' price at a particular point in time. For the latter, the use of mean or median matters. If the distribution of prices is positively skewed because low- to middle-value properties are sold more frequently than high-value properties, the mean price will be higher than half of the sale prices, a distortion that is usually not wanted. In such a case, it is better to use the median, which is less affected by outliers (a small number of extremely low or high values). Nevertheless, the mean is still commonly used because it is easy to understand.

Several studies have compared mean/median methods with other methods (Case and Shiller, 1987, Mark and Goldberg, 1984, Crone and Voith, 1992, Gatzlaff and Ling, 1994, Wang and Zorn, 1997). Although a sufficiently large number of transactions might iron out quality differences in mean/median price indices, they still do not control the quality sufficiently well, as transacted properties are not homogenous (even within a submarket). To improve the accuracy of the index, attempts have been made to adjust transaction prices with information on quality difference before calculating the mean/median. We refer to the resulting index as a quality-adjusted mean/median price index (see section Quality-adjusted: A Hong Kong example).

Mean/median – A Northern Ireland example

Figure 10.1 is a comparison of the mean and median prices with the hedonic-based Northern Ireland Residential Property Price Index (NIRPPI; see section – A Northern Ireland example) as a benchmark, over the period first quarter 2005 to fourth quarter 2015.

In this figure, a gap could be seen between the mean and median prices. This suggests that, as expected, the distribution of prices is not symmetric but is skewed to the right, probably due to more sales in the low to middle price range but many fewer sales of high-value properties. If the hedonic-based NIRPPI is taken as the constant-quality benchmark, the median index appears to underestimate the growth during the boom before 2007, while the mean index tends to underestimate the decline during the bust after 2007.

Quality-adjusted mean: a Hong Kong example

One of the sets of indices that adopt the quality-adjusted mean is the official Hong Kong Property Price Indices, which are based on prices per floor area adjusted by appraised

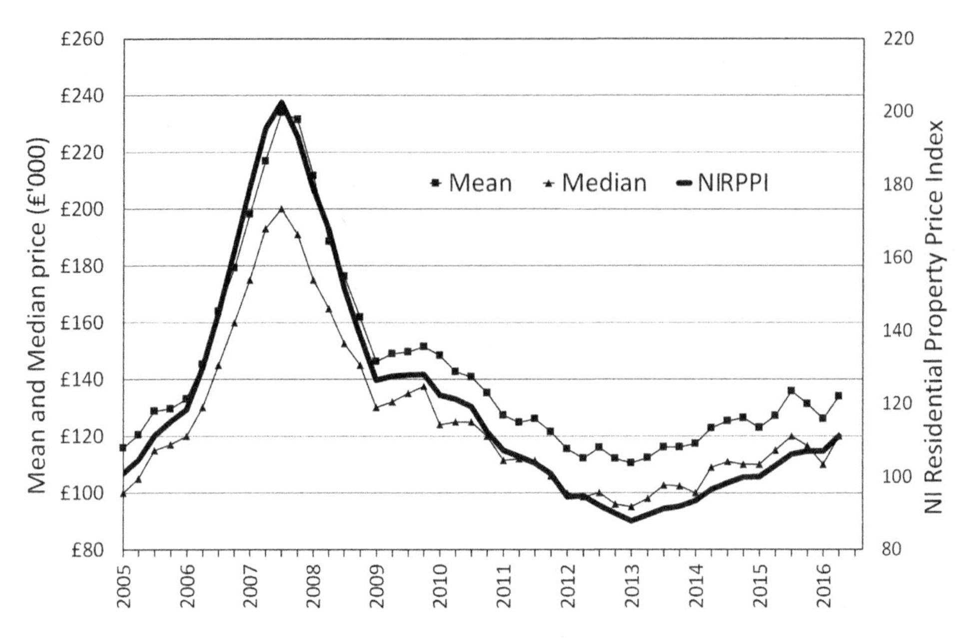

Figure 10.1 Mean and median prices versus hedonic price index, Northern Ireland Residential Property Price Index (NIRPPI) in Northern Ireland

rental values for tax purposes (rateable values). In Hong Kong, the Rating and Valuation Department assesses the rateable value,[3] which is similar to open-market rent of newly let property, of all properties in Hong Kong for the purposes of assessment of the rates and government rent payable by the property owners. Hedonic price models are used to estimate the initial rateable values, which will then be verified and modified manually if necessary to arrive at the final estimates. Since higher-quality properties will have a higher rateable value per saleable floor areas, they can be used as an aggregate measure of property quality; that is, the rateable values per floor area can be considered to be a cross-sectional quality index. Transaction prices of heterogeneous properties can be adjusted to the prices of similar qualities by dividing the observed transaction price per saleable floor area by its own rateable value. The mean value of the rateable value-adjusted price per saleable floor areas is then taken as the quality-adjusted property price index.[4] Because of its wide coverage (both residential and non-residential sectors by location, size and quality) and long history, the RVD's quality-adjusted mean indices are still regarded as the primary source of property price indices in Hong Kong (Chau *et al*, 2005b).

Figure 10.2 shows a comparison of the mean price with the quality-adjusted mean price index for small flats (40–70 m^2) and large flats (100–160 m^2). Two observations are made. For both types of flats, there is a noticeable difference between movements of mean price and the quality-adjusted mean price index. If the quality-adjusted mean price index is taken as a constant-quality benchmark, the faster growth in mean prices means that the quality distribution of transacted properties is not stable. In fact, more high-quality properties were sold during the boom market. The use of a mean price index could have overestimated the growth in property prices during boom periods. The other observation is that mean prices are more

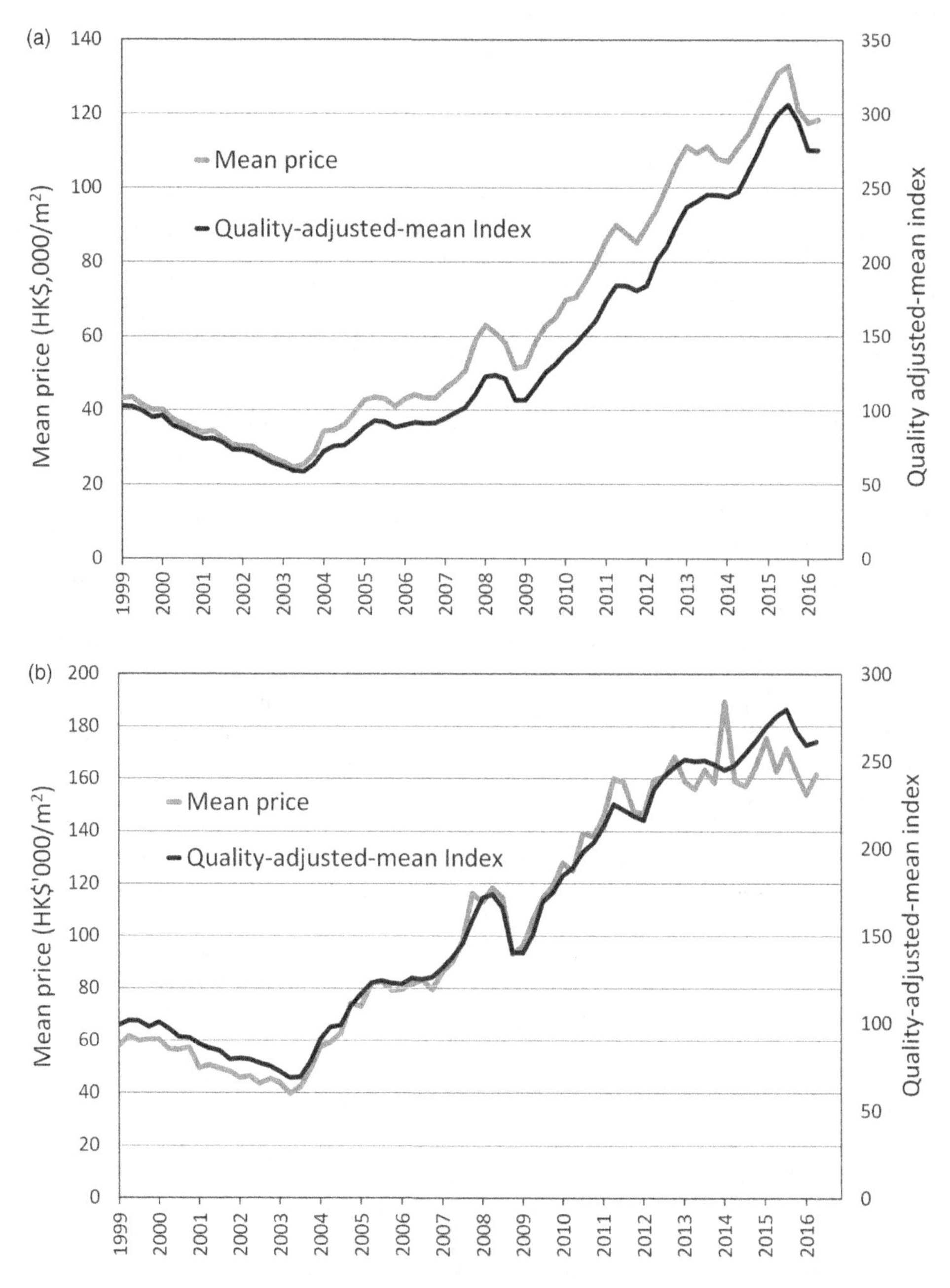

Figure 10.2 Mean price versus rateable value-adjusted mean price indices in Hong Kong; (a) small flats (40–70 m^2); (b) large flats (100–160 m^2)

volatile than the quality-adjusted mean price index, especially for the large flats. This could be caused by fewer transactions and the greater quality variation in the large flats submarket.

Hedonic price index

The origin of hedonic-based price indices for heterogeneous goods can be traced back to the constant-quality price indices for automobiles and computers (Adelman and Griliches, 1961; Court, 1939). Later on, the same approach became popular for the construction of real estate price indices. However, the theoretical foundation was not laid until Rosen (1974). The popularity of hedonic price indices has increased significantly in recent years as a result of increased computation capacity and data availability.

The hedonic price method provides a more general framework than the mean or median method to address the issue of quality heterogeneity. It assumes that heterogeneous goods are priced for their observed attributes. A property, for example, can be viewed as a bundle of attributes such as property size, age, view, build class, house type and nearby amenities, which can be separately priced. The hedonic model controls quality constant by regressing transaction prices on a set of observable property attributes. A series of price indices is then computed either from the coefficients of time dummies in a single regression that covers several time periods (for example, 10 years), or from the values of a standard property estimated from the coefficients of the hedonic model in each period (for example, annually).

The starting point for the modelling is the assumption that the price P_{it} of property i in period t, is a function of its J number of attributes, $X_{1it},\ldots,X_{Jit}$. The attributes can be divided into categorical variables (such as building quality and location) and numerical variables (such as the size of the property and the number of bedrooms). Numerical variables could be divided into two types, continuous and discrete. For example, age and floor area of the property are continuous numbers, but the number of bedrooms, number of bathrooms and floor level of the property are discrete numbers. While numerical variables can be easily quantified (such as size) or counted (such as number of rooms), categorical variables have first to be converted to a numerical value called a 'dummy' variable, which is used to indicate the absence or presence of an attribute and which takes the values of 0 or 1. For example, a dummy variable SV can be created to represent presence of a sea view such that when the there is a sea view, SV is set to 1; when there is no sea view, SV is set to 0, which is the benchmark or base. The estimated coefficient of SV in the hedonic price model shows how much more expensive a property is compared with a property with exactly the same set of attributes but no sea view (base). This is also known as the implicit or shadow price of sea view, since it represents how much more a buyer has paid for the sea view alone (compared with the base – no sea view), controlling for the influence of other attributes (or keeping other attributes constant). It is 'implicit' in the sense that there was no actual transaction of 'sea view' alone. In general, the coefficient of an attribute can be interpreted as its own implicit price.

The set of implicit prices from the hedonic model estimated for each period can be used to price a standard property[5] in different periods to obtain the change in price levels. The standard property can defined based on property transacted at the base or current period; that is, a hypothetical property with the mean attributes of properties transacted in base or current period. The former is analogous to a constant-weight (La Laspeyres) index while the latter is analogous to a current weight (Passche) index. The two indices produce different results; each has its own justifications. The choice between constant and current weights is the known as the index number problem. Fisher (1922) proposed to take the geometric mean of the two, which is known as the Fisher Ideal Index. Although Diewert (1998), has shown that the Fisher Ideal Index has many desirable properties, Balk (1995) argues that it is not necessarily the best index and that constant and current-weight official price indices can be justified in some cases.

Another hedonic method is to pool together data from different periods and to include time dummy variables in one single hedonic price model. For example, in a sample covering three periods (t_0, t_1 and t_2), two dummy variables, D1 and D2, should be created: when a transaction takes place in t_1, D1 is set to 1; when it takes place in t_2, D2 is set to 1; when it takes place in t_0 (base period), both D1 and D2 are set to 0. As with the interpretation of the coefficients of other attributes, the coefficient of a time dummy represents how much more a buyer has paid in time t_1 compared with what s/he could have had to pay if s/he were to have purchased *exactly the same property* (identical attributes, thus constant quality) in the base period (t_0). The coefficients of the time dummies are therefore price indices with quality controlled by a hedonic price model.[6]

More formally, each property i sold will differ in price due to differences in its characteristics X_{jit}. Any price differences not attributable to the observed differences in characteristics will be captured by an error term, ε_{it}. A general way to express the relationship between the price and characteristics is:

$$P_{it} = f(X_{1it}, \ldots, X_{Jit}, \varepsilon_{it}) \tag{10.1}$$

There are many ways to specify the function $f(.)$. It is possible to start with a highly general functional form and then use a statistical method to choose a special case for final estimation.[7] As the distribution of sale prices is usually positively skewed, one special case that appears in many applications is the semi-log functional form[8] with time dummies:

$$P_{it} = \sum_{j=1}^{J} \beta_j X_{jit} + \sum_{t=1}^{T} \alpha_t D_{it} + \varepsilon_{it} \tag{10.2}$$

where P_{it} denotes the log transaction price of property i at time t ($i = 1,\ldots,n$; $t = 1,\ldots T$), β_j denotes the implicit price for the jth property characteristic X_{jit} ($j = 1,\ldots,J$), and ε_{it} is a random error with zero mean and constant variance. In Equation (10.2), D_{it} is an additional set of time dummy variables introduced to capture general changes in price over time. It is set to 1 if the ith property is sold at time t and to 0 if otherwise. Its coefficient, α_t, represents the logarithm of the hedonic price index at time t. Equation (10.2) can be estimated by the ordinary least squares method.

As discussed above, rather than using time dummies, another approach is to estimate Equation (10.2) for each period, without time dummies, to obtain the implicit prices to construct the price index. This is known as the characteristics method.

Technical and practical issues

Despite the popularity of hedonic real estate price indices, there are a number of problems with this approach. A comprehensive review of advantages and disadvantages of different types of hedonic housing price index can be found in Hill (2013). Many problems arise from the assumption that the hedonic price model is correctly specified or close to the unobservable true underlying relationship between price and attributes. Since the correct functional form is unknown, in practice, the most commonly used form of the hedonic model is the semi-log model, where the log of price is regressed on a linear combination of the hedonic attributes. Time dummies are often used (Palmquist, 1980). However, this may not be the correct form and thus may lead to biased results. In theory, the unknown underlying relationship can be approximated by flexible functional forms such as the Box–Cox function (the semi-log model is a special case of the general Box–Cox form). However, this will dramatically increase computational time and the interpretation of coefficients is not nearly as straightforward.

Another serious model specification issue is that some important price influencing attributes are not included in the model due to lack of data. This is known as the missing variable problem. These attributes include, for example, neighbourhood and location variables (Case *et al.*, 1991), which are expected to affect property prices. For example, we know that location attributes such as proximity to shopping centres, parks, airports, public transportations and club facilities may affect housing prices, but if there is no information on these attributes, they cannot be included in the hedonic model to control for their effects. Greenlees (1982) shows that a hedonic price index with a large amount of descriptive and locational information could improve the accuracy of price indices.

In practice, data on many known price-influencing attributes are not available. A practical solution is to build a hedonic price index for a relatively homogeneous subset of properties, such as properties in the same housing estate. A small number of attributes (the independent variables) is sufficient to specify the hedonic model since they have similar location and quality of construction. The estimated price indices for each housing estate are then aggregated together to form a market-wide index (such as the Centa-City Index, CCI, in Hong Kong described in in the section A Hong Kong example: Centa-City Index). This method is particularly useful when the markets are segmented (Wilhelmsson, 2009).

Another issue related to model specification is that the coefficients of the attributes may vary over time and space. Subdividing the transaction by location can partly solve the problem of spatial variation if the implicit prices within a small geographical location can be assumed to be stable. The characteristics method can deal with temporal varying implicit prices better than the time dummy variable method since implicit prices need not be assumed to be constant over time.

The time dummy variable method also suffers from the problem of index revision since the coefficients of all time dummies have to be re-estimated with new information. The repeat-sales price index also suffers from this problem. Revision is a major issue if the index is used for derivative trading. One practical solution is to estimate the hedonic price model with data from two adjacent periods to obtain the changes in price level over the previous period (Gatzlaff and Ling, 1994; Knight *et al.*, 1995). This method is also known as the adjacent period method (Triplett, 2004), which is based on the assumption that the implicit prices will not change over a short time interval. The adjacent period method is essentially the same as 'chaining' pairs of price indices of two adjacent periods to a form an index series. In between the adjacent period method and the single equation time dummy regression is the moving window regression (Song and Wilhelmsson, 2010), which uses data from a few rolling periods (window) to estimate the coefficients.

Studies have shown that properties are spatially autocorrelated (Can and Megbolugbe, 1997; Pace and Gilley, 1997; Pace *et al.*, 1998; Kelejian and Prucha; 1998, Dubin *et al.* 1999; Kim *et al.*, 2003; Sun *et al.*, 2005; Wong *et al.*, 2013), which means that property prices are affected by nearby transaction prices. One of the reasons for spatial autocorrelation is missing variables that have localised effects, which induces spatial clustering of unexplained price variations that appear to be correlated with each other. In this sense, including spatial information such as coordinates of the properties to model the spatial autocorrelation can solve some of the missing variable problems.

In summary, the key issue of the hedonic price index originates from the difficulties in specifying the correct model, which include specification of the functional relationship between property price and the hedonic attributes and the choice of these attributes (the independent variables). A related issue the choice of means to segment the data, temporally and spatially, so that simpler models can be specified and estimated with results aggregated to produce a single index. In general, more detailed model specification should be closer to the reality and, thus, provide a more accurate index. However, the costs are an increase in computational complexity and more time and resources needed for data collection. In many cases, certain information is simply not available. However, given the increasing trend of market transparency and technological progress, models that appeared to be too computational and information demanding today may have a practical use in the future.

A Northern Ireland example

The NIRPPI is referenced to January to March (Q1) 2005; that is, the value at Q1 2005 is set to 100. The proposed hedonic modelling approach uses a semi-log model. The approach ensures that, although the actual properties sold may be skewed in favour of one property type or a certain property characteristic, the value of a 'standardised' house can still be calculated, using the sample averages of characteristics in a period to define it. The hedonic price methodology is used to produce the NIRPPI and, specifically, a characteristics method of hedonic modelling is applied.

The characteristics approach to compiling a hedonic price index is defined by Eurostat within the *Handbook on Residential Property Price Indices* (Eurostat, 2013). It involves separate regressions being run for each time period with the index constructed by making use of the predicted prices based on the regression coefficients.

The coefficients of the regression function give the implicit price, in natural logarithm terms, of the characteristics of the property. The implicit price can be estimated for specific values of the characteristics of a property. To 'construct' and price the 'standardised' residential property, and to allow for the varying mix of characteristics between one time period and another, the average values of each characteristic of residential properties sold in the previous year are used in the equation. For quantitative characteristics, the mean value from all sales in the previous year is input and, for qualitative characteristics, the proportions of that characteristic from all sales in the previous year are used.

The average values for quantitative variables and percentage proportions can be thought of as a standard 'representative' set of weights. The index numbers calculated represent the movement in price paid for a 'standardised' residential property possessing the same characteristics as those sold in the previous year. The index numbers themselves are computed by comparing the weighted (that is, mix-adjusted) prices in each current quarter with the weighted average price in the base period. The base period of the NIRPPI has been chosen as January to March 2005.

The hedonic modelling process can be summarised as follows:

- From the sales and property characteristics database, remove any sales that are: (1) sales at a discounted price (such as right to buy); (2) sales with a sale price less than £20,000; and (3) sales with floor size outside identified limits.

- To obtain the average value of each characteristic of properties sold in the previous year (that is, standardised weights, X_j), calculate the proportions of the qualitative characteristics and the means of the quantitative characteristics in the appropriate year (Table 10.1).
- Transform sale price to its natural log form and use ordinary least squares regression to estimate the coefficients β_j for the j explanatory characteristics, in all time periods from January 2005. Regression equations are calculated separately for houses (h) and apartments (a) using this equation:

$$ln\,P_i^t = \beta_0^t + \sum_{j=1}^{J} \beta_j^t X_{ji}^t + \varepsilon_i^t \qquad (10.3)$$

- Calculate the price paid for a 'standardised' house/apartment in period t as:

$$P_h^t = \exp\left(\frac{\beta_0^t + \sum \beta_j^t X_j^t}{\beta_0^0 + \sum \beta_j^0 X_j^0}\right) \quad P_a^t = \exp\left(\frac{\beta_0^t + \sum \beta_j^t X_j^t}{\beta_0^0 + \sum \beta_j^0 X_j^0}\right) \qquad (10.4)$$

where P_h^t = Price paid for a 'standardised' house in period t and P_a^t = Price paid for a 'standardised' apartment in period t.

- Calculate an overall average price paid for a 'standardised' property in Northern Ireland in period t as the weighted average of the price paid for a 'standardised' house, h, and the price paid for a 'standardised' apartment, a.

$$P^t = \exp\left(\frac{1}{S_h^t + S_a^t}\left(S_h^t ln\left(p_h^t\right) + S_a^t ln\left(p_a^t\right)\right)\right) \qquad (10.5)[9]$$

P^t = Price paid for a 'standardised' property in period t.
S_h^t = Number of house sales in period t.
S_a^t = Number of apartment sales in period t.
P_h^t = Price paid for a 'standardised' house in period t.
P_a^t = Price paid for a 'standardised' apartment in period t.

- Produce a weighted (Laspeyre's type) index (Ix) for the current quarter, calculating the ratio between price in the current period and the base period:

$$Ix = \frac{P^t}{P^0} \qquad (10.6)$$

The index is an annual chain-linked Laspeyre's type index. Chain-linking involves 'joining together two indices that overlap in one period by rescaling one of them to make its value equal to that of the other in the same period, thus combining them into single time series'.[10] An annual chain-linked index is preferred to a fixed-base index as it takes better account of changes in the mix of properties being sold over time. The graphs of individual property indices in NIRPPI by property type are shown in Figure 10.3.

The development of the NIRPPI was seen as an important tool in monitoring changes in residential property prices. While several index-based methodologies were investigated

Table 10.1 Variable weights

Characteristic variable	*Average value from sales in previous calendar year – used as weights*
Habitable space	120.5 m^2
Privately built	83%
Publicly built	17%
Wealthy achievers*	21%
Urban prosperity*	5%
Comfortably off*	41%
Moderate means*	21%
Hard-pressed*	11%

*Geodemographic segmentation of the area in which the property is located.

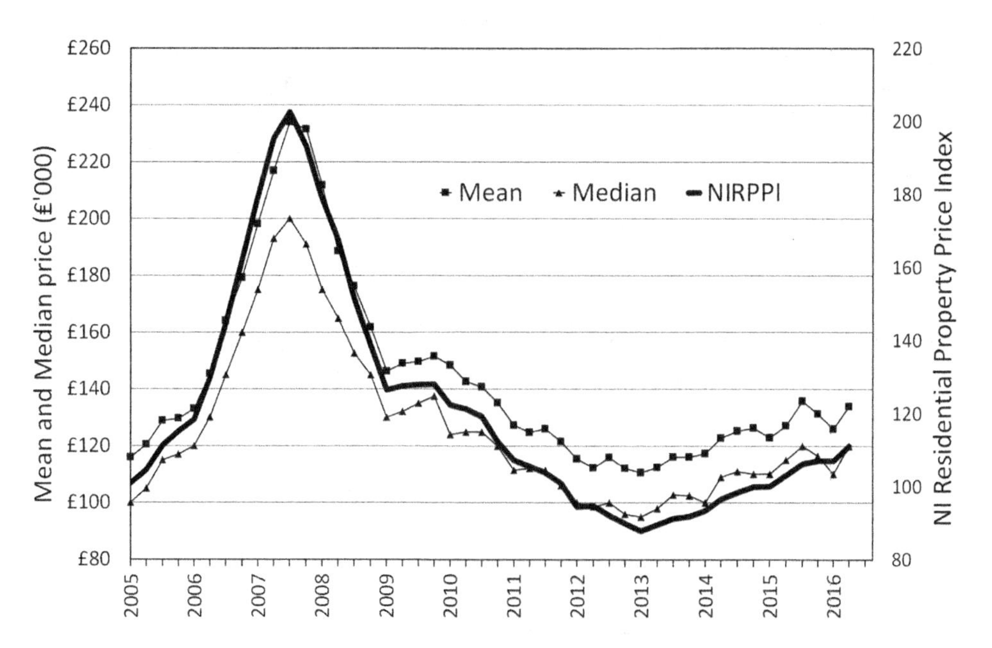

Figure 10.3 Quarterly individual property indices in the Northern Ireland Residential Property Price Index (NIRPPI), 2005–2015

the decision was taken to develop a characteristics based approach using a semi-log regression model.

A Hong Kong example: Centa-City Index

The CCI, which was developed by Centaline Property Agency Limited in Hong Kong, is a hedonic transaction-based residential price index. It is a monthly index using secondhand market transactions registered with the Hong Kong Land Registry.[11]

Hedonic price models for each of the major large private housing estates (constituent estates) are estimated to derive the total market value of the each constituent estate, which are aggregated into the market-wide housing price indices using the following formula:

$$CCI_i = \frac{TMV_i}{TMV_{i-1}} \cdot CCI_{i-1} \tag{10.7}$$

where CCI_i is the CCI in the i_{th} month and TMV_i is the total market value of the constituent estates in the i_{th} month. The criteria for choice of the constituent estates are:

- it has a high transaction value;
- it has a large number of transactions;
- it has been in the market for at least 12 months after occupancy; and
- it is representative of the region.

This approach is feasible as there are abundant transactions of in each of the constituent estates and the properties are relatively homogeneous within each constituent estate, so that only a small number of attributes are needed to define each hedonic price model.

Figure 10.4 shows the CCI in different categories. CCI (Large Units), CCI (Small/Medium Units) and CCI Mass are the Centa-City Indices, respectively, for large units, small/medium units and mass estates. As only transactions of housing units on estate type developments are used, strictly speaking, the CCI index represents price movements of properties in major housing estates in Hong Kong.

Repeat-sales price index

The repeat-sales model was established by Bailey *et al.* (1963). As its name implies, the model controls quality by measuring the price change of a property with repeated sales over time. Intuitively, this model makes use of the fact that the quality of the same property does

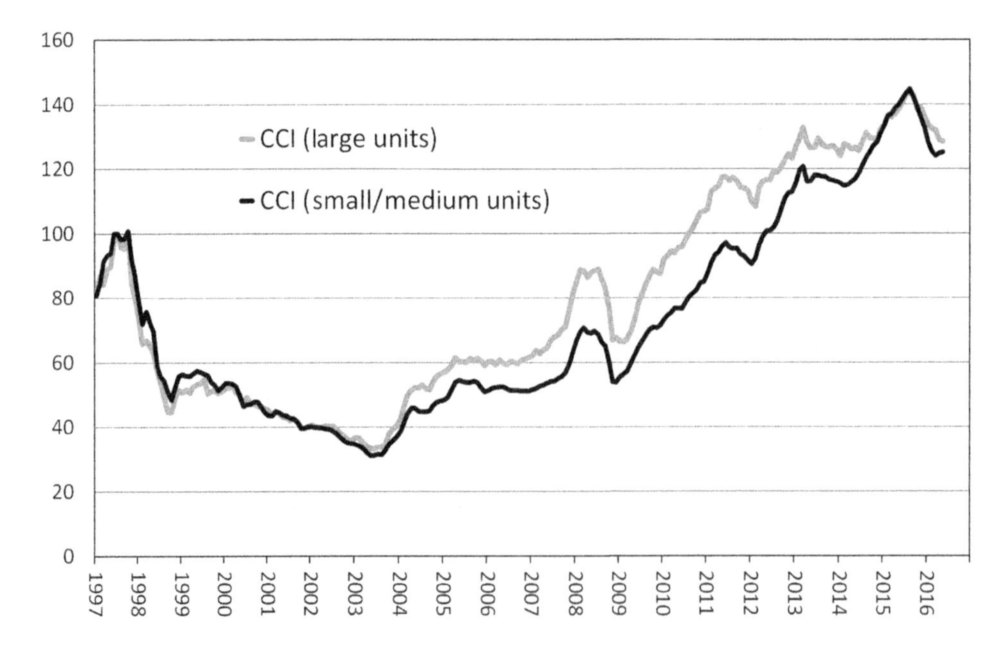

Figure 10.4 Centa-City Index (CCI) by categories (1997–2016)

not change much over time, so that the property attributes need not be specified. Technically speaking, the repeat-sales model is the $(t_2 - t_1)^{th}$ difference of the hedonic pricing equation for property i (Equation 10.8) under the assumption that all property attributes cancel out each other for each j (Equation 10.9):

$$lnP_{it_2} - lnP_{it_1} = \sum_{j=1}^{J} \beta_j \left(X_{jit_2} - X_{jit_1}\right) + \sum_{t=1}^{T} \alpha_t \left(D_{it_2} - D_{it_1}\right) + (\varepsilon_{it_2} - \varepsilon_{it_1}) \tag{10.8}$$

$$lnP_{it_2} - lnP_{it_1} = \sum_{t=1}^{T} \alpha_t D_{i,\tau} + \varepsilon_{i\tau} \tag{10.9}$$

where the subscript t_1 and t_2 denotes the first sale and the second sale of property i, and $D_{i,\tau}$ and $\varepsilon_{i\tau}$ denote $D_{it_2} - D_{it_1}$ and $\varepsilon_{it_2} - \varepsilon_{it_1}$, respectively. The time coefficient α_t in the following repeat-sales model is estimated using repeat-sales pairs in each subregion:

$$\ln \frac{P_{i,t_2}}{P_{i,t_1}} = \sum_{t=1}^{T} \alpha_t D_{i,\tau} + \ln \varepsilon_i \tag{10.10}$$

where the dependent variable is the natural logarithm of the ratio of the second to first sales prices of each repeat-sales pair. The independent variable ($D_{i,T}$) is a series of time indicators which equal –1 (when first sale took place), +1 (when second sale took place) or 0 (any other time). These time indicators take 'month' as the unit of measurement so as to construct a monthly price index. The time coefficient α_t, which determines the index value, is estimated using regression analysis techniques. The resultant index is found by converting the time coefficients to index values. All indices are scaled to the have the same value of 100 at a specific time period, which is chosen as the base period.

The repeat-sales model controls quality by measuring the price change of a property with repeated sales over time. They have converted the problem of combining price relatives of repeat sales to a regression problem so that standard techniques of regression analysis could be used to estimate the index. This method does not require information on the price influencing attributes of the transacted properties, which alleviate problems of model specification of the hedonic price indices such as the missing variable and choice of functional forms. This, however, relies on the assumption of constant quality for the same property

Technical and practical issues

The problems of the repeat-sales method mainly come from two sources. First, the assumption of constant quality may not hold. Second, this method only uses a subsample of all the transactions, which means that the estimation is not efficient (it does not fully use the available data) and the subsample used for estimation may not be representative of the entire data set, so there may be sample selection bias (Case *et al.*, 1991; Clapp and Giaccotto, 1992; Gatzlaff and Haurin, 1997). In addition to these issues, the repeat-sale index is also subjected to revision – when new information arrives, the entire model needs to be re-estimated with newly added data (Clapp and Giaccotto, 1999; Clapham *et al.*, 2006).

Age is the attribute that must have changed over time for the same property. Ignoring the age effect would lead to underestimation of the growth rate of the index, since the effects of physical deterioration and functional obsolescence are not properly controlled. The age effect and time effect (the pure change in the price level over time) cannot be separately estimated in a repeat-sales model if the age effect on price is assumed to be linear (Chau, *et al.*, 2005a). Palmquist (1980) proposes the use of an independent estimation of age effects from the hedonic regression model, which is then incorporated into the repeat-sales model. This method can be more elegantly incorporate into the hybrid model developed later (see section A hybrid model). Chau *et al.* (2005a) suggest that a linear-age effect is unrealistic. Dropping this assumption and incorporating a flexible-age effect in the repeat-sales model allows simultaneous estimation of age and time effect, but at the expense of computational complexity. A practical solution proposed by Chau (2006) is to use a 10-year rolling window of repeat-sales pairs (see section A Hong Kong example).

Case and Shiller (1987) and Case and Shiller (1988) propose the use of a three-step regression to solve the problem of possible change in attributes of the same property over time (for example due to renovation, remodelling, neighbourhood and amenities). Intuitively, this method assumes that a one-period return implied by repeat-sales pairs over longer holding periods are less reliable (larger deviation from the mean) and thus less weight is given in the regression model to repeat-sales pairs with longer holding periods. Graddy *et al.* (2012) have proposed a modification that takes account of possible serial correlation in the deviations from the mean one-period returns.

Clapp and Giaccotto (1992) found that properties more frequently transacted are of lower quality. This may cause bias in the repeat sales index if prices of the lower-quality properties grow at a different rate compared with other properties, as shown in Hill *et al.* (2009). Gatzlaff and Haurin (1997), Wallace and Meese (1997) and Steele and Goy (1997) also show evidence of sample selection bias.

The index revision problem is unavoidable for the repeat-sales method. This is less a problem if the revision is not biased. However, Clapp and Giaccotto (1992) found that index revision is downward biased. They also found that, when very-short-term transactions (with holding periods of less than two years) are excluded, the bias disappeared. Although index revision cannot eliminated, Simon (2009) has proposed a theoretical model of predicting the magnitude of revision, which is potentially useful for pricing repeat-sales index-based property derivatives.

There are also a number of studies that use alternative estimation procedures to improve the repeat-sales index. They include, for example, use of a semiparametric estimator to relax the normality assumption (Hodgson *et al.*, 2006) and robust estimators to reduce the influence of extreme observations (Bourassa *et al.*, 2013).

A Hong Kong example

One of the applications of the repeat sales index is the University of Hong Kong All Residential Price Index (HKU-ARPI).[12] HKU-ARPI is a monthly real estate price index that tracks the changes in the general price level of residential properties in Hong Kong over time. The index is constructed using actual secondhand market transactions of private residential properties registered with the Hong Kong Special Administrative Region Government (the Land Registry).

Hypothetical transactions, shown in Table 10.2, can be used to illustrate the basic idea of the repeat-sales index. Property A was transacted in 2000 and 2001 at prices of HKD$10 million and HKD$11 million, respectively. This pair of transactions implies that its price has increased by 10% during 2000–2001. Similarly, transactions of property B imply that its price has increased by 15% during 2001–2002. The price index derived from

Table 10.2 Illustration of the repeat-sale index

	2000	*2001*	*2002*
Property A	\$10 million	\$11 million	
Property B		\$20 million	\$23 million
Property C	\$10 million		\$12.5 million
Index (AB)	100	110	127
Growth (AB)		10%	15%
Index (C)	100		125
Growth (C)		12%	12%
Growth (ABC)		11%	13%
Index (ABC)	100	111	126

the transaction prices of property A and property B can, therefore, be determined. However, during the same period, there are other repeat-sales pairs that may imply a different change in price levels. For example, property C implies that the cumulative growth rate during 2000–2002 was 25% as opposed to a cumulative growth of 26.5%, implied by property A and B. The index, being a market-wide indicator represents a 'compromise' with growth rates somewhere between those implied by properties A, B and C. The repeat-sales model uses regression analysis to find the set of changes in price levels that best fit the changes in price levels implied by all the repeat-sales pairs.

The University of Hong Kong Real Estate Index Series in period *t* is estimated using repeat sales in the immediate past 10 years only. It covers the entire Hong Kong Special Administrative Region and is a weighted average of sub-indices for three sub-regions in Hong Kong, namely the University of Hong Kong's Hong Kong Island Residential Price Index (HKU-HRPI), the Kong Kowloon Residential Price Index (HKU-KRPI), and the New Territories Residential Price Index (HKU-NRPI). The weights reflect the market value of the total stock of residential units in each of the three sub-regions. The indices are constant-quality indices that are designed to capture only changes in price levels over time.

The residential price indices for the three sub-regional areas are aggregated to form the market-wide residential price index using the following weighted average formula:

$$HKU-ARPI_t = \left(w_H \frac{HKU-HRPI_t}{HKU-HRPI_{t0}} + w_K \frac{HKU-KRPI_t}{HKU-KRPI_{t0}} + w_N \frac{HKU-NRPI_t}{HKU-NRPI_{t0}} \right) \times HKU-ARPI_{t0} \tag{10.11}$$

where w_H, w_K and w_N represent the weightings for Hong Kong Island, Kowloon and the New Territories, respectively. To ensure that the HKU-ARPI tracks capital returns of a fully diversified portfolio of residential properties in Hong Kong, the weights should reflect the relative size of the market value of the stock of residential properties in each subregion. We use total rateable values of completed residential units in each subregion as proxies for market value weight. Table 10.3 shows the sub-regional index weights based on rateable values in 2015. In future, the weights will be updated when new rateable values become available, usually on an annual basis. The weights will be updated in the first month of the year that follows the year of publication of the new rateable values. Since the weights only change slowly from year to year, the updates should have little immediate effect on the index.

Table 10.3 Percentage rateable value of all completed residential units in 2015

	Weights (%)
Hong Kong Island	35
Kowloon	26
New Territories	39
Total	100

Source: Annual Summary, Rating and Valuation Department, Hong Kong Special Administrative Region Government.

The University of Hong Kong Real Estate Index Series (HKU-REIS) is estimated using the repeat-sales pair within the last 10 years. The sampling window will roll forward as new transaction data arrives each month. The underlying assumption is that changes in attributes and their effects on price (including age) is negligible within a 10-year holding period. The index values published earlier will not be updated, regardless of any revision, as the average magnitude of revision within a two-year period is less than half a percentage point. The new index value at the latest period will be chain linked to the published index based on the percentage in the last period. For example, given information up to time T, the published index values are $\{\overline{P}_1,\ldots,\overline{P}_T\}$. At T+1, the estimated index values are $\{P_1,\ldots,P_T,P_{T+1}\}$. With all previously published index values retained, the new index value is calculated by:

$$\overline{P}_{T+1} = \frac{P_{T+1}}{P_T} \times \overline{P}_T \tag{10.12}$$

Similarly to Clapp and Giaccotto (1999), flips (repeat-sales pair with short holding periods) are a major source of biased index revision, which can be largely resolved by dropping flips (holding periods less than two years). However, the definition of flips is an empirical question. Experiments with the Hong Kong data suggest that dropping transactions with holding periods of less than four months can substantially reduce index revision and that the remaining revision is not biased systematically.

The HKU-REIS method illustrates practical solutions to well-known problems of repeat-sales indices. These solutions largely take advantage of the abundant repeat-sales transactions in Hong Kong, which allows some observations to be dropped (only included are repeat-sales pairs with holding periods of more than four months in the immediate past 10 years). Obviously, the method may not necessarily applicable to other less liquid markets.

The historical trend of the HKU-ARPI and Hong Kong University residential price regional sub-indices for three subregions are shown in Figure 10.5:

Hybrid model

The hybrid model is basically a method which incorporates repeat-sales information into the hedonic pricing model. It was first proposed by Case and Quigley (1991), who estimated a system of equations of single sales and repeat-sales simultaneously. The price appreciation over time could be estimated by combing data from single transactions where one sale is observed, multiple transactions where the physical and locational characteristics of properties are unchanged, and multiple transactions where the physical or locational characteristics have been modified between sale dates by rehabilitation or other forms of investment. The

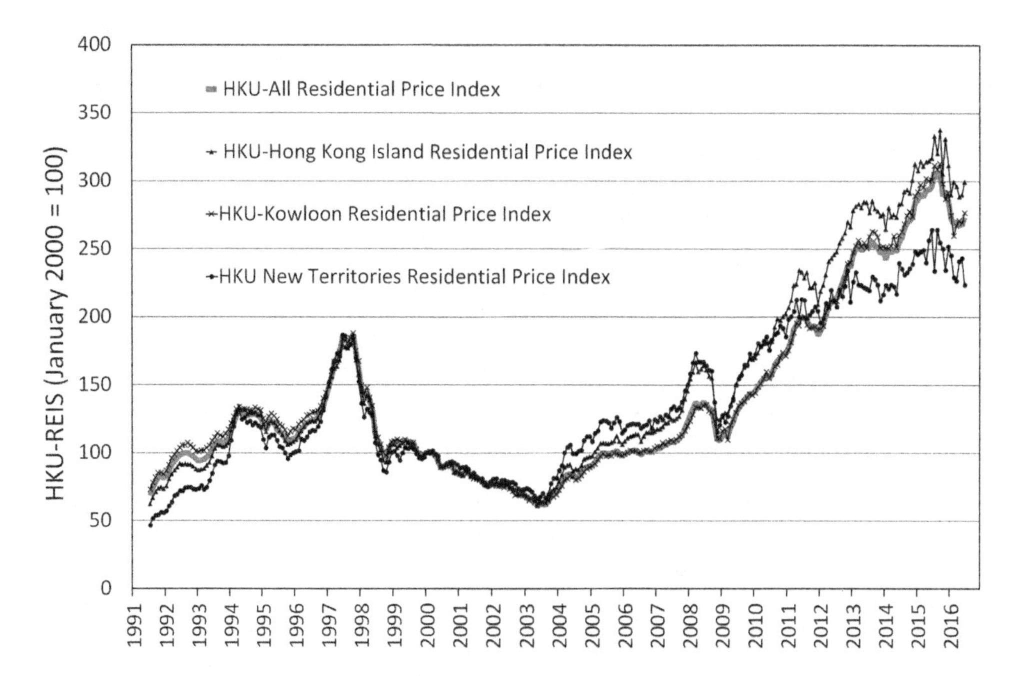

Figure 10.5 Historical trend of the Hong Kong University (HKU) indices
HKU-REIS: University of Hong Kong Real Estate Index Series

hybrid model has been improved by incorporating some error structures explicitly (Quigley, 1995; Knight *et al.*, 1995; Hill *et al.*, 1997; Englund *et al.*, 1998).

Quigley (1995) presented an explicit model for combining samples of single sales and repeat sales, which is based on an explicit error structure, incorporating a random walk in housing prices. It is also based on robust generalised least squares methods to improve the efficiency of estimation. Knight *et al.* (1995) introduced a method that combined repeat-sales observations with single sales, while permitting characteristic prices from hedonic regressions to vary over time. They provided a test for inter-period parameter stability with location and repeat-sales information in the database, which produces intertemporal error correlations that can be exploited by the seemingly unrelated regression technique. Hill *et al.* (1997) jointly estimated conventional hedonic and repeat-sales models using all the data that are available, capturing depreciation (in the hedonic model) within the systems of equation. Their method can improve the precision of the estimation by smaller standard errors and narrower interval estimates for the resulting price indices.

Englund *et al.* (1998) proposed a method to analyse housing price dynamics by exploiting extensive descriptive and financial information on every house sale in a certain period. The method extends and synthesises several techniques including hedonic and repeat-sales methods. It also distinguishes between the effects of observable and unobservable aspects of quality and between the effects of depreciation and vintage upon asset prices. The results suggest that unusually short turnover periods between sales of any house are associated with atypical price movements, reflecting distressed sales or uninformed initial offer prices.

Goetzmann and Peng (2006) have developed a model to analyse the bias in transaction-based price indices, in which the ratio of sellers' reservation prices to the market value affects trading volume and biases of observed transaction prices. They proposed an econometric procedure to mitigate the bias and constructed a reserve-conditional unbiased index, which substantially differs from traditional repeat-sale indices. Bourassa *et al.* (2006) presented the sale price appraisal ratio (SPAR) method for constructing house price indices, which uses ratios of transaction prices and previous appraised values to produce semiannual price indices. They observed that the SPAR method produces an index similar to the constant-quality repeat-sales index. Shi *et al.* (2009) applied the SPAR method to develop monthly SPAR house price indices. It suggested that the monthly SPAR index is possible with a large sample but difficult to apply for medium and small samples. In addition, the correlation of index returns between SPAR and the repeat-sales index is high at the quarterly level but low at the monthly level, which might result from noise in price changes.

De Vries *et al.* (2009) compared the SPAR method with the repeat-sales method and hedonic method. This showed that sample selection bias is most likely to be smaller for the SPAR index than a repeat-sales index as the latter excludes houses that have been sold only once. Maury (2009) has applied the spatiotemporal hedonic approach to the analysis of office transaction prices and found that spatial and temporal dependence effects are strongly present in submarkets. Additionally, a hybrid model is proposed incorporating both spatio-temporal dependences and temporal heterogeneity, which is different to the usual hedonic price index. Mason and Pryce (2011) developed a method for correcting transaction bias in house price indices where information exists at neighbourhood level on factors that influence the probability of sale. The results show that sample selection bias is present and not constant. Consequently, the unadjusted index tended to overestimate the true rate of price appreciation. They suggested that the approach could be adapted to correct for transaction bias in repeat-sale indices and indices based on subsamples of the traded stock.

McMillen (2012) suggested using a matching pairs as an alternative to the hedonic and repeat-sales approaches. A matching pair are pairs of transactions of properties with similar attributes. The matching pair approach preserves larger sample sizes than the repeat-sales estimator but requiring less pre-imposed structure than the hedonic approach. This approach is useful for markets with scarce repeat pairs and has been applied by Deng *et al.* (2012) to construct a quality-adjusted price index for private residential market in Singapore.

In contrast to a focus on different data samples or more information about sales and property characteristics in the early literature, studies on hybrid models mainly concentrate on the improvement of models (such as bias correction and matching estimator). Although the hybrid model is more efficient than the hedonic pricing model, it still subject to a charge of functional form misspecification and omitted variable bias (Wallace and Meese, 1997).

Conclusion

This chapter introduced the problems of constructing real estate price indices and methods of solving these problems. The mean/median price index cannot effectively control quality constant. The hedonic price model has been criticised for its functional form assumption and difficulty in specifying and quantifying a correct and complete set of property characteristics. The repeat-sales model has been mainly accused of the inefficient use of data, sample selection bias and ignoring age effects. The hybrid model is more efficient than the hedonic pricing model but is still subject to possible functional form misspecification and the possible bias resulting from omitted variables.

In principle, the repeat-sales model can be viewed as a special case of the hedonic pricing model, which in turn is a special case of the hybrid model. The more general a model is, the fewer assumptions it imposes and the less vulnerable it will be to attacks on its assumptions. The generality, however, does not come without cost. Much more information is required to operate the more general model. Both the hybrid model and the hedonic pricing model require a full set of data including transaction prices, dates and property characteristics, whereas the repeat-sales model does not require the property attributes. Thus, in practice, the choice of models is largely governed by the availability of data and the purpose for which an index is used (Wang and Zorn, 1997).

Notes

1 This chapter has drawn from the index construction method for the University of Hong Kong All Residential Price Index and the Land and Property Services/Northern Ireland Statistics and Research Agency Residential Property Price Index methodology report (Land and Property Services, 2016).

2 Commonly used submarket classifications are by property types (such as residential, offices, retail, and industrial), by building structure (detached houses, semidetached and apartments) by location and by quality (such as office grades). An example is the monthly average transaction prices of submarkets published by the Rating and Valuation Department of the Hong Kong Special Administrative Region Government, which is available at www.rvd.gov.hk/en/property_market_statistics/index.html (accessed 14 August 2018).

3 See Hong Kong Rating and Valuation Department (www.rvd.gov.hk/en/faqs/rates.html) for a more detail definition of rateable value. For the purpose of our discussion here, it is sufficient to know that rateable value is good approximation of market rent for private properties.

4 The data are available at: Hong Kong Rating and Valuation Department (RVD), Property Market Statistics, www.rvd.gov.hk/en/property_market_statistics/index.html (accessed 14 August 2018). The RVD valuation-based index is compiled by converting the transaction prices to constant-quality property value based on the RVD's assessed 'rateable value' for the purposes of assessing the rates, which is a form of tax based on the market rent of the property under certain assumptions. Since higher rateable value per floor area implies higher quality, the observed price per saleable floor area is deflated by the rateable value per floor areas before they are used to compile the RVD price indices (that is, rateable-value-adjusted price indices; Technical Notes, p.4).

5 In addition to pricing a hypothetical standard transacted property, price indices can also be used to price actual transacted properties or even unsold properties (Miles *et al.*, 1990; Gatzlaff and Haurin, 1998).

6 If the dependent variable is the natural log of the transaction price, the coefficients of the time dummies can be interpreted as percentage change in price from the base period.

7 For example, one can apply the Box–Cox transformation to each variable in Equation (10.1) and use a likelihood ratio test to choose among a linear, log-linear, and semi-log equation.

8 Some of the advantages of the semi-log model are discussed in Diewert (2003) and Malpezzi (2003).

9 The NIRPPI is no longer calculated as a composite index. Prices for apartments and houses are now determined by incorporating variables for all property types in the model. This change occurred in May 2016.

10 OECD Glossary of Statistical Terms: http://stats.oecd.org/glossary/detail.asp?ID=5605 (accessed 14 August 2018).

11 All property transactions in Hong Kong must be registered with the Land Registry of the Hong Kong Special Administrative Region Government.

12 A detailed description of the construction of the University of Hong Kong Real Estate Index Series can be found in Chau (2006).

References

Adelman, I. and Griliches, Z. (1961) On an index of quality change, *Journal of the American Statistical Association*, 56, 535–48.

Bailey, M. J., Muth, R. F. and Nourse, H. O. (1963) A regression method for real estate price index construction, *Journal of the American Statistical Association*, 58, 933–42.

Balk, B. M. (1995) Axiomatic price index theory: a survey, *International Statistical Review*, 63, 69–93.

Bourassa, S. C., Cantoni, E. and Hoesli, M. (2013) Robust repeat sales indexes, *Real Estate Economics*, 41, 517–41.

Bourassa, S. C., Hoesli, M. and Sun, J. (2006) A simple alternative house price index method, *Journal of Housing Economics*, 15, 80–97.

Can, A. and Megbolugbe, I. (1997) Spatial dependence and housing price index construction, *Journal of Real Estate Finance and Economics*, 14, 203–22.

Case, B. and Quigley, J. M. (1991) The dynamics of real estate prices, *Review of Economics and Statistics*, 50–8.

Case, B., Pollakowski, H. O. and Wachter, S. M. (1991) On choosing among house price index methodologies, *Real Estate Economics,* 19, 286–307.

Case, K. E., and Shiller, R. J. (1987) Prices of single-family homes since 1970: new indexes for four cities, *New England Economic Review*, (Sep), 45–56.

Case, K. E. and Shiller, R. J. (1988) *The efficiency of the market for single-family homes*, National Bureau of Economic Research, Cambridge, MA.

Chau, K. W. (2006) *Index construction method for the University of Hong Kong (All Residential Price Index and its sub-indices)*, Versitech Limited, University of Hong Kong, Hong Kong.

Chau, K. W., Wong, S. K. and Yiu, C. Y. (2005a) Adjusting for non-linear age effects in the repeat sales index, *Journal of Real Estate Finance and Economics*, 31(2), 137–53.

Chau, K. W., Wong, S. K., Yiu, C. Y. and Leung, H. F. (2005b) Real estate price indices in Hong Kong, *Journal of Real Estate Literature*, 13, 337.

Clapham, E., Englund, P., Quigley, J. M. and Redfearn, C. L. (2006) Revisiting the past and settling the score: index revision for house price derivatives, *Real Estate Economics*, 34(2), 275–302.

Clapp, J. M. and Giaccotto, C. (1992) Estimating price indices for residential property: a comparison of repeat sales and assessed value methods, *Journal of the American Statistical Association*, 87, 300–6.

Clapp, J. M. and Giaccotto, C. (1999) Revisions in repeat-sales indexes: here today, gone tomorrow?, *Real Estate Economics*, 27(1), 79–104.

Court, A. (1939) Hedonic price indexes with automobile examples, pp. 99–117 in *The dynamics of the automobile demands*, General Motors Company, New York, NY.

Crone, T. M. and Voith, R. P. (1992) Estimating house price appreciation: a comparison of methods, *Journal of Housing Economics*, 2(4), 324–38.

De Vries, P., De Hann, J., Van der Wal, E. and Marien, G. (2009) A house price index based on the SPAR method, *Journal of Housing Economics*, 18, 214–23.

Deng, Y., McMillen, D. P. and Sing, T. F. (2012) Private residential price indices in Singapore: a matching approach, *Regional Science and Urban Economics*, 42, 485–94.

Diewert, W. E. (2003) Hedonic regressions: a review of some unresolved issues, in *7th Meeting of the Ottawa Group, Paris, May* 2003, Vol. 29.

Diewert, W. E. (1998) Index number issues in the consumer price index, *Journal of Economic Perspectives*, 12(1), 47–58.

Dubin, R. A., Pace, R. K., and Thibodeau, T. G. (1999) Spatial autocorrelation techniques for real estate data, *Journal of Real Estate Literature*, 7(1), 79–95.

Englund, P., Quigley, J. M. and Redfearn, C. L. (1998) Improved price indexes for real estate: measuring the course of Swedish housing prices, *Journal of Urban Economics*, 44, 171–96.

Eurostat (2013) *Handbook on residential property price indices*, Eurostat, Brussels.

Fisher, I. (1922) *The making of index numbers: a study of their varieties, tests, and reliability (No. 1)*, Houghton Mifflin, Boston, MA, and New York, NY.

Gatzlaff, D. H. and Haurin, D. R. (1997) Sample selection bias and repeat-sales index estimates, *Journal of Real Estate Finance and Economics*, 14, 33–50.

Gatzlaff, D. H. and Haurin, D. R. (1998) Sample selection and biases in local house value indices, *Journal of Urban Economics*, 43, 199–222.

Gatzlaff, D. H. and Ling, D. C. (1994) Measuring changes in local house prices: an empirical investigation of alternative methodologies, *Journal of Urban Economics*, 35, 221–44.

Goetzmann, W. and Peng, L. (2006) Estimating house price indexes in the presence of seller reservation prices, *Review of Economics and Statistics,* 88, 100–12.

Graddy, K., Hamilton, J. and Pownall, R. (2012) Repeat-sales indexes: estimation without assuming that errors in asset returns are independently distributed, *Real Estate Economics,* 40, 131–66.

Greenlees, J. S. (1982) An empirical evaluation of the CPI home purchase index, 1973–1978, *Real Estate Economics*, 10, 1–24.

Hill, R. C., Knight, J. R. and Sirmans, C. (1997) Estimating capital asset price indexes, *Review of Economics and Statistics*, 79, 226–33.

Hill, R. J. (2013) Hedonic price indexes for residential housing: a survey, evaluation and taxonomy, *Journal of Economic Surveys*, 27(5), 879–914.

Hill, R. J., Melser, D. and Syed, I. (2009) Measuring a boom and bust: the Sydney housing market 2001–2006, *Journal of Housing Economics*, 18(3), 193–205.

Hodgson, D. J., Slade, B. A. and Vorkink, K. P. (2006) Constructing commercial indices: a semiparametric adaptive estimator approach, *Journal of Real Estate Finance and Economics*, 32, 151–68.

Kelejian, H. and Prucha, I. (1998) A generalized spatial two stage least squares procedure for estimating a spatial autoregressive model with autoregressive disturbances, *Journal of Real Estate Finance and Economics*, 17, 99–121.

Kim, C. W., Phipps, T. T. and Anselin, L. (2003) Measuring the benefits of air quality improvement: a spatial hedonic approach, *Journal of Environmental Economics and Management*, 45, 24–39.

Knight, J. R., Dombrow, J. and Sirmans, C. (1995) A varying parameters approach to constructing house price indexes, *Real Estate Economics*, 23, 187–205.

Land and Property Services (2016) *Northern Ireland House Price Index methodology 2016*, Northern Ireland Statistics and Research Agency, Belfast.

Malpezzi, S. (2003) Hedonic pricing models: a selective and applied review, pp. 67–89 in O'Sullivan, T. and Gibb, K. (eds.), *Housing economics and public policy: essays in honor of Duncan Maclennan*, Blackwell Science, Oxford.

Mark, J. H. and Goldberg, M. A. (1984) Alternative housing price indices: an evaluation, *Real Estate Economics*, 12, 30–49.

Mason, P. and Pryce, G. (2011) Controlling for transactions bias in regional house price indices, *Housing Studies*, 26, 639–60.

Maury, T. P. (2009) A spatiotemporal autoregressive price index for the Paris office property market, *Real Estate Economics*, 37, 305–40.

McMillen, D. P. (2012) Repeat sales as a matching estimator, *Real Estate Economics*, 40, 745–73.

Miles, M., Cole, R. and Guilkey, D. (1990) A different look at commercial real estate returns, *Real Estate Economics*, 18, 403–30.

Nagaraja, C., Brown, L. and Wachter, S. (2014) Repeat sales house price index methodology, *Journal of Real Estate Literature*, 22, 23–46.

Pace, R. K. and Gilley, O. W. (1997) Using the spatial configuration of the data to improve estimation, *Journal of Real Estate Finance and Economics*, 14, 333–40.

Pace, R. K., Barry, R., Clapp, J. M. and Rodriquez, M. (1998) Spatiotemporal autoregressive models of neighborhood effects, *Journal of Real Estate Finance and Economics*, 17(1), 15–33.

Palmquist, R. B. (1980) Alternative techniques for developing real estate price indexes, *Review of Economics and Statistics*, 442–8.

Quigley, J. M. (1995) A simple hybrid model for estimating real estate price indexes, *Journal of Housing Economics*, 4, 1–12.

Rosen, S. (1974) Hedonic prices and implicit markets: product differentiation in pure competition, *Journal of Political Economy*, 82, 34–55.

Shi, S., Young, M. and Hargreaves, B. (2009) Issues in measuring a monthly house price index in New Zealand, *Journal of Housing Economics*, 18, 336–50.

Simon, A. (2009) Quantifying the reversibility phenomenon for the repeat-sales index, *Journal of Real Estate Research*, 31, 27–62.

Song, H. S. and Wilhelmsson, M. (2010) Improved price index for condominiums, *Journal of Property Research*, 27, 39–60.

Steele, M. and Goy, R. (1997) Short holds, the distributions of first and second sales, and bias in the repeat-sales price index. *Journal of Real Estate Finance and Economics*, 14(1–2), 133–54.

Sun, H., Tu, Y. and Yu, S. M. (2005) A spatio-temporal autoregressive model for multi-unit residential market analysis, *Journal of Real Estate Finance and Economics*, 31(2), 155–87.

Triplett, J. E. (2004) Handbook on hedonic indexes and quality adjustments in price indexes: special application to information technology products, *STI OECD Working Paper 2004/9*, Organisation for Economic Co-operation and Development, Paris.

Wallace, N. E. and Meese, R. A. (1997) The construction of residential housing price indices: a comparison of repeat-sales, hedonic-regression, and hybrid approaches, *Journal of Real Estate Finance and Economics*, 14, 51–73.

Wang, F. T. and Zorn, P. M. (1997) Estimating house price growth with repeat sales data: what's the aim of the game?, *Journal of Housing Economics*, 6, 93–118.

Webb, R. B., Miles, M. and Guilkey, D. (1992) Transactions-driven commercial real estate returns: the panacea to asset allocation models?, *Real Estate Economics*, 20, 325–57.

Wilhelmsson, M. (2009) Construction and updating of property price index series: the case of segmented markets in Stockholm, *Property Management*, 27, 119–37.

Wong, S. K., Yiu, C. Y. and Chau, K. W. (2013) Trading volume-induced spatial autocorrelation in real estate prices, *Journal of Real Estate Finance and Economics*, 46(4), 596–608.

Part IV

Portfolios and risk management

11 Pricing models

Bryan D. MacGregor, Rainer Schulz and Yuan Zhao

Introduction

Asset pricing models try to explain how prices are set in asset markets and how these prices relate to the risk of asset cash flows. To achieve this, asset pricing models start from assumptions about investors and the market structure, and derive conditions that asset prices must fulfil in market equilibrium. These models have both a positive and a normative role.

The *positive* role of asset pricing models is to describe and help us to understand how investors behave in actual asset markets. As always, a model requires that simplifying assumptions are made about investor behaviour and the market structure. Such simplifications can assume that investors care only about specific aspects of future cash flows, such as their mean return and their volatility, or that aspects of a market can be ignored, such as transaction costs. By making such simplifications, an asset pricing model may lose some realism but gain clarity. This should lead to clear model predictions, which can be tested empirically. An appropriate asset pricing model combines a good dose of realism with the potential to explain asset prices observed in asset markets.

The *normative* role of asset pricing models is to give advice to investors about investment decisions. The first form of advice that a model can give is qualitative, because asset pricing models *explain* more or less explicitly why specific assets have value. The intuition behind this should be useful to investors who have to choose assets for their portfolios or who have to enter new contracts to hedge some of the risks to which they are exposed. The second form of advice is quantitative. Asset pricing models often provide explicit formulas that allow the asset's value in market equilibrium to be calculated. Knowing this value helps investors to decide how much they should be prepared to pay for existing assets on offer or how to set prices for novel financial instruments, such as real estate index derivatives. Real estate developers will also benefit if an asset pricing model enables the market value of a completed building to be derived based on general principles and not only on the current sentiment in the market.

The dual purpose of asset pricing models means that it is unsurprising that more than one model exists. This does not mean, however, that all models are equally good. Some early models are still useful as long as only intuition is needed, whereas newer and refined models usually better explain asset prices. Asset pricing models can also differ with respect to the degree of realism they allow. This realism can depend on the particular application. For instance, it may be reasonable to ignore transaction costs in the case of fairly liquid securities such as real estate investment trusts (REITs). But for direct real estate, such asset pricing models might provide only approximate results. Nevertheless, approximate results still might be good enough for practical decision making.

The argument in subsequent sections proceeds as follows. First, a simple two-period portfolio decision model is introduced, where an investor decides on how much to save for the second period and how to allocate the saving among different assets. From there, it is assumed that there are many such investors and that these investors agree on the distributions of the returns of the available assets. Investors differ, however, with respect to their degree of risk aversion. While it may not seem realistic that investors share homogenous beliefs on asset returns all the time, this position does keep the presentation simple. Furthermore, if it is assumed that investors interact frequently, their beliefs should converge over time. Risk preferences, on the other hand, will not be affected by interaction and are, thus, much more fundamental for asset pricing. This is in line with the widely held perception that the main purpose of asset markets is to allocate risk efficiently.[1]

The solution to an investor's portfolio problem and the assumption of asset market equilibrium leads to the core pricing formula. While this formula provides solid economic intuition on what affects asset prices, it is not useful in a practical context. Further assumptions are needed to make it useful for actual investment decisions. These assumptions relate to investor preferences, return distributions, or both.

In the next stage of the argument, the capital asset pricing model (CAPM) is presented. The CAPM results from the core valuation formula if either asset returns follow a specific type of distribution or if investors share a specific type of utility function. The CAPM is used frequently in the real estate industry and some examples are provided. This is followed by a discussion of multifactor asset pricing models. Multifactor models have been applied extensively in real estate studies and such models are also popular in the investment industry.

Finally, and before proceeding, it should be noted that only the pricing of primary assets is covered; that is, assets whose returns cannot be replicated with assets already traded and priced in the market. If such comparables exist, then reference to the asset pricing models might not be necessary for the pricing of new assets.[2] Even then, however, the models presented in this chapter could be useful in practical applications to check if a comparable value can be justified by economic principles.

Formal framework

Asset pricing models characterise market clearing – equilibrium – prices. At these prices, the total demand for each asset equals its supply. While the characterisations of equilibrium prices have intuitive content, which can be described verbally, it is helpful for the presentation to introduce a simple formal framework.

Asset demand of an investor

We focus on a risk-averse investor who wants to set up a portfolio in period 0 for retirement in period 1. The market consist of $J \geq 2$ assets. The vector $\mathbf{p}$ contains the prices of the assets. The $S \times J$ pay-off matrix $\mathbf{X}$ contains the cash flows for each asset in each of the $S \geq 2$ possible states in period 1. The investor has assumptions about these cash flows and their probability distribution. The quantity invested in each of the assets is collected in the vector $\mathbf{q}$. The portfolio costs $\mathbf{p'q}$ in period 0. The portfolio return in the different possible states in period 1, is given by c_{1s}, which are the rows of $\mathbf{c}_1 = \mathbf{Xq}$. For example, assume that there are two assets that cost $p_1 = 0.75$ and $p_2 = 0.5$ per unit. In period 1, one of two possible states will occur. The cash flows of the two assets in the two states are given in the matrix:

$$\mathbf{X} = \begin{bmatrix} 1.0 & 2.0 \\ 1.5 & 1.0 \end{bmatrix} \tag{11.1}$$

Thus, a portfolio that holds one unit of each asset ($q_1 = 1$ and $q_2 = 1$) has returns in each of the two possible states given by:

$$\begin{bmatrix} c_{11} \\ c_{12} \end{bmatrix} = \begin{bmatrix} 1.0q_1 + 2.0q_2 \\ 1.5q_1 + 1.0q_2 \end{bmatrix} = \begin{bmatrix} 3.0 \\ 2.5 \end{bmatrix} \tag{11.2}$$

The portfolio costs $p_1q_1 + p_2q_2 = 0.75 \times q_1 + 0.5 \times q_2 = 1.25$ in the current period.

The investor already owns some units of the J assets, denoted by $\bar{\mathbf{q}}$. The investor now has to decide how much of her current wealth $\mathbf{p}'\bar{\mathbf{q}}$ she wants to consume immediately in period 0 and how much she wants to save for retirement and how to allocate the savings to the J available assets. To find the optimal portfolio, she will maximise her utility from consumption:

$$U = u(c_0) + \delta E[u(c_1)] \tag{11.3}$$

with $c_0 \equiv \mathbf{p}'(\bar{\mathbf{q}} - \mathbf{q})$. The period utility $u(c)$ is a function of consumption. The period utility function is strictly increasing and concave. $E[\cdot]$ is the expectation operator and is taken over the probability distribution of the S states with probability of occurrence $0 \le \pi_s \le 1$ for state s; the probabilities sum to one. Given a portfolio $\mathbf{q}$, $E[u(c_1)] = \pi_1 u(c_{1,1}) + \pi_2 u(c_{2,1}) + \cdots + \pi_S u(c_{S,1})$ is then the investor's probability-weighted expected utility over all possible states in period 1, as seen from period 0. The time preference parameter $0 < \delta \le 1$ allows that the investor prefers current to future utility. Maximising U with respect to the elements of $\mathbf{q}$, that is, the investor's portfolio, leads to J first order conditions:

$$p_j = E\left[\frac{\delta u'(c_1)}{u'(c_0)} x_j\right] \tag{11.4}$$

These conditions define implicitly the optimal portfolio $\mathbf{q}^*$. Reformulating gives:

$$-u'(c_0)p_j + E\left[\delta u'(c_1)x_j\right] = 0 \tag{11.5}$$

This formula shows that the investor chooses the portfolio such that the trade-off between current and expected future utility is equalised at the margin. A small change Δq_j^* of the investment in asset j would change current consumption by $\Delta c_0 = -p_j \Delta q_j^*$, but would change future consumption in each state by $\Delta c_{1s} = x_{js} \Delta q_j^*$. This affects current utility by $u'(c_0)\Delta c_0$ and expected future utility by $E\left[\delta u'(c_1)\Delta c_1\right]$. The equation shows that this trade-off is exactly equalised for the optimal portfolio. If this were not the case, the overall utility could be increased be altering the portfolio. Finally, it is assumed that asset J is risk-free and costs $p_J = 1$ in the current period. It then pays in each possible future state $x_{Js} = 1 + r_f$. Combining this with the expression from above gives:

$$\frac{1}{1 + r_f} = E\left[\frac{\delta u'(c_1)}{u'(c_0)}\right] \tag{11.6}$$

Equilibrium

The perspective is now changed to ask what can be said about asset prices in equilibrium. To do so, it is assumed that there are $I \geq 2$ investors. The asset market is in equilibrium if the following condition holds for each of the J assets:

$$\sum_{i=1}^{I} \bar{q}_{j,i} = \sum_{i=1}^{I} q^{*}_{j,i}(\boldsymbol{p}^{*}) \tag{11.7}$$

The condition states, for each asset j, that the total stock of the asset over all investors – the left hand side of Equation (11.7) – equals the total demand for the asset. It is made explicit that the individual asset demand functions depend on all asset prices. The price vector $\boldsymbol{p}^{*}$ is the one that ensures that all J asset markets clear. What can be said about the characteristics of these equilibrium prices? First, an individual investor's first-order conditions hold as before, but this time for the equilibrium prices. This gives for each asset:

$$p^{*}_{j} = E\left[\frac{\delta_i u'_i(c^{*}_{1,i})}{u'_i(c^{*}_{0,i})} x_j\right] \tag{11.8}$$

Using the definition of the covariance and the expression for the risk-free asset from Equation (11.6), this can be rewritten as:

$$p^{*}_{j} = \frac{E\left[x_j\right]}{1+r_f} + \mathrm{Cov}\left[\frac{\delta_i u'_i\left(c^{*}_{1,i}\right)}{u'_i\left(c^{*}_{0,i}\right)}, x_j\right] \tag{11.9}$$

This is an instructive expression and shows that the equilibrium price of asset j in the current period is the asset's expected cash flow discounted with the risk-free rate plus an adjustment for asset's cash flow risk. The risk adjustment depends on the *covariance* of the asset's cash flows with marginal utility, not on the risk of these cash flows themselves.

If the investor were risk-neutral and u' constant, the covariance term would be zero. The asset price would be simply the discounted expected cash flow. For a risk-averse investor, however, $u'(c^{*}_{j})$ becomes smaller, the higher the consumption. It follows that if asset j had, on average, high cash flows in states where the marginal utility is low (because consumption is high), then the covariance term will be negative. Intuitively, the asset pays well in states where most other assets also pay well (that is why consumption is high in these states), but does not pay well in states where income for consumption is needed. The price of such an asset in equilibrium will be smaller than the expected cash flow discounted at the risk-free rate. Contrast this with an asset that pays well in states where consumption is low and marginal utility is high. In this case, the covariance term will be positive and the asset price higher than the expected cash flow discounted at the risk-free rate.

The above pricing formula shows that asset prices should be positively related to their diversification potential. Some assets will have a higher diversification potential than others, and such assets must come at higher prices, so that in the end all assets find a home in investors' portfolios. For instance, if office buildings are less exposed to market-wide shocks than other assets, because their rental income is fixed and has priority, then buildings provide high cash flows in exactly those states where other assets deliver only meagre income. This implies that the covariance of the cash flows with marginal utility in Equation (11.9) will be positive. Compared with an asset that has the same expected cash flow as the office building, the office building price will be higher.

We can use Equation (11.9) to derive an intuitive expression for the expected return rate of asset j in market equilibrium. We divide Equation (11.9) first by the equilibrium price and multiply through with one plus the risk-free rate. Rearranging and using Equation (11.6) gives:

$$E\left[r_j\right] = r_f + \mathrm{Cov}\left[-\frac{\delta_i u_i'\left(c_{1,i}^*\right)}{\mathrm{E}\left[u_i'\left(c_{0,i}^*\right)\right]}, r_j\right] \tag{11.10}$$

In equilibrium, the expected return rate of asset j is equal to the risk-free rate – to compensate for waiting – plus a risk premium. The risk premium is the covariance between a function of consumption $c_{1,i}^*$ and the return rate r_j of the asset. The function increases strictly in $c_{1,i}^*$.[3] This implies that the risk premium will be the higher the stronger the overall correlation between consumption in the different states and r_j. Intuitively, the risk premium will be higher for an asset that pays well in states where most other assets pay well too. The high risk premium compensates for the fact that such an asset is not very useful to hedge against consumption risk.

The above formulas reveal that it is not the variance that matters for asset pricing, but the covariance. Equation (11.9) shows that an asset that has cash flows that are highly correlated with those of most other assets will command a low *price*; Equation (11.10) tells us that such an asset will command a high risk premium and will provide a high *expected return* rate. In equilibrium, the low price and, correspondingly, the high expected return rate simply compensate for the fact that the asset does not provide much diversification. While the formulas provide these qualitative insights, they do not have enough structure to be useful for investment decisions. For applications, more structure is needed.

The capital asset pricing model

If it is assumed that all investors share beliefs about asset returns and either have quadratic utility functions or asset returns are elliptically distributed, then the famous CAPM pricing formula results from Equation (11.10):

$$E\left[r_j\right] = r_f + \frac{\mathrm{Cov}\left[r_m, r_j\right]}{\mathrm{Var}\left[r_m\right]}\left(E\left[r_m\right] - r_f\right) \tag{11.11}$$

The subscript m stands for the market portfolio, that is, the portfolio that includes *all* risky assets in proportion to their respective total value. The intuition is as follows: quadratic utility or elliptically distributed asset returns lead investors to care only about the expected return and the risk of portfolios. When investors share beliefs on the returns, they also share beliefs about the expected return and risk of each possible portfolio. Investors are risk averse and will only hold well-diversified portfolios. In market equilibrium, investors as a group must be willing to hold all available assets in their well-diversified portfolios. In the CAPM market equilibrium, investors hold portfolios that combine two 'funds': the risk-free asset and a portfolio of *all* risky assets. The latter is the *market portfolio*. This result is known as the two-fund theorem or as the mutual fund separation (Tobin, 1958). An investor's risk aversion determines how the money invested is allocated between the two funds. A higher risk aversion leads to more money being allocated to the risk-free asset and less to the market portfolio.

The CAPM formula in Equation (11.11) shows that the risk premium of asset j in market equilibrium is the market-wide risk premium on the market portfolio, $E[r_m]-r_f$, times a measure of the diversification potential of asset j. The diversification potential of asset j will be small if its cash flows co-vary strongly with the market. In this case, the scaled covariance term in Equation (11.11) will be high and so will be the risk premium. The intuition for this relationship has been given already above, in the discussion of Equation (11.10). In equilibrium, all risky assets must be part of the market portfolio. Assets that do not diversify risk must offer a high risk premium to become attractive; assets that diversify risk have to offer only a small risk premium.

The scaled covariance term in Equation (11.11) is often written simply as β_j, so that:

$$E[r_j] = r_f + \beta_j \left(E[r_m] - r_f\right) \tag{11.12}$$

According to the CAPM, in asset market equilibrium, the expected return rate of asset j has to compensate for the *delay* and the *riskiness* of its future cash flows. The CAPM formula depends on variables that should be, in principle, observable. However, because the market portfolio contains *all* risky assets, it is effectively unobservable. Empirical studies must rely on proxies when applying the CAPM. Assuming that a good proxy for the market portfolio exists, beta can be estimated by fitting the regression:

$$r_{jt} - r_{ft} = \beta_j \left(r_{mt} - r_{ft}\right) + \epsilon_{jt} \tag{11.13}$$

The last term on the right-hand side is an unsystematic regression error term with expectation zero.[4] The least squares estimator for beta in the regression is the estimated covariance between the excess return rates of asset j and the excess return rate of the market portfolio divided by the variance of the excess return rates of the market portfolio. This estimator is easy to calculate and has only minimal data requirements. It seems, therefore, natural that the CAPM has been widely used in the context of listed stocks.

The underlying assumptions of the CAPM are strong. Quadratic utility implies that risk aversion increases with income, which is not a reasonable assumption. There is empirical evidence that return rates do not follow elliptical distributions. More important is the direct empirical evidence against the CAPM. Equation (11.13) shows that a regression constant, if included, should be zero if the CAPM were true. However, empirical studies have established for different data sets and time periods that the regression constant is typically positive and statistically significant. This result is robust with respect to the choice of the market portfolio proxy. Stambaugh (1982) studied this for a wide set of proxies, some of which also included residential real estate, house furnishing, and automobiles. Fama and French (2004) give an overall assessment on the strong empirical evidence against the CAPM.

The CAPM in real estate applications

According to Brown and Matysiak (2000, 495), there is a widespread 'misconception' in the real estate industry that 'the CAPM applies to the equity market only.' However, as Brown and Matysiak continue, 'there is nothing in the theory that says that this should be the case.

... the CAPM is a general equilibrium asset-pricing model and is quite capable of accommodating [direct real estate].' In particular, they refer to the work of Mayers on the CAPM with non-marketable assets (see Brown and Matysiak, 2000, Appendix 10E). Geltner *et al.* (2007, Sec. 22.2.2) share the view that the CAPM applies also to direct real estate, but they emphasise that applications have to consider a broad market index, including real estate, and potential appraisal smoothing in observed direct real estate index return rates. If this is done, then the CAPM should be useful for applications that consider broad asset classes, such as real estate stocks, stocks from other sectors, government bonds and direct real estate. The CAPM is covered in real estate investment textbooks, such as, in addition to those books already mentioned, Hoesli and MacGregor (2000) and Baum and Hartzell (2012). The CAPM has been used in the academic literature to assess the performance of unlisted real estate portfolios (see, for example, Brueggeman *et al.*, 1984), but typically only as one of several factor models.[5]

Multifactor pricing models

Multifactor pricing models start with the assumption that return rates are generated by the process:

$$r_{jt} = \alpha_j + \boldsymbol{\beta}_j' \mathbf{f}_t + \epsilon_{jt} \tag{11.14}$$

with the $(K \times 1)$ vector of risk factors $\mathbf{f}_t$. The vector $\boldsymbol{\beta}_j$ collects the exposure coefficients of asset j to each of these factors. Equation (11.14) is not, in itself, an asset pricing model. To obtain an asset pricing model with testable restrictions, it is assumed that the marginal rate of substitution in Equation (11.8) is, or can be approximated by, a linear function of the factors. If we then divide both sides of the equation by the price, the result is:

$$1 = E\left[(\theta_0 - \boldsymbol{\theta}_1' \mathbf{f}_t)(1 + r_{jt})\right] \tag{11.15}$$

From this, after some redefinitions, it can be shown that in asset market equilibrium:

$$E\left[r_{jt}\right] = \gamma_0 + \boldsymbol{\beta}_j' \gamma_1 \tag{11.16}$$

The gamma coefficients are functions of the preference parameters (the theta coefficients from Equation (11.15)) and the unconditional first two moments (mean and variance) of the risk factors. The exact formulas for the gamma coefficients can be found in Jagannathan *et al.* (2010, 55). The multifactor pricing model was first derived by Ross (1976) as arbitrage pricing theory, assuming only that return rates are generated by the process in Equation (11.14) and that all arbitrage opportunities have been exploited. The exact factor representation of the arbitrage pricing theory corresponds to Equation (11.16). The economic interpretation of Equation (11.16) is straightforward. In equilibrium, investors will be compensated for the cost of delay by the return on the zero-beta asset (usually the risk-free rate) plus a risk premium that consists of the sum of the risk premium γ_k for each of the K factors, times the exposure β_{jk} of asset j to each of these risk factors. Obviously, if there is only one priced risk factor and this factor is the excess return rate of the market portfolio, then Equation (11.16) reduces to the CAPM from Equation (11.12). The zero beta return will be equal to the risk free rate, the factor exposure equals β_{mj} and γ_1 equals the market-wide risk premium.

It should be stressed that a factor model consists of *two* equations: Equation (11.14) and Equation (11.16). There might be many variables related to asset return returns and, thus, have a non-zero beta in Equation (11.14), but which are not priced in the market and carry no risk premium, that is, the gamma of the factor is zero in Equation (11.16). In the academic literature, the risk factors in Equation (11.14) are sometimes called *ex post* factors and those in Equation (11.16) *ex ante* factors. While *ex post* factors might be useful for short-term return forecasting, only *ex ante* factors are of importance for long-term investment strategies (Bender *et al.* 2013, 7). Factor pricing models are highly relevant to portfolio managers, who call them *smart* or *alternative beta* models (Ang, 2014, 450). For example, Ang *et al.* (2009) use factor pricing models to assess the performance of the Norwegian Government Pension Fund. The investments of the fund are exposed to priced risk factors and the fund's performance must at least compensate for this exposure.

The academic literature has used many different sets of variables and applied statistical methods to generate factors $\mathbf{f}_t$. Three approaches to identify factors exist: purely statistical, macro-economic and fundamental.

Statistical factors extract systematic components out of the cross-section of asset return rates. Such dimension reduction uses factor analytical or principal components methods. The resulting factor series $\mathbf{f}_t$ are effectively portfolios of all available assets in the market. Conceptually, each of these *mimicking portfolios* represents a systematic component that affects all asset return rates. While some of these components can be easily identified and interpreted, such as market risk, others reject simple interpretation and economic content. Huberman *et al.* (1987), Lehmann and Modest (1988) and Connor and Korajczyk (1988) are influential studies using this approach.

Macro-economic factors are economic variables such as gross domestic product growth rate, inflation rate expectations and the term spread. Chen *et al.* (1986) is an influential study using this approach. Chen *et al.* (1986, 384) choose those economic variables as the factors for the regression in Equation (11.14) that influence the 'economy's pricing operator or that influence dividends'. Equation (11.9), while only derived for a simple two-period world, provides intuition for this choice. Cash flows such as dividends enter the expression on the right-hand side directly, the marginal rate of substitution enters it indirectly as pricing operator. Factors that influence both over time should influence expected return rates, the left-hand side. Chen *et al.* (1986) consider the following macro-economic factors for their monthly return rate data regression: growth of monthly and annual industrial production, expected and unexpected inflation, change in the expected inflation, the *ex post* real interest rate, the risk premium between risky and government bonds, and the slope of the term structure. They find that most of these factors play a role for the return rate generating process from Equation (11.14) and also, more importantly, that these factors are priced *ex ante*.

Fundamental factors are traits of companies that have been found to explain excess return rates above the market average. For instance, the average of return rates of stocks of small companies over those of large companies have been positive in many stock markets. Economists motivate this either with a risk premium for the higher exposure to business cycle risk of small companies or with overconfidence of investors investing in small companies. Influential studies in this area are the papers by Fama and French (1993; 2015). Fama and French (1993) find that a three-factor model can explain the cross-section of return rates in the US market. The factors are the market factor (excess return rate on a broad market index over the risk-free rate), the size factor (excess return rate on a portfolio of small capitalisation companies above large capitalisation companies) and the value factor (excess return rate on a portfolio of companies with a high book-to-market value ratio to a portfolio of companies which have a low ratio).

Many other factors have been suggested and debated in the academic literature and among financial professionals. This might make multifactor pricing models appear arbitrary. However, this arbitrariness is a result of the weak structural assumptions of such models. The CAPM is based on strong structural assumptions about preferences and return rate distributions. Correspondingly, the CAPM gives clear guidance that the market index is the only risk factor that should count. The multifactor pricing model is based on weaker structural assumptions, which corresponds then to less guidance. For instance, in the derivation of the multifactor pricing model above, the structure of the marginal rate of substitution was reduced by linearising it as function of some factors. The link with the marginal rate of substitution makes some economic factors more plausible than others, but there is still an abundance of candidate factors. The fact that there are three different methods in the literature to derive risk factors contributes to the appearance of arbitrariness. Strictly speaking, if assets are priced in the market in a structured and not a haphazard way, then factors generated with different methods – statistical, macro-economic, and fundamental – that are relevant for asset pricing must be related to each other.[6]

This implies that multifactor factor pricing models must rely heavily on *empirical testing* to discriminate between factors that play a role for pricing and those which do not. Without going into too much detail, this requires not only that a factor plays a significant role in Equation (11.14), but also that Equation (11.16) holds. For instance, if a risk-free asset exists and all factors $\mathbf{f}_t$ are the excess return rates of traded portfolios (such as size or value), then arbitrage will prevent an asset from earning a premium if it is not related to the corresponding risk exposure. The risk-free asset is the zero-beta asset and γ_0 equals the (unconditional) expected risk-free rate. The risk factors are traded portfolio premiums and $\mathrm{E}[\mathbf{f}] = \boldsymbol{\gamma}_1$. Under these assumptions, Equation (11.16) becomes:

$$E[r_j] = \mathrm{E}[r_f] + \boldsymbol{\beta}_j' \, \mathrm{E}[\mathbf{f}] \tag{11.17}$$

It holds for the ordinary least squares estimators of the regression in Equation (11.14) that:

$$\overline{r}_j = \hat{\alpha}_j + \hat{\boldsymbol{\beta}}_j' \, \overline{\mathbf{f}} \tag{11.18}$$

The bar indicates the sample average. Comparing the two equations reveals that if Equation (11.17) is indeed the correct asset pricing model then, from Equation (11.18), the estimated $\hat{\alpha}_j$ must equal the average risk-free rate. As both the estimated coefficient of the constant and the average risk-free rate are based only on a sample, equality has to be tested statistically; the test gains power if a panel of assets or portfolios of assets is used for testing.

In the literature that tests factor asset pricing models, the regression in Equation (11.14) is often estimated with the return rate in excess of the risk-free rate as dependent variable. In this case, the estimated coefficient for the regression constant should not be statistically different from zero for the pricing model to be valid. Intuitively, the dependent variable is the risk premium – the return rate in excess of the risk-free rate – and the factors should explain its variation completely. The estimation and testing of multifactor pricing models without a risk-free asset require more complicated statistical approaches – see, for instance, Campbell *et al.* (1997, ch. 6) and Jagannathan *et al.* (2010). Given that empirical testing is essential for multifactor pricing models, much academic research has been conducted and is still being conducted on the statistical methodology. Such research is needed, because multifactor models are always exposed to the criticism that, owing to the weak structural guidance, results might be simply statistical artefacts. Expressed differently, if a researcher ponders long enough over a data set, some relationship will be found among the variables. It is, thus, essential to guard against such 'data snooping' by the use of appropriate statistical techniques and by replicating the analysis for different data sets.

The multifactor model presented in Equation (11.14) and Equation (11.16) is unconditional in the sense that it assumed that the coefficients of factor exposure (betas) and expected premiums (gammas) remain constant over time. However, it is likely that some of these coefficients vary over time. For example, the premium for real interest rate risk could depend on the current term structure and the premium for stock market risk could depend on the current dividend yield. Conditional factor models have been implemented for the single (CAPM) and multifactor models, for an overview, see Jagannathan *et al.* (2010). Important studies in this area are Fama and MacBeth (1973) for the CAPM and Ferson and Harvey (1991) for a multifactor pricing model.

Practical relevance of multifactor pricing models

Investors and portfolio managers are interested in advice on the exposure to risk factors of different assets. Investors also want to know the risk premiums paid by the market when such risks are taken on. Investors can then set up portfolios that give exposure to some risk factors but not others. Portfolio management becomes then more than diversifying idiosyncratic risk away and more of a fully-fledged strategy that takes all aspects of the investments into account. For instance, if illiquidity of an asset is priced in the market, because most investors have a short-term investment horizon, then long-term investors will be able to achieve this premium. Such long-term investors will then invest in illiquid assets, such as certain bonds or office buildings, and will be able to earn, on average, the premiums these assets bring.

While this seems sensible and clear advice, investors and portfolio managers might be bewildered by the many risk factors that have been proposed in the academic and industry literature. It is clear that only *ex ante* factors are of interest, as the market will deliver only premiums for exposure to those. What factors are relevant then? Ang (2014, ch. 14.3) lists conditions that factors should fulfil to be of interest to practitioners. These conditions are paraphrased here.

First, factors should have an *intellectual foundation* and should be *justified by academic research*. Both aspects are helpful to understand the risk exposure of the assets under management or, if a new investment strategy should be implemented, from where the returns will come and to what risks the strategy is exposed.

Second, factors should have exhibited a premium of *significant magnitude*. And the investor should be convinced that the *premium persists in the future*. This immediately requires some understanding as to why the premium has existed in the past and why it will continue to exist in the future. The literature predicts that a factor premium will persist if it corresponds to a *systematic* risk factor – risk exposure that cannot be diversified away – or if it corresponds to *behavioural* tendencies of market participants. An example of the latter is *momentum*, the observed pattern that stock prices continue in a particular direction over time. While such a pattern is hard to square with the assumption of rational investors, it is a pattern that persists and that has be found in many studies to be priced in the market.[7]

Third, factors must have been tested with sufficiently long data series. In particular, the data of such tests must have covered *bad times*. Systematic risk premiums reward the willingness to suffer losses during bad times. If such periods are not observed in the data, such risk premiums cannot be identified. Behavioural premiums may disappear if market participants learn over time that their behaviour is not rational or if astute investors find ways to exploit the behavioural tendencies, thereby arbitraging away the premium.

Multifactor pricing models in real estate applications

Factor pricing models have been used widely in studies on real estate. The focus here is on a selection of papers. Some papers estimate only the risk-exposure of return rates to factors, that is, only $\boldsymbol{\beta}_j$ is estimated, whereas other papers also test the pricing model as such. First, papers that examine the pricing of US REITs using different multifactor models are considered. These papers establish the factors that affect real estate returns. This is followed by a discussion of papers that compare the pricing of REITs with the pricing of other securities. From an investor perspective, investors are interested to learn if different types of assets are exposed to the same risk factors and to the same extent. Then there is a discussion of studies that examine if public and private real estate is priced differently. The section concludes with a discussion of papers that examine the pricing of real estate securities traded in international markets. While the papers reviewed differ in approach and method, the main results are rather robust. Real estate securities are related in the expected manner to risk factors and there is also evidence that this applies to direct real estate.

Pricing of US real estate investment trusts

Studies on REITs pricing have used single- and multifactor models. The studies differ with regard to the method used to obtain the factors. Practitioners are likely most interested in a pricing model based on macro-economic factors, as these factors can have an intuitive economic interpretation. However, if the explanatory power of such a model is inferior to models using statistical or fundamental factors, this might change. Another aspect relevant for practitioners is that the models are estimated. This comes with estimation uncertainty, a fact of which decision makers must be aware.

Titman and Warga (1986) provide evidence that a multifactor model using *statistical factors* is better at explaining REIT return rates than the CAPM. Titman and Warga (1986, 415) explain that real estate investments 'are particularly sensitive to unexpected changes in inflation and interest rates'. A multifactor model 'may provide better estimates of the riskiness of real estate investments' as these factors 'should mimic changes in inflation, interest rates, and any other macro-economic variables that generate returns on capital assets'. For the analysis, Titman and Warga (1986, 416) use the five statistical factors of Lehmann and Modest (1988). Titman and Warga find that the CAPM and the five-factor model lead to quite different conclusions regarding the pricing of REITs. The first factor of the multifactor model is statistically significant in all sample periods. This factor is highly correlated with the market index, the sole factor of the CAPM. However, most of the remaining four factors of the multifactor model are statistically significant too. While it is not obvious what systematic risk exposure these remaining factors represent, the results indicate that the CAPM does not explain REITs pricing completely.

Chan *et al.* (1990) provide evidence that a multifactor model using *macro-economic factors* is better at explaining REIT return rates than the CAPM. In the first step of their analysis, Chan *et al.* examine which economic factors affect REIT return rates; in the second step, they test under which pricing model REITs seem to be priced. To implement this testing procedure, they construct portfolios of traded assets that are highly correlated with the economic factors they consider as relevant for REIT pricing. To do so, Chan *et al.* use the method suggested in Huberman *et al.* (1987). After estimation of the factor exposures, Chan *et al.* test if the coefficient of the constant in time series regressions of excess return rates on excess return rates of the factor portfolios is zero – see the discussion for Equations (11.17) and (11.18) above. Chan *et al.* find that the following four economic factors impact on REIT return rates: unexpected inflation, the risk premium on low grade bonds, the slope of the term structure and the closed end fund discount. Chan *et al.* (1990, tables 4 and 6) find that the CAPM is not the correct pricing model for REITs, whereas the multifactor model of factor portfolios leads to a regression constant that is statistically undistinguishable from zero. The average REIT excess return rate is thus explained completely by the multifactor model.

The two studies presented use either statistical or macro-economic risk factors. Chen *et al.* (1997) compare both approaches for US REITs. They find that macro-economic factors have a higher explanatory power for REIT return rates. This is an encouraging result, as macro-economic factors can be understood and explained by economic reasoning, whereas purely statistical factors often remain opaque. However, Chen *et al.* (1997) receive only inconclusive results when they test if the macro-economic factors are priced *ex ante*.

Peterson and Hsieh (1997) examine if the *fundamental factors* of Fama and French (1993) can explain the return rates of US equity REITs. They find that this is the case, as the constant in the time series regression of REIT excess return rates on the factors market, size, and value, is not statistically different from zero. The estimate of the constant from a CAPM regression applied to the same data is statistically different from zero (Peterson and Hsieh, 1997, table 4). This provides further evidence that the CAPM is not the appropriate model to explain REIT pricing. Peterson and Hsieh also examine the pricing of mortgage REITs. Such REITs invest mainly in individual mortgages and mortgage-related products. Whereas equity REITs carry only risk premiums for the market, size and value factors, it is reasonable that mortgage REITs are also exposed to bond market risk factors. Peterson and Hsieh consider all of the five factors used by Fama and French (1993) in their regression analysis, two of which are related to the bond market. The coefficient of the constant is statistically different from zero. While the Fama-French three-factor model captures the pricing of equity REITs, even the extended five-factor model does not capture the pricing of US mortgage REITs.[8]

Pricing of US real estate investment trusts and other securities

Liu and Mei (1992) and Karolyi and Sanders (1998) are two studies that examine similarities and differences in the pricing of US securities, including REITs. Both papers use multifactor models that allow for time variation of risk premiums and also allow that the risk premiums can be predicted in part by observable economic variables. Ignoring such predictable variation could lead to poor real estate investment decisions.

Liu and Mei (1992) examine the predictable components of excess return rates of the market portfolio, a bond portfolio, a portfolio of small cap stocks and a portfolio of REITs. They use a conditional multifactor model, where the factor exposure (betas) stays constant over time, but the factor risk premiums (gammas) depend linearly on observable market variables. The risk premiums in Equation (11.16) are now functions of variables observed in the current period. Liu and Mei consider the following variables that could relate to risk premiums: the January effect (a behavioural factor), the short-term risk-free bond yield, the default spread, the dividend yield and the real estate cap rate. Their empirical analysis shows that the cap rate has high explanatory power for the expected REIT return rates and that economic variables that help to predict the risk premiums of small cap stocks also help to predict REIT premiums (Liu and Mei, 1992, table 3). The variation of the premium and, therefore, the variation of expected REIT return rates, is substantial. Working with a constant required return rate could lead to poor real estate investment decisions.

Similar to Liu and Mei (1992), Karolyi and Sanders (1998) examine whether US stocks, bonds, and REITs differ with respect to their exposure to macro-economic risk factors and if these risks are priced differently. Karolyi and Sanders use a multifactor model that allows for variation over time of both factor exposure (betas) and risk premiums (gammas). A risk-free asset is no longer assumed and the premium for the zero beta portfolio – γ_0 in Equation (11.16) – becomes a coefficient that has to be estimated as well.[9] To implement this, Karolyi and Sanders estimate, in a first step, time series of risk premiums for each economic risk factor using the return rates of a cross-section of security portfolios. To do so, they estimate the exposure (betas) of the portfolios to the risk factors using rolling windows and estimate for the last month of each window the risk premiums of each factor; see Equation (11.16). In a second step, they regress the return rates of a given portfolio in excess of γ_0 on the estimated risk premiums. The coefficients of the regression indicate that the sensitivities of REITs to the risk premiums are similar to those of other stock portfolios and are larger than those for bond portfolios (Karolyi and Sanders, 1998, 254). In a last step, Karolyi and Sanders (1998) examine if the risk premiums can be predicted with observed variables. They find this to be the case for all three asset classes under investigation. For the REIT return rate variation, changes in the risk premiums are more important than changes in factor exposure. They find that their model does not explain the return rate variation of REITs as well as for other sectors. Karolyi and Sanders (1998, 259) attribute this to an 'important economic risk premium for REITs that is not represented in conventional multiple-beta asset pricing models.'

Pricing of public and private US real estate

Examining the pricing of real estate securities has the advantage that data on transactions are readily available. However, public and private real estate could be priced differently.[10] Ling and Naranjo (1997) approach this question and estimate multifactor models for both public and private US real estate return rates. The macro-economic risk factors are similar to those of Chen *et al.* (1986) and Chan (1990). Ling and Naranjo (1997, table 1) focus on four factors in particular: the market index, the growth of consumption expenditures, the real Treasury-bill rate, the term structure and unexpected inflation. Ling and Naranjo fit unconditional factor models, where factor exposure (betas) and risk premiums (gammas) are assumed to be constant throughout the sample period, and conditional models, where both the exposure and premiums can vary between periods. For the unconditional model, they find that the growth of consumption expenditures and the real Treasury-bill rate carry a risk premium in both the public and the private real estate market. Estimating conditional models, in which the risk premiums are allowed to vary over time, they obtain a similar result for about half of the quarters in the sample.

In a similar vein, Ling and Naranjo (1999) examine whether public and private real estate markets in the US are integrated with or segmented from the general stock market. Integration implies that the risk premiums (gammas) that investors can expect to receive are the same in both markets. Segmentation implies that the risk premiums differ and, in the extreme, the assets in the different markets are exposed to different risk factors. Ling and Naranjo (1999) find that the public REITs market is integrated with the general stock market. The private real estate market, however, is segmented from the general stock market. In one study, Peng (2016) assesses the evidence that common risk factors do not play a role for the pricing of private real estate. According to Peng, this result could be a statistical artefact caused by the use of index data. For his analysis, Peng uses the actual returns of individual buildings as the dependent variable instead of an index of a portfolio of appraised buildings. He finds that the three Fama and French fundamental equity factors not only explain REIT return rates, but also the actual return rates of the commercial buildings.

Pricing of international real estate securities

The studies discussed so far were all conducted with data from the US. Multifactor pricing models have also been applied in the context of internationally traded real estate securities. Bond *et al.* (2003) examine the risk and return of securitised real estate companies from 14 countries in Asia, Europe and North America. They use the CAPM with a global market index and also several different multifactor models. The multifactor models can include fundamental factors and country-specific real estate risk factors. To interpret their econometric results, we must assume that the real estate risk corresponds effectively to a traded security portfolio. The coefficient of the regression constant in the most general model is statistically insignificant for the majority of countries (Bond *et al.*, 2003, table 6). This indicates that this model explains the pricing of real estate securities well overall. However, this does not apply to the US, Japan, Singapore and Sweden.

While Bond *et al.* (2003) focussed on fundamental risk factors, Pavlov *et al.* (2015) examine the role of macro-economic risk factors for the pricing of international real estate securities, such as exchange and inflation rate shocks. The authors are interested in the relationship between credit market conditions and returns on real estate securities. They obtain plausible results for their models. For instance, the factor exposure (betas) for country risk, exchange rate fluctuations, inflation and firm size are all positive and statistically significant. Pavlov *et al.* (2015) do not test whether their multifactor model explains the pricing of international real estate securities.

Practical relevance of multifactor pricing models

Multifactor models provide evidence about the factors that affect risk premiums and on the economic conditions under which these effects will be stronger or weaker. This should help real estate investors to make informed decisions. However, multifactor models are estimated and this comes with estimation and specification uncertainty. Fama and French (1997) examine the first aspect when the aim of the analysis is to estimate the *cost of capital*; that is, the return rate investors will require in equilibrium given a project's risk. Fama and French conduct this exercise for many different sectors, including real estate. For each sector, they compare the cost of capital estimated with the CAPM to the one estimated with their three factor model (Fama and French, 1993). For real estate, they find that the cost of capital estimated with the CAPM seems too low. Fama and French (1997) also assess the standard errors of the cost estimates, which depend on the standard errors of the estimates of factor exposure (beta) and risk premiums (gamma). The standard errors at sector level are sizable and Fama and French are sceptical that the precision of cost of capital estimates are useful at the project level.

Conclusion

This chapter gives an overview of asset pricing models. Pricing models are useful for the valuation of existing assets, for the decision on the production of new assets (such as buildings or structured securities), for the assessment of fund manager performance and for portfolio construction. The CAPM has not withstood the test of time, because factors in addition to the market have been found to explain expected return rates. These additional factors are often related to economic variables, which opens them up to economic interpretation and understanding. Multifactor models allow fund managers to set up portfolios with a specific exposure towards relevant risk factors. This is a slightly different allocation approach than one that works with the concept of asset classes.

The chapter has focussed on the broad concepts to keep the discussion as intuitive as possible. A critical reader may object that essential aspects that play a role in the practice of real estate investments were not covered. For instance, neither transaction costs, the effect of taxes nor liquidity issues were covered. Such aspects can be considered in asset pricing models, at the cost of making them more complex. The simple two-period framework used throughout the chapter seems also rather restrictive. In empirical work, this restrictive framework is used implicitly if return distributions are assumed to be unchanged over time. Most of the factor models discussed above make this assumption by assuming that factor exposures (betas) and risk premiums (gammas) are constant over time. A few of the multifactor studies assumed that exposures and premiums can vary over time conditional on investors' information set. Readers interested in an in-depth discussion of dynamic asset pricing models should consult Cochrane (2005) or Singleton (2006).

Notes

1 Information aggregation is another widely recognised function of asset markets, so that it is assumed that this aggregation has taken place.
2 Chapter 12 discusses how assets can be priced by 'replicating' future cash flows with assets that are already traded. If such 'replication' is not practicable, an asset pricing model must be used.
3 As explained above, the marginal utility is a decreasing function in the level of consumption; the negative of this function is thus increasing.
4 Observe that the expectation of Equation (11.13) leads directly back to Equation (11.12).
5 Brueggeman *et al.* (1984) use an 'extended' CAPM that considers inflation as second risk factor. The authors note that liquidity risk is important for private vehicles too, but they do not consider it in their study.
6 Chen *et al.* (1986, Footnote 7), for example, examine if factors extracted statistically from asset return rates and their economic factors are related, which they are.
7 It could, therefore, be the case that the momentum factor stands for a systematic risk factor that is not yet understood.
8 Peterson and Hsieh (1997) discuss potential reasons for this result.
9 The zero beta portfolio has no exposure to the other risk factors.
10 Important contributions to this debate include Gyourko and Keim (1992) and Pagliari *et al.* (2005).

References

Ang, A. (2014) *Asset Management: a systematic approach to factor investing*, Oxford University Press, Oxford.

Ang, A., Goetzmann, W. N. and Schaefer, S. M. (2009) *Evaluation of active management of the Norwegian Government Pension Fund–Global*, Report to the Norwegian Ministry of Finance.

Baum, A. and Hartzell, D. (2012) *Global property investment: strategies, structures, decisions*, Wiley-Blackwell, Chichester.

Bender, J., Briand, R., Melas, D. and Subramanian, R. A. (2013) *Foundations of factor investing*, MSCI Research Insight, December 2013, MSCI.

Bond, S. A., Karolyi, G. A. and Sanders, A. B. (2003) International real estate returns: a multifactor, multicountry approach, *Real Estate Economics*, 31, 481–500.

Brown, G. R. and Matysiak, G. A. (2000) *Real estate investment: a capital market approach*, Pearson, Harlow.

Brueggeman, W. B., Chen, A. K. and Thibodeau, T. G. (1984) Real estate investment funds: performance and portfolio considerations, *AREUEA Journal*, 12, 333–54.

Campbell, J. Y., Lo, A. W. and MacKinlay, A. C. (1997) *The econometrics of financial markets*, Princeton University, Princeton, NJ.

Chan, K. C., Hendershott, P. H. and Sanders, A. B. (1990) Risk and return on real estate: evidence from equity REITS, *AREUEA Journal*, 18, 431–52.

Chen, N-F., Roll, R. and Ross, S. A. (1986) Economic forces and the stock market, *Journal of Business*, 59, 383–403.

Chen, S-J., Hsieh, C-H. and Jordan, B. D. (1997) Real estate and the arbitrage pricing theory: macrovariables vs. derived factors, *Real Estate Economics*, 25, 505–23.

Cochrane, J. H. (2005) *Asset pricing*, Princeton University Press, Princeton, NJ.

Connor, G. and Korajczyk, R. A. (1988) Risk and return in equilibrium APT: application of a new test methodology, *Journal of Financial Economics*, 21, 255–90.

Fama, E. F. and French, K. R. (1993) Common risk factors in the returns on stocks and bonds, *Journal of Financial Economics*, 33, 3–56.

Fama, E. F. and French, K. R. (1997) Industry cost of capital, *Journal of Financial Economics*, 43, 153–93.

Fama, E. F. and French, K. R. (2004) The capital asset pricing model: theory and evidence, *Journal of Economic Perspectives*, 18, 25–46.

Fama, E. F. and French, K. R. (2015) A five-factor asset pricing model, *Journal of Financial Economics*, 116, 1–22.

Fama, E. F. and MacBeth, J. D. (1973) Risk, return, and equilibrium: empirical tests, *Journal of Political Economy*, 81, 607–36.

Ferson, W. E. and Harvey, C. R. (1991) The variation of economic risk premiums, *Journal of Political Economy*, 99, 385–415.

Geltner, D. M., Miller, N. G., Clayton, J. and Eichholtz, P. (2007) *Commercial real estate: analysis and investments*, Thomson South-Western, Mason, OH.

Gyourko, J. and Keim, D. B. (1992) What does the stock market tell us about real estate returns?, *AREUEA Journal*, 20, 457–85.

Hoesli, M. and MacGregor, B. D. (2000) *Property investment: principles and practice of portfolio management*, Pearson Education, Harlow.

Huberman, G., Kandel, S. and Stambaugh, R. F. (1987) Mimicking portfolios and exact arbitrage pricing, *Journal of Finance*, 42, 1–9.

Jagannathan, R., Schaumburg, E. and Zhou, G. (2010) Cross-sectional asset pricing tests, *Annual Review of Financial Economics*, 2, 49–74.

Karolyi, G. A. and Sanders, A. B. (1998) The variation of economic risk premiums in real estate returns, *Journal of Real Estate Finance and Economics*, 17, 245–62.

Lehmann, B. and Modest, D. M. (1988) The empirical foundations of the arbitrage pricing theory, *Journal of Financial Economics*, 21, 213–54.

Ling, D. C. and Naranjo, A. (1997) Economic risk factors and commercial real estate returns, *Journal of Real Estate Finance and Economics*, 15, 283–307.

Ling, D. C. and Naranjo, A. (1999) The integration of commercial real estate markets and stock markets, *Real Estate Economics*, 27, 483–515.

Liu, C. H. and Mei, J. (1992) The predictability of returns on equity REITs and their co-movement with other assets, *Journal of Real Estate Finance and Economics*, 5, 401–18.

Pagliari Jr., J. L., Scherer K. A. and Monopoli R. T. (2005) Public versus private real estate equities: a more refined, long-term comparison, *Real Estate Economics*, 33(1), 147–88.

Pavlov, A., Steiner, E. and Wachter, S. (2015) Macroeconomic risk factors and the role of mispriced credit in the returns from international real estate securities, *Journal of Real Estate Finance and Economics*, 43, 241–70.

Peng, L. (2016) The risk and return of commercial real estate: a property level analysis, *Real Estate Economics*, 44, 555–83.

Peterson, J. D. and Hsieh, C-H. (1997) Do common risk factors in the returns on stocks and bonds explain returns on REITs?, *Real Estate Economics*, 25, 321–45.

Ross, S. A. (1976) The arbitrage theory of capital asset pricing, *Journal of Economic Theory*, 13, 341–60.

Singleton, K. J. (2006) *Empirical dynamic asset pricing: model specification and econometric assessment*, Princeton University Press, Princeton, NJ.

Stambaugh, R. F. (1982) On the exclusion of assets from tests of the two-parameter model: a sensitivity analysis, *Journal of Financial Economics*, 10, 237–68.

Titman, S. and Warga, A. (1986) Risk and the performance of real estate investment trusts: a multiple index approach, *AREUEA Journal*, 14, 414–31.

Tobin, J. (1958) Liquidity preference as behavior towards risk, *Review of Economic Studies*, 25, 65–86.

12 Real options in real estate

Bryan D. MacGregor, Rainer Schulz and Tien Foo Sing

Introduction

Options are an integral part of real estate investments. Defined loosely, an option represents the flexibility to take an action regarding an asset if this action generates value. If the action does not generate value, then the holder of the option will not take it. Options can be standardised financial contracts related to the purchase or disposal of real estate securities. Such options do not differ from other financial options. But direct real estate investments bring many so-called *real options*. These options have a real asset underlying them. For instance, the ownership of land allows decisions on what and when to develop. Ownership of a building carries with it options to alter the building, such as the refurbishment of an existing office building or the extension of an industrial warehouse. Operational lease contracts for the use of commercial real estate often contain options, such as rights to cancel or renew the contract or to adjust the rent. Such contractual claims on the use of real estate display option-like characteristics and should be considered as such.

In this chapter, we focus on real option models and present them in the context of real estate applications. The real option literature is usually less asset-specific, and research and development, production processes and foreign direct investments have been modelled with real option models. The theory of real options is based on the theory of financial options but, depending on the context, adaptation might be required. First, the use of the replicating portfolio approach as pricing tool might not be appropriate. This approach is based on the reasoning that whenever cash flows of a new asset can be replicated – in principle – by a portfolio of traded securities, then the price of the asset must be identical to the cost of this portfolio. However, once real assets are exposed to risks that are not yet priced and traded in securities markets, the replicating portfolio approach is no longer useful. Real option models must then rely instead on equilibrium pricing models (see also Chapter 11). Second, adaptation will be necessary if relevant variables are not exogenous. In the case of real estate, rents and construction costs are such variables. Whereas exercising a financial call option on a stock leaves the price process of the underlying asset unchanged, the construction of a new building will alter the future rental cash flows of all buildings through the increased building supply. Third, strategic interactions are usually ignored for financial options, but they are important aspect for real options.

The chapter is organised as follows. In the next section, we illustrate real options using simple models; in particular, we discuss timing and scale choice in land development and options embedded in lease contracts. Then, we show how real option models can be implemented in a more complex setting. Closed form solutions are often not available, so that numerical procedures are required. Following this, we discuss the empirical literature on real options in real estate. The final section assesses the potential future use of real option models for real estate investment decision making.

Three examples using a two-period model

We use a simple two-period framework to illustrate the basic concepts of real options in real estate. We apply this framework to land development and upward-only adjustments in operational lease contracts.

Example 1: land development

In his seminal paper, Titman (1985) observes that urban land can remain vacant despite high building prices. Delaying development can be advantageous because additional information allows better decision making about the type of building to be developed and when to build. To show this, we use the numerical example of Trigeorgis (1996, 347).

A developer owns a site on which she could develop a block of apartments. Two specifications are possible with, respectively, six or nine apartment units. Construction costs are 480 for the former and 810 for the latter. For simplicity, it is assumed that construction is instantaneous. The current price per unit is 100 and the price next period will be either 150 or 90 (Table 12.1). The security market is complete and replication of the cash flows from the development project is possible. There is no need to be specific about the probabilities with which each of the two states occurs.[1]

If the developer developed immediately, the six unit design would be chosen because:

$$6 \times 100 - 480 = 120 > 9 \times 100 - 810 = 90 \tag{12.1}$$

If the developer wanted to sell the site instead of developing it herself, she should accept an offer that is not less than the residual value of 120.

Now assume that the developer can also wait until the next period and decide then on the development. Construction costs for both designs in the next period will be the same as in the current period, but the unit price will either be 150 or 90. If the developer chooses not to develop in the current period, she will learn which unit price is realised next period and will – based on this information – decide if and what to develop. Developing in the current period means that she gives up this option to learn.

Should she wait to develop? While the developer does not know in the current period *which* of the two states will occur in the next period, she can anticipate what she will do in each of the states. If she ends up next period in the state where the unit price is 150, she would implement the nine unit design, because:

$$150 \times 9 - 810 = 540 > 150 \times 6 - 480 = 420 \tag{12.2}$$

Table 12.1 Price per apartment unit

Price in current period	*State-dependent price next period*
100	150
	90

If she ends up instead in the state where the unit price is 90, she would implement the six unit design, because:

$$6 \times 90 - 480 = 60 > 9 \times 90 - 810 = 0 \tag{12.3}$$

Table 12.2 summarises this position. In each of the two states, the developer would choose the design that maximises her profit. However, this leaves the question if it is better to develop in the current period and to earn a profit of 120, or to delay development to the next period for the chance to earn either 540 or 60?

Before showing how to derive the current value of land if kept undeveloped, we discuss the important aspects of the example.

First, the example provides the major conceptual insight that even though the developer does not know *which* of the two states will occur next period, she knows exactly *how she will act* in each of the states. Comparing the value of land if developed immediately with the present value of either the nine or six unit building would not be correct, because it ignores that she will have better information next period than she has now.

Second, the example assumes that ownership of land gives the owner flexibility in choosing the timing and scale of development. But there are factors that can curtail such flexibility. For example, flexibility will be reduced if a building permission is about to expire, or if zoning prevents specific kinds of buildings. Flexibility will be reduced if a competitor can pre-empt development and thereby reduce the value of waiting. For instance, it might be worthwhile to wait and see what happens to prices before committing to a new apartment block. However, if there are other potential competitors and only one project will be economically feasible, timing flexibility may be eroded.

We use the replicating portfolio approach to value the land if held undeveloped in the current period. In particular, we assume that the variable that drives the value of the development option – the price per apartment unit – has a traded equivalent in the security market. This could be, for instance, a portfolio of stocks of apartment developers. This portfolio shows exactly the same behaviour as the apartment price given in Table 12.1. We assume also that money can be borrowed and loaned at the same interest rate of 10% per period. Given these assumptions, it is possible to set up a notional portfolio that replicates the state-dependent cash flows next period, as shown in Table 12.2. Once the composition of this portfolio is known, we can compute its current price and this must be the price of the site if development is delayed.

Suppose an investment of a quantity q_s in the security portfolio and borrowing of an amount q_b, so that the replicating portfolio has exactly the same cash flows as the development in the next period (Table 12.2). This requires that we find q_s and q_b that solve the two equations:

$$150 \times q_s + 1.1 \times q_b = 540 \quad \text{and} \quad 90 \times q_s + 1.1 \times q_b = 60 \tag{12.4}$$

Table 12.2 Value of site if development is delayed

Value in current period	*State-dependent value next period*
?	max[540,420] = 540
	max[60,0] = 60

The solution is $q_s = 8$ and $q_b = -600$ and the replicating portfolio would cost, in the current period:

$$100 \times 8 - 600 = 200 \tag{12.5}$$

The replicating portfolio and postponed development deliver the exact same cash flows next period. Therefore, the current value of the site – if held undeveloped –must be also 200.

The conclusion is that it is better to wait with the development, because the value of land if held undeveloped in the current period is 200, whereas it is only 120 if land were developed immediately. The difference $200 - 120 = 80$ is the *option premium of waiting*. Readers who are familiar with financial option theory will see immediately that land is a call option on the building, where the exercise price depends on the chosen design. Developing in the current period is like exercising the option now, while waiting is like keeping the option alive.

Example 2: land development with price and cost uncertainty

A natural way to extend the setting just used is to assume that more than one source of uncertainty exists. Take the developer from Example 1 and assume that, not only is the price of each apartment unit is uncertain, but also the construction costs. For simplicity, assume that only the six unit design is feasible. From Table 12.1, the building price is then 600 in the current period and either 900 or 540 in the next period. The construction costs are 480 in the current period as before, but suppose that the costs will be now either 620 or 420 in the next period. The exercise price of the development option is now uncertain.

This implies that there are now four possible states in the next period: the state with a high building price and a low cost (900, 420), the state with a high building price and a high cost (900, 620), the state with a low building price and a low cost (540, 420) and the state with a low building price and a high cost (540, 620). In the last of these states, development would imply incurring a loss and the developer should not go ahead. The value of land in this state next period is, therefore, zero.

To find the current value of land if held undeveloped, we suppose that liquid securities exist that can be used – in principle – to replicate the cash flows of the development option in the four possible states next period. The securities are two stocks, the risk-free asset and a call option on an equal-weighted index of the two stocks. The first stock is perfectly correlated with the building price and the second stock is perfectly correlated with construction costs. Money can be lent or borrowed at the risk-free rate of 10% per period. Let us assume that the fourth security – the call option – has an exercise price of 700 and costs 38 in the current period. Next period, this stock index call option will only be exercised if the state (900, 620) occurs, because this is the only state where the call option is in the money. The call option's cash flow in this state is $(0.5 \times 900 + 0.5 \times 620) - 700 = 60$.[2]

Given the security market, the current value of the land if kept undeveloped is 108.6; see Appendix 12A. The residual value of immediate development is $600 - 480 = 120$. Therefore, it is better to develop immediately then to wait until next period.

Example 3: upward-only rent adjustment

Operating leases often have option-type covenants. The landlord may have the right, but not the obligation, to adjust the rent at predetermined review dates to the market rate. The tenant may have the right, but not the obligation, to terminate or renew the contract at some

Table 12.3 Market rent per square metre of space

Rent in current period	*State-dependent rent in all future periods*
	24
20	
	16

Table 12.4 Present value of future rental income per square metre of space

Value in current period	*State-dependent value next period*
	$\frac{1.1}{0.1} \times 24 = 264$
216	
	$\frac{1.1}{0.1} \times 16 = 176$

specified future date. In both cases, the other party, in effect, grants an option. For instance, in the case of the upward-only rent adjustment, the tenant writes an option for the landlord. Even though the tenant does not know if the landlord will exercise the option, which will only happen if the market rent at the review date is above the current going contract rent, the tenant knows that if the landlord exercises the option, then it will be to the tenant's detriment. A rational tenant should, therefore, ask for an upfront compensation when granting such an option; for example by insisting on a reduction of the base rent.

Table 12.3 shows that the current market rent is 20 per square metre and that the rent will either increase to 24 or reduce to 16 in the next period. The rent will then stay at this level in all future periods. Therefore, all uncertainty about the market rent is resolved in the next period and the landlord will know which rent can be received in perpetuity. Assuming that the risk-free interest rate is 10% in the current and all future periods, the values of rentable space per square metre in the two possible states next period are given in the second column of Table 12.4. If the market rent moves up to 24, the value is $24 + 24/0.1 = (1.1/0.1) \times 24 = 264$; if the market rent moves down to 16, the value is $16 + 16/0.1 = (1.1/0.1) \times 16 = 176$.

To obtain the value of the building in the current period, we suppose a traded security that pays next period 2.64 per unit in the up-state and 1.76 in the down-state. The security costs 2.16 per unit in the current period. Obviously, a portfolio of 100 units of this security has cash flows next period identical to the value of the building in each of the two possible future states (Table 12.4, second column) The security portfolio costs $100 \times 2.16 = 216$ in the current period. The value of the building in the current period is thus the current rent plus the present value of the uncertain future building value, which is $20 + 216 = 236$ per square metre in total.

Assume now that the building is currently vacant and three different parties approach the landlord. The first party offers to pay the going market rent in each period. This offer has – as derived above – a total value of 236 in the current period. The second party offers to pay a rent of 21.45 in perpetuity. The third party offers to pay a base rent of 17, but grants the landlord the right to adjust the rent to the market rent in the next period.

Table 12.5 Rent with landlord's adjustment option per square metre of space

Rent in current period	*State-dependent rent in all future periods*
17	max[24,17] = 24
	max[16,17] = 17

Table 12.6 Present value of future rental income with adjustment option per square metre of space

Value in current period	*State-dependent value next period*
?	$\frac{1.1}{0.1} \times 24 = 264$
	$\frac{1.1}{0.1} \times 17 = 187$

It is immediately obvious that the landlord is indifferent between the offers of the first two parties, because 236 = (1.1/0.1) × 21.45. But what about the offer of the third party? Given the market rent process from Table 12.3, it is clear that the landlord will exercise the adjustment option in the up state, but not in the down state. Taking this optimal behaviour into account, the landlord is confronted with the effective rent process given in Table 12.5 and the corresponding building values in each of the two possible future states are given in the second column of Table 12.6.

To find the present value of these two possible future building values, we have to find a replicating portfolio of the traded and the risk-free securities that fulfils:

$$2.64 \times q_s + 1.1 \times q_b = 264 \quad \text{and} \quad 1.76 \times q_s + 1.1 \times q_b = 187 \tag{12.6}$$

The solution is $q_s = 87.5$ and $q_b = 30$, so that, in the current period, the replicating portfolio would cost:

$$2.16 \times 87.5 + 30 = 219 \tag{12.7}$$

The total value of the rental contract that the third party proposes is 17 + 219 = 236, which is identical to the offers by the other two parties.

The above three examples show that real options models are useful in a real estate context. The models have the potential to describe how decisions are made (*positive aspect*), but the models can also inform how decisions should be made (*normative aspect*). In many situations, real estate market participants do not make all decisions at the same time. For instance, a developer does not let office space before a building permission has been granted; the developer will construct a new building sequentially from ground up and financing might be staggered depending on the development phase of a project.

Real estate market participants may also delay some decisions, so that they can learn new information whenever available. For instance, a shopping centre might be developed while keeping some land undeveloped and used as parking space. Once the owner learns that the centre is a success, the car park land could then be used for the expansion of the shopping centre. If the owner learns that the centre space is not fully leased, the land should remain as parking space. While the owner does not know which of the two possible events (success or not success) will occur in the future, they have already anticipated that it might be worthwhile to keep the car park land for future expansion. Having the car park land is analogous to having an option, but not an obligation, to expand in the future.

Making real option models more realistic

Whereas the three examples above provide intuition into the basic concepts of real option models, they ignore aspects that are important in practice. The following will now be considered:

- The discrete two state framework is not realistic for real world applications.
- Financial markets might not be sufficiently complete for the – notional – replication of real option cash flows.
- It is possible to wait before implementing an investment, but it is also possible to abandon an investment.
- Delays between exercising the option and the arrival of cash flows might exist (time to build).
- Real option holders may interact strategically or competition might erode the value of waiting.

All the aspects above have been treated in the literature, mostly separately. It is natural that higher realism comes with more complex real option models.

Continuous time framework

Future asset prices typically change rapidly. This cannot be modelled with a simple binomial model. It is possible, however, to divide the interval into many short sub-intervals, and to set up a binomial tree that grows with each sub-interval. Such a tree starts at the current asset price, which can either go up or down in the first sub-interval. Over the second sub-interval, the price can go up or down from each of the two levels reached in the first sub-interval. At the end of the second sub-interval, the asset value has four possible realisations and so on. The resulting tree becomes complex rather quickly and option problems have to be solved by backward induction, which is complex and time consuming. In the limit, as the sub-intervals approach zero, the tree approaches the behaviour of a continuous process. Working with the limiting continuous process can have the advantage that an explicit solution for the particular real option model might exist.

Most of the papers mentioned below work within the continuous time stochastic framework. As will be seen, real option models in this framework lead to differential equations that need to be solved. If no explicit solution exists, numerical methods can be used. Numerical methods include simulation, lattice approaches, and finite differences (Trigeorgis, 1996, ch. 10). Simulation of the risk-adjusted price process leads to the distribution of the relevant variables over which expectations can be formed (Boyle, 1977). The binomial approach is an example for a lattice approach. Finite differences solve the differential equations numerically.

Asset pricing framework

The assumption that a replicating portfolio exists is strong:

...capital markets must be sufficiently 'complete' so that, at least in principle, one could find an asset or construct a dynamic portfolio of assets (that is, a portfolio whose holdings are adjusted continuously as asset prices change), the price of which is perfectly correlated with [... the market value of the underlying asset]. This is equivalent to saying that markets are sufficiently complete that the firm's decisions do not affect the opportunity set available to investors. The assumption of spanning should hold for most commodities, which are typically traded on both spot and futures markets, and for manufactured goods to the extent that prices are correlated with the values of shares or portfolios. However, there may be cases in which this assumption will not hold; an example might be a project to develop a new product that is unrelated to any existing ones, or an R&D venture, the results of which may be hard to predict.

(Dixit and Pindyck, 1994, 147)

An alternative to the replicating portfolio approach is to assume an asset pricing model and to use this model to derive the value of a project. It is assumed that there are no transaction costs nor taxes. Constantinides (1978) gives an early application of this approach that uses a continuous time framework. The next example shows how this approach works for the land development option. As the derivation is rather technical, the reader might wish just to skim through it and focus on the resulting valuation formulas that will be motivated in detail after the derivation.

Example 4: land development option

We consider the owner of a piece of land who could develop an office building on it. We derive the value of the office building first. By exercising the development option, the land owner will obtain the building. We discuss the optimal development-timing rule and the value of the piece of land.

Rental cash flows $x(t)$ follow a geometric Brownian motion:

$$dx = \mu x dt + \sigma x dz \tag{12.8}$$

The cash flows grow with the expected rate $\mu \geq 0$, are disturbed by shocks with volatility $\sigma > 0$, and dz is the increment of the Wiener process $z(t)$. If the geometric Brownian motion reaches zero, it will not recover. The owner of an office building will receive the rental income. It could, therefore, be said that the office building *derives* its value from the *underlying* rental process. While being a derivative in this sense, there is no flexibility regarding the rental income. Such flexibility would exist if the landlord could review rents or had the right to break the contract at specific dates. As we focus solely on the development option, such additional flexibility is not considered.

Let $v(x)$ denote the value of the developed office building. Over a short interval, the building owner receives the change in capital value dv and rental income of xd. The *ex-ante* return rate is therefore:

$$\frac{dv + xdt}{v} = \frac{\mu x v_x + 0.5\sigma^2 x^2 v_{xx} + x}{v} dt + \frac{\sigma x v_x}{v} dz \tag{12.9}$$

On the right-hand side, Ito's lemma has been used for the change in building's value over a short time period, see, for instance, Trigeorgis (1996, 89). The expressions v_x and v_{xx} stand for the first- and second-order derivatives of the value function with respect to variable x.[3]

In market equilibrium, the expected return rate of the building must be equal to the required return rate. To determine the required return rate, it is necessary to decide on an asset pricing model. We use the capital asset pricing model (CAPM; see Chapter 11). According to the CAPM, the required return rate for an investment in the developed office building is:

$$h = r + \lambda \frac{\sigma_{vm}}{\sigma_m} \tag{12.10}$$

Here, r is the risk-free rate, $\lambda \equiv (r_m - r)/\sigma_m$ is the market price of risk (r_m is the expected return rate of the market portfolio and σ_m its volatility) and σ_{vm} is the covariance between the return rates of the building and the market portfolio. The risk of the building comes from the stochastic rental income, see Equation (12.8), giving:

$$\sigma_{vm} = \frac{v_x}{v}\sigma_{xm} = \frac{v_x}{v}\rho\sigma x \sigma_m \tag{12.11}$$

The coefficient ρ measures the correlation between dz and the Wiener process driving the whole market. Taking the expectation of Equation (12.9), which must equal h in equilibrium, and using Equation (12.11), leads after reformulation to this non-homogeneous equation:

$$x - rv + (\mu - \rho\sigma\lambda)v_x x + 0.5\sigma^2 v_{xx} x^2 = 0 \tag{12.12}$$

It is standard that the solution of the homogenous part of this equation (that is, excluding the x term) will be of the form $v(x) = x^\gamma$. It can then be shown that the two roots of the homogenous part are:

$$\gamma_{1,2} = \frac{1}{2} - \frac{\mu - \rho\sigma\lambda}{\sigma^2} \pm \sqrt{\left(\frac{\mu - \rho\sigma\lambda}{\sigma^2} - \frac{1}{2}\right)^2 + \frac{2r}{\sigma^2}} \tag{12.13}$$

Observe that the first root is strictly positive and the second strictly negative ($\gamma_1 > 0 > \gamma_2$). Further, the first root is larger than one if $r + \rho\sigma\lambda > \mu$. It is assumed throughout that this inequality holds, which implies that the growth of cash flows alone is not sufficient to compensate for the risk taken. As will be seen below from Equation (12.17), this assumption ensures that the present value of cash flows from the developed building will be bounded. The particular part of the solution for the differential equation in Equation (12.12) is obtained using a polynomial of order one. Combining the solutions of the homogenous and particular parts gives the general solution:

$$v(x) = c_1 x^{\gamma_1} + c_2 x^{\gamma_2} + \frac{x}{r + \rho\sigma\lambda - \mu} \tag{12.14}$$

To determine the two constants c_1 and c_2, the following two boundary conditions are used. First, if the rental process falls to zero, it will not recover. In such a case, the building will also have no value. The first boundary condition is thus $v(0) = 0$. This can only hold if $c_2 = 0$. Second, the value of the building over time should be driven only by fundamentals and not a speculative component. The rent process is the fundamental and grows forever with an expected rate of μ. Imposing this condition on the expected value growth of the building leads to the restriction that $c_1 = 0$ (see also the discussion in Dixit and Pindyck, 1994, 181).[4] The value of the building is therefore:

$$v(x) = \frac{x}{r + \rho\sigma\lambda - \mu} \tag{12.15}$$

The building is priced so that the income yield θ equals the required return rate – risk-free rate plus risk premium – minus the rent growth rate: $\theta = r + \rho\sigma\lambda - \mu$.[5] The value formula in Equation (12.15) should look familiar, because it corresponds to the Gordon growth model, used frequently in the real estate industry (Geltner *et al.*, 2007, 594). The Gordon growth model starts from the present value:

$$\tilde{v}(x) = E\left[\int_0^\infty x(\tau) e^{-\int_0^\tau h(u)du} d\tau\right] \tag{12.16}$$

It assumes then that both the required return rate and the expected rental growth rate are constant. If we set the required return rate to $h(\tau) = (r + \rho\sigma\lambda)$, let the rent follow the geometric Brownian motion $x(\tau) = exp\{(\mu - 0.5\sigma^2)\tau + \sigma z\}$ for $\tau \geq 0$, so that $E[x(\tau)] = xexp\{\mu\tau\}$, then we obtain from Equation (12.16):

$$\tilde{v}(x) = \int_0^\infty xe^{-(r+\rho\sigma\lambda-\mu)\tau} d\tau \tag{12.17}$$

The present value converges, because – by assumption – the required return rate is larger than the rental growth rate. Solving leads immediately to $\tilde{v}(x) = v(x)$ from Equation (12.15), as was stated above.

Applying Ito's lemma to $v(x)$ from Equation (12.15), it follows that the building value follows a geometric Brownian motion:

$$dv = \mu v dt + \sigma v dz \tag{12.18}$$

Note that the expected capital growth rate is μ.

Why did we choose a rather complicated approach to derive $v(x)$? First, the approach starts from the elementary principle that, in asset pricing equilibrium, expected and required return rates must be the same. Second, given the model assumptions, the approach is rather general and can be applied to value real options that have the rental process as underlying. We show this next.

Let $l(v)$ denote the value of a piece of land on which an office building with current value $v(x)$ could be erected. The piece of land derives its value effectively from the underlying rental cash flows, because by developing a building these cash flows can be earned. Different to the erected building, which came with no flexibility, the land comes with timing flexibility. Land is an American call option on the building value and ultimately an option on when to receive the rental cash flows.[6] To obtain the building, the landowner has to invest in the construction of the building, which costs c. Not developing immediately has the advantage that the land owner can wait until a favourable rent level has been reached. While waiting to develop, the land owner benefits from the land value growth – driven by the building value v – but receives no rental cash flows. In asset pricing equilibrium, the expected and the required return rates for holding the land must be the same. This leads to an expression similar to Equation (12.12):

$$-rl + (\mu - \rho\sigma\lambda) l_v v + 0.5\sigma^2 l_{vv} v^2 = 0 \tag{12.19}$$

The general solution is:

$$l(v) = c_1 v^{\gamma_1} + c_2 v^{\gamma_2} \tag{12.20}$$

The three boundary conditions are $l(0) = 0$, $l(v^*) = v^* - c$ and $l'(v^*) = 1$. Here, v^* denotes the critical building value that will trigger immediate land development. The trigger level could also be expressed for the rental process, because this process drives the building value. Equation (12.18) shows that the building value follows a geometric Brownian motion and will not recover if the value drops to zero. The first boundary condition simply states, therefore, that land has no value if the underlying asset – the building – has no value. The second boundary condition states that the value of land upon development is just the residual value. The third boundary condition is the so-called *smooth-pasting* condition (Dixit, 1992). The first boundary condition requires that we set $c_2 = 0$ in Equation (12.20). From the remaining two conditions, we obtain:

$$v^* = \frac{\gamma_1}{\gamma_1 - 1} c \tag{12.21}$$

and

$$l(v) = \begin{cases} (v^* - c)\left(\frac{v}{v^*}\right)^{\gamma_1} & \text{for} \quad v < v^* \\ v - c & \text{for} \quad v \geq v^* \end{cases} \tag{12.22}$$

The building value has to reach v^* before land development is triggered. It is obvious that $v^* > c$ (recall from above that $\gamma_1 > 1$). This contrasts with the net present value rule according to which development should be triggered whenever $v - c \geq 0$. Following this rule could lead to premature development, because it does not consider that keeping the land undeveloped allows the developer to wait for better outcomes, to which she will then adapt. Development should only go ahead if the current building value is sufficiently high – as determined by Equation (12.21) – to compensate for annulling the benefits of waiting.

The completed building is itself a traded asset and its expected return rate consists of capital growth at rate μ and the income yield θ. In asset market equilibrium, the expected return rate must be equal to the required return rate and we know from above that $\mu + \theta = r + \rho\sigma\lambda$. In this case:

$$\gamma_1 = \frac{1}{2} - \frac{r - \theta}{\sigma^2} + \sqrt{\left(\frac{r - \theta}{\sigma^2} - \frac{1}{2}\right)^2 + \frac{2r}{\sigma^2}} \tag{12.23}$$

This is a function of variables that are either observable (such as the interest rate r) or can be estimated easily (such as the initial yield θ and the volatility of the rent process σ). It is convenient for practical applications that the risk premium and the expected rental growth rate are not explicitly present in Equation (12.23). Establishing magnitudes for both variables would be difficult in most applications.[7]

The model used in Example 4 can be extended and becomes more realistic once we assume that the construction costs are uncertain as well and follow a geometric Brownian motion (McDonald and Siegel, 1986). If traded securities span this additional uncertainty, then the setting is similar to Example 2, but now modelled in continuous time. McDonald and Siegel also analyse the comparative statics of the volatility on the decision to invest and the value of the investment opportunity, in this case the value of undeveloped land. They find that a larger volatility σ makes it optimal to postpone development further (v^* increases); larger volatility also increases the value of the project $l(v)$. This is a standard result from financial option models. However, as McDonald and Siegel discuss, this comparative result depends crucially on the impact of the volatility on the required return rate (McDonald and Siegel, 1986, note14). Once the required return rate is affected, the overall effect is no longer clear-cut – see also McDonald and Siegel (1985, 343). The comparative results of McDonald and Siegel (1986) are frequently cited, but often without this qualification. If $\rho = 0$, then the required return rate reduces to the risk-free rate and the effect is clear. Zero correlation implies that the cash flows of a project are unrelated with the rest of the market. In real estate context, this might be justifiable for infrastructure projects, but much less so for other commercial sectors.

Abandonment

The owner of a real asset has always the option to abandon operation and, in the extreme, to abandon the asset. In the real estate context, a landlord could leave a building vacant whenever the net rent receivable is negative. In the extreme, the landlord could demolish the building. The present value does not consider such flexibility, as it treats future cash flows as being beyond the influence of the landlord. Real option models consider dynamic behaviour of the asset owner explicitly. The real option value of a building will be, therefore, at least as large as its present value.

McDonald and Siegel (1985) model the value of a firm that can abandon its operation and take it up later at no additional costs. Such operational options have value, because future net cash flows can never become negative. Assuming geometric Brownian motions for income and cost, McDonald and Siegel (1985) derive closed-form formulas for the value of the firm. McDonald and Siegel (1986, 714) analyse the case of abandonment, with the exit option being the opposite of the decision to enter a market.

Dixit (1989) analyses the case when a firm has both an entry option into and an exit option out of a market. For instance, the owner of developable land in the City of London holds an entry option into the commercial office market with the construction costs as exercise price. The rental cash flows net of operating costs can become negative. If this happens, it might be worthwhile to demolish the building and keep it as a vacant site with future development potential. The abandonment option has the demolishing cost as the strike price. Owning the building with this embedded option has value above the net present value as the formula in Dixit (1989, eq. 7) shows: the building value is the Gordon growth model value *plus* the value of the abandonment option. Dixit (1989) shows that the critical net operating cash flow at which the market should be entered – the building should be constructed – is higher than the break-even level. All else equal, the critical entry cash flow increases with higher exit (demolition) cost and the critical exit cash flow decreases with higher entry (construction) cost. Comparative statics show that cash flow volatility increases the critical entry cash flow and reduces the critical exit cash flow. Dixit's results seem very reasonable in the context of real estate development and investment. Land ownership gives an option to develop whenever this is most profitable. Once completed, a building will generate rental income, but will also incur variable cost. Just like in the development option case, in which the land owner will not develop immediately when the building value is just equal to the construction cost, the building will not be demolished the moment the rental income is just below the variable cost. In both cases, Dixit's model predicts a trigger rental cash flow that is above the break-even rental income (development) and below the variable cost (abandonment). Williams (1991) applies these ideas explicitly to real estate development and treats the flexibility of scale as well.

Gestation lags

Time to build is an essential aspect of many projects. Majd and Pindyck (1987) assume that once project construction has started, the *rate* of construction can be adjusted during the process whenever new information about project's market value arrives. Such investment in stages can be observed in residential settlement developments, where the early construction stage needs to be completed before the next stage starts. Majd and Pindyck assume that the market value of the completed project follows a geometric Brownian motion. Finding the optimal investment programme requires numerical solution techniques. The numerical results show that construction should not start immediately when a project's market value equals total construction cost. The flexibility to 'mothball' a project and complete it once market conditions have changed brings additional value. Bar-Ilan and Strange (1996) examine projects that require time to build, but can be abandoned. Effectively, they extend the model of Dixit (1989) by considering the time it takes to complete the project. Given that a project can be abandoned, there is less harm in committing to it. They find that it is now even possible that investment is triggered when the current cash flow is below the break-even level (Bar-Ilan and Strange, 1996, Table 1, last column). This is certainly something observed in real estate markets, when new projects are started even in a falling market. However, it is essential for this result that the project can be abandoned at reasonable cost.

Competition and strategic interaction

The discussion so far presumed that an individual firm faces no competition from other firms. Such a firm can take its time and wait for the optimal demand conditions for its products. However, what happens if other firms are active in the same market? This can happen in real estate markets, in which firms compete for development opportunities, and when waiting can mean that a valuable opportunity is foregone. Further, unlike financial options, the exercise of real estate development options will change the available stock of buildings and, therefore, affect the rent process.

Grenadier (1995) focusses on a perfectly competitive real estate industry and derives the endogenous spot rent process. The spot rent is determined by the current building stock and demand for space that is exposed to shocks. Given the value of existing buildings and construction costs, new construction will start whenever this promises profits. This limits the upward drift of spot rents. Competition prevents developers from reaping excess profits, but it does not erode the value of waiting. Even under perfect competition, it is never optimal to develop immediately when rents just cover the required return.[8] Grenadier (2005) extends the analysis to other modes of market conduct and shows that a monopolist will wait the longest with new construction after a series of positive demand shocks, followed by an oligopolistic real estate industry. The shortest waiting time is found in an industry facing perfect competition. Once the process for the spot rents is derived, Grenadier values different lease contracts. A simple lease is a portfolio consisting of owning a building and writing a call option with zero exercise price (see also Smith, 1979, 105). During the lease term, the tenant can use the building *as if* she were the owner. However, at the end of the lease period, the building and its full use value go back to the previous owner. Based on this reasoning and the value of the building underlying the call option, Grenadier (1995) derives the term structure of lease rates for a perfectly competitive real estate market. He also derives equilibrium rents on pre-leasing contracts, overage rents and several other contracts. Grenadier (2005) conducts similar analysis for the case when strategic interaction between developers takes place.[9] In particular, he values lease contracts that have embedded options, such as renewal options at the end of the stipulated term, cancellation options, lease concessions, and sale-and-leaseback contracts.

Grenadier (1996) analyses the behaviour of two developers who interact in a two-stage situation. Using the concept of leader–follower competition, Grenadier shows that development timing can be sequential or simultaneous. In the latter case, 'too much' construction takes place. This is not a sign of irrationality, but a rational reaction to the specific situation.

Empirical testing and real estate applications

The real option models discussed so far can motivate many aspects observed in real estate markets. However, the discussion has shown that such models ignore aspects such as transaction costs, which are important in the real world. As Geltner (1989, 157) remarks 'empirical testing of the option model[s] ... is important prior to application to real world problems'.

Empirical applications can be broadly divided into those with a *structural* approach and those with a *reduced form* approach. Structural applications of real option models start with assumptions about the processes of the underlying value drivers (market values, construction cost, rents, operation cost etc.) and solve for the option value using these drivers. The solution might be either in a closed form or solved with numerical techniques. The theoretical real option values are then compared with actual land prices, building prices and agreed rents. Depending on the researchers' standpoints, deviations between predicted and observed values are either signs that market participants do not assess the value of respective real assets correctly or that the model misses out on important aspects. If the former seems more likely, practitioners can learn from real option models, if the latter is more likely, academics have to make their models more realistic.

Reduced form applications test if data are in line with the broad behaviour predicted by real option models. For instance, we have seen above that land values should increase with the volatility of building prices, irrespective of the exact price process. A reduced form test would then regress land prices from local office markets on the volatility of office prices or rents to establish if this prediction holds for the data. If the relationship between land prices and volatility of prices or rents is positive and statistically significant, then this would provide evidence for the existence of real options. As became obvious in the discussion of the theoretical literature, real option values will depend on several other economic variables, such as the level of prices and construction cost, so that reduced form tests must ensure that such other value drivers are accounted for properly.

Structural applications

Paddock *et al.* (1988) use a real option model that has a closed form solution to examine offshore petroleum leases in the Gulf of Mexico. The paper finds that real option valuations for the leases are close to industry bids. The average real option valuation error is similar to the one of static discounted cash flow valuations. This indicates only a small option premium on average. Quigg (1993) examines the predictive power of a real option model using 5900 transactions of developed (3200) and undeveloped (2700) sites from Seattle. Quigg's real option model is similar to the one proposed by Williams (1991), which allows for stochastic building prices, development costs and scale flexibility. Quigg (1993, table VII) computes the real option and the 'intrinsic' value for each site of undeveloped land, where the latter assumes zero timing flexibility. The average option premium is sizable, estimated at 6%, and premiums vary by building type from 1–30%. Quigg (1993, table IX) runs a regression of the land price on a constant, the intrinsic value and the option premium (the difference between option and intrinsic value), and finds that the regression coefficients are significantly positive, but mostly smaller than one. As Quigg (1993, 638) states, this supports 'the hypothesis that the option valuation model has some explanatory power for prices, over and above the intrinsic value.'

Patel and Paxson (2001) use a case study of Canary Wharf to show how the real options model can be used to value developed and undeveloped parts of a project. Brenner *et al.* (2007) use the real option model of McDonald and Siegel (1986) to value unused buildings of a large utility in Berlin, Germany. They find that real option values have high predictive power for actual transaction prices and that real option values are nearly as good as surveyor valuations. The best valuations result if the real option values and surveyor valuations are combined. Brenner *et al.* (2007) find that the real options model is good at predicting the actual development timing. They conduct a detailed qualitative examination to understand any deviation between prices and real option values.

Reduced form applications

Holland *et al.* (2000) examine whether new supply (starts) of commercial real estate in the US is better described by real option or neoclassical investment models. While systematic risk plays a role in both approaches, idiosyncratic risk plays a role only in real option models. Holland *et al.* (2000) find that idiosyncratic price risk delays starts, which is to be expected if real options exist. Somerville (2001) conducts a similar analysis for Canada and obtains a similar result. Capozza and Li (2001) test if an increase of the interest rate brings real estate developments forward. This effect is possible if the scale of a project can be adjusted. Capozza and Li find that a higher interest rate can have a positive influence on building permits if the growth rate and/or the volatility of the growth rate are high. Using individual lots from Seattle, Cunningham (2006) tests whether house price volatility is correlated negatively with time to development and positively with land values. In each of Cunningham's three empirical specifications for development timing, the price volatility coefficient is negative and highly statistically significant. In the preferred specification, an increase in the standard deviation by one standard deviation unit reduces the development probability by 11%. Regressing land prices on price volatilities yields a positive and statistically significant coefficient. Evaluated at the median price, an increase in the house price volatility by one standard deviation increases the land price by 1.6%. After conducting several robustness checks of his results, Cunningham (2006, 27) concludes: 'These results suggest that real estate investors do account for real options, even in competitive and economically important sectors, like new home construction. The presence of real options in land markets is further evidence for the necessary inclusion of real options in models of capital investment.'

Schwarz and Touros (2007) test the qualitative predictions of the models of Grenadier (2002; 2005) for the commercial real estate market. In particular, a higher degree of competition should bring developments forward leading to more starts of projects, all else being equal. This also applies to a higher growth rate in demand. An increase in the volatility of the demand, however, should lead to a reduction of development, all else being equal. To test these predictions, Schwartz and Torous use data from 28 US metropolitan areas. Their dependent variable is the number of starts of commercial buildings. The main explanatory variables are the market concentration measured by the Hirschman–Herfindahl index, the rental growth rate and its volatility. The regressions confirm all predictions. In a similar study, Bulan *et al.* (2009) use data from apartment building developments in Vancouver and test if development timing is influenced by cash flow risks. They find that price volatility as forecasted by generalised autoregressive conditional heteroskedasticity models tempers the development propensity, exactly as predicted by the real option models. An increase in the price growth rate by one standard deviation reduces the development probability by 13%. Prices had to fall by 9% to have the same effect on the development probability. The degree of competition has no *direct* and statistically significant effect, but affects development timing through the interaction with the volatility.

Conclusion

As this chapter has shown, real option models have received much attention by academics. They provide an appropriate framework for modelling development decisions, which come with flexibility in timing, scale and use. Empirical studies indicate that real option models are successful in explaining land prices and development timing. The models have, therefore, a *positive aspect* and are able to describe how real estate investment decisions are made and flexibility is valued. However, compared with the popularity of option modelling in the financial industry, the *normative aspect* of the real options models seems to be underused in the investment industry. In the study of Graham and Harvey (2001, fig. 2), only about 25% of chief financial officers mention real option models as a technique that they always use for investment decisions. The most popular techniques are the static net present value and the internal rate of return, which are always used by more than 75% of the surveyed chief financial officers. Nor is there evidence that real option models are used frequently by real estate practitioners. Rather, it seems that practitioners often feel compelled to apply methods such as the internal rate of return and to 'fudge' cash flow predictions until the outcome fits their intuitive assessment of a project. If 'intuition' relates to the inherent flexibility of real estate projects, then real option models should be much better suited for decision making than static investment criteria. Whenever the investor can affect cash flows in the future, the option premium will indicate the value of this flexibility. Therefore, practitioners might benefit from a deeper understanding of this more flexible investment decision technique.[10]

Appendix 12A

We discuss the solution for Example 2. The following matrix contains the cash flows of the four securities. Each row corresponds to one of the four possible states:

$$\mathbf{M} = \begin{bmatrix} 900 & 420 & 1.1 & 0 \\ 900 & 620 & 1.1 & 60 \\ 540 & 420 & 1.1 & 0 \\ 540 & 620 & 1.1 & 0 \end{bmatrix} \tag{A1}$$

The first column contains the prices of the stock that is perfectly correlated with the building price; the second column contains the prices of the stock that is perfectly correlated with the construction costs; the third column contains the return of the risk-free security; and the last column contains the cash flows of the stock index option. For instance, if state 2 is realised, the first stock has a price of 900, the second of 620, the risk-free security pays 1.1, and the stock index call option pays 60.

In each state, the developer will develop the land only if the building price is at least as large as the construction costs. The vector of land values in the different possible states is:

$$\mathbf{l} = \begin{bmatrix} 480 \\ 280 \\ 120 \\ 0 \end{bmatrix} \tag{A2}$$

Using matrix algebra, the replicating portfolio $\mathbf{q}$ is defined implicitly as $\mathbf{Mq} = \mathbf{1}$ and explicitly:

$$\mathbf{q} = \mathbf{M}^{-1}\mathbf{1} \tag{A3}$$

Holding this portfolio gives the same cash flows in the next period as owning the land and to develop it when this has value. Solving for $\mathbf{q}$ and pre-multiplying with the vector of the current security prices, which is (600, 480, 1, 38), shows that the replicating portfolio costs 108.6 in the current period.

Notes

1 Probabilities are strictly positive and sum to one.
2 The specific assumptions on the securities and their prices are arbitrary. They are made to conduct the calculations. Other assumptions would lead to different results. All that is needed is that the security market is sufficiently complete to replicate the future possible cash flows from land development.
3 Hirsa and Neftci (2013) give a good introduction to Ito calculus.
4 The rental income x is net of operating cost. If it were assumed instead that operating cost grew deterministically with rate μ and x is gross rental income, then the building owner might want to abandon the current building and obtain the development option again. In this case, the solution has to consider this option, which would lead to another boundary condition.
5 Observe from Equation (12.15) that $(vx/v) = (1/x)$, so that the required return rate from Equation (12.10) becomes, with Equation (12.11), $h = r + \rho\sigma\lambda$.

6 An American option can be exercised anytime from inception until expiry. In the case of land, this would be the moment the building permission is granted until this permission expires.
7 From Equation (12.15), $\theta = r + \rho\sigma\lambda - \mu$, so that the initial yield depends on both variables. But the two variables have not to be observed separately to be able to compute γ_1.
8 See also Leahy (1993) for this result.
9 The analysis uses the concept of a Nash equilibrium. The perfect competition and the monopoly outcome are limiting cases.
10 Readers who are interested in learning more should consult the textbooks on real options by Chevalier-Roignant and Trigeorgis (2011), Copeland and Antikarov (2003), Dixit and Pindyck (1994), Smit and Trigeorgis (2004) and Trigeorgis (1996).

References

Bar-Ilan, A. and Strange, W. C. (1996) Investment lags, *American Economic Review*, 86, 610–22.
Boyle, P. P. (1977) Options: a Monte Carlo approach, *Journal of Financial Economics*, 4, 323–38.
Brenner, S., Schulz, R. and Härdle, W. K. (2007) Realoptionen und Immobilienbewertung: Eine Umsetzungsstudie, *Schmalenbachs Zeitschrift für betriebswirtschaftliche Forschung* (zfbf), 59, 1002–28.
Bulan, L., Mayer, C. and Somerville, C. T. (2009) Irreversible investment, real options, and competition: evidence from real estate development, *Journal of Urban Economics*, 65, 237–51.
Capozza, D. R. and Li, Y. (2001) Residential investment and interest rates: an empirical test of land development as a real option, *Real Estate Economics*, 29(3), 503–19.
Chevalier-Roignant, B. and Trigeorgis, L. (2011) *Competitive strategy: options and games*, MIT Press, Cambridge, MA.
Constantinides, G. M. (1978) Market risk adjustment in project valuation, *Journal of Finance*, 33, 603–16.
Copeland, T. and Antikarov, V. (2003) *Real options: a practitioner's guide*, Thomson Texere, New York, NY.
Cunningham, C. R. (2006) House price uncertainty, timing of development, and vacant land prices: evidence for real options in Seattle, *Journal of Urban Economics*, 59, 1–31.
Dixit, A. K. (1989) Entry and exit decisions under uncertainty, *Journal of Political Economy*, 97, 620–38.
Dixit, A. K. (1992) Investment and hysteresis, *Journal of Economic Perspectives*, 6(1), 107–32.
Dixit, A. K. and Pindyck, R. S. (1994) *Investment under uncertainty*, Princeton University Press, Princeton, NJ.
Geltner, D. M. (1989) On the use of the financial option price model to value and explain vacant urban land, *AREUEA Journal*, 17, 142–57.
Geltner, D. M., Miller, N. G., Clayton, J. and Eichholtz, P. (2007) *Commercial real estate: analysis and investments*, 2nd ed., Thomson South-Western, Mason, OH.
Graham, J. R. and Harvey, C. R. (2001) The theory and practice of corporate finance: evidence from the field, *Journal of Financial Economics*, 60, 187–243.
Grenadier, S. R. (1995) Valuing lease contracts: a real-options approach, *Journal of Financial Economics*, 38, 297–331.
Grenadier, S. R. (1996) The strategic exercise of options: development cascades and overbuilding in real estate markets, *Journal of Finance*, 51, 1653–79.
Grenadier, S. R. (2002) Option exercise games: an application to the equilibrium investment strategies of firms, *Review of Financial Studies*, 15, 691–721.
Grenadier, S. R. (2005) An equilibrium analysis of real estate leases, *Journal of Business*, 78, 1173–213.
Hirsa, A. and Neftci, S. N. (2013) *An introduction to the mathematics of financial derivatives*, 3rd ed., Academic Press, San Diego, CA.

Holland, S., Ott, S. H. and Riddiough, T. J. (2000) The role of uncertainty in investment: an examination of competing investment models using commercial real estate data, *Real Estate Economics*, 28, 33–64.

Leahy, J. V. (1993) Investment in competitive equilibrium: the optimality of myopic behavior, *Quarterly Journal of Economics*, 108, 1105–33.

Majd, S. and Pindyck, R. S. (1987) Time to build, option value, and investment decisions, *Journal of Financial Economics*, 18, 7–27.

McDonald, R. and Siegel, D. (1985) Investment and the valuation of firms when there is an option to shut down, *International Economic Review*, 26, 331–49.

McDonald, R. and Siegel, D. (1986) The value of waiting to invest, *Quarterly Journal of Economics*, 101, 707–27.

Paddock, J. L., Siegel, D. R. and Smith, J. L. (1988) Option valuation of claims on real assets: the case of offshore petroleum leases, *Quarterly Journal of Economics*, 103, 479–508.

Patel, K. and Paxson, D. (2001) *Real urban development options at Canary Wharf*, pp. 163–76 in Howell, S., Stark, A., Newton, D., Paxson, D., Cavus, M. and Pereira, J., *Real options: evaluating corporate investment opportunities in a dynamic world*, Pearson, Harlow.

Quigg, L. (1993) Empirical testing of real option-pricing models, *Journal of Finance*, 48, 621–40.

Smit, H. T. J. and Trigeorgis, L. (2004) *Strategic investment: real options and games*, Princeton University Press, Princeton, NJ.

Smith, C. W. (1979) Applications of option pricing analysis, pp. 79–121 in Bicksler, J. L. (ed.), *Handbook of financial economics*, North-Holland, Amsterdam.

Schwartz, E. S. and Torous, W. N. (2007) Commercial office space: testing the implications of real options models with competitive interactions, *Real Estate Economics*, 35, 1–20.

Somerville C. T. (2001) Permits, starts, and completions: structural relationships versus real options, *Real Estate Economics*, 29, 161–90.

Titman, S. (1985) Urban land prices under uncertainty, *American Economic Review*, 75, 505–14.

Trigeorgis, L. (1996) *Real options: managerial flexibility and strategy in resource allocation*, MIT Press, Cambridge, MA.

Williams, J. T. (1991) Real estate development as an option, *Journal of Real Estate Finance and Economics*, 4, 191–208.

13 Behavioural real estate finance

Michael White

Introduction

There has been a significant growth in the literature using behavioural approaches to understand financial decision making. This literature recognises that economic actors operate in a world characterised by uncertainty and asymmetric information. This can lead to market frictions, transaction costs and even to market failure. Behavioural approaches, however, go further than this and question whether the assumption of actor rationality is appropriate. These approaches do not only consider that economic actors have limited information processing capabilities (bounded rationality), but also that actors may process information within these limits incorrectly.

Behavioural finance has produced many stylised facts on financial markets that contradict predictions coming from models assuming rational investor behaviour. It attempts to understand how actual investors make investment decisions instead of modelling how neoclassical economic theory suggests they should make decisions. Translating Kahneman (2011, 4) to an investment context, only once we understand how actual investors make their investment decisions, and where and why they commit judgemental errors, can we potentially give the right advice and design the right institutional settings and regulations to nudge investors towards correct investment decision making. Hodgson (2003, 163) notes that individual economic actors 'must always be considered in their evolutionary, historical and institutional contexts. Rational deliberation is not possible except through interaction with the fabric of social institutions.'

In this chapter, we examine the role and contribution of behavioural real estate finance. We start with a short section summarising the core results of financial investment theory as it is used throughout most chapters in this book. This provides the background against which we contrast the facts on actual investment behaviour in the real estate industry. We define behavioural finance and its core concepts of sentiment, heuristic and rule of thumb. This is followed by a discussion of applications in real estate, in particular regarding investment valuation and forecasting. The chapter concludes with a critical assessment on the value that a behavioural approach can bring to an understanding of real estate investment markets.

Results of modern investment theory

Modern investment theory assumes that individual investors form beliefs about future cash flows of assets and base their investment decisions on these beliefs in line with their own preferences regarding risk and expected return. Modern portfolio theory (Markowitz, 1952) shows that investors, under these assumptions, should strive for well-diversified asset portfolios. Assuming that information on cash flows is freely available and that rational investors process this information correctly, they will all end up with homogenous beliefs regarding the future cash flows of assets. Asset markets are assumed to be perfectly competitive and asset exchange comes at no other cost than the agreed price. The two-fund theorem (Tobin, 1958) tells us then that all investors will hold the same portfolio of risky assets (market portfolio) and the capital asset pricing model (Sharpe, 1964) tells us that the risk premium of each of the risky assets is proportional to the risk premium of the market portfolio (the beta pricing relation). The Modigliani–Miller (1958) theorem tells us that the value of a project does not change by the way it is financed (in the absence of differential tax treatment). Even if not all investors begin with correct beliefs about future cash flows, they might learn while trading with others. This has led to the efficient markets hypothesis (Fama, 1970), which says that asset prices will fully reflect available information of future cash flows. This hypothesis also implies that asset prices will always reflect their fundamental value.

This body of theory cannot explain why financial intermediaries exist or why capital structure choice seems so important to actual investors. The application of models from information economics, in particular with respect to asymmetric information and contract design, can explain many of the regularities that are observed in financial markets. However, while asymmetric information and contract design can explain in principle why investment funds are structured the way they are, the theory is still based on the underlying assumption that actors are rational. Behavioural finance doubts that this is a useful assumption to understand actual investment behaviour.

Conflicts between theory and actual investment behaviour

Research has detected behaviour that has led to persistence and repetition of errors in investment decision making. It has been argued that such mistakes have led to bubbles. Manias from history are hard to explain when rationality is assumed. As far back as the 1630s, the tulip mania swept Holland, causing a bubble in prices for bulbs. More recently, Shiller (1981) argues that stock price volatility is too high if explained only by changes in expected dividends. It seems more likely that investor sentiment causes the excess volatility. This empirical result, which has been replicated for other markets shows a clear contradiction of the efficient market hypothesis. Other studies on real estate markets have confirmed that real estate markets might not be informationally efficient. For instance, Quigley (1999) finds that fundamental market drivers explain changes in real estate prices only by 10–40%. This indicates that other factors, such as investor sentiment, may play an important role for real estate prices. This also suggests that real estate investment research needs to encompass, in addition to any quantitative analysis of fundamentals, an analysis of psychological factors that may affect the investors (Black *et al.*, 2003).

Investment professionals might be able to exploit wrong investment decision making, thereby generating excess profits and drive irrational investors out of the market. Behavioural economists show that this is not the case.

First, this arbitrage process might be limited if rational investors cannot overcome mistakes made by those less rational. Betting against irrational investors comes with the additional risk that sentiments can be volatile. This makes arbitrage risky and, if it is too risky, will prevent it in the first place. As Barberis and Thaler (2003, 1057) state, ‘even when an asset is wildly mispriced, strategies designed to correct the mispricing can be both risky and costly, rendering them unattractive. As a result, mispricing can remain unchallenged’.

Second, even professional investors might have no interest in correcting market prices. Professional investors fall within heterogeneous groups, some of which might be mainly interested in short-term gains, while others might be interested in long-term fundamental values. Real estate agents, for one, may have a clear monetary incentive to talk up a market. For instance, real estate agents may encourage their clients to sell, because agents' contractual incentives might be skewed in favour of a quick transaction instead of a best price transaction. Levitt and Syverson (2008) find for residential real estate agents that prices are relatively higher and houses stay on the market for longer if the agent sells his own house than a client's home. This shows that real estate agents are better informed than their clients, but also that they will not share their better knowledge.

Fundamentals of behavioural finance

Concepts from cognitive psychology and limits to arbitrage are the two building blocks of behavioural finance (Ritter 2003). Cognitive psychology has provided a huge body of evidence on 'the biases that arise when people form beliefs, preferences and the way in which they make decisions, given their beliefs and preferences' (Kishore, 2004, 109). Economics has provided many 'puzzles' that are observed in investment markets, but which should not be observed if some investors were rational and could benefit from exploiting mispricing. Limits of arbitrage are a potential explanation and examples include: the closed-end fund puzzle, where prices of fund shares deviate from fund's net asset value (Shleifer, 2000) and mispricing of financial assets that give effectively the same cash flow on an underlying real asset (Lamont and Thaler, 2003).

Cognitive psychology focusses on how individuals think and make systematic errors of judgement in their thinking. For example, they place more importance on recent events than past events. Cognitive biases may lead to irrational investment decision-making. Next, we discuss important concepts from cognitive psychology.

Heuristics

Heuristics in general are cognitive *shortcuts* or *rules of thumb* that reduce the computational cost of decision making. While making life easier, such shortcuts can lead to biased and suboptimal decisions. Kahneman and Tversky (1974, 1124) discuss how people, in practice, calculate probabilities of uncertain events happening or probabilities of valuing uncertain quantities. They argue that 'these heuristics are quite useful, but sometimes they lead to severe and systematic errors'. For instance, in the context of investment allocation, an investor could use the $1/N$ rule, which implies that, of N assets in a portfolio, all receive a share of $1/N$. While simple, this rule may ignore that the assets may have very different risk and expected return outcomes.

We discuss next several of such heuristics in more detail and exemplify them with examples relevant to real estate investments.

Anchoring

As highlighted by Kahneman and Tversky (1974), initial conditions have often an important impact on decisions. For example, the market value estimate of a property may be based upon recently observed prices for similar properties. The expected price for the property is then anchored on these initial observed values. An expectation of the asset's value is formed based upon the information assumed to be contained in the (possibly limited) set of observed prices of comparables. Hence, there are processes of both anchoring and adjustment of real estate values. Kahneman and Tversky (1974, 1128) suggest that adjustments are unlikely to be sufficient as 'different starting points yield different estimates, which are biased towards the initial conditions'. They show that anchoring relates not only to initial conditions (for example, an observed transactions price of a comparable real estate investment) but when people base their estimates or expectations on 'incomplete computation[s]' (Kahneman and Tversky 1974, 1128). Such incomplete computations were found to lead to insufficient adjustment. The adjust-and-anchor heuristic, as pointed out by Kahneman (2011, 120), was preferred by Tversky as 'a strategy for estimating uncertain quantities'. Epley and Gilovich (2001) viewed adjustment as requiring effort and information. In processing complex information, or in dealing with limited information upon which to base judgments, people may adjust less.

Representativeness

People often put too much emphasis on recent events when predicting future events. For instance, if real estate prices have been increasing over recent years, this generates an expectation that this increase will continue. Such reasoning was in place before the financial crisis 2007/08, when house prices were thought to be increasing permanently, because they had done over the previous 15 years.

Overconfidence

Overconfidence can be reflected in under-diversified portfolios, 'because of a tendency to invest too much in what one is familiar with' (Ritter 2003, 431). People are also inaccurate when it comes to estimating probabilities of event occurrence (Barberis and Thaler, 2003). Overconfidence may be related to self-attribution bias and hindsight bias. With self-attribution bias, people think their success is due to their talents but any failure is due to bad luck. Hindsight bias leads people to believe that they predicted past events accurately and, therefore, can predict the future with more accuracy than they actually can (Barberis and Thaler 2003, 1066).

Mental accounting

People often make decisions separately that should be combined. For example, is a loss on one investment subtracted for a gain on another or are they considered separately? Thaler (1999) provides a detailed discussion and shows how this links with prospect theory, as discussed later in this chapter.

Framing

The way in which information is presented to individuals can impact on their decision making. When given individual investment decisions, investors often treat them separately rather than considering them as part of a portfolio.

Conservatism

People often adapt only slowly to change. In this situation people will, for example, anchor expected sale price of real estate on recent comparable prices or actual asking prices and only slowly change their anchor over time as new evidence emerges.

It could be expected that people making mistakes repeatedly would learn that the approach they have adopted results in systematic errors. Ultimately, they should change their behaviour. We would expect that people who invest infrequently might rely on heuristics much more than professional fund managers, who should have better market knowledge due to repeated trades and market exposure. Barberis and Thaler (2003, 1068), however, suggest that this is not the case and that the 'effect of learning is often muted by errors of application: when the bias is explained, people often understand it, but then immediately proceed to violate it again in specific applications'. They also suggest that experts in a given field are more likely to display overconfidence and this too can lead to persistent biases in decision making.

Prospect theory

Investors decide to purchase assets with some expected return or target rate of return. However, they do not know the future, hence they face a problem of making choices under conditions of uncertainty. Under these conditions, it has been assumed that investors' decisions fit models for choice under uncertainty following Von Neumann and Morgenstern (1944) expected utility theory. However, research evidence has suggested that people do not follow expected utility theory when choosing between uncertain alternatives. Kahneman and Tversky (1979, 263) propose an alternative explanation in prospect theory. They argue that 'people underweight outcomes that are … probable in comparison with outcomes that are obtained with certainty. This tendency, called the certainty effect, contributes to risk aversion in choices involving sure gains and to risk-seeking in choices involving sure losses.' In an experiment, the authors consider a game of chance with non-zero outcomes. They offer subjects choices of gains and losses with certainty and equivalent value outcomes under uncertainty. In their experiments, they found that, for gains, the participants preferred the certain outcome and for losses they preferred the risky outcome. Hence, the two sets of choices had the same final wealth states, but different choice patterns, indicating the behaviour of the participants considered only the gains or losses they could face.

In addition to choosing certain outcomes for gains and uncertain ones for losses, Kahneman and Tversky argue that the value function is non-linear. This is reflective of individuals' utility being considered over gains and losses. Figure 13.1 shows the value function. The figure indicates that there is a greater sensitivity of participants to losses than to gains. This is referred to as *loss aversion* and implies that we need to diverge from expected utility theory to explain behaviour under conditions of uncertainty. Not unrelated is regret theory. 'It implies that people anticipate … the regret of making a bad investment decision' (Salzman and Zwinkels, 2013, 12). Regret theory can also explain why investors will participate in markets that have already experienced significant price rises as they wish to avoid the regret of not benefitting from further value increases even though prices may already exceed fundamentals. The figure also reflects the disposition effect, which refers to the desire of people to avoid losses and realise gains. Hence, when real estate prices fall, people do not want to sell if the transaction price is below the purchase price. The effect can also manifest in the sale of well-performing assets while investors hold on to underperforming assets. The fact that transactions volumes are procyclical is also consistent with this effect.

While the above is based upon games of chance where the uncertain outcome is presented to participants with a fixed probability, in practice probabilities may not be known in advance. To deal with this Savage (1964) developed subjective expected utility. However, as with expected utility theory, this has also been shown to be unable to explain actual behaviour under uncertainty. People do not like uncertainty about the probability of an outcome,

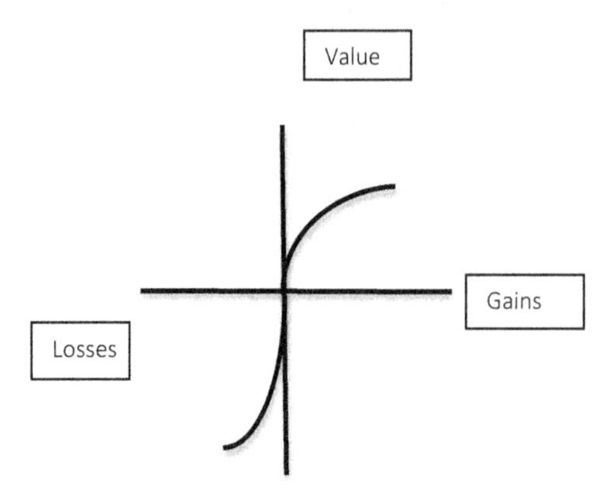

Figure 13.1 Value function
Drawing based on Kahneman and Tversky (1979, 1070).

referred to as *ambiguity aversion*. They display a preference for the familiar related to the competence hypothesis where people feel that they can more accurately evaluate uncertain outcomes in familiar subject (or investment) areas.

Behavioural finance applications in real estate markets

This section considers applications of behavioural finance in real estate. We examine behavioural forces in valuation, investment decision making and in forecasting real estate values.

Valuation

Northcraft and Neale (1987) discuss anchoring in real estate markets causing bias in appraisals towards the initial value (for example, asking price). The anchoring heuristic has been found to be at work not only with those who may trade infrequently (home sellers) but also for those whose professional roles are within real estate markets (Black, 1997). The heuristic is also found to act strongly for valuers in markets that they do not know (Diaz and Hansz, 2001). Havard (2001) also notes the role of anchoring and argues that valuers set initial values and these act as a bias, and the valuers display a tendency to ignore market information. This could also be due to client pressure on the valuation process (Kinnard *et al.*, 1997; Levy and Schuck, 2005) that also generates biased values. These biased values may then act as anchors for future adjustment processes.

Diaz (2002) notes that investors may calculate the 'probability of tenant bankruptcy by considering how many similar instances can be recalled. The use of this "availability" heuristic is influenced by the ease of recall. When actual probabilities are not correlated with the ease of recall, bias can occur' (Diaz 2002, 1). The use of comparables in valuation can be related to the representativeness heuristic. However, the inclusion of irrelevant characteristics can lead to valuation bias. 'Numerical estimates can be made with the "anchoring and adjustment" heuristic' (Diaz 2002, 1). Adjustment is then made from the anchor point when new evidence becomes available, but this adjustment may be too little. However, the anchor or starting point can be wrong if it is influenced by subjective value opinions. This again generates bias. Research by Gallimore (1994) suggested that recent evidence was most heavily weighted by valuers and hence the sequence in which information was received was important in influencing valuations. Diaz (1997) also found that comparable evidence was not used by valuers in markets with which they were familiar but only in unfamiliar markets, the former reflecting overconfidence heuristics and the latter the anchoring heuristic, also confirmed in Diaz and Wolverton (1998). Further, they found that adjustment was slow and insufficient given market evidence.

Barkham and Geltner (1994; 1995) suggest that the valuation process may cause smoothing in published indices, thus underestimating market volatility and risk. They argue that the true or fundamental price of a real estate asset is unobserved but assumed to evolve via a random walk process:

$$P_t^F = P_{t-1}^F + \eta_t \tag{13.1}$$

where P_t^F is the fundamental asset price, η_t is the error term with mean zero and constant variance. However observed prices differ from fundamentals as follows:

$$P_t^O = P_t^F + v_t \tag{13.2}$$

where P_t^O is the observed asset price and v_t is the error term. Valuations are then updated based upon the following process:

$$V_t = KP_t^O + (1-K)V_{t-1} \tag{13.3}$$

where V_t is the valuation of the asset and K is calculated from:

$$K = \frac{\sigma_\eta^2}{\sigma_\eta^2 + \sigma_v^2} \tag{13.4}$$

The error variance from the fundamental price equation, σ_η^2, appears on both the numerator and denominator of the formula and hence the only way to change the value of K is if the error variance from the observed price equation, σ_v^2, changes. With limited market information on observables or comparable transactions, the error variance on the observed price equation will increase making K closer to zero and the current valuation in equation (13.3) will place a heavier weight on the last period's valuation; hence, there is a clear anchoring effect and heuristic in decision making. When there is more market information on similar observed transactions then the error variance on the observed price equation will decrease, meaning that K will approximate one. Therefore, the current valuation will rely more heavily on current market information and less on the previous period's valuation. However, there remains a sample size issue and perhaps therefore over-confidence as outlined above. While K is a signal-to-noise ratio, in practice, the use of comparables in valuation processes provides an example of anchoring when there is limited information in the market. The addition of market evidence reflects the anchoring and adjustment heuristic.

Securitised real estate

The illiquidity of unsecuritised real estate can lead to lumpy portfolios with perhaps limited diversification. Investment diversification can be found to follow naïve rules, such as the 1/

N heuristic, and is evidenced by Benartzi and Thaler (2001). This mental shortcut is a data reduction exercise but implies that cognitive behaviour differs from that suggested by theories based upon perfect rationality.

Wofford *et al.* (2010) discuss the management of cognitive risk in real estate. They state that, 'While attention has been paid to deviations from instrumental rationality, these deviations ... have been viewed as anomalies rather than as a natural and expected result of human cognition. Likewise, these deviations have often been viewed in isolation and not as part of systems producing cognitive risk in which deviations may either offset one another or amplify, potentially in a non-linear manner, overall cognitive risk' (Wofford *et al.* 2010, 274–5).

Such systematic and persistent deviations are inconsistent with traditional finance theory, rational expectations and investor rationality. Many authors provide evidence against market efficiency: in housing markets (Case and Shiller, 1990; Clayton, 1998; Cutler *et al.*, 1991) and in commercial real estate markets (Brown and Matysiak, 2000). Real estate investment decision making may require information that is incomplete and difficult to obtain.

Considering that direct real estate assets requiring valuation are illiquid and slower at processing new information than securitised markets, it may be that the latter are less likely to suffer from bias in investment decision making. However, 'Newell and Kishore (1998) have identified that listed property trusts (LPTs) stratified by small size and high value render profitable trading rules inconsistent with the EMH and CAPM' (Kishore and Demas, 2011, 11). Pricing anomalies in listed real estate may be due to the same sources of investor irrationality as in the direct market.

Kishore and Demas (2011, 11) suggest that securitised real estate markets can be considered as being similar to stock markets and that the equity premium and volatility puzzles can be explained by the 'application of preference and ambiguity aversion biases, under prospect theory'. Using rational expectations, listed property trust yields should exceed bond yields. However investors usually make a comparison between them, which would seem irrational.

Overconfidence and regret avoidance can cause investors to trade excessively and to hold on to losing assets respectively. These characteristics are exhibited in stock and property markets. High market volatility is also difficult to explain. Kishore (2004, 108) states that, 'in an economy with rational investors, long-term stock return volatility should [be] equal to the volatility of dividend growth, holding discount rates and variation in the price/dividend (P/D) ratios constant. Rational investors would only allow variation in future discount rates and P/D ratios, based on the rational approach to risk aversion as per the CAPM'. However, asymmetry in investor behaviour with respect to expected gains and losses seems to fit the data better and provide a better explanation of observed volatility.

Investment decision making

Gallimore *et al.* (2000) research investment decision-making processes in property companies. They find that actual investment behaviour diverges from that postulated in neoclassical models. They note that market information is often received by word of mouth and can, therefore, make the decision-making process rely on limited information – the availability heuristic comes into play. Gallimore and Gray (2002) argue that UK investors are influenced by sentiment that leads to suboptimal investment outcomes. They suggest that lack of quantitative data leads to a reliance on more qualitative factors. Roberts and Henneberry (2007) examine institutional investment into real estate in France, Germany and the UK, and find evidence of investors taking cognitive 'shortcuts' in their decision-making processes. Farragher and Kleiman (1996) considered how decisions on real estate investment were made in real estate investment trusts (REITs) and institutions. These investment decisions followed from firms setting their overall investment strategy, benchmark returns and forecasting risks and returns. Instinct and experience were also valued more so than formal risk return models.

An availability bias is indicated in research by Adair *et al.* (1994). They found that investors choose to invest where there is available information. Salzman and Zwinkels (2013) suggest that the availability heuristic can also lead to a representativeness bias as investors make inaccurate inferences from recently observed value changes. The representativeness heuristic means that investors overweight recently observed prices when forming their return expectations. Investors, such as commercial banks, were found to be trend-chasing, consistent with the availability and representativeness heuristics. Real estate forecasters also were found to adopt similar behaviour (Ling, 2005).

The results above suggest an overconfidence in prediction of asset return performance. Wang *et al.* (2000) examine developer behaviour when there is private information and public (market) information. They suggest that, when public information is received that confirms private information, irrationality will increase, together with reliance on private information. Investors become overconfident in the use and interpretation of private information. The authors argue that this overconfidence will lead to excess supply and greater cyclical volatility.

Evidence on the importance of learning is provided by Gervais and Odean (2001, 2) in the context of overconfidence. They suggest that traders in markets learn about their abilities from their successes and failures, but that they take too much personal credit for their successes and attribute failures to external factors. They may suffer from an illusion of validity (attribute observed successes to their own efforts rather than, say, luck). Hence, they become overconfident and this subsequently influences trading behaviour, profitability and price volatility. This particular research determines overconfidence endogenously so that it changes over the trader's life. The authors suggest that 'aggregate [market] overconfidence [will] be higher after market gains and lower after market losses. Since ... greater overconfidence leads to greater trading volume, this suggests that trading volume will be greater after market gains and lower after market losses.' Evidence in real estate markets is consistent with this prediction. Gervais and Odean also suggest that overconfidence will be greatest for investors who are less experienced and that they will become more realistic regarding their abilities over time.

Evidence also points to younger investors being more active, making more trades, than more experienced investors. The 'buy-and-hold' older traders also tend to make higher returns (Barber and Odean 2001). Hence, younger traders may be more affected by herding behaviour reflected in the pro-cyclicality of transactions volumes. Their limited experience may make them more reliant on recent available information in computing expected values and initial success, through a self-attribution heuristic, may lead to overconfidence.

The availability heuristic and over reliance on recent values to compute expected future returns generates an autoregressive process that is frequently observed in real estate asset values. This process can be referred to as a momentum effect. Investors might buy assets because they observe short-term price increases. Hence, momentum and herding reinforce the direction of price movement without regard for fundamentals in decision making. Lux (1995) explains bubble formation using momentum and herding, and Shiller (2005) also notes the role of herding in bubble formation and mispricing.

Market psychology influenced by herding behaviour can lead to irrational exuberance. This can cause markets to reach pricing levels that are unsustainable (Shiller, 2005) and not supported by fundamentals.

Empirical evidence points to an increase in the volatility of capital values relative to cap rates and rental movements. Expected utility theory cannot explain this change. However, there could be changes in preferences as a result of changes in relative risk aversion. Hence, investor beliefs and sentiment affect behaviour in the market place.

Ling *et al.* (2014) discuss the role of investor sentiment and the limits to arbitrage in private commercial real estate markets. As sentiment can cause a divergence from fundamental values, the authors state that, 'sentiment-induced asset mispricing arises from a combination of sentiment-driven investor demand and limits to arbitrage' (Ling *et al.*, 2014, 532). In private real estate markets, characterised by information asymmetry and illiquidity, there are constraints on short selling. In addition, there is limited information on pricing and the impact of sentiment on price may only be discovered slowly over time. 'Moreover, the inability to short-sell in private markets impedes the opportunity for informed arbitrageurs to counteract mispricing, particularly during periods of overvaluation' (Ling *et al.*, 2014, 532). This in turn creates persistence to mispricing into the longer term that could impact on the sentiments of new investors entering the market who anchor their expectations on current inaccurate expectations. Lamont and Thaler (2003) describe these investors as being sentiment-induced investors.

Explaining non-rational behaviour

Bokhari and Geltner (2011) examine the impact of the anchoring and adjustment heuristic and loss aversion in commercial real estate pricing. The authors argue that 'it is only the behaviour of agents who are to the left of the prospect theory value function "kink-point" [see Figure 13.1] … who are in a position to exhibit the sort of psychological loss aversion that is distinguished by prospect theory' (Bokhari and Geltner, 2011, 8). The authors call this 'behavioural loss aversion'.

Loss aversion and the disposition effect are related. Crane and Hartzell (2008) report that REIT managers have a greater tendency to sell well-performing assets at low prices. Applying the anchoring and adjustment heuristic, setting asking prices too high or too low could impact on the potential buyer's valuation (anchoring) and could affect the transaction price. Black and Diaz (1996) confirmed this anchoring effect.

Yavas and Yang (1995), however, using game theory, argue that price setting will be strategic and will reflect the relative strength of the buyer and seller, given market conditions. Using anchoring, a seller might set a high price but this could result in a longer than average market duration, which would signal that the property is overpriced to potential buyers. Hence, sellers would have an incentive to set an asking price close to the observed transactions prices for similar properties. Thus, sellers anchor their selling price in addition to buyers anchoring their valuations.

Bokhari and Geltner (2011) construct an empirical model to test for non-rational behaviour. They analyse anchoring and loss aversion in investor behaviour, finding evidence that investors are more sensitive to losses than gains. They suggest that 'commercial property sellers faced with a loss relative to their purchase price tend to post asking prices higher than otherwise-similar sellers not facing a loss' (Bokhari and Geltner, 2011, 19). They further note that it is the difference in the coefficients on losses and gains, reflecting psychological loss aversion, from prospect theory, that rejects the expected utility theory of investor rationality. The authors further explore the role of the anchor. Their results indicate that investors who face a gain set lower asking prices than otherwise. Investors facing losses set higher asking prices but there is no symmetry between under- and overpricing by gaining and losing investors. These results support the disposition effect of selling winners and holding losers. In relation to investor experience, gains did not show any difference between the more and less experienced investors. However, Bokhari and Geltner (2011) found that more experienced investors displayed more loss aversion than less experienced investors. Institutional investors and equity fund managers showed the highest loss aversion levels. Sah *et al.* (2010) found that experienced market actors took more time and displayed more cross-checking than inexperienced investors.

The data used by Bokhari and Geltner (2011) cover the start of the global financial crisis. During this initial phase they found an increase in loss aversion. Consistent with downward price rigidity, sellers did not sell at significantly reduced prices but, when sales did occur, the buyers in the market seemed willing to accept the 'high' prices set by loss averse sellers. However, the number of transactions fell substantially as the crisis unfolded. By 2008/09, the results suggested that sellers' loss aversion declined. Loss-averse sellers perhaps became more rational and/or their expectations were reset by the recent information from the crisis itself. Bokhari and Geltner (2011) created hedonic indices that incorporated behavioural components to create an index reflecting these phenomena. They found that the inclusion of behavioural variables improved the fit of the index, particularly making it better at capturing the 2007–09 market downturn.

Ling *et al.* (2014) can be seen as an extension of the work by Bokhari and Geltner (2011) in examining aggregate returns in a private real estate market. Ling *et al.* found that sentiment caused prices to diverge from fundamental value in the short run. Even in the longer term, private real estate markets were found to be subject to mispricing due to sentiment influences in investment decision making. In contrast, they found that in public real estate markets positive sentiment effects did not persist in the long run.

Seiler *et al.* (2012) consider the use of heuristics in real estate investment choice. They consider mental accounting where, 'an investor's willingness to sell differs when considering the asset in isolation versus the willingness to sell as part of an overall portfolio' (Seiler *et al.*, 2012, 18). This behaviour is inconsistent with expected utility theory. They found that less than 7% of their sample behave rationally. Almost 75% of their sample would sell an asset as the investment return rises. In addition, they found that the value function (as in Figure 15.1) was not always S-shaped. Just over 7% of their sample had a U-shaped value function.

Kallberg *et al.* (1996) examine the role of direct real estate in investment portfolios. They employ rational mean-variance efficient portfolios before considering a heuristic approach, 'to reflect the practice of many firms that do not solve the problem of allocating resources into real and financial assets simultaneously' (Kallberg *et al.*, 1996, 10). Firms, such as pension funds, might decide to allocate a certain amount of money to real estate and other assets in a discrete process (the 'separation heuristic') and the use of modern portfolio theory might be limited to more liquid assets of the overall fund. They find relatively small impacts on overall fund performance, although the size of the effect varies with the proportion of real estate in the overall fund size.

Jin and Gallimore (2010) examine the framing heuristic. While there is a greater range of real estate information available in terms of both quantity and quality, the authors suggest that this will lead to greater use of short-cuts to help people process information for decision-making purposes. In relation to the framing heuristic, the authors consider how decision-making is affected by '"distortions" and "amplifications" in the visual and verbal presentation of factual data. The use of charts and other such exhibits, and of "executive summaries", has become pervasive as an aid to helping people deal with complex and extensive data. [The authors] argue that the ways in which such aids are presented will differentially influence people's interpretation of the same information' (Jin and Gallimore, 2010, 210).

In the framing heuristic, 'frames define what counts as relevant for attention and assessment ... [and] ... they represent people's worlds in ways that already call for particular styles of decision or of behavioural response' (Perri 6, 2005, 94). Thus, the 'frame significantly affects how we infer meaning and hence understand the situation' (Jin and Gallimore, 2010, 240). In real estate, investors make decisions on investment strategies based upon limited information from which they infer expected return performance. The information is the frame through which people perceive outcomes, of investment in this case.

Jin and Gallimore (2010) conduct research on framing using a market report on commercial real estate that contains graphical and verbal analysis of the market. They split their sample of subjects into a control group and a treatment group, where the latter received optimistically framed information. The property market information given used variables for rental value, transactions prices and vacancy rates. The groups received the same information with the graphical representations made to look visually different. The results of the test suggested that a framing effect was present. Both groups expected there to be a positive change in market performance. However, the group receiving optimistically framed information had a statistically significantly higher positive expectation of market performance than the group receiving pessimistically framed information. Thus, information could be manipulated that could affect investor decision making. Even if the investor thought their choices were rational based upon risk and expected return evaluations, they were biased by the effect of framing.

Real estate forecasts: econometrics versus heuristics

Forecasting future performance in an uncertain environment is widespread in real estate analysis. Mostly, these forecasts use 'rational' economic models of market structure identifying key market drivers and development response. As data availability has increased, more complex models can be constructed.

However, 'many heterodox economists, including behaviouralists, institutionalists and evolutionary theorists, challenge the assumption that decisions are made by rational individualistic economic agents. They would argue that decisions are actually heavily influenced by the social and cultural context within which they are embedded' (Watkins *et al.*, 2012, 11). This view suggests that investors' decision-making is affected by word-of-mouth information as well as mood and sentiment rather than reflecting a rational objective process. Habits, norms, and culture influence market processes and outcomes. Individuals' perceptions and emotions will influence their choices, and this will extend to professional decision-makers. The cognitive shortcuts people take may lead to non-rational outcomes and people may satisfice (settle for second best) rather than optimise, particularly if the latter takes more cognitive power.

Thus, if behaviour is not based upon optimality, forecasters may reject econometric models 'and try instead to find methods that capture opinions that might be held more because of the influence of social norms or habits, emotions, mood or sentiment rather than as the outcome of perfectly informed cost-benefit calculations' (Watkins *et al.*, 2012, 20). Heterodox economists use surveys and interviews to capture attitudes or sentiment regarding the area of study.

Watkins *et al.* (2012) find that the forecasters in general base their predictions on quantitative econometric models that forecast the future values of key market drivers but also engage in an in-house market overlay process in which the 'house view' of the real estate market is overlaid on the econometric analysis. This latter was also thought to embody mood or sentiment as there was evidence that forecasters' views of performance were seen to be unrelated to economic fundamentals and expected property market outcomes. When asked to predict two or three years ahead, forecasters exhibited caution, or risk aversion, or limited adjustment, anchoring their views on recent short term market performance. Further, the qualitative market overlay process was thought to be more important in some periods rather than others. During periods of market volatility and uncertainty, the overlay process was perceived to be more important than at times of more stability or movements along trend. Clayton *et al.* (2009) also find evidence for investor sentiment on commercial real estate prices after controlling for fundamentals.

Discussion and conclusions

This chapter has discussed behavioural approaches to real estate analysis. While this is a growing field of research, much analysis of real estate investment is conducted within the mainstream expected utility maximising framework. Increasingly, these models fall short in explaining investment decision making and market performance. The characteristics of real estate provide fertile ground for behavioural approaches to shed light on market processes and outcomes. The valuation process may be subject to the anchoring and representativeness heuristics that induce potential bias. Slow and inaccurate adjustment of value perceptions may also develop from such starting points.

Loss aversion and the disposition effect have been found in real estate investment selling decisions. Investors sell winners and hold on to losers. There is evidence of overconfidence and putting too much weight on recent information. Regret avoidance has also been found to be present and consistent with loss aversion as well as excessive trading.

Recent research has also pointed to experienced investors being more sensitive to loss aversion than novices. Institutional investors were also found to adopt a separation heuristic where higher level management would follow a discrete process when deciding between real estate and non-property investment allocations.

Also of note is the use of information and how it is presented (the framing heuristic) was found to affect market perceptions and hence potentially influence investment decision making.

The area of real estate forecasting is also of interest. The practice adopted by in-house forecasters of the use a qualitative overlay process that can capture the house view of the market provides an in-road for mood and sentiment to play a role in driving expectations of future market performance and diverges from more 'rational' approaches. Recent research on this topic has uncovered conservatism reflected in the anchoring-and-adjustment heuristic. Failure to embody new information or 'black swans' increases the probability of persistent forecast errors.

While the chapter has not discussed other potential explanations of observed behaviour, it seems clear that there is a substantive role for a behavioural approach in understanding real estate decision making. There is evidence of anchoring, overconfidence, framing, representativeness, conservatism and loss aversion. All of these cause divergence from the expected utility framework and suggest that alternative views need to be considered to aid understanding of real estate investment decision making.

References

Adair, A. S., Berry, J.N., and McGreal, W. S. (1994) Investment decision making: a behavioural perspective, *Journal of Property Finance*, 5(4), 32–42.

Barber, B. and Odean, T. (2001) Boys will be boys: gender, overconfidence, and common stock investment, *Quarterly Journal of Economics*, 116(1), 261–92.

Barberis, N. and Thaler, R. (2003) A survey of behavioural finance, in G. M. Constantinides, M. Harris and R. Stulz (eds.), *Handbook of the Economics of Finance*, Elsevier, Amsterdam.

Barkham, R. J. and Geltner, D. M. (1994) Unsmoothing British valuation-based returns without assuming an efficient market, *Journal of Property Research*, 11, 81–95.

Barkham, R. J. and Geltner, D. M. (1995) Price discovery in American and British property markets, *Real Estate Economics*, 23(1), 21–44.

Benartzi, S. and Thaler, R. (2001) Naïve diversification strategies in defined contribution savings plans, *American Economic Review*, 91, 79–98.

Black, R. T. (1997) Expert property negotiators and pricing information, revisited, *Journal of Property Valuation and Investment*, 15(3), 274–81.

Black, R. T. and Diaz, J. III (1996) The use of information versus asking price in the real property negotiation process, *Journal of Property Research*, 13(4), 287–97.

Black, R. T., Brown, M. G., Diaz, J., Gibler, K. M. and Grissom, T. V. (2003) Behavioral research in real estate: a search for the boundaries, *Journal of Real Estate Practice and Education*, 6(1), 85–112.

Bokhari, S. and Geltner, D. (2011) Loss aversion and anchoring in commercial real estate pricing: empirical evidence and price index implications, *Real Estate Economics*, 39(4), 635–70.

Brown, G. R. and Matysiak, G. A. (2000) *Real estate investment. A capital market approach*, Pearson Education, Harlow.

Case, K. E. and Shiller, R. J. (1990) Forecasting prices and excess returns in the housing market, *Journal of the American Real Estate and Urban Economics Association*, 18, 253–73.

Clayton, J. (1998) Further evidence on real estate market efficiency, *Journal of Real Estate Research*, 15, 41–57.

Clayton, J. and Ling, D. C. and Naranjo, A. (2009) Commercial real estate valuation: Fundamentals versus investor sentiment, *Journal of Real Estate Finance and Economics*, 38, 5–37.

Crane, A. and Hartzell, J. (2008) *Is there a disposition effect in corporate investment decisions? Evidence from real estate investment trusts*, SSRN Working Paper, 16 July. University of Texas, Austin, TX. Available at: https://papers.ssrn.com/sol3/papers.cfm?abstract_id=1031010 (accessed 14 August 2018).

Cutler, D. M., Poterba, J. M. and Summers, L. H. (1991) Speculative dynamics, *Review of Economic Studies*, 58(3), 529–46.

Diaz, J. III (1997) An investigation into the impact of previous expert value estimates on appraisal judgment, *Journal of Real Estate Research*, 13(1), 57–66.

Diaz, J. III (2002) *Behavioural research in appraisal and some perspectives on implications for practice*, RICS Foundation Research Review Series, August, RICS Foundation, London.

Diaz, J. III and Hansz, J. A. (2001) The use of reference points in valuation judgment, *Journal of Property Research*, 18(2), 141–8.

Diaz, J. III and Wolverton, M. L. (1998) A longitudinal examination of the appraisal smoothing hypothesis, *Real Estate Economics*, 26(2), 349–58.

Epley, N. and Gilovich, T. (2001) Putting adjustment back in the anchoring and adjustment heuristic: differential processing of self-generated and experimenter-provided anchors, *Psychological Science*, 12, 391–6.

Fama, E. F. (1970) Efficient capital markets: a review of theory and empirical work, *Journal of Finance*, 25, 383–420.

Farragher, E. J. and Kleiman, R. (1996) A re-examination of real estate investment decision-making practices, *Journal of Real Estate Portfolio Management*, 2(1), 31–9.
Gallimore, P. (1994) Aspects of information processing in valuation judgment and choice, *Journal of Property Research*, 11(2), 97–110.
Gallimore, P. and Gray, A. (2002) The role of investor sentiment in property investment decisions, *Journal of Property Research*, 19(2), 111–20.
Gallimore, P., Hansz, J. A. and Gray, A. (2000) Decision making in small property companies, *Journal of Property Investment and Finance*, 15(3), 261–73.
Gervais, S. and Odean, T. (2001) Learning to be overconfident, *Review of Financial Studies*, 14(1), 1–27.
Havard, T. (2001) An examination of the relationship between the anchoring and adjustment heuristic and variance in commercial property, *Journal of Property Research*, 18(1), 51–67.
Hodgson, G. M. (2003) The hidden persuaders: institutions and individuals in economic theory, *Cambridge Journal of Economics*, 27, 159–75.
Jin, C. and Gallimore, P. (2010) The effects of information presentation on real estate market perceptions, *Journal of Property Research*, 27(3), 239–46.
Kahneman, D. (2011) *Thinking, fast and slow*, Penguin, Harmondsworth.
Kahneman, D. and Tversky, A. (1974) Judgement under uncertainty: heuristics and biases, *Science* 185, 1124–31.
Kahneman, D. and Tversky, A. (1979) Prospect theory: an analysis of decision under risk, *Econometrica*, 47(2), 263–91.
Kallberg, J. G., Liu, C. H. and Greig, D. W. (1996) The role of real estate in the portfolio allocation process, *Real Estate Economics*, 24(3), 359–77.
Kinnard, W. N., Lenk, M. M. and Worzala, E. M. (1997) Client pressure in the commercial appraisal industry: how prevalent is it?, *Journal of Property Valuation and Investment*, 15(3), 233–44.
Kishore, R. (2004) Theory of behavioural finance and its application to property market: a change in paradigm, *Australian Property Journal*, 38(2), 105–10.
Kishore, R. and Demas, D. (2011) An examination of the wealth effect of REIT shares due to the introduction of Sarbanes Oxley Act: an event study approach, *Journal on Banking, Financial Services and Insurance Research*, 1(3), 63–76.
Lamont, O. A. and Thaler, R. H. (2003) Can the market add and subtract? Mispricing in tech stock carve-outs, *Journal of Political Economy*, 111(2), 227–68.
Levitt, S. D. and Syverson, C. (2008) Market distortions when agents are better informed: the value of information in real estate transactions, *Review of Economics and Statistics*, 90(4), 599–611.
Levy, D. and Schuck, E. (2005) The influence of clients on valuations: the clients' perspective, *Journal of Property Investment and Finance*, 23(2), 182–201.
Ling, D. C. (2005) A random walk down main street: can experts predict returns on commercial real estate? *Journal of Real Estate Research*, 27(2), 1–15.
Ling, D. C., Naranjo, A. and Scheick, B. (2014) Investor sentiment, limits to arbitrage and private market returns, *Real Estate Economics*, 42(3), 531–77.
Lux, T. (1995) Herd behaviour, bubbles and crashes, *Economic Journal*, 105, 881–96.
Markowitz, H. M. (1952) Portfolio selection, *Journal of Finance*, 7(1), 77–91.
Modigliani, F. and Miller, M. H. (1958) The cost of capital, corporation finance and the theory of investment, *American Economic Review*, 48(3), 261–97.
Newell, G. and Kishore, R. (1998) The accuracy of commercial property valuations, paper presented at the 4th Pacific Rim Real Estate Society Conference, Perth, Australia, January.
Northcraft, G. B. and Neale, M. A. (1987) Experts, amateurs, and real estate: an anchoring-and-adjustment perspective on property pricing decisions, *Organizational Behavior and Human Decision Processes*, 39(1), 84–97.
Perri 6. (2005) What's in a frame? Social organization, risk perception and the sociology of knowledge, *Journal of Risk Research*, 8(2), 92–118.
Quigley, J. M. (1999) Real estate prices and economic cycles, *International Real Estate Review*, 2(1), 1–20.

Ritter, J. R. (2003) Behavioral finance, *Pacific-Basin Finance Journal*, 11, 429–37.
Roberts, C. and Henneberry, J. (2007) Exploring office investment decision-making in different European contexts, *Journal of Property Investment and Finance*, 25(3), 289–305.
Sah, V., Gallimore, P. and Clements, J. S. (2010) Experience and real estate investment decision-making: a process-tracing investigation, *Journal of Property Research*, 27(3), 207–19.
Salzman, D. and Zwinkels, R. C. J. (2013) *Behavioral real estate*, Discussion Paper, TI 13–088/IV/DSF 58, Tinbergen Institute, Amsterdam.
Savage, L. (1964) *The foundations of statistics*, Wiley, New York, NY.
Seiler, M. J., Seiler, V. and Lane, M. A. (2012) Mental accounting and false reference points in real estate investment decision making, *Journal of Behavioral Finance*, 13, 17–26.
Sharpe, W. F. (1964) Capital asset prices: a theory of market equilibrium under conditions of risk, *Journal of Finance*, 19(3), 425–42.
Shiller, R. J. (1981) Do stock prices move too much to be justified by subsequent changes in dividends?, *American Economic Review*, 71, 421–36.
Shiller, R. J. (2005) *Irrational exuberance*, 2nd ed., Princeton University Press, Princeton, NJ.
Shleifer, A. (2000) *Inefficient markets: an introduction to behavioral finance*, Oxford University Press, Oxford.
Thaler, R. H. (1999) Mental accounting matters, *Journal of Behavioral Decision Making*, 12, 183–206.
Tobin, J. (1958) Liquidity preference as behavior towards risk, *Review of Economic Studies*, 25(2), 65–86.
Von Neumann, J. and Morgenstern, O. (1944) *Theory of games and economic behavior*, Princeton University Press, Princeton, NJ.
Wang, K., Zhou, Y., Chan, S. H. and Chau, K. W. (2000) Over-confidence and cycles in real estate markets: cases in Hong Kong and Asia, *International Real Estate Review*, 3(1), 93–108.
Watkins, C., White, M. and Keskin, B. (2012) *The future of real estate forecasting, report for the IPF Research Programme 2011–2015*, Investment Property Forum, London.
Wofford, L. E., Troilo, M. L. and Dorchester, A. D. (2010) Managing cognitive risk in real estate, *Journal of Property Research*, 27(3), 269–87.
Yavas, A. and Yang, S. (1995) The strategic role of listing price in marketing real estate: theory and evidence, *Real Estate Economics*, 23(3), 347–68.

14 Commercial real estate investment in a portfolio of risky assets

Mark J. Eppli and Charles C. Tu

Introduction

Humans prefer certainty to uncertainty. Across most personal and business transactions, we pursue the safe option over the risky one, especially for the important or large decisions that involve our health or economic livelihood, all else equal. However, that is not the case across all actions in our daily lives. For instance, United States Census data reports that US$59.4 billion in lottery tickets or just over US$190's worth per person were purchased in 2012, the most recent year for which lottery data was collected, while only US$37 billion was distributed in prize money.[1] Bets or investments in the lottery paid out only US$0.62 for every dollar invested. While most residents of the United States may not know the specifics of the 62% payout rate when purchasing lottery tickets, most are aware that less than a dollar is paid out for each dollar in ticket sales – so why do we do it?

Across small portions of our wealth, a majority of adults gamble each year, revealing risk-seeking behaviour.[2] We are willing to take the risk of losing one dollar, five dollars or ten dollars on a bet with a potentially large payoff as that bet involves a very small portion of our wealth that, if lost, will not impact our quality of life. Similarly, many US citizens place bets on sports games, both formally through legal betting channels and informally with friends and family, with an average return that is either neutral or a loss.[3] In short, humans are not risk averse across all spectrums of investment.

Conversely, US citizens, corporations and organisations also pay over US$500 billion a year in property and casualty insurance premiums that reimburse us for unexpected or unplanned losses (Federal Insurance Office, 2013); losses that could place individuals and organisations in financial distress, if not bankruptcy, if these insured risks are not transferred to another party to manage. Property and casualty insurance loss ratios are approximately 60–65% of premiums paid, so here again Americans engage in contracts realising that they will not receive a dollar of loss coverage for each dollar of insurance paid, as there are insurance sales expenses, insurance adjuster expenses, among many other costs in creating and delivering an insurance policy. The purchase of insurance reveals strong risk aversion behaviour.[4] When large portions of our wealth are placed at risk, we shy away from uncertainty. So human actions generally reveal that we are risk seekers with small portions of our wealth and simultaneously are very risk averse when large portions of or wealth or personal health are at stake.

So what does the purchase of lottery tickets and insurance have to do with investing in real estate as part of a portfolio of risky assets? It helps us to understand the investment behaviours of individuals and institutions. It also helps in crafting government policies as they relate to investment risk levels, how they should be measured and why they are important.

In subsequent sections, we consider uncertainty, risk and risk aversion, defined benefit retirement plans and commercial real estate investment in a mixed asset portfolio.

Uncertainty, risk and risk aversion

The 2017 Nobel Prize for Economics was awarded to Richard Thaler for his work in behavioural economics in analysing how human psychology influences economic and financial decisions, and showing that humans may not always be rational economic actors. Limited rationality and limited self-control are human traits that direct human behaviour, as human psychology depends on the circumstances, abilities and knowledge of individuals, and different individuals make different decisions.

Human behaviour generally reveals risk aversion across a large range of economic opportunities, and that is the case for most investment behaviour. Investment returns come with uncertainty requiring humans to make decisions that are often based on limited information, differing personal circumstances or an incomplete understanding of investment products. This limitation means that many individuals may follow a simplified approach to portfolio diversification, such as 'don't put all your eggs in one basket'. And if individual stocks or bonds or real estate investments are thought of as the eggs, how should we think about contents of these baskets or should we hold more than one basket?

Over 40 years ago, the US Employee Retirement Income Security Act (ERISA) of 1974 was established to direct and limit investment adviser behaviour. One of the significant elements of this regulation is that investor advisers are expected to diversify investment plan assets to mitigate the risk of large losses to retirement plans and protect individual investors from investment fraud and negligent behaviour. ERISA applies to US investment professionals, who manage defined benefit pension plans. Defined benefit retirement plans require investment professionals to invest company or municipally sponsored retirement plans to meet a promised stream of future retirement payouts. To ensure that investment managers operate in the client's best interest, a fiduciary standard was established by ERISA that requires investment plan advisers to act in the best interest of individual investors, which includes investing in a diverse set of assets that minimise the risk of large losses. To reduce or minimise the risk of a large loss, pension fund managers must consider the diversification standards forwarded in Section 404(c) of ERISA, where the Act requires investment plans be diversified into assets that maintain *materially different risk and return characteristics*.[5]

ERISA required that defined benefit plan investment managers seek investment opportunities beyond investing in stocks and bonds, as stock and bond investments maintain a relatively high correlation; that is, they go up and down together, thus providing limited ability to minimise the risk of large loss in market downturns.[6] To reduce the risk of large loss, other investments that maintain different risk and return characteristics than those of stocks and bonds are needed. The size of the defined benefit investment plan market is large in the United States and globally. According Willis Towers Watson, a pension consultancy, US defined benefit investment funds were US$14.7 trillion on 4 September 2017 in the United States.[7] Across 22 large global pension markets, including the US, the global defined benefit market was US$36.4 trillion in 2016.

However, the need to reduce portfolio variance is far broader than the regulatory requirements of defined benefit plans in the United States and internationally. Defined contribution plans, such as Section 401(k) and 403(b) plans are growing rapidly and, based on Investment Company Institute data, hold US$7.0 trillion in assets.[8] To reduce the risk of investing in individual assets, individuals invest in stock, bond, diversified mutual and exchange-traded funds. Rapid growth in the mutual fund market provides evidence of the market acceptance of the benefits of portfolio diversification. In 2016, 9511 mutual funds managed US$16.3 trillion in assets in the US.[9] There are twice as many publicly traded mutual funds as publicly traded stocks (there are 4331 publicly traded companies in the United States).[10] Exchange-traded funds hold an additional US$2.5 trillion in assets.

The wisdom of risk reduction through investing in a portfolio of stocks and bonds, as opposed to investing in a small handful of securities, is broadly accepted by the investment profession and most lay people. What is less widely accepted and understood is how many 'baskets' of assets (that is different investment classes such as stock, bond, real estate, private equity and so on) an investor should hold as opposed to the number of eggs in each basket (that is the number of stocks or number of bonds). A requirement of ERISA is for plan investment professionals to invest in baskets of investment that maintain materially different risk/return profiles.

Defined benefit retirement plans and the need for many baskets

So far, we have learned that investors have different risk profiles, that regulation requires investment plans to diversify, and that individual investors recognise the benefits of investing in portfolios or baskets of stocks and bonds, but may be less informed about the benefits of investing in a range of baskets with different risk/return profiles. This brings us back to the purpose of including real estate in a mixed asset portfolio and whether investments in commercial real estate have materially different return characteristics to stocks and bonds.

Let us begin with a discussion of market-based investment return expectations. The *discount rate* or target rate of return on defined benefit pension plans is the actuarially determined return on invested funds needed to meet future employee retirement obligations.[11] If the discount rate is not met, additional funds must be set aside by the plan to meet plan retirement obligations. Figure 14.1 reveals how an investment portfolio needs to change across time if a pension fund wants to maintain the same target rate of return. Using information provided

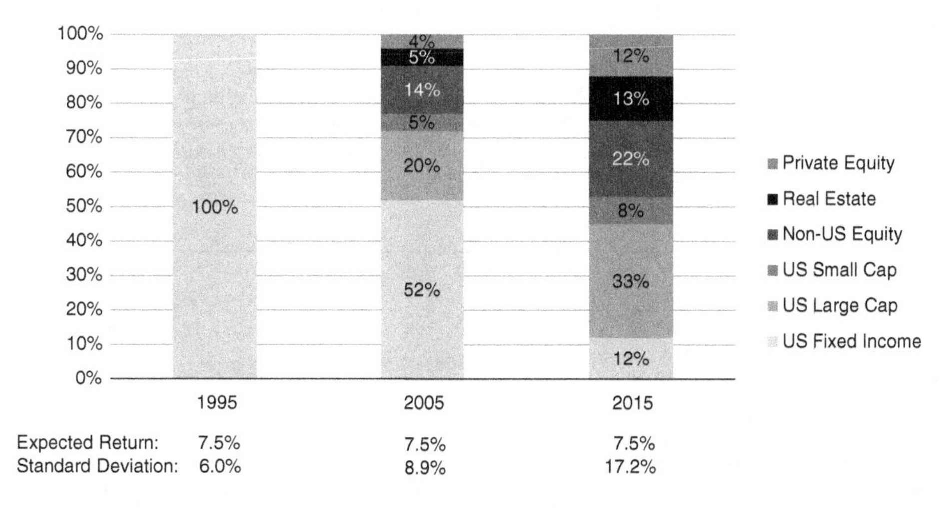

Figure 14.1 Same return, increasing risks
Note: The investment portfolio needed to obtain a 7.5% return across time.
Source: Callan and Associates (2016).

by Callan and Associates, an investment consultancy, Figure 14.1 reveals that, in 1995, a 7.5% return could be achieved by investing all funds in bonds. Bonds also have a fairly low risk profile, with a standard deviation, at 6% in 1995 (Callan and Associates, 2016). Moving forward to 2015 and a market that anticipates considerably lower investment return per unit of risk, to achieve a 7.5% return, Callan suggests that only 12% of the portfolio be invested in bonds, with 63% in stocks (that is US large capitalisation stocks, US small capitalisation stocks and non-US equities), 13% in real estate and 12% in private equity investments. To maintain the 7.5% investment yield in a low return rate environment, pension funds in 2015 need to take on much greater investment risk than in 1995, with portfolio risk almost tripling from the 1995 case of 6.0% to 17.2% for the 2015 case.

Alternatively and interestingly, in the Callan and Associates (2016), they hold the standard deviation at 6.0% across investment scenarios and find that the investment return falls from 7.5% in 1995 to 4.8% in 2015. If a pension fund like California Public Employees Retirement System (CalPERS) were to reduce the discount rate to 4.8%, the increase in retirement contributions would be dramatic and would require significantly larger pension contributions to the retirement system, thus increasing the cost of public services. Thus, organisations like CalPERS actively seek investments that provide a reasonably high return without generating outsized increases in risk to the portfolio.

In short, corporations and municipalities with defined benefit retirement plans have a very difficult choice: continue to invest in bonds and receive a ± 3.65% rate of return, which is what BBB bonds are yielding today (January 2018) and make much higher fund contributions cutting into corporate profitability or increasing municipal expenses, and/or invest in a portfolio of assets that has a higher return profile but comes with significantly higher risk. CalPERS, the largest non-federal pension plan in the United States is doing both. First, the CalPERS board voted to reduce the investment discount rate from 7.5% to 7.0% between 2017 and 2020.[12] To meet future pension obligations, the State of California or its employees will need to contribute larger amounts to the fund, increasing municipal or employee expenses. Second, it also appears that CalPERS is taking on more risk to maintain the 7.0% investment discount rate. Table 14.1 shows how CalPERS is increasing its allocation to real estate from 9.3% in 2002 to 13% in 2017 and beyond.

Table 14.1 California Public Employees Retirement System investment allocation to real estate

Year	*Assets under management (US$ billion)*	*Allocated to real estate*	
		(US$ billion)	*(%)*
2002	143	13	9.3
2004	133	11	8.3
2006	164	11	6.9
2008	205	20	9.8
2010	199	22	11.0
2012	212	23	10.9
2014	232	24	10.1
2016	293	31	10.6
2017+			13.0

Source: CalPERS press release: CalPERS to lower discount rate to seven percent over the next three years, 21 December 2016; www.calpers.ca.gov/page/newsroom/calpers-news/2016/calpers-lower-discount-rate (accessed 17 August 2018).

Asset returns and risk

The 2005 and 2015 mixed asset portfolios in Figure 14.1 reveal the need to invest in a broad portfolio of assets to maintain a 7.5% investment return while keeping the variance in returns relatively low, which brings us to the risk and return of a mixed asset portfolio. The first goal of pension fund investment is to maintain the purchasing power of the investment corpus or principal. Inflation as measured by the Consumer Price Index had an average annual increase of 2.65% over the past three decades (Table 14.2), so investments need to exceed inflation to preserve the purchasing power of a dollar. During that same three-decade period, short-term US Treasuries outpaced inflation by 73 basis points maintaining a 3.38% average annual return, while long-term government bonds beat inflation by 3.52% during this period. However, as of the January 2018, 10-year US Treasury bonds, yield a meagre 2.55% providing limited opportunity for capital gains as rates cannot fall much further.

Thirty years ago, corporate bonds had an average annual return of 7.25%, or approximately one percentage point higher than long-term government bonds, and high-yield bonds, with less than a BBB-minus rating, provided an 8.93% average annual return. So, in 1995, investment returns on a portfolio of bonds-only could achieve a 7.5% annual yield, but that is not the case today as 10-year US Treasuries yield in the mid-2% range, BBB bonds yield in the mid-3% range and B-rated high-yield bonds return a yield in the upper 5% range. In 2018, bond yields alone provide a yield that is woeful relative to a 7.5% pension fund target return.

To maintain a 7.5% investment yield in 2018, pension fund investment managers must secure investments that provide higher yields that come with an increased risk profile. Large capitalisation stocks, small capitalisation stocks and real estate investment trusts (REITs) all maintained double-digit average historic annual returns and many investment advisers expect stocks to provide investment returns in the high single-digit range, however that comes with increased risk. Large capitalisation and small capitalisation stocks have a standard deviation of 17–19%, more than three times the standard deviation of corporate bonds. Private investment in commercial real estate in the National Council of Real Estate Investment Fiduciaries (NCREIF) index earned a lower historic return, at 8.2%, but also has a lower standard deviation.[13]

As one might expect, the standard deviation of returns, which is the most common measure of investment risk, increases across the investments discussed in Table 14.2, with US Treasuries having the lowest risk and risk growing with high-yield bonds and stock

Table 14.2 Comparison of annual returns by asset class and index, 1987–2017 second quarter

Asset Class	*Index*	*Mean (%)*	*Standard deviation (%)*
Inflation	Consumer Price Index	2.65	1.33
Risk-free rate	3-month Treasury Bills	3.38	2.60
Government bonds	Bloomberg Barclays US Government	6.17	4.95
Corporate bonds	Bloomberg Barclays US Credit	7.25	5.74
High-Yield bonds	Barclays Capital US High Yield Corporate	8.93	11.95
Large cap stocks	Standard & Poor's 500	11.58	17.04
Small cap stocks	Russell 2000	10.92	18.80
Public real estate	FTSE Nareit Equity Real Estate Investment Trusts Index	12.21	19.99
Private real estate	National Council of Real Estate Investment Fiduciaries Property Index	8.20	7.86

investments. Given the relatively high mean return for commercial real estate with a fairly muted standard deviation, private investment in commercial real estate may have risk and return characteristics that are different from other investments.

Investment risk, returns and risk-adjusted returns

Table 14.3 presents the annual returns of the NCREIF National Property Index. The average return for the 30-year 1987–2017 second-quarter period reveals an 8.20% average annual holding period return with a 7.86% standard deviation. Holding period returns are calculated on a rolling basis, or for example, the one-year holding period return calculations are for sequential one-year return horizons quarter-after-quarter.[14] After all one-year holding period returns are calculated for the 30-year investment horizon, the average of those holding periods is reported.

Table 14.3 also provides the three-, five- and seven-year holding period returns, which reveal investment returns that are slightly over 8.0% for each of those holding periods. While average holding period returns for successive holding periods, range from 8.06–8.10%, holding period standard deviations drop by more than half to 3.38% for a seven-year holding period from a one-year holding period standard deviation of 7.86%. As holding periods lengthen, the standard deviation of the NCREIF index declines, revealing a mean-reverting reduction in risk for longer holding periods, which is evident in most investment asset returns.

As most all institutional investors have a holding period that extends beyond one year, Figure 14.2 reveals commercial real estate holding period returns for one-, three-, five- and seven-year holding periods. The mean-reverting nature of commercial real estate returns is graphically presented, as the seven-year holding period return line is much less volatile than the one-year holding period return line.

Table 14.4 subdivides the Table 14.3 NCREIF index into each of the primary property types, presenting the one-, three-, five-, and seven-year annual holding period returns and holding period return standard deviations for apartments, industrial, office, and retail investments.

The importance of including the one-, three-, five- and seven-year holding period returns (Figures 14.3 to 14.6) is to reveal graphically that for all property types, the longer the holding period the lower the property variance as property returns mean revert. Apartment and retail holding period returns are generally higher than other property types with a lower variance, which is more easily seen in the five- and seven-year holding period return graphs (Figures 14.3 and 14.4).

Table 14.4 also reveals the Sharpe ratios for each of the four holding periods. The Sharpe ratio is the average return minus the risk-free rate divided by standard deviation of the

Table 14.3 National Council of Real Estate Investment Fiduciaries Property Index holding period return comparison, 1987–2017 second quarter

	Annual return (%)	*Holding period return (%)*		
		3-year	*5-year*	*7-year*
Mean	8.20	8.10	8.06	8.06
Standard deviation	7.86	5.89	4.36	3.38
Maximum	20.19	18.03	15.13	12.77
Minimum	–22.11	–4.71	–0.08	2.09

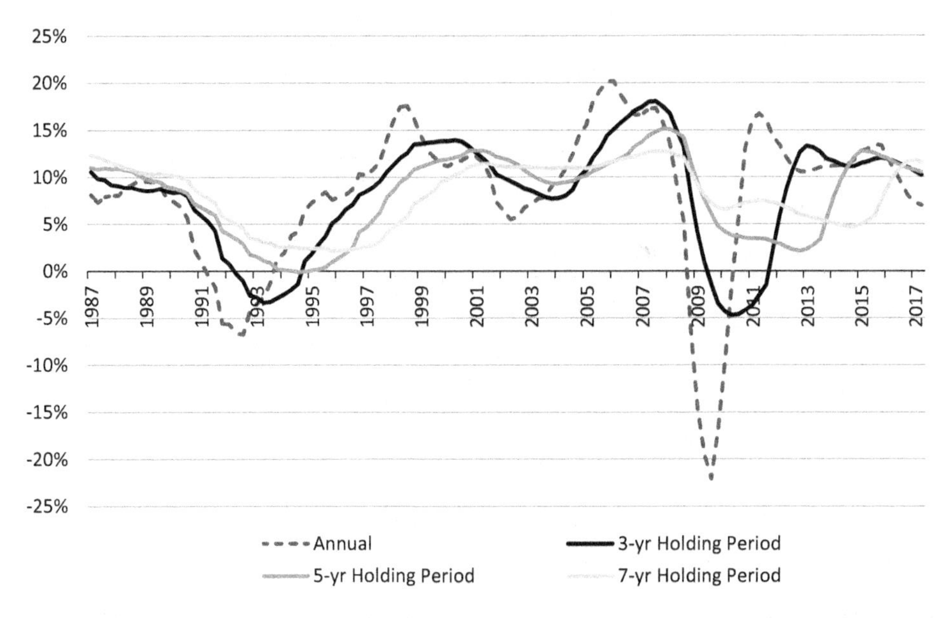

Figure 14.2 National Council of Real Estate Investment Fiduciaries holding period return comparison, 1987–2017 second quarter

Table 14.4 National Council of Real Estate Investment Fiduciaries holding period returns by property type 1987–2017 second quarter

	Annual			*3-year holding period*		
	Mean (%)	*SD (%)*	*Sharpe ratio*	*Mean (%)*	*SD (%)*	*Sharpe ratio*
All	8.20	7.86	0.58	8.10	5.89	0.63
Apartment	9.16	7.34	0.75	9.05	5.07	0.92
Industrial	8.85	8.08	0.65	8.64	6.24	0.68
Office	7.05	9.56	0.36	6.88	7.38	0.34
Retail	9.43	7.18	0.81	9.44	5.68	0.89
	5-year holding period			*7-year holding period*		
	Mean (%)	*SD (%)*	*Sharpe ratio*	*Mean (%)*	*SD (%)*	*Sharpe ratio*
All	8.06	4.36	0.69	8.06	3.38	0.71
Apartment	9.11	3.50	1.16	9.21	2.77	1.28
Industrial	8.53	4.64	0.75	8.50	3.53	0.80
Office	6.79	5.66	0.31	6.82	4.52	0.26
Retail	9.43	4.47	0.98	9.36	3.44	1.08

SD = standard deviation from the mean.

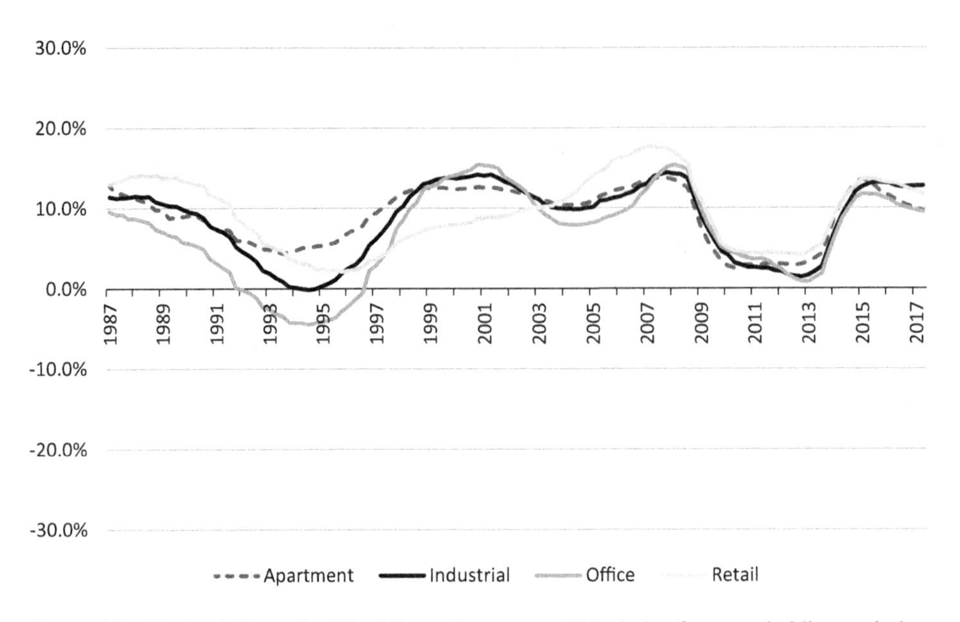

Figure 14.3 National Council of Real Estate Investment Fiduciaries five-year holding period returns by property type, 1987–2017 second quarter

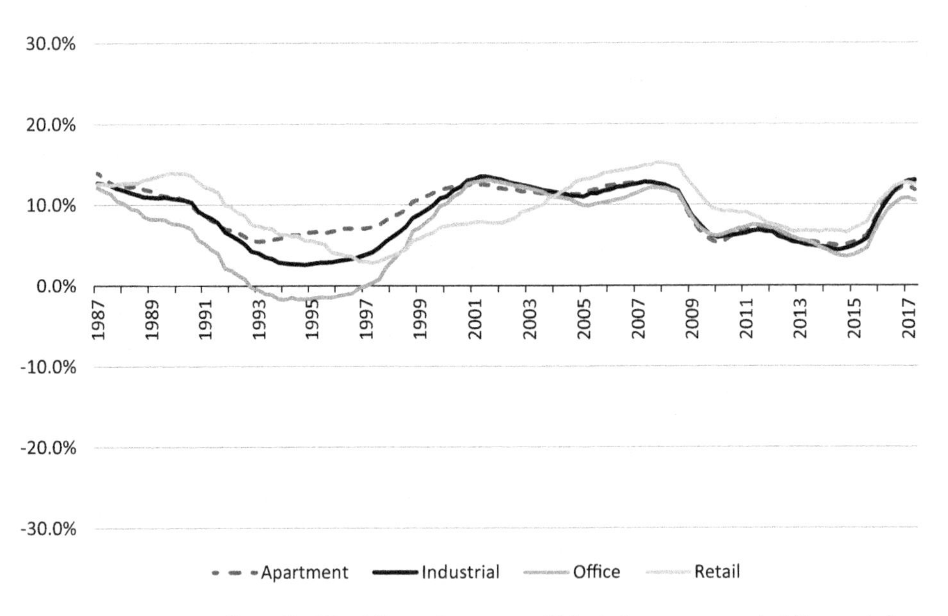

Figure 14.4 National Council of Real Estate Investment Fiduciaries seven-year holding period returns by property type, 1987–2017 second quarter

Figure 14.5 National Council of Real Estate Investment Fiduciaries annual holding period returns by property type, 1987–2017 second quarter

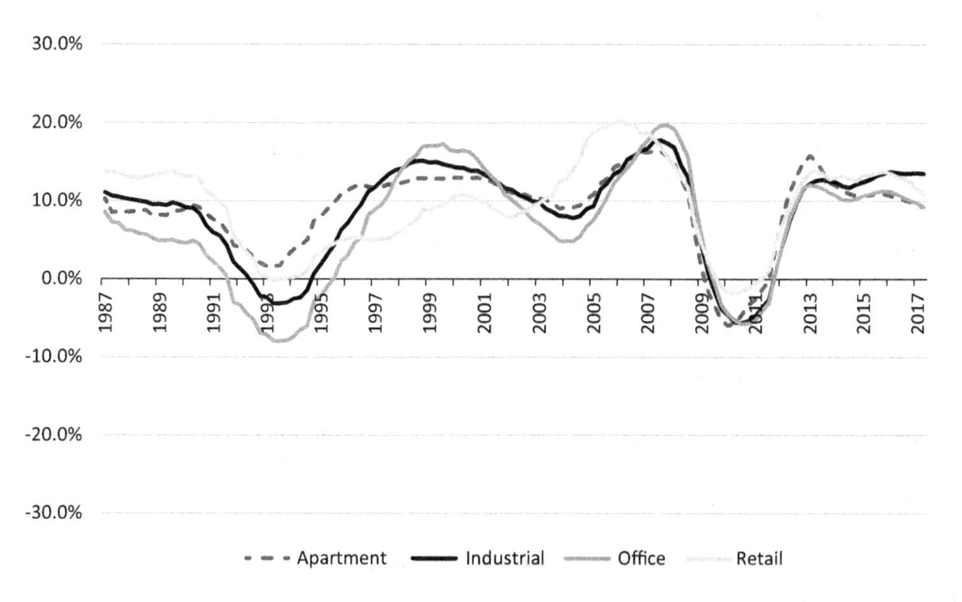

Figure 14.6 National Council of Real Estate Investment Fiduciaries three-year holding period returns by property type, 1987–2017 second quarter

Table 14.5 Comparison of holding period returns, 1987–2017 second quarter

Asset class	*Annual*			*3-year holding period*		
	Mean (%)	*SD (%)*	*Sharpe ratio*	*Mean (%)*	*SD (%)*	*Sharpe ratio*
Inflation	2.65	1.33		2.68	0.96	
Risk-free rate	3.38	2.60		3.62	2.47	
Government bonds	6.17	4.95	0.56	6.72	3.30	0.94
Corporate bonds	7.25	5.74	0.67	7.76	3.57	1.16
High-yield bonds	8.93	11.95	0.46	8.91	5.87	0.90
Large cap stocks	11.58	17.04	0.48	11.25	10.95	0.70
Small cap stocks	10.92	18.80	0.40	9.89	8.67	0.72
Public real estate	12.21	19.99	0.44	11.25	10.32	0.74
Private real estate	8.20	7.86	0.61	8.10	5.89	0.76
Asset Class	*5-year holding period*			*7-year holding period*		
	Mean (%)	*SD (%)*	*Sharpe ratio*	*Mean (%)*	*SD (%)*	*Sharpe ratio*
Inflation	2.76	0.80		2.88	0.81	
Risk-free rate	3.91	2.40		4.26	2.49	
Government bonds	7.12	2.96	1.08	7.55	2.97	1.11
Corporate bonds	8.19	3.19	1.34	8.61	3.23	1.35
High-yield bonds	9.07	3.88	1.33	8.93	2.67	1.75
Large cap stocks	11.24	8.59	0.85	11.13	6.66	1.03
Small cap stocks	9.90	6.27	0.96	9.92	4.29	1.32
Public real estate	11.39	6.88	1.09	11.53	4.88	1.49
Private Real Estate	8.06	4.36	0.95	8.06	3.38	1.12

investment return. A higher Sharpe ratio indicates a higher return per unit of risk. Across the four property types, the risk-adjusted Sharpe ratios were 0.26–1.28, with office properties maintaining the lowest Sharpe ratios in the 0.26–0.36 range and apartments maintaining a 0.75–1.28 Sharpe ratio. Thus, over the last 30 years, apartments outperformed office properties on a risk-adjusted basis, maintaining an average return per unit of risk of about 1%, and office properties underperforming with an average 0.3% return per unit of risk.

Table 14.5 presents one-, three-, five- and seven-year holding period returns for stocks, bonds, real estate and inflation. The average holding period return, across the one-through seven-year holding periods, remains roughly the same across each of the asset classes, however, the standard deviation drops precipitously as the holding period expands from one to seven years, with the highest risk investment indices (that is for stocks and high yield bonds) standard deviation falling the most. The reversion to the mean is revealed across all property types, with significantly lower standard deviations as the holding period lengthens. Finally, the Sharpe ratios reveal a fairly narrow range of risk adjusted returns. The private real estate Sharpe ratios are similar to stock returns which is consistent with Edelstein and Quan (2006).[15]

Investment correlation

In the previous section we highlighted the importance of individual asset class risk/return profiles; however, the more important metric is the risk return profile of the entire portfolio.

As asset class returns do not move in lock step, diversification benefits of investing in a portfolio of assets offset some of the risk of holding individual asset classes.

The primary purpose of portfolio diversification is to invest in a set of assets that do not correlate highly with each other and therefore mute the impact of market movements during the holding period of the pool of assets. Correlation coefficients range from +1.0 to –1.0, where a +1.0 correlation reveals that two securities perfectly positive correlated and therefore go up and down in lock step and provide no diversification benefits. Conversely, securities that have a –1.0 correlation are perfectly negatively correlated and when paired can eliminate portfolio risk as, when one security moves up, the other moves down pushing the combined standard deviations to zero. A zero correlation coefficient means that two securities move in a random manner relative to each other. Diversification benefits can be achieved by any two securities that do not maintain a perfect positive correlation; however, the lower the correlation coefficient, the more that diversification can reduce portfolio volatility. For an asset class to have materially different risk return characteristics from other asset classes, it needs to have a correlation coefficient that approaches zero or preferably is negative relative to other securities in the portfolio.

Table 14.6 presents one-, three-, five-, and seven-year holding period return asset correlations where one-year holding period returns are presented in the top panel. The correlation matrices in Table 14.6 use greyscale shades for ease of understanding. The lighter the shade the higher the correlation coefficient between two indices and the lower the diversification benefits from investing in that combination of securities. For instance, the annual return correlation for corporate and government bonds is 85.5%, meaning that the two securities move up and down roughly in tandem, much as expected. The Standard & Poor's and Russell stock indices also co-move with a correlation coefficient of 84.4%. Again, diversification benefits are greatest for securities that have low or negative correlations.

On the other end of the spectrum are the darker shaded correlation coefficients, indicating relationships that are materially different from each other. Looking down the right-hand portion of the correlation matrices in Table 14.6, the NCREIF index of privately held real estate reveals low to negative correlations with all other asset classes across all four holding periods. In the annual return matrix in the top panel, the NCREIF index maintains a negative correlation with all the long-term bond indices indicating material diversification possibilities with that asset class. Similarly, a negative correlation between bonds and the NCREIF index exists for the three-, five- and seven-year holding periods. While stock and the NCREIF indices have a positive, albeit low, correlation with each other, as the holding periods lengthen correlations become negative for all of the correlations for stock and NCREIF investments. In summary, based on the one year through seven-year holding period analyses, it appears as if the NCREIF real estate index has materially different return characteristics than those of stocks and bonds.

Some observers might expect correlation coefficients between the Nareit and NCREIF indices to be higher than the reported 14–42% correlations across the different holding period analyses in Table 14.6, as both indices reflect portfolios of commercial real estate. To provide a partial explanation for the relatively low correlations, Table 14.7 presents an overview of how the two indices differ across a series of characteristics. The Nareit index is based on publicly traded securities, uses leverage, and generally invests in assets of typical quality. However, the NCREIF index is privately held, does not use leverage and invests in top quality, institutional-grade properties. As such, it should be expected that while these two indices hold commercial real estate, they are not highly correlated.

Table 14.6 Correlation matrix

Annual returns

	CPI	*T bill*	*US Govt*	*US Corp*	*US HY*	*S&P*	*Russell*	*Nareit*	*NCREIF*
CPI	1.000	0.754	0.157	-0.021	-0.194	0.020	0.074	0.050	0.288
T Bill		1.000	0.496	0.304	-0.169	0.126	0.059	0.010	0.220
US Govt			1.000	0.855	0.078	0.104	0.060	0.112	-0.071
US Corp				1.000	0.404	0.361	0.329	0.392	-0.168
US HY					1.000	0.519	0.499	0.562	-0.300
S&P						1.000	0.844	0.568	0.172
Russell							1.000	0.700	0.068
Nareit								1.000	0.144
NCREIF									1.000

3-year holding period returns

	CPI	*T Bill*	*US Govt*	*US Corp*	*US HY*	*S&P*	*Russell*	*Nareit*	*NCREIF*
CPI	1.000	0.696	0.613	0.514	-0.137	0.169	0.250	0.167	0.100
T Bill		1.000	0.829	0.691	-0.158	0.305	0.190	0.116	0.150
US Govt			1.000	0.917	0.119	0.183	0.115	0.192	-0.097
US Corp				1.000	0.329	0.309	0.317	0.417	-0.098
US HY					1.000	0.419	0.454	0.459	-0.318
S&P						1.000	0.758	0.435	0.341
Russell							1.000	0.748	0.272
Nareit								1.000	0.373
NCREIF									1.000

5-year holding period returns

	CPI	*T Bill*	*US Govt*	*US Corp*	*US HY*	*S&P*	*Russell*	*Nareit*	*NCREIF*
CPI	1.000	0.549	0.747	0.643	0.098	0.221	0.174	0.207	-0.035
T Bill		1.000	0.905	0.790	0.048	0.426	0.225	0.209	0.100
US Govt			1.000	0.941	0.180	0.339	0.206	0.249	-0.028
US Corp				1.000	0.377	0.441	0.383	0.415	-0.034
US HY					1.000	0.466	0.566	0.381	-0.419
S&P						1.000	0.780	0.392	0.174
Russell							1.000	0.761	0.170
Nareit								1.000	0.408
NCREIF									1.000

7-year holding period returns

	CPI	*T Bill*	*US Govt*	*US Corp*	*US HY*	*S&P*	*Russell*	*Nareit*	*NCREIF*
CPI	1.000	0.419	0.880	0.805	0.350	0.408	0.305	0.276	-0.096
T Bill		1.000	0.956	0.875	0.229	0.598	0.385	0.314	0.054
US Govt			1.000	0.957	0.318	0.566	0.368	0.313	0.003
US Corp				1.000	0.443	0.634	0.478	0.401	-0.023
US HY					1.000	0.553	0.562	0.186	-0.637
S&P						1.000	0.801	0.305	-0.140
Russell							1.000	0.632	-0.061
Nareit								1.000	0.418
NCREIF									1.000

Notes: Corp = corporation; CPI = Consumer Price Index; Govt = government; HY = high yield; NCREIF = National Council of Real Estate Investment Fiduciaries; S&P = Standard & Poor's; T bill = Treasury bill.

Table 14.7 Characteristics of the National Council of Real Estate Investment Fiduciaries and Nareit Indices

Characteristic	*FTSE Nareit Equity REITs Index*	*NCREIF Property Index*
Ownership	Publicly traded	Privately held
Index size	US$1.1 trillion	US$539 billion
Properties	225 REITs	7161 properties
Valuation	Daily (equity markets)	Quarterly (appraisal)
Use of leverage	Use leverage	No leverage
Property quality	Investment quality	High quality institutional

FTSE = Financial Times stock Exchange; NCREIF = National Council of Real Estate Investment Fiduciaries; REIT = real estate investment trust.

Overall, the risk, return, and risk-adjusted returns for the NCREIF index fit well into the risk–return spectrum for stocks and bonds. However, the NCREIF index reveals characteristics that are different from the other asset classes with correlation coefficients that are low to negative with stocks and bonds. As such, private investment in commercial real estate may provide diversification benefits when invested with other asset classes. However, it should be noted that the NCREIF National Property Index is an appraisal-based index and there is a sizeable literature on the impact of appraisal smoothing on the variance of real estate returns that reveals a lag in property valuations and other possible value distortions. The impact of appraisal-based property values become less meaningful as property holding periods lengthen. The combined risks of the asset classes, along with the interaction of risk between and among the asset classes, is at the core of measuring the quantitative impact of diversifying investment holdings.

Commercial real estate investment in a mixed asset portfolio

Thus far, we have assessed the risk and return profile of commercial real estate and other assets held individually and how well the different asset classes correlate with each other. However, we have not formally placed the different asset classes into a mixed asset portfolio. The ultimate measure of an asset's ability to reduce or moderate portfolio risk, and as ERISA requires, find assets that have materially different risk and return characteristics.

The first step in analysing the risk of a two, then three, then four asset portfolio is to calculate the risk and return on the assets as if held individually. Table 14.8 reveals average annual returns for stocks, bonds, the Nareit index, and the NCREIF index for the period 19987–2017 second quarter. Publicly traded stocks and REITs had the highest return for the 30-plus year investment horizon at 11.47% and 12.21%, respectively. However, with higher returns come greater risk. The standard deviation of the stock and Nareit indices are 17.04% and 19.99%, respectively, which is two- to four-fold the standard deviation of bonds and the NCREIF index. Average one-year investment returns for bonds and the NCREIF were 6.52% and 8.20% with standard deviations of 4.78% and 7.86%, respectively.

With annual returns and standard deviations calculated for each of the investments, we then calculate the correlation coefficient between each of the asset classes which are presented in Table 14.9.[16] During the period 1987–2017 second quarter, stock and Nareit returns maintained a 60% correlation, as such, a portfolio of those two somewhat highly correlated securities will provide limited diversification benefits. This should not be a surprise as the Nareit index is an index of publicly traded real estate investment trusts that are traded on the New York, American and Nasdaq stock exchanges, and a number of the REIT

Table 14.8 One-year holding period returns and standard deviations (1987–2017 second quarter)

	Stocks	*Bonds*	*Nareit*	*NCREIF*
Mean (%)	11.47	6.52	12.21	8.20
Standard deviation (%)	17.04	4.78	19.99	7.86

NCREIF = National Council of Real Estate Investment Fiduciaries.

Sources: Wilshire 5000 Index; Bloomberg Barclays US Aggregate Index.

Table 14.9 Correlation matrix for one-year holding periods (1987–2017 second quarter)

	Stocks	*Bonds*	*Nareit*	*NCREIF*
Stocks	1.0000	0.2145	0.6002	0.1512
Bonds		1.0000	0.2483	–0.1113
Nareit			1.0000	0.1447
NCREIF				1.0000

NCREIF = National Council of Real Estate Investment Fiduciaries.

stocks, are included in the Wilshire 5000 index. Bonds maintain a 21% and 25% correlation with stocks and Nareit. The lowest correlations in Table 14.9 all involve the NCREIF index. With correlations ranging from –0.11 to 0.15, the commercial real estate index is weakly to negatively correlated with stocks, bonds and NCREIF. This weak to negative correlation should generate material diversification benefits for portfolios that include the NCREIF commercial real estate index.

To assess the impact of investing in a portfolio of securities, it is necessary to calculate the returns and standard deviations for a range of portfolio allocations. The benefits of a mixed asset portfolio are best presented graphically with the efficient frontier for a two-asset, stock and bond indices portfolio (Figure 14.7). The line represents different allocations of assets (weights) to stocks and bonds, if the entire portfolio is allocated to bonds, the graph reveals a 6.5% return and a 4.8% standard deviation, and if the entire allocation is to stocks, the graph reveals an 11.5% return and a 17.5% standard deviation. The slightly curved line between these points reveals the portfolio return and portfolio risk for different investment allocations to stocks and bonds. Recall that annual stock and bond returns for the period 1987–2017 second quarter maintained a 0.21 correlation coefficient, which means that the diversification benefits of investing in a two-asset portfolio will generate higher returns for the same level of risk than a single asset portfolio for that same risk preference level. As can be seen in Figure 14.7, the efficient frontier bows out to the northwest, which is the measure of the benefits of portfolio diversification. If bonds and stocks were perfectly positively correlated, the line between the risk and return for stocks and bonds would be straight between the two observations. If stocks and bonds were perfectly negatively correlated, the diversification benefits would push portfolio standard deviation to zero. Diversification benefits are revealed by the bowing of the line to the northwest, where investors receive a higher return per unit of risk as the line bows.

In Figure 14.8, the Nareit index is added to the stock and bond portfolios. Portfolios that include Nareit investments are depicted with the yellow line. Adding REITs to the two-asset portfolios of stocks and bonds (red line), expands the feasible set, so there are many possible combinations that are incrementally better when including the Nareit index with the

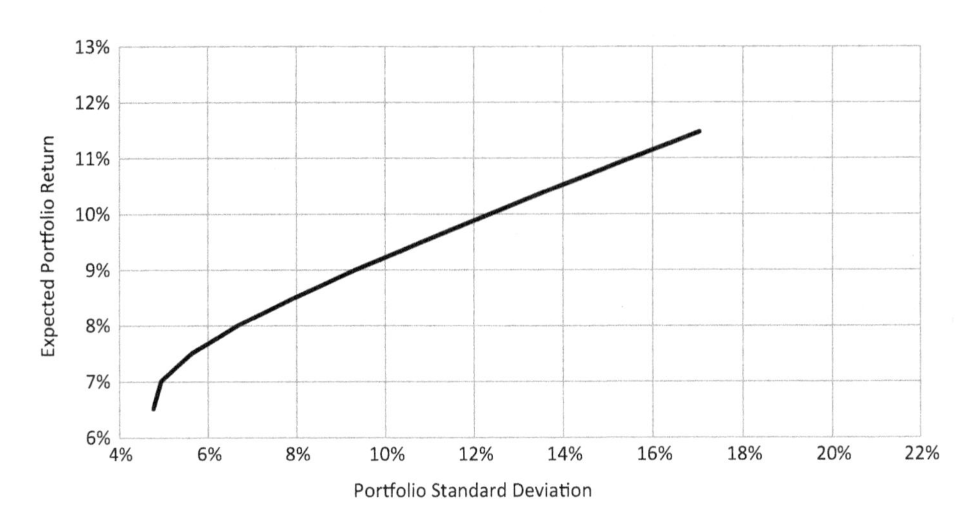

Figure 14.7 Two-asset, stock and bond efficient frontier

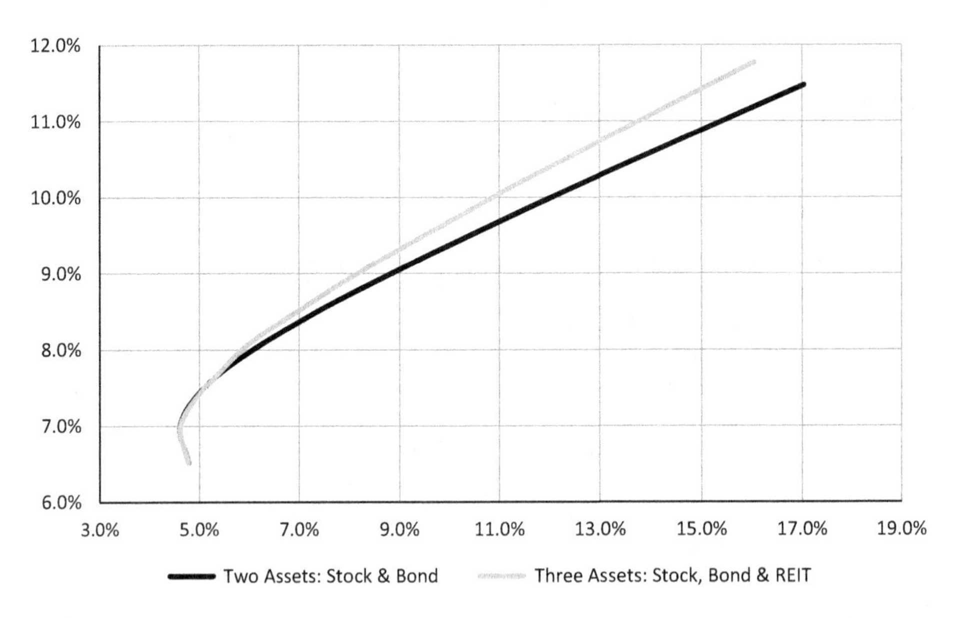

Figure 14.8 A three-asset, stock, bond and real estate investment trust (REIT) efficient frontier

two-asset, stock and bond portfolios presented efficient frontier. Including the Nareit index in a stock and bond portfolio pushes the efficient frontier incrementally out to the northwest of the graph, either reducing risk per unit of return or increasing return per unit of risk.

When the lower correlated NCREIF index is added to the stock, bond and REIT portfolio (Figure 14.9), much greater diversification benefits are revealed as can be seen by the green line on the graph. Including the NCREIF index with the stock, bond, and Nareit portfolios

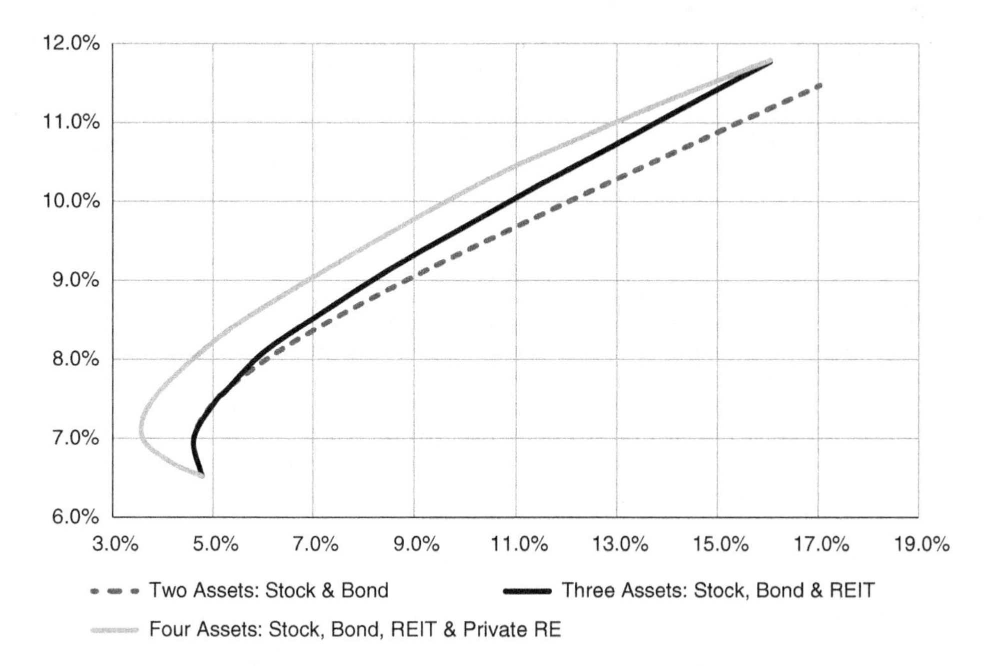

Figure 14.9 A four-asset, stock, bond, real estate investment trust (REIT) and private real estate (RE) efficient frontier

materially expands the feasible set of efficient investment portfolios (that is, those portfolios that have a better risk–return profile than without the NCREIF investment) and pushes the efficient frontier out to the northwest. For example, in Figure 14.9, for a two-asset portfolio (red line) with a standard deviation of 10%, the expected return is approximately 9.25%. However, as is depicted with the green line that include four assets – stocks, bonds, Nareit and NCREIF indices – the new efficient set of investments provides an expected return of 10.10%, at a 10% standard deviation. Alternatively, including the NCREIF index in the three-asset portfolio, investors could achieve a 9% portfolio return with a much lower 7% portfolio standard deviation.

Across a range of portfolios, adding the NCREIF pushes the efficient frontier to the northwest (also known as the trade-off between risk and return) increasing return per unit of risk. Alternatively, if an investment manager is targeting a certain rate of return, as is the case of CalPERS, the same rate of return can be achieved with a lower portfolio risk profile.

Conclusion and summary

The goal of investment managers, whether they are ERISA driven defined benefit plan managers in the United States or other investment managers, is to either increase the level of return per unit of risk or reduce the risk per unit of return, with a particular focus on minimising the possibility of large losses. Adding the Nareit index to a stock and bond portfolio has some diversification benefit, but those benefits are rather muted as REITs are positively correlated with stocks and bonds. However, when the NCREIF index is added to a portfolio stock, bond, and Nareit indices, a significant reduction in risk per unit of return, or alternatively return per unit of risk, is achieved. While the presented analysis was restricted to US data, the results using the United States are similar across other countries' data. Finally, while our analysis uses 'best in class' data, the NCREIF data is appraisal based and subject to potential data smoothing. In closing, adding commercial real estate to a portfolio of stock and bond investments has material positive portfolio diversification benefits.

Notes

1 See https://factfinder.census.gov/faces/tableservices/jsf/pages/productview.xhtml?pid=SGF_SG1500A2_FTP&prodType=document for national and state-by-state lottery statistics.
2 Conlisk (1993) provides a model that reveals risk seeking in small payoff gambles, large-prize lotteries and other patterns of risk seeking in experimental evidence that is puzzling from the viewpoint of standard economic theory.
3 While most bets return a neutral or negative outcome in gambling, through informed and strategic betting, a small handful of gamblers are able to profit from gambling.
4 It should be noted that mortgage lenders require borrowers to purchase homeowners' insurance and many states require drivers to carry automotive insurance.
5 See Section 404(c) of ERISA at: www.legisworks.org/GPO/STATUTE-88-Pg829.pdf.
6 A correlation matrix is provided in Table 14.6 of this paper. For one- and three-year holding periods the correlations are relatively low, however, for seven-year holding periods the Standard & Poor's 500 correlation across a series of bond indices is about 60%, limiting the diversification benefits of holding a portfolio of only stocks and bonds.
7 For detailed plan investment information see Willis Towers Watson, Global Pension Assets Study 2017: www.willistowerswatson.com/en/insights/2017/01/global-pensions-asset-study-2017 (accessed 15 August 2018).
8 For more on the size of the defined contribution investment market see chapter 7 of the Investment Company Institute's (2017) *2017 Investment Company Factbook*: http://www.icifactbook.org/ch7/17_fb_ch7 (accessed 17 August 2018).
9 Information on the number of funds, fund managers and investment asset size can be found at: www.statista.com/statistics/255590/number-of-mutual-fund-companies-in-the-united-states (accessed 17 August 2018) and the *2017 Investment Company Handbook*, published by the Investment Company Institute, 57th edition.
10 Data secured from the World Bank World Federation of Exchanges database, Listed domestic companies, total: https://data.worldbank.org/indicator/CM.MKT.LDOM.NO (accessed 17 August 2018).
11 For a detailed discussion and comparison of pension plan discount rates, see Schilling (2016).
12 CalPERS News, 'CalPERS to lower discount rate to seven percent over the next three years', 21 December 2016; www.calpers.ca.gov/page/newsroom/calpers-news/2016/calpers-lower-discount-rate (accessed 17 August 2018).
13 The NCREIF National Property Index is an appraisal-based index with a sizable literature on the impact of appraisal smoothing of property variance that reveals a lag in property valuations and other possible value distortions. The impact of appraisal-based property values become less meaningful as property holding periods lengthen. For more on this topic, see Edelstein and Quan (2006) and Fisher (2005).
14 There are 102 five-year holding periods – starting with the initial five-year hold from 1987 Q1 to 1991 Q4, then rolling forward for the next 102 quarter from 1987 Q1 to 2017 Q2.
15 See footnote 14.
16 We analysed the portfolio effects for each of the stock, bond, and real estate indices in Table 14.2. As the stock and bond indices are highly correlated with other stock and bond indices, respectively, we do not include them in the mapping of the efficient frontier as they create additional clutter to the example and cloud the discussion.

References

Callan and Associates (2016) Risky business, Callan Institute, San Francisco, CA. www.callan.com/wp-content/uploads/2016/12/Risky-Business.pdf (accessed 17 August 2018).

Conlisk, J. The utility of gambling, *Journal of Risk and Uncertainty*, 6, 255–75.

Edelstein R. H. and Quan, D. C. (2006) How does appraisal smoothing bias real estate returns measurement?, *Journal of Real Estate Finance and Economics*, 32(1), 41–60.

Federal Insurance Office (2013) *Annual report on the insurance industry, Completed pursuant to Title V of the Dodd-Frank Wall Street Reform and Consumer Protection Act*, US Department of the Treasury, Washington, DC.

Fisher, J. D. (2005) US Commercial real estate indices, pp 359–367 in Bank for International Settlements (eds.), *Real estate indicators and financial stability*, volume 21, Bank for International Settlements, Basel, www.bis.org/publ/bppdf/bispap21zc.pdf (accessed 17 August 2018).

Investment Company Institute (2017) *2017 Investment company handbook: a review of trends and activities in the investment company industry*, 57th ed., Investment Company Institute, Washington, DC.

Schilling, L. (2016) *US pension plan discount rate comparison 2009–2014*, Society of Actuaries, Schaumburg, IL.

15 Risk management

Shaun Bond and Simon Stevenson

Introduction

Real estate differs from mainstream capital market assets in a wide variety of aspects. Its nature as a privately traded, illiquid and largely indivisible asset means that it has quite different characteristics than asset classes such as stocks. These features have been extensively considered when examining the investment characteristics of the asset and they have important implications for how a real estate fund manager assesses risk. Risk management techniques in the capital markets primarily focus on market risk using well-established techniques and risk measures such as value at risk (VaR), while the quantitative modelling of volatility and its importance is well established. In addition, there is, in most large and mature capital markets, a wide variety of derivative products and vehicles that aid in the successful implementation of risk management strategies. However, the assessment and management of risk are far more problematic in a real estate context.

There are a number of issues in the application of market risk measures in a real estate context, due to the characteristics of the asset. This is not only directly as a result of the nature of property as an asset class but also because many of the risks that a real estate fund manager faces are not as easily and simply quantifiable. This is seen no more so than with respect to illiquidity. In equities, bonds and other capital market asset classes, information is incorporated into prices, and therefore returns, more efficiently. This means that investors can largely assume that prices capture the vast majority of the risk factors to which those assets are exposed. Risk managers can, therefore, focus their attention on market risk. In contrast, in real estate, we frequently rely on valuation/appraisal-based data. While many of the issues concerned with valuation data, such as smoothing (see Chapter 9), are well established in the real estate literature, the implication is that information is less efficiently processed into prices than in the capital markets. The result is that we are less able to proxy risk by focussing attention on market risk. Rather, real estate investors are required to more explicitly consider the full spectrum of risk factors that can affect the asset as they may not be fully captured by prices and therefore returns. While clearly evident in real estate, these issues are not unique to real estate. Indeed, the problems that conventional risk measures have in capturing non-market risk factors was seen in both the collapse of the Long Term Capital Management hedge fund in 1998 and during the subprime mortgage-backed security crisis in 2007–08.

This chapter initially considers the risk factors that real estate fund managers face, highlighting the limitations that can sometimes arise from relying upon the same frameworks a manager in the capital markets would use. It then considers the challenges faced in using property derivatives for risk management purposes. Not only does real estate have a limited range of derivative products in comparison to other asset classes, but there also are a number of specific issues that make it challenging for them to be effectively used for hedging.

Investment risk

We can subdivide risk factors into three key areas which we refer to as market, asset and operational, and governance.

Market risk

Market risk is the form of risk that has the most similarities with those concentrated on in mainstream asset classes. It is concerned with more easily identifiable and quantifiable investment risk factors and, therefore, also has the most commonalities in terms of the methods used. Thus, risk-adjusted performance, volatility and downside exposure can all be examined, at least in part, using conventional approaches. However, even in this case, it is necessary for investors to be fully aware of the impact the characteristics of real estate as an asset class have on the application of such measures. The most well-known issue in this context is that of smoothing in appraisal-based data.

The implications of smoothed appraisal data are well established in the literature (see, for example, Geltner, 1989, 1991, 1993a, 1993b; Fisher *et al.*, 1994; Barkham and Geltner, 1995; Cho *et al.*, 2003; Geltner *et al.*, 2003; Bond and Hwang, 2007; Bond *et al.*, 2012; Cho *et al.*, 2014), and especially that appraisal data can lead to an underrepresentation of the actual risk of the asset. Much of the academic literature has focussed on the issues raised in the context of asset allocation and real estate's role in a mixed-asset portfolio (such as Bond *et al*, 2007; Rehring, 2012). However, even from the more isolated perspective of a real estate portfolio there are issues.

First, as mentioned above, the assessed volatility of the asset can be underestimated. This is especially so at a fund or portfolio level. It is important to recognise that not only do index providers, such as the National Council of Real Estate Investment Fiduciaries (NCREIF) and MSCI/Investment Property Databank (IPD), rely on valuation data but so do fund managers. Owing to the lack of transactions, the investment performance of private real estate funds relies primarily on valuations. Therefore, many of the issues that have been extensively documented with respect to indices are also relevant from a portfolio perspective. Furthermore, given that valuation methods vary across countries, there are complications in directly comparing performance and risk at a global level. Authors such as Lai and Wang (1998) have illustrated that individual valuations are not themselves susceptible to smoothing but that fund level data displays heightened levels of smoothing. This is due to factors such as index aggregation and also, more generally, the heterogeneity observed in real estate. There are a number of implications from this disparity between asset and portfolio level measures of risk. One is a positive note as it illustrates that real estate fund managers can benefit from enhanced diversification benefits due to the heterogeneity of the asset. This is consistent with Brown's (1997) early work on risk reduction, which showed that, when considering real estate, risk falls further than in comparison with stock portfolios. However, it can also mean that at a portfolio level the fund manager is obtaining an undue positive impression of the risk inherent in their portfolio.

The underestimation of risk from a quantitative perspective also has practical implications with respect to the risk measures commonly used, even down to the traditional use of standard deviation/variance as the measure of risk. The impact of smoothing on the estimation of variance is well researched ground in both the academic and industry literature. However, it has broader connotations. Risk measures, such as VaR, are commonly used in capital market assets. VaR provides a monetary value of the potential exposure to downside movements in asset value. It can be defined as the loss level which the investor is x% confident will not be exceeded over a set horizon. For example, based upon a portfolio value of US$750 million, a confidence level of 90% and a horizon of three months, a VaR of US$50 million would indicate that you could be 90% confident that you would not lose more than US$50 million over the next quarter. A VaR estimate can be calculated as

$$VaR = \sigma N^{-1}(X) \tag{15.1}$$

Where σ is the standard deviation, N^{-1} is inverse cumulative normal distribution and X is the confidence level. While there are several variations of this approach, in its simplest form the volatility figure is monetarised based upon the value of the portfolio, merely multiplying the standard deviation by the value of the portfolio. There are a number of issues with VaR generally. For example, basic versions assume that asset returns conform with the assumptions of a normal distribution. This is of particular interest in the context of property due to the empirical evidence that asset returns are often not normal (Bond and Patel, 2003). However, there are issues with the assumption of normality even in the case of assets such as stocks due to the presence of leptokurtosis, or fat tails. Basing the measure simply on a normal distribution will underestimate the likelihood of losses in excess of the VaR estimate.

There are also concerns over how investors interpret a VaR and specifically that they may misinterpret what it actually means. First, our estimate of US$50 million means that we would anticipate not losing more than US$50 million based on a 90% probability. If however, that 10% chance was realised the VaR estimate does not inform us of the likely actual loss. It is merely saying there is a 90% probability we would not lose more than US$50 million. Similarly, there is also the risk that investors will underestimate the frequency of extreme events. This perhaps can be illustrated better using a daily example from the capital markets. Let us assume an active fund manager with a portfolio currently valued at US$200 million with a daily VaR of US$15 million based upon a 99% probability. Even with this high level of probability, it means that it is likely that losses in excess of US$15 million will be observed once every 100 trading days, or 2.5 times a year. VaR does not actually measure the risk of losses from extreme events, rather fairly regular bad trading days. In addition to these general issues with VaR, there are other issues that have specific relevance for real estate, not least that, once the desired level of confidence is decided, the estimate is entirely dependent on the measure of volatility input. This raises additional concerns over the measurement of volatility.

The problems which arise with real estate data are a major constraint for a fund manager being able to simply apply techniques such as VaR in the accurate assessment of investment risk. This also applies more generally in the quantitative modelling and use of volatility in a risk context. Quantitative techniques such as generalised autoregressive conditional heteroskedasticity or GARCH and exponential moving averages are commonly used in the capital markets to model volatility. However, the frequency of the data available and the smoothed nature of appraisal data raise concerns over their use in a property context.

There are further issues. For example, the difference in holding period also raises important issues over how investors can interpret risk measures such as standard deviation. There is an implicit assumption in finance that the data frequency is also the assumed holding period. However, in real estate we will inevitably have a mismatch here, owing to the illiquidity present in the asset and the resulting long holding periods. The long holding periods also raise additional risk factors discussed in the following section with respect to leverage and refinancing risk.

The stability of income flows from real estate is one of the primary advantages of the asset because of the structure of leases. However, this stability does have some consequences. First, it can lead to potential complacency if investors focus too much upon it. Figure 15.1 displays the monthly returns of the MSCI-IPD Index for UK Real Estate from 1986 to 2015. It can be seen that, even at a relatively high monthly frequency, there are very few negative observations, certainly in comparison with what would be observed in the equity and fixed income sectors. This effect is enhanced with respect to the total return, when the income return is added. Of 346 observations, there are only 44 months, over a nearly 30-year period, which see a negative total return. These observations also tend to be clustered in the crash of the early nineties and the financial crisis of 2007–09. Indeed, every single one of the negative observations is within these two periods (February 1990 to December 1992 and August 2007 to June 2009). This observation has a number of implications. First, it highlights the smoothed nature of the assets returns. Second, it highlights that real estate as a real asset has in many respects more similarities with macro-economic indicators than the return performance of capital market assets. Third, the smoothing of valuations has implications for the accurate assessment of risk on a time-varying basis. This is in part due to the clustering of negative events.

Figure 15.2 reports the time-varying standard deviation and skewness of the total return series based on five-year (60-month) rolling windows. This simple analysis highlights several issues. First, due to the relative stability of real estate returns, the volatility of the asset is not only relatively low but also consistent. However, this means that, with respect to the

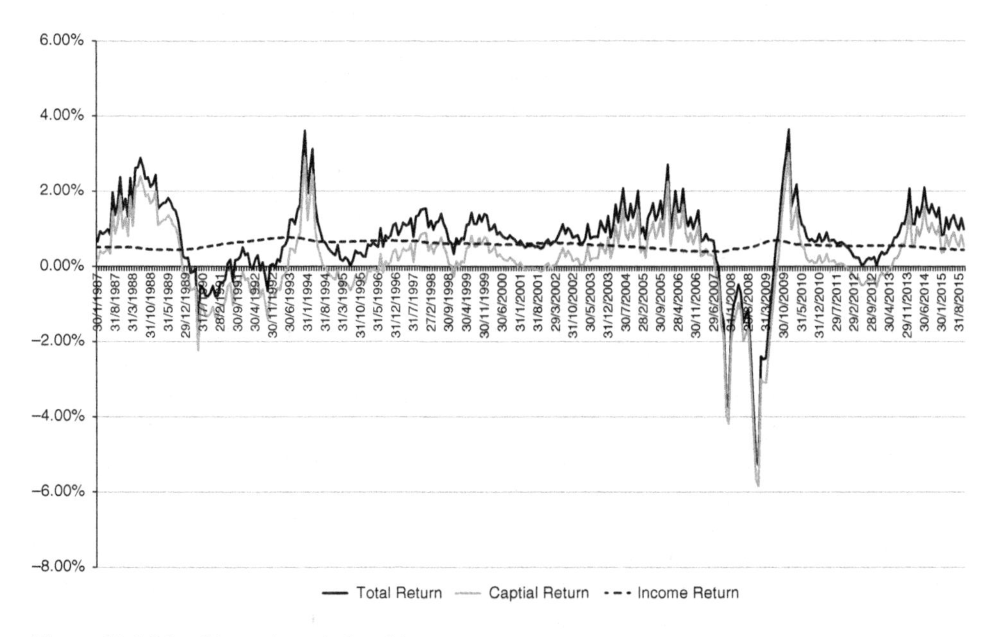

Figure 15.1 Monthly total, capital and income returns
Source: MSCI-IPD.

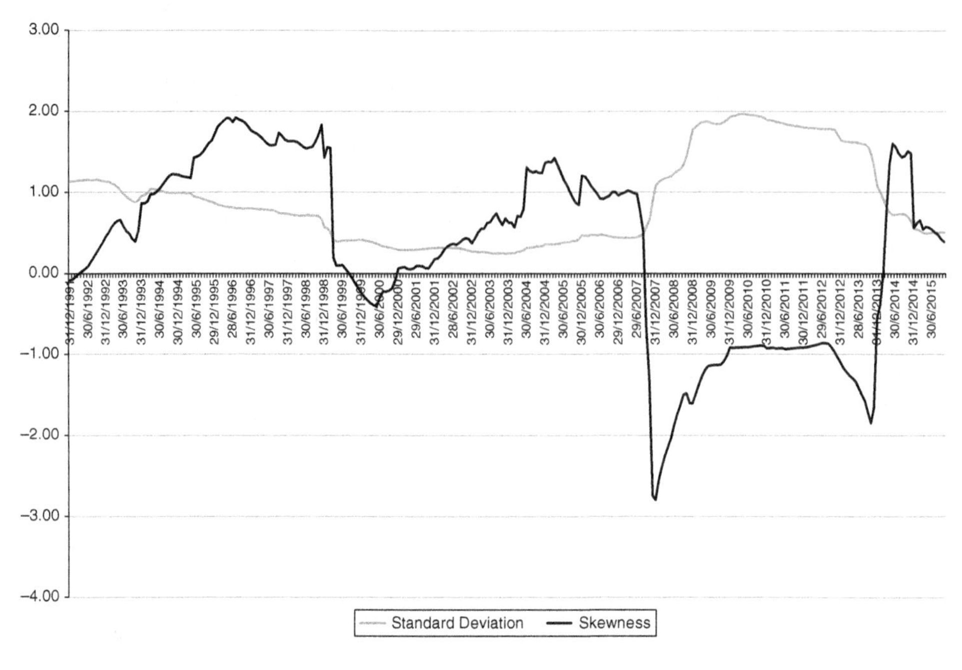

Figure 15.2 Volatility and skewness of monthly total returns
Source: MSCI-IPD.

2007 crisis, the prior estimates of standard deviation, and hence conventional measures of volatility, significantly underestimated the risks present in the asset. As can be seen, the five-year rolling standard deviation rises substantially during the second half of 2007, only falling back in 2013 once 2007 and 2008 have fallen out of the data. A similar effect can be observed with regard to skewness with a substantial divergence observed around the financial crisis. There is a large literature that has highlighted that real estate returns can often be non-normally distributed (such as Bond and Patel, 2003). However, there is a far smaller literature on the time-varying nature of that non-normality. Again based upon very simple five-year rolling estimates of the third moment, it can be seen that during strong market conditions real estate tends to display positive skewness. This is in part due to protection that the income component provides, as previously noted. The large swing to negative skewness in 2007–09 highlights that this effectively underestimates the risk of negative events.

For a long time it was considered that, because of the heterogeneity of real estate, there was reduced portfolio risk. Research (such as Brown and Matysiak, 2000) has highlighted that the average correlation between individual property assets is very low in comparison with equities. However, this research has not really considered how stable this heterogeneity is. The financial crisis, and the resulting collapse in property values in many markets, highlighted that real estate can be as vulnerable to aggregated portfolio level crashes as any asset. The old adage that correlations veer towards one as values fall was clearly seen during the 2007–2009 period. Figure 15.3 illustrates this using residential real estate data for the United States. This is of particular interest as the assumption that correlations would not increase, and that all markets could not decline at the same time, was one of the key errors of Wall Street with respect to the subprime mortgage-backed securities market.

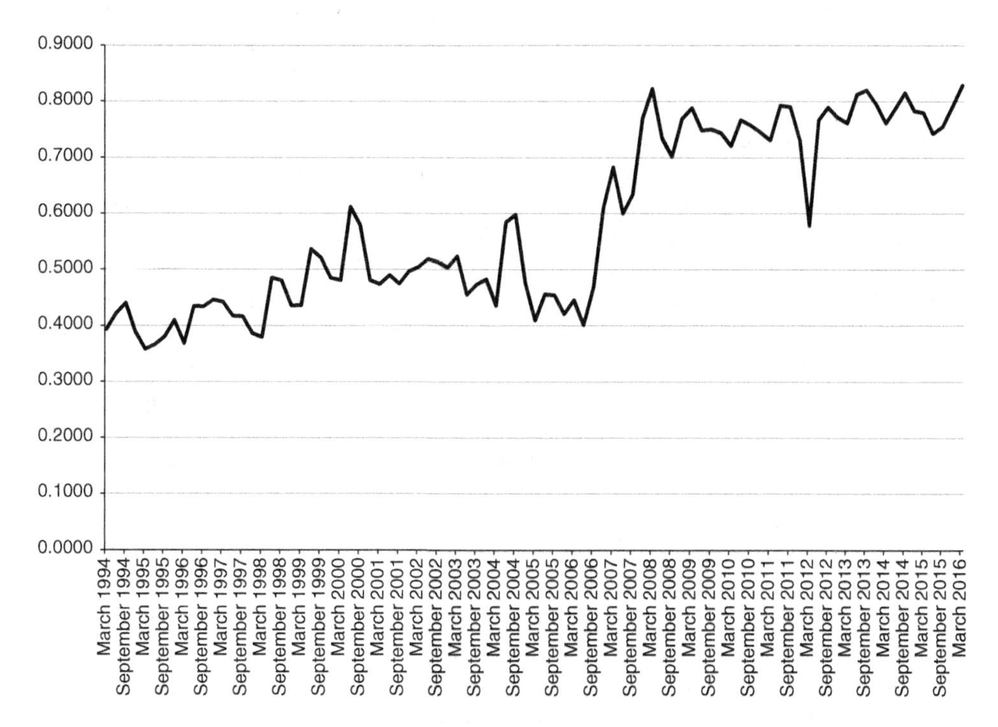

Figure 15.3 Average correlation across US metropolitan housing markets
Source: S&P Case-Shiller.

The analysis is based on the S&P CoreLogic Case-Shiller Home Price index data for a total of 19 cities. The correlations are estimated for each pairing over, in this case, a three-year horizon. Although the S&P Case-Shiller Indices are released monthly, they are estimated on a rolling quarterly basis. Quarterly data are therefore used. The simple average of all the bilateral correlations is then estimated and then displayed in Figure 15.3. It can be clearly seen that the correlations rose in 2006 and 2007 as the crisis in the US housing market gathered pace. The average correlation increased from 0.40 in June 2006 to 0.82 in March 2008, highlighting that, despite the fact that real estate is more heterogeneous than capital market assets, this characteristic is far less evident in periods of crisis. In a commercial real estate setting the same issues are present.

Asset risk

The problems inherent in simply using market risk are far more apparent in a real estate context. This means that real estate portfolio and fund managers need to consider explicitly the full range of factors that contribute to investment and portfolio risk, rather than rely on market risk measures as proxies. Specific risk factors obviously also play a role in other asset classes. However, there is a greater ability to capture and proxy them through broadly based market risk measures.

In addition to data driven issues, some of the heightened importance of the underlying risk factors in a real estate context arises from the heterogeneity present in the asset. If one were to base the analysis on the conventional separation of risk into systematic and unsystematic factors in comparison with assets such as stocks, unsystematic factors take on greater importance when considering property. Callender *et al.* (2007) highlight this heterogeneity through an examination of the City of London office market. As the financial district of London, the City market is not only economically focussed around financial services, but it is very small, only one square mile in size. Callender *et al.* (2007) reported that, over a ten-year period, the average annual return for office properties was 5%. However, one-third of the properties reported average annual returns of either below minus 5% per annum or in excess of plus 10% per annum.

Many of the issues that come into play with respect to risk, and also drive returns, are not market wide, but are rather in some way spatial in nature. However, they vary in scale from broader sector base issues to extremely specific property level factors. At a broader level, the importance of factors such as broad regional location and the property type play a key role. In turn, factors influencing properties at that level also come into the equation, such as the underlying economic base, regional economic performance and demographic factors. However, at a national level these are not systematic factors, especially when one is considering large markets such as the United States, where significant variations may be observed in regional economic performance. From this level, all of the way down to property level, factors such as the specific location, design and functional condition, tenants, depreciation, vacancy rates, lease structure and resulting income flows, mean that real estate is much more exposed to unsystematic risk than are other assets. Systematic, or non-spatial, risk factors are in contrast relatively few in number, limited to factors such as interest rates and government policy at a national level (such as on tax). Even in the case of economic performance, the degree to which it impacts nationally is dependent on their being limited regional variation in underlying economic conditions.

Thus, real estate investors need to be acutely aware of the characteristics of their portfolio. This includes issues such as the broad focus or diversification of the portfolio. An important element here is the economic focus and the possibility that tenants are concentrated in certain industries. For example, an investor with a large office portfolio in the City of London is not only focussed by property type and geography but will also, in all likelihood, have an overconcentration of firms focussed on financial services.

Further, while unsystematic factors will not impact every property identically, there may be common factors that affect a disproportionate number of assets in the portfolio. For example, an ageing portfolio may see similar impacts in terms of depreciation and obsolescence, and a large number of leases expire at the same time. It is, therefore, important to identify those risks which, while unsystematic, are correlated across the portfolio. Thus, at a portfolio level, investors need to be aware of how risk factors at an individual asset level may be correlated, and especially the risk that the correlation may increase during market and economic downturns.

The nature of real estate as a real asset means that the core property management issues need to be considered at a portfolio as well as at an asset level. It is, therefore, important that, at a portfolio level, allocation decisions are closely examined to assess how they will affect the overall risk that a real estate fund manager faces. This includes both sector and geographical asset allocation decisions. Investors need to be aware how local level drivers and market risk factors, such as economic growth, supply and vacancy rates, demographics and rental trends, are similar across the markets to which the portfolio is exposed. Even in this case, however, there are important areas of divergence between property and assets such as stocks. Owing to the illiquidity present in real estate, it is extremely difficult for a fund manager to make meaningful allocation changes with any speed. This, therefore, means that an investor in real estate must be aware of potential risk factors knowing that they will be only able to reduce their exposure at the margins. Thus, the accurate forecasting of medium to long-term performance trends is extremely important. Effectively, real estate is a medium- to long-term play with extremely limited ability to participate in short-term tactical asset allocation.

Governance and operational risk

The effective management of operational factors is essential for all investors; it is not a unique issue for the real estate sector. Therefore, in common with all investors, it is imperative that real estate investors have strong and effective corporate governance procedures and have effective mechanisms for the reporting of financial data. However, the nature of the asset can again mean that some of these issues take on heightened importance, often due to the twin elements of indivisibility and illiquidity.

In most markets, real estate assets are indivisible. One of the implications of this is that the size of the investment in real estate is far greater than in asset classes such as equities or fixed income. Purely due to the resulting size of real estate investments, this in itself contributes to the illiquidity present in the sector. Whichever side of a trade an investor is involved with, the scale of property investments can encourage a heightened level of caution. This is especially so when an investor is disposing of an asset. Because of the indivisibility of real estate, an investor effectively has to view a sale of any property as a permanent transaction – they cannot guarantee being able to buy it back again in the future. The contrast with assets like stocks is noticeable. In the case of equities, an investor is dealing with millions of identical assets. If they sell shares in a firm they can reverse that trade immediately by purchasing different yet identical shares in the same firm. The nature of real estate makes investors potentially more conservative and also means that the importance of medium- to long-term views and strategic asset allocation decisions is heightened.

These elements mean that the general concerns over operational efficiency are amplified in a property context. In many respects, investment in real estate has more in parallel with the investment decision making and risk factors that corporations face rather than with fund managers in the capital markets. It is, therefore, imperative that investors have effective procedures in place with respect to due diligence and, especially with respect to development, cost control. As a real asset, property can also be exposed to political risk in a very direct manner. Investors, therefore, need to have sufficient safeguards in place that can adapt to and respond to changes in legislation and regulation in areas such as planning, building regulations and environmental issues.

Issues surrounding financial structure are key operational risk factors with real estate. In part due to the indivisibility of the asset, and the resulting high unit cost, debt is extensively used in the asset. Leverage and the use of debt financing is, therefore, a key risk factor at a portfolio level. Fund managers must be aware of the risk factors associated with the debt they have used, including the structure of the debt, any hedging instruments put into place and the maturity profile.

In addition to the above, the use of leverage will, by itself, increase the volatility in the performance of the fund. The sensitivity and potential exposure due to different market conditions are important considerations. This is not isolated to the credit market and changes in underlying interest rates and the availability of credit. It is also associated with the underlying real estate. For example, in early 2009, a number of UK REITs had problems with minimum debt-to-asset ratios at a corporate level and then current property values. A fall in property values and the adoption by UK REITs of a fair-value accounting system meant that a number of firms were in danger of breeching their debt covenants. This meant that, in extremely unfavourable market conditions in the spring of 2009, firms were forced into raising equity capital from the market to shore up their balance sheets. Conversely, simple analysis of loan-to-value ratios can provide unduly optimistic impressions at the top of a cycle when risk may be likely to increase.

A further issue is the risk involved in loan refinancing. The combination of the size of loans, and the fact that few commercial real estate loans extend beyond ten years, means that it is relatively rare for commercial real estate loans to be fully amortising. This results in considerable risk factors with respect to balloon payments, which, is turn, means that the ability to refinance and the state of the real estate and credit markets at the time when loans mature is of extreme importance. It is for this reason that the maturity structure of debt and its effective management are so important.

It is, however, not just debt financing that can be affected by market conditions. Open-ended real estate funds have considerable risk factors relating to redemption. The holding of an illiquid underlying asset can limit the ability to source funds quickly to fulfil large-scale redemption requests. This was seen in the UK both in 2007 and in 2016, following the Brexit referendum, when an increase in redemption requests meant that a number of funds imposed restrictions on investors' ability to redeem. In general, it is likely that redemption requests will increase during market downturns or heightened uncertainty, as shown following the 2016 UK referendum. Therefore, market risk and redemption requests may be highly correlated.

For closed-end funds, timing issues are also of importance, but from a slightly different perspective. In this case, it is concerned with the vintage of the fund. With the majority of modern-day closed-end funds adopting a fixed maturity structure, the performance of the fund and therefore also the risk factors, is highly related to the vintage/launch of the fund and its maturity, owing to the cyclical nature of real estate. These factors not only need to be considered by the individual fund but also by 'fund of funds' managers, who need to be aware of and mitigate against any systematic exposure they may have to specific vintages.

Property derivatives and risk management

There are a number of issues surrounding the use of derivatives in a risk management context. As noted in the introduction to the chapter, of immediate concern is that there are a limited number of potential options in comparison with the choice of hedging instruments available for capital market assets. However, there are additional concerns, specifically the ability of property derivatives to act as effective hedging instruments. This section initially details the primary derivatives currently available and then discusses the detailed issues surrounding their use in a risk management context.

Property derivative contracts

At present, there are two primary forms of property derivatives available in the market place, namely futures contracts and total return swaps. Futures contracts are currently available in the United States with respect to housing. The contracts were launched in 2006 and are traded on the Chicago Mercantile Exchange (CME). In the UK, commercial real estate futures were launched by the EUREX Exchange in 2009. There is also the total return swap market. This over-the-counter (OTC) market was launched in the UK in 2004 and deals have been subsequently been undertaken in a wide variety of markets.

The housing futures traded on the CME use the S&P Case-Shiller House Price Indices for both a composite national index and ten specific cities, namely Boston, Chicago, Denver, Las Vegas, Los Angeles, Miami, New York, San Diego, San Francisco and Washington DC. The contracts are priced such that each index point is monetarised at US$250. For the national composite and each of the ten cities there are four contract dates each year, in February, May, August and November. However, as the indices have a delay in their release, these actually relate to the December, March, June and September indices. The indices are released and the contracts mature on the last Tuesday of the respective contract month. The contracts operate just as normal index futures in that they are not only standardised with respect to value and maturity but are also cash settled. As with all other futures contracts, the futures price and the spot price, in this case the actual released index value, have to converge by maturity. The EUREX contracts in the UK are similar cash settled futures. The underlying asset is the MSCI/IPD Annual Index.

The swaps are structured differently due to their OTC nature. This does make them more flexible as they are bespoke to the parties concerned. However, in practice, they have in the majority of cases been LIBOR-All Property Swaps. That is, the two assets in the trade are the LIBOR rate and the MSCI/IPD All Property Total Return Index for the UK. While they have the broad structure of a swap there are subtle differences. The two counterparties take a long position in the respective asset. For example, fund A takes a long position in real estate and fund B a long position in LIBOR. Each party, therefore, by definition, has a corresponding short position in the other asset. A notional principal is agreed between the two parties. This notional acts as the basis on which the actual payments are based. It is, however, in this area where property swaps differ from, for example, interest rate swaps. The payments are not just based on the performance/rate of return of the two assets. For example, if LIBOR was 2% and real estate delivered 12%, based upon an agreed notional amount of £10 million the party that was long on real estate would receive a net payment of £1 million (12% of £10m – £2% of 10m).

The problem is that, if such a structure were adopted, it would be extremely hard to find counterparties. As discussed earlier in the chapter, real estate displays high levels of auto-correlation. It would, therefore, be relatively easy to forecast whether real estate would out-perform or underperform LIBOR on an annual basis. And it would be very hard to find counterparties who would take the opposing view and thus maintain an active market across all points in a cycle. There would be significant amounts of time where there would be an overwhelming demand for long real estate positions, and also periods where the vast majority of investors would wish to take a short potion. The swap contracts are, therefore, priced relative to LIBOR.

In practice, this means that the quote observed by the market is effectively an expectation regarding the relative performance of real estate relative to LIBOR. If, for example, an investor observed a quote of LIBOR plus 5%, it can be interpreted that the market is already pricing into the quote an outperformance of 5% over and above the LIBOR rate. The decision of whether to go long or short is now based on whether an investor believes that real estate will do better or worse than that specific quote. If at maturity the contract expires at LIBOR plus 7.5% then the party that is long real estate receives a cash flow equal the outperformance, in this case 2.5% multiplied by the notional principal. If real estate still outperformed LIBOR but did not achieve the 5% priced in, say it matured at LIBOR plus 4%, the party with the short position would receive a cash flow of 1% of the notional. The decision is now based on the performance of the two assets relative to the quote observed, rather than the absolute performance of real estate and LIBOR. This means that there will be far higher degrees of disagreement across investors, something that is necessary for there to be sufficient traders willing to go both long and short and thus create the market.

This form of quoting does have complications and investors need to be very clear as to what the quotes mean. This can be seen especially in down markets, and was seen in practice in 2008 and 2009. Figure 15.4 displays quotes for the one-year total return contracts in the UK over the period June 2007 to December 2009. At the turn of 2007, the December 2008 contract was trading at LIBOR minus 7.65%. This meant that an under performance of the MSCI/IPD index of 7.65 relative to LIBOR was already priced in. Therefore, even if an investor were to take a pessimistic view of real estate in 2008, that degree of under-performance was already priced in. Therefore, the party with the short position would only benefit by the extent to which real estate did even worse than 7.65%. A year later, even more extreme market conditions were observed. As of the end of 2008 the December 2009, contract was quoting minus 19.50%. It matured at LIBOR plus 3.50%. In this case, the party that went long profited. Investors cannot simply base their trading decision on the direction they feel the underlying asset will go; that is, to hedge against a fall in the underlying asset or go short. Rather, the trading decision has to be based on the quote observed and whether the trader feels that the underlying asset, that is, real estate, will do better or worse against LIBOR than that quote.

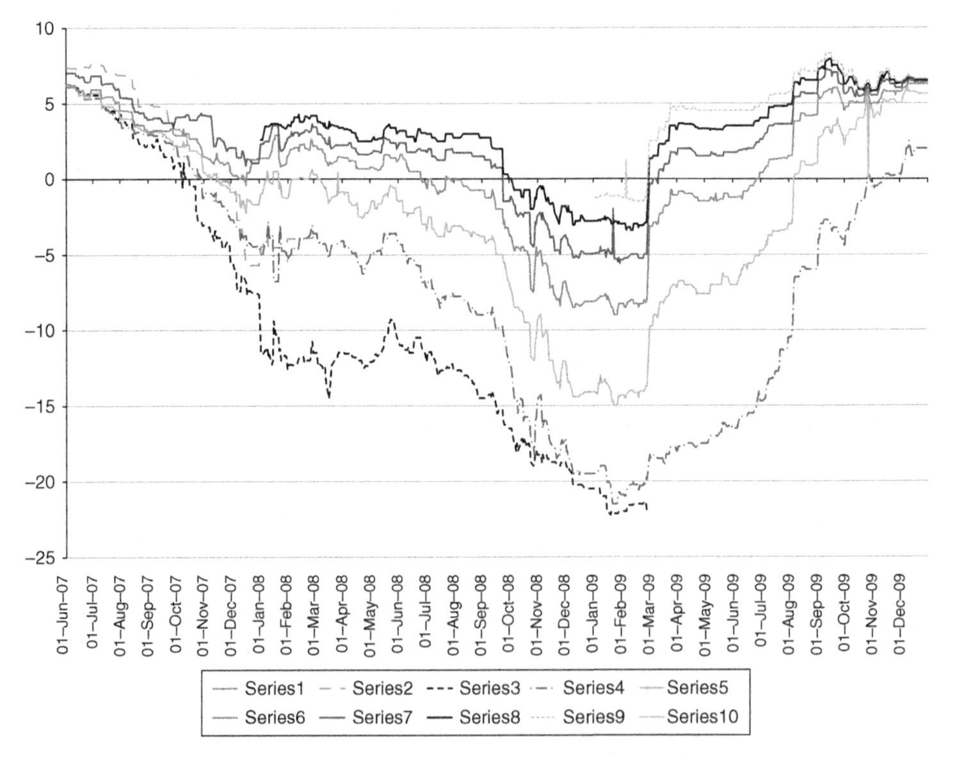

Figure 15.4 One-year total return swap quotes
Source: CBRE/GFI.

Property derivative pricing and hedging

The primary issues with property derivatives, both futures and swaps, centre on the pricing and, specifically, that the arbitrage relationship that underpins equilibrium prices does not hold in a real estate context. This is easy to show in non-dividend paying forwards where the equilibrium price is:

$$F_0 = S_0 e^{(r)(T)} \tag{15.2}$$

Where F is the forward price, S the spot, e the exponential, r is the risk-free rate and T the maturity. If this did not hold, an investor could partake in risk-free arbitrage. If the price was substantially above this value then an investor could borrow funds to buy the asset and could then enter into a forward to sell the asset at maturity. If the forward was significantly less than the equilibrium, arbitrage profits would be available by shorting the asset, investing the proceeds and then using the forward to buy back the asset by maturity to satisfy the short. Similar arbitrage arguments apply in all derivatives whether they be OTC forwards, traded futures, option contracts or swaps. The key issue here is that it is extremely problematic for those arbitrage opportunities to be exploitable in a real estate context. This is because you cannot short real estate and, in addition to the underlying assets being indices of real estate markets, it is extremely hard effectively to 'buy the index'. Not only is an investor dealing with an indivisible asset but factors, such as transaction costs and the heterogeneity present, mean that it is extremely hard to buy the asset and for it to behave like the index. This means, as papers such as Lizeiri *et al.* (2012) note large potential deviations from the equilibrium. This is in contrast with equivalent contracts in the equity market. Because the arbitrage conditions hold a lot more effectively it means that the spreads observed in equity–LIBOR swaps are extremely small, certainly in comparison with those observed with respect to real estate swaps.

Indeed, those deviations are to such an extent that effectively the prices become expectations from the derivative market as to where the contract will mature. For example, Figure 15.4, shows that substantial discounts were observed in the quotes from late 2007 to late 2009. Indeed, not only are they driven by expectations but Bond and Mitchell (2011) show that forecasts derived from the swap market are more accurate than consensus forecasts of published actual forecasts. However, the fact that the quotes, in both the swap and futures markets, are largely expectations concerning the price at which the contract will mature, does severely hamper their ability to act as effective hedging tools. A simple example from the swap market can illustrate this.

Say an investor feels that real estate will underperform LIBOR by 10% and they wish to hedge against this potential downturn. However, if the quote is already standing at LIBOR minus 10% that underperformance is already priced into the derivative market. Even if the investor is proved correct they will be unable to hedge against any fall in the value of their property portfolio through the derivative market. If the quote is currently LIBOR minus 15% then first the investor needs to make the correct call and go long in the derivative as they have the view that real estate will perform better than expected by the market. However, even if they make the correct call with respect to the trade, they will have only hedged half of their exposure and received 5% from the derivative market. Therefore, at best, property derivatives can only be viewed as a partial hedge, and their ability effectively to be used in a risk management and hedging context is highly dependent on the current quote in the market.

Conclusion

This chapter has reviewed the key components of risk management for real estate assets. A number of challenges were presented related to the underlying data on real estate returns that make applying widely used market risk models, based on publicly traded securities, difficult to apply to real estate. Where investors have focussed on risk management, this is often more heavily concentrated on aspects of operational risk. Finally, the chapter concluded with a discussion on real estate derivatives. The topic of risk management remains a relatively under researched area within the real estate field. However, as databases improve and a growing body of research helps shed light on the nature of individual asset risk, it is expected that analytical approaches to risk management in real estate will grow in importance.

References

Barkham, R. and Geltner, D. (1995) Price discovery in American and British property markets, *Real Estate Economics*, 23(1), 21–44.

Bond, S. A. and Hwang, S. (2007) Smoothing, nonsynchronous appraisal and cross-sectional aggregation in real estate price indices, *Real Estate Economics*, 35(3), 349–82.

Bond, S. A., Hwang, S. and Marcato, G. (2012) Commercial real estate returns: an anatomy of smoothing in asset and index returns, *Real Estate Economics*, 40(4), 637–61.

Bond, S. A., Hwang, S., Mitchell, P. and Satchell, S. E. (2007) Will private equity and hedge funds replace real estate in mixed-asset portfolios?, *Journal of Portfolio Management*, 33(5), 74–84.

Bond, S. A. and Mitchel, P. (2011) The information content of real estate derivatives, *Journal of Portfolio Management*, 35(5), 170–81.

Bond, S. A. and Patel, K. (2003) The conditional distribution of real estate returns: are higher moments time varying?, *Journal of Real Estate Finance and Economics*, 26(2), 319–39.

Brown, G. R. (1997) Reducing the dispersion of returns in U.K. real estate portfolios, *Journal of Real Estate Portfolio Management*, 3(2), 129–40.

Brown, G. R. and Matysiak, G. A. (2000) Sticky valuations, aggregation effects, and property indices, *Journal of Real Estate Finance and Economics*, 20(1), 49–66.

Callender, M., Devaney, S., Sheahan, A. and Key T. (2007) Risk reduction and diversification in UK commercial property portfolios, *Journal of Property Research*, 24(4), 355–75.

Cho, Y., Hwang, S. and Lee, Y-K (2014) The dynamics of appraisal smoothing, *Real Estate Economics*, 42(2), 497–529.

Cho, H., Kawaguchi, Y., and Shilling, J. D. (2003) Unsmoothing commercial property returns: a revision to Fisher-Geltner-Webb's unsmoothing methodology, *Journal of Real Estate Finance and Economics*, 27(3), 393–405.

Fisher, J. D., Geltner, D. M., and Webb, R. B (1994) Value indices of commercial real estate: a comparison of index construction methods, *Journal of Real Estate Finance and Economics*, 9(2), 137–64.

Geltner, D. (1989) Bias in appraisal-based returns, *Journal of the American Real Estate and Urban Economics Association*, 17(3), 338–52.

Geltner, D. (1991) Smoothing in appraisal-based returns, *Journal of Real Estate Finance and Economics*, 4(3), 327–45.

Geltner, D. (1993a) Temporal aggregation in real estate return indices, *Journal of the American Real Estate and Urban Economics Association*, 21(2), 141–66.

Geltner, D. (1993b) Estimating market values from appraised values without assuming an efficient market, *Journal of Real Estate Research*, 8(3), 325–45.

Geltner, D., MacGregor B. D. and Schwann, G. M. (2003) Appraisal smoothing and price discovery in real estate markets, *Urban Studies*, 40(5–6), 1047–64.

Lai, T-Y. and Wang, K. (1998) Appraisal smoothing: the other side of the story, *Real Estate Economics*, 26(3), 511–35.

Lizieri, C., Marcato, G., Ogden, P. and Baum, A. (2012) Pricing inefficiencies in private real estate markets using total return swaps, *Journal of Real Estate Finance and Economics*, 45(3), 774–803.

Rehring, C. (2012) Real estate in a mixed-asset portfolio: the role of investment horizon, *Real Estate Economics*, 40(1), 65–95.

16 Evaluation of fund manager performance

Rainer Schulz, Yuan Zhao and Si Zhou

Introduction

Investors, such as private households, trustees and financial institutions, often delegate the management of their wealth to fund managers. Delegation can take place in different ways. Investors could buy units of existing investment products offered by fund managers. Such collective investment schemes pool monies of many investors and the manager will be in the position to hold a well-diversified portfolio. The manager will also be able to trade under wholesale conditions and use cost-effective record keeping. It will be possible to invest in assets with high unit values, such as commercial buildings. Most individual investors do not have enough wealth to be able to exploit such economies of scope and scale efficiently. Even if financial institutions, such as pension funds and insurance companies, could exploit such economies, it might still be better to rely on the expertise of an external manager. However, investors with sufficient capital are not constrained to invest in products that are already on offer. They could also instruct managers to provide tailored investment products that suit their specific needs and objectives. It is also possible that a manager would invite a selected group of such investors as limited partners into a newly created closed-ended investment scheme.

Before investing with a particular manager, investors want to know how well the manager has performed in the past. While good past performance on its own does not guarantee that the manager will also perform well in the future, it is a starting point for manager evaluation. If an investor ponders about investing in an existing established investment product, then a sufficiently long history of the product's monthly return rates will allow performance assessment over different market cycles. If an investor plans to instruct a manager for a tailored product, such as a portfolio of commercial buildings, direct evidence on past performance will – by definition – not be available. However, relevant information on the manager's skills could be produced by calculating the composite performance of all assets under the manager's management that fall into the same investment category. For example, assume a manager is responsible for two discretionary accounts of different sizes, both invested exclusively in commercial real estate, but with slightly different country composition. The value-weighted composite return rates of both accounts would indicate to the client how well the manager's real estate investments have performed in the past.

Once investors have placed their monies with a manager, they continue to be interested in receiving information on the performance of the investment product. This information should allow investors to assess whether fund managers continue to do what they have promised. Such information includes the performance of the assets under the manager's control and the fees the manager charges. For instance, it is common for private equity and hedge funds that managers receive a flat fee on assets under management (AUM). Such managers can also claim a performance-related fee and assure the investors that this additional fee is paid only when justified. Investors are interested that the manager sticks to the advertised or agreed investment strategy, which makes detailed information on the composition of the managed portfolios important. Obviously, investors are not only interested in the performance of a fund, but also in the people who are behind this performance. For instance, assume that a fund management firm has a very knowledgeable and successful direct real estate fund management team. However, members of the team decide to leave the firm. If the fund management firm is unable to find suitable replacements for those leaving, investors in the firm's real estate offerings might decide to disinvest.

Information on past performance is the essential input for any assessment of the likely *future* performance of individual fund managers. As even an unskilled manager might be able to produce good returns in a bullish market, the challenge for such assessment is to disentangle skill from luck. This requires sufficient data, risk-adjusted comparable return rates and a statistical framework.

In this chapter, we provide an introduction into the evaluation of fund managers. We consider not only how performance can be measured and assessed after it has been realised (*ex post*), but also provide an account of statistical methods that should allow us to spot managers (*ex ante*) who might be better skilled than their peers. The rest of the chapter is organised as follows. In the next section, we give an overview of the fund management industry, followed by a discussion of the computation of *total return rates*, the crucial data input for performance measurement. While the computation for total return rates is straightforward for portfolios that consist only of highly liquid assets, such as blue chip stocks and government bonds, the computation becomes more intricate for assets with low liquidity and trading in private markets. Direct real estate is a prime example of such a type of asset. The following sections present different performance measures and motivate their economic background. We discuss statistical methods that should help to distinguish fund managers that are really skilled from those that are just lucky. We close the chapter with a short discussion of potential data issues.

Fund management industry

The fund management industry has been growing at a high rate since the 1980s. For instance, AUM in regulated funds in the United States have increased from US$134.76 billion in 1980 to US$16.34 trillion in 2016 (Investment Company Institute, 2017). The number and types of collective investment schemes offered by the fund management industry have also increased substantially over this period. The same trend can be observed for other regions. At the end of 2016, schemes had US$14.12 trillion AUM in Europe and US$5.01 trillion in the Asia Pacific region. Worldwide, US$40.36 trillion were invested in regulated collective schemes in 2016 (Investment Company Institute, 2017). The same trend has applied to unregulated schemes; for example private equity and hedge funds that are targeted at professional investors such as financial institutions, sovereign wealth funds and wealthy individuals.[1]

To bring a collective investment scheme to life, the fund manager will set up a legal vehicle, such as an investment company or a limited partnership, and will invite investors to place their money with the fund. If the fund targets only professional investors, this will be conducted under private law. If the target audience for the scheme are retail investors, registration of the investment vehicle is required and the investment activities are exposed to oversight by the financial regulatory authority. Once set up, the collected money is used to buy assets. Units of the fund might be traded in private markets only – if at all – or it might be possible to sell units back to the respective scheme.[2] Some schemes can have their units listed on an exchange. By the end of 2016, of all US schemes regulated by the Securities and Exchange Commission (SEC), open-ended funds accounted for 85.06% of all AUM, exchange-traded funds 13.14% and close-ended funds, which are usually traded on an exchange, accounted for 1.36%. Unit investment trusts, which have units that are either redeemed by the trust itself or which are traded on an exchange, accounted for less than 0.44% of AUM.

US open-end managed registered investment companies – commonly known as 'mutual funds' – are a prominent and much researched example of regulated collective investment schemes. Such funds must register with the SEC and can invest only in financial securities. The management and business of mutual funds are strictly regulated.[3] For instance, laws impose a fiduciary duty on fund managers regarding the compensation received. Further, fees and expenses of a mutual fund must be disclosed in detail in a fund's prospectus. Leverage or borrowing by issuing debt securities is strictly prohibited.[4] Bank borrowing (up to 33% of a fund's net assets) and engagement in derivatives (including the use of options, futures, forward contracts, and short selling) are allowed as long as the fund can provide coverage (Galkiewicz, 2014).

Institutional investors usually place their monies with managers in unregulated or only lightly regulated schemes, such as hedge or private equity funds. Such funds are set up in such a manner to be exposed to as little regulation as possible. Hedge funds, for example, achieve this by accepting only professional investors and by restricting the number of investors in a scheme to avoid regulation. Running unregulated schemes allows hedge fund managers to use unconventional investment strategies, such as leveraging through borrowing, taking of short positions and making extensive use of derivatives to gain from market downturns (Stulz, 2007).

The delegated management of an investment scheme comes with costs, which include administrative cost, trading costs and, in particular, the fee that has to be paid to the fund manager. This fee depends mainly on the investment style of the manager. 'Passive' managers mimic the performance of a market segment – represented by an index – and give investors access to a well-diversified portfolio. 'Active' managers, on the other hand, promise to generate extra risk-adjusted return by the timing of sales and purchases and/or by finding mispriced assets. For this promise, active managers charge higher fees. For instance, the fees of active mutual funds are about 80 basis points higher than those of passive funds (Investment Company Institute, 2017). Schemes targeted at institutional investors charge typically a management fee of 1–2% per annum on AUM. The manager of such a fund also obtains typically 10–20% of scheme's profits, however, often only once profits are above a preset hurdle rate. This remuneration model should incentivise managers to produce good returns (for details see Bacon, 2008, 57).

All the types of collective investment schemes that can be found in other investment sectors can also be found in real estate. In particular, real estate investments can be conducted through joint ventures (partnerships), private equity and hedge funds (limited partnerships), open-ended and closed-end funds, such as tax-transparent public and private real estate investment trusts (REITs).

Return rate calculation

Performance evaluation is based on the total return rates of the investment products managed by a particular manager. Investors might be, however, also interested in receiving information on how the total return rate is divided into the income and the capital return. Depending on the type of assets the manager invests in, the computation of return rates can range from being easy to being complicated. Consider first the easy case and assume a managed portfolio that is invested solely in blue chip stocks. The stocks are traded in a liquid market and, using the stock prices, we can establish that the value of the portfolio at the beginning of the first period is $V_0 = 100$. During the period, the manager buys and sells stocks, and investors will neither take money out nor place new money into the portfolio. In other words, there are no exogenously triggered cash flows. At the end of period one, the portfolio has a market value of $V_1 = 110$. Obviously, the absolute money return at the end of period one is $V_1 - V_0 = 10$ and the total return rate is $r_1 = 10\%$. Let us assume that the return rate over period two is $r_2 = 10\%$, which implies that the market value of the portfolio at the end of period two is $V_2 = 121$. The return rate over both periods is then:

$$r_{12} = \frac{(121-100)}{100} = 21\%$$

exactly the same as the cumulated individual period return rates $(1 + r_1)(1 + r_2) - 1$. The cumulative per period return rate over the two periods is:

$$r_{12}^{c} = \sqrt{(1+r_1)(1+r_2)} - 1 = 10\%$$

It is useful for the comparison of fund managers to express return rates for the same frequency, such as monthly or quarterly. For example, let us assume that manager A increased the market value of a portfolio from 100 to 161.1 over five years. Manager B increased the market value of a portfolio from 150 to 219.6 over four years. It seems that manager B has produced a higher absolute return over a shorter period of time than manager A. This ignores, however, that manager B started out with a portfolio that had a higher market value. Annualised return rates help to make more meaningful comparisons. The rates are defined implicitly by $100 \times (1 + r_A)^5 = 161.1$ and $150 \times (1 + r_B)^4 = 219$. Solving gives $r_A = r_B = 10\%$ and the two portfolios show exactly the same performance.

Return rate calculation becomes a bit more intricate once cash flows in and out of the portfolio occur *between* dates at which the market value of the assets in the portfolio is assessed. Such external cash flows can occur because new investors invest in an open-ended fund or some existing investors claim their investments back. Such external cash flow activity impacts on a portfolio's value, but should not be considered for the return rate calculation. Imagine a portfolio manager whose activities during the first 29 days of a month have no effect on the value of a managed portfolio. During these 29 days, the portfolio's value remains unaltered at $V_0 = 100$. At the last day of the month, a new investor pays 10 into the portfolio. The value of the portfolio at the end is thus $V_1 = 110$ and 10% higher than the value at the beginning of the period. However, the increase in portfolio's value is caused *solely* by the external cash flow and has nothing to do with manager's skill. To deal with this problem, the monthly return rate should be calculated as the cumulative return rate of the sub-period return rates of investments in the portfolio. This leads to:

$$\frac{100}{100} \times \frac{110}{110} - 1 = 0\% \tag{16.1}$$

The first wealth relative on the left-hand side applies to the first 29 days. During this sub-period of the month, the manager could not generate any additional portfolio value. On the last day of the month, the second sub-period, AUM increased, but the manager was again not able to generate additional portfolio value. Using daily cumulative return rates for the two sub-periods, Equation (16.1) can be expressed equally as:

$$\left(1+r_1^s\right)^{29}\left(1+r_2^s\right)-1=0\% \tag{16.2}$$

The calculations just conducted correspond to the *time-weighted rate of return* (TWR; see Bailey *et al.*, 2007 for further discussion). The Global Investment Performance Standards require the use of TWR with only few exceptions (CFA Institute 2012).

The calculation of TWR requires that the values of all assets in the current portfolio are assessed each time when an external cash flow occurs. This is easy for securities that are traded in highly liquid markets, such as a portfolio of blue chip stocks. Matters become complicated for portfolios that are invested in illiquid assets. Market prices will not be readily observable and appraisals must be used instead. Such appraisals cost time and money and may be carried out only at the minimum required statutory frequency. If cash flows arrive between two appraisal dates, it is important that return rates are adjusted properly for such cash flows. Given the low frequency at which appraisals are computed, an *exact* computation of time-weighted return rates will not be possible. In this case, approximations must be used. Prominent examples are the so-called simple and modified Dietz formulas (Christopherson *et al.*; 2009 Travers, 2004). Given its illiquid nature, the Global Investment Performance Standards contain specific provisions regarding the computation of TWR if a fund invests in direct real estate (Hendricksen and Stout, 2014). For instance, portfolio assets must be valued only every quarter and such valuations can be done internally. However, every 12 months an external appraiser should value the properties. Based on the asset valuations, income and external cash flow information, quarterly TWRs have to be calculated. Closed-end real estate funds should use – like other private equity funds – the internal rate of return since inception to measure performance (CFA Institute, 2012).

Performance evaluation

Investors who have monies placed with *passive* managers are interested in answers to the following two questions. How accurately does the portfolio return rate track the returns of the market index it intends to mimic? What are the fees charged by the manager and how do these compare with the fees charged by peer group competitors? Investors who have monies placed with *active* managers are interested further in an answer to the question: does the manager have skills in finding mispriced assets and is the manager able to time the market? Market timing skill requires that the manager moves into market segments when these are likely to outperform and moves out of segments when these are likely to underperform. Being able to detect active managers who are skilled is what all investors are looking for. However, skill is not directly observable and fund managers act in a risky environment. Realised return rates of an active managed portfolio could be low because a skilled manager had bad luck. Equally possible, an unskilled manager might be lucky in a short run, but will not be able to replicate this success in the future.

Performance measures

Once return rates have been computed, these can be used to assess the past performance of a manager (see Bacon, 2013, for a detailed summary of performance measures). For example, the annualised total return rate over the past five years could be calculated and compared with the annualised return rate from a market index (CFA Institute, 2012). It might be that the manager promised at inception to mimic or beat a particular index, such as the IPD UK Monthly Property Index. Given the actual performance information, this can then be assessed. To be meaningful, it is important that the benchmark portfolio and the managed fund are comparable. For instance, if funds compute return rates based on a specific approximation, then a benchmark should be based on the same approximation. The CFA Institute (2017) discusses this in the context of closed-end real estate funds that use the internal rate of return. It is also possible that indices with the same purpose are computed differently depending on the particular country. For example, the IPD computes fund return indices for the United States and Canada based on the modified Dietz formula 'to address client requirements' (MSCI, 2017, 2.4).

If an investor sets a target return rate for a managed account, performance evaluation is straightforward. For instance, assume that an investor has set a target rate of 6% per annum but the managed account delivered only 5%. Obviously, the manager did not deliver what was agreed on. The manager's performance can also be compared with the performance of peers in the same industry segment, such as commercial real estate investments. However, even if a manager is among the top decile in the segment, this does not necessarily imply a good performance if commercial real estate did not perform well. It depends then on the specific investment policies of the fund or the scheme how the manager's performance should be rated. For example, if the manager was restricted to commercial real estate investments, then being in top decile in an otherwise poorly performing market segment should be assessed as good performance. If the manager was allowed to implement a mixed strategy and could have invested in corporate bonds, which performed very well, then the performance cannot be rated highly. In addition to information on return rates over particular holding periods, investors will also be interested in the variability of return rates. This variability can be measured, for instance, with the standard deviation. Investors might also be interested in information on the number of times the manager produced return rates below the target rate of 6%. If the magnitude of the deviations matters as well, the investor is interested in the downside risk, which is measured with the semi-variance.

While summary information on return rates and return rate risk are useful, a performance measure should relate the average return rate and the risk of these rates in one number. The best-known risk-return measure is the one suggested by Sharpe (1966). In *ex ante* form, the Sharpe ratio of managed portfolio p is:

$$SR_p = \frac{\mathrm{E}\left[r_p\right] - r_f}{\sigma_p} \tag{16.3}$$

To gain intuition, assume that investors have mean variance preferences. They care only about the expected return rate and the risk of this return rate. The trade-off relationship between risk and return will depend on an investor's specific preferences. Figure 16.1 shows a risk-return diagram.

All investors would like to have portfolios that have risk-return combinations in the upper-left part. Figure 16.1 shows also the risk-return combinations of the two managed portfolios A and B indicated by the two triangles. If investors had to decide between the two, some would choose A, others would choose B. Those who choose A will have a lower degree of risk aversion and will be satisfied by the extra amount of expected return for the extra risk.

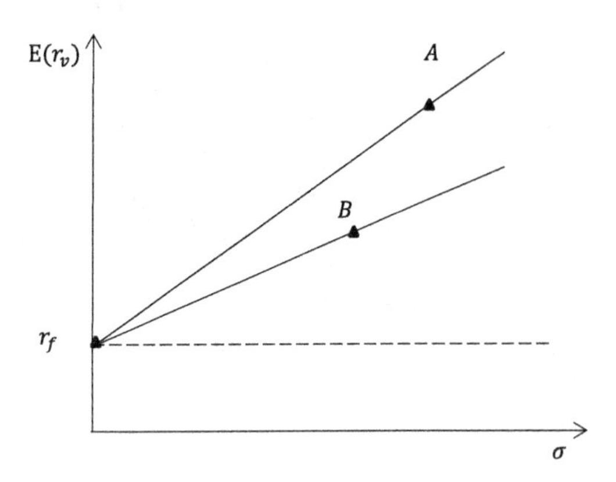

Figure 16.1 Risk–return diagram and portfolio frontiers

Those who choose B will have a higher degree of risk aversion and accept a lower return for lower risk.

What would happen if the investors could split their monies between a managed portfolio and cash? The return rate of a portfolio where the investor places share v of monies with a manager and the remaining $1-v$ in cash is:

$$r_v = r_f + v(r_p - r_f) \tag{16.4}$$

The expected return rate of this investor-augmented portfolio is:

$$\mathrm{E}[r_v] = r_f + v(\mathrm{E}[r_p] - r_f)$$

and its risk is:

$$\sigma_v = v\sigma_p$$

Combining both equations by eliminating v gives:

$$\mathrm{E}[r_v] = r_f + \left(\frac{\mathrm{E}[r_p] - r_f}{\sigma_p}\right)\sigma_v \tag{16.5}$$

This equation gives all the risk-return combinations an investor can achieve by combining the risk-free asset and the managed portfolio p. Observe that the term in brackets on the right-hand side is the Sharpe ratio. These combinations are plotted in Figure 16.1 for the two managed portfolios A and B. It is clear that every investor will prefer an investment in A to an investment in B. Portfolio A gives access to better a better portfolio allocation line. Observe from Equation (16.5) that this implies that $SR_A > SR_B$. Using realised return rates of a managed fund allows the computation of *ex post* Sharpe ratios, which can be used to rank portfolios or to examine the persistence of fund manager performance.[5] The average of return rates can be used as estimator for the expected return rate and the standard deviation as an estimator for the risk of the return rates.

Treynor (1965) emphasises that asset prices fluctuate widely and managers should be assessed relative to this market-wide variation. In particular, assume that return rates of a managed fund are represented well by the single-index model (Sharpe 1963):

$$r_p = \alpha_p + \beta_p r_m + \epsilon_p \tag{16.6}$$

where r_m is the return rate of *some* market index and ϵ_p is the return rate component unrelated to market variation. Assume, for instance, that we want to rank managers of open-ended investment schemes that invest in REITs. The market index would then be a REIT index. Observe from Equation (16.6) that the total risk of the return rates of the managed fund p is:

$$\sigma_p = \beta_p \sigma_m + \sigma_\epsilon \approx \beta_p \sigma_m$$

Using this approximation in Equation (16.5) leads to:

$$\mathrm{E}[r_v] = r_f + \left(\frac{\mathrm{E}[r_p] - r_f}{\beta_p} \right) \frac{\sigma_v}{\sigma_m} \tag{16.7}$$

The term in brackets on the right-hand side of Equation (16.7) is the *ex-ante* Treynor ratio. Equation (16.7) gives all the risk-return combinations an investor can achieve by combining the risk-free asset and the managed portfolio p. The difference between Equations (16.5) and (16.7) lies in the fact that the Treynor ratio ignores transitory effects. 'By concentrating on the systematic part of a fund's variability … we can avoid paying attention to these transitory effects and concern ourselves with the more permanent relationship' (Sharpe 1966, 128). In a plot similar to Figure 16.1, more desirable managed portfolios would lead to steeper portfolio allocation lines. It is possible that the Sharpe and the Treynor ratios lead to different ranking outcomes.[6]

Fund managers often market investment schemes with the promise to beat a specific market index. For instance, there are many active investment schemes investing in securitised real estate that promise to outperform an appropriate index. The risk that investors have to bear is that there are months where the manager cannot fulfil this promise. The *information ratio* – also known as *appraisal ratio* – introduced by Treynor and Black (1973) relates the performance of fund p relative to some market benchmark index m and takes account that there is uncertainty that the manager is always able to fulfil the promise of outperforming the respective market index. The *ex ante* information ratio is:

$$IR_p = \frac{\mathrm{E}[r_p] - \mathrm{E}[r_m]}{\sigma_{pm}} \tag{16.8}$$

The numerator is the expected excess return rate of fund p over the benchmark m and the denominator is the so-called *tracking error risk*. It measures the volatility of the monthly difference between the return rates of the managed portfolio and the index. Observe that this uncertainty treats outperformance and underperformance symmetrically. The use of the term *information* in the name of the ratio can be motivated as follows. An informed investor is able to avoid securities in the sector that are likely to underperform and to get excess exposure to those securities that are likely to outperform. Deviating in segments of the sector, however, introduces the risk of not performing like the sector. The information ratio can be a very useful tool for an investor who employs different internal and external managers in the same sector, as it allows for ranking these managers *ex post*.[7] The investor will choose the appropriate benchmark and the information ratio allows them to assess how well the different managers perform (see Goodwin, 1998 for a detailed discussion of the information ratio).

For investors who give a mandate with a target return rate to an active fund manager, performance can be assessed with the *Sortino ratio*. In its *ex ante* form, this ratio is:

$$SorR_p = \frac{\mathrm{E}\left[r_p\right] - r_{tr}}{\sigma^{-}_{ptr}} \tag{16.9}$$

The numerator in this ratio is the expected performance of the managed portfolio in excess of the target rate r_{tr} set by the investor. The denominator is the target semi-deviation, that is, the standard deviation of the portfolio return rate and the target rate conditional on the differences being negative. The semi-deviation is also called *downside risk*, because it measures the risk of the managed portfolio not delivering what is required given the target rate.

While fund managers often declare which benchmark they try to beat, for instance the FTSE100, it is also useful to assess the performance of such fund managers relative to the opportunity cost of capital. Active managers take on risk and, in a well-functioning asset market, risk taking will be compensated. Implementing this approach necessitates the use of an asset price model. Jensen (1968) was the first to suggest this approach and he used the capital asset pricing model (CAPM) model. Many other asset pricing models have been suggested since then. In *ex ante* form, Jensen's original approach is:

$$\mathrm{E}\left[r_p - r_f\right] = \alpha_p + \beta_p \mathrm{E}\left[r_m - r_f\right] \tag{16.10}$$

The left-hand side is the expected return rate of the managed portfolio p in excess of the risk-free rate. This risk premium equals the risk premium for the portfolio under the CAPM – the market-wide risk premium times the fund's beta – plus *alpha* (α_p), which measures the extra performance the manager generates, if any. Given sufficient return rate data for fund p, ideally at least five years of monthly data, alpha can be estimated by fitting the linear regression:

$$r_{pt} - r_{ft} = \alpha_p + \boldsymbol{\beta}'_p \, \mathbf{x}_t + \epsilon_{pt} \tag{16.11}$$

with $\mathbf{x}_t = r_{mt} - r_{ft}$. The last term in Equation (16.11) is the unsystematic return rate component, which will be zero on average. In line with the CAPM, the market index m in Equation (16.10) is understood in the broadest sense and represents *all* risky assets, including illiquid asset and returns from human capital. It is clear that such an index is hard to construct in reality. Empirical applications have to settle for a *proxy* when fitting the regression in Equation (16.11). The quality of the proxy will obviously affect the measured alpha, but – because the market index that covers all risky assets is practically unobservable – it will be impossible to decide to what extent. In addition, a second problem arises regarding the correctness of the asset pricing model. Jensen (1968) used the CAPM as the model to measure the return rate that investors require, given a managed fund's risks. Other pricing models have superseded the CAPM in recent decades (see also Chapter 11). Jensen's alpha approach is versatile, however, and can be implemented with other asset pricing models. For instance, if – in addition to the market-wide risk premium – the fundamental factors *size* and *growth* are included in the vector $\mathbf{x}_t$ in Equation (16.11), then the three-factor model of Fama and French (1993) results. The three-factor model is explained in more detail in Chapter 11. If the fundamental factors *market*, *size*, *growth* and *momentum* are included in the vector $\mathbf{x}_t$, then the Carhart (1997) four-factor model results. The momentum factor is computed as difference of equal-weighted average return rates of the best and the worst performing stocks to over the previous 11 months. Pastor and Stambaugh (2003) and Liu (2006) propose the *liquidity risk factor* as a further potential fundamental pricing factor. Liu (2006) measures liquidity risk by counting the number of days on which individual stocks are not traded during the previous 12 months. Liu (2006) constructs then portfolios for high and low liquid stocks and finds that the return rate differences – the liquidity factor – improves the explanatory power of the CAPM. Fama and French (2015) have suggested a five-factor model as an extension of their three-factor model. The two additional factors are *profitability* and *investment risk*. After sorting companies by their operating profitability into two groups as *robust and weak*, the *profitability factor* is the average return of robust companies minus the average return of weak companied. The *investment factor* is constructed in a similar manner by sorting companies into *conservative and aggressive* and computing the difference of the average return rates of the conservative and aggressive companies.

Factor pricing models have also been applied for performance evaluation of hedge funds. Hedge fund managers engage in multiple strategies and these strategies can often not be replicated with existing indices. This implies that benchmarks are needed that take appropriate account of the risks of these different strategies. For instance, Fung and Hsieh (2004) identify seven risk factors in hedge fund styles and propose that these should be used in a factor pricing model for hedge fund performance evaluation. These factors include the return rate of a market index in excess of the risk-free rate; the return rate of a small cap index in excess of return rates of a large cap index; yield changes of bonds; and a measure of credit risk.

The asset pricing approach seems ideally suited to evaluate fund managers. It allows benchmarking a managed fund's return rates against the opportunity cost of what the market requires given the risk taken. However, as the discussion above indicates, there seems no end to models proposed to serve this purpose. Every time a new credible asset pricing model is suggested, active fund managers have to be evaluated again. This will likely have an effect on the results of performance evaluation. For instance, Ippolito (1993) and Elton *et al.* (1993) use the same fund performance data, but assess it with different benchmarks. Ippolito (1993) finds that the average fund manager has a significantly positive alpha, whereas Elton *et al.* (1993) find a significantly negative alpha.

Statistical aspects

Testing for fund manager skill

The performance measures discussed are always computed using a sample of *historical* return rate data. Investors usually want to learn if a manager has true skills or was just lucky over the observation period. A decision on this question requires the use of *statistical inference*. This is an area where much research is taking place and our discussion can only be indicative. To understand the problem, take Equation (16.11): the coefficient of interest is α_p and can be estimated with the ordinary least squares (OLS) estimator. Given that Equation (16.11) is specified correctly, the OLS estimator for alpha, α_p, is unbiased – for a general discussion, see Wooldridge (2013, Chapters 2–4). Applying the OLS estimator to our data sample results in a point estimate for alpha, for example $\hat{\alpha}_p = 0.25$. This point estimate seems to indicate that the manager of fund p has some skill. However, applying the estimator to a different sample – all else equal – would likely result in a different point estimate for alpha. To understand this, assume that the initial sample is short and that the factors of the asset pricing model do not vary much during the sample. The OLS estimator will separate the systematic component in Equation (16.11) from the unsystematic ϵ_{pt} and will provide a set of estimates $(\hat{\alpha}_p, \hat{\boldsymbol{\beta}}_p)$. Assume that we obtain new data that allows us to extend the current short sample. The factors of the asset pricing model now show substantial dispersion over the extended sample. If we obtained $\hat{\alpha}_p = 0.25$ for the extended sample, we would feel more confident that the manager of fund p has skill then we do for the same estimated alpha for the original, shorter, sample. Applied to the extended sample, the estimator will separate the systematic component from the noise as before, but this task is now easier because the sample is longer. It is also easier to separate the effects of the individual fundamental factors – the individual beta coefficients – from each other, because the factors show more dispersion in the extended sample.

There are several approaches to deal rigorously with the problem of sampling variability. First, we could rely on the theoretical derivation of the standard error of the estimator for alpha and could use this formula and the data to obtain an estimate of the standard error, for example $\hat{\sigma}_{\hat{\alpha},p} = 0.14$. We would use the two point estimates to construct the test statistic:

$$\hat{t}_p = \frac{\hat{\alpha}_p}{\hat{\sigma}_{\hat{\alpha},p}} \tag{16.12}$$

Using the numbers from our example, we obtain the estimate $\hat{t}_p = 1.786$. Under particular assumptions on the data generating process, the test statistic will be asymptotically standard-normally distributed under the null hypothesis that the manager of fund p has no skills and that $\alpha_p \leq 0$.[8] The distributional result can be used to assess if $\hat{t}_p = 1.786$ is too large to be compatible with the null hypothesis (as would be the case if the manager had skills and $\alpha_p > 0$). Applied to our example, the probability that the standard-normally distributed variable z is at least as large as $\hat{t}_p = 1.786$ is $P(z \geq 1.786) = 0.037$. This probability is small and it is unlikely that the observed test statistic comes from the null distribution.[9] We are, therefore, able to reject the null hypothesis and would therefore conclude that we have statistical evidence that the manager of fund p has skills.

Relying on the asymptotic assumption for inference can be inappropriate because most samples are 'small' and variables such as fund return rates and factors obey complicated data generating processes. For instance, stock return rate distributions show heavy tails and the unsystematic return rate components exhibit volatility clustering. The unsystematic component of stock portfolio return rates will exhibit the same characteristics. This does not affect the unbiasedness, consistency and asymptotic normality of the OLS estimator.[10] However, inference based on asymptotic normality might be misleading in small samples.

The bootstrap is the second approach to deal with sampling variability. This approach can lead to effective improvements of inference in small samples (for an overview in the context of time series see Kreiss and Lahiri, 2012). Bootstrap methods can be used to simulate the distribution of the t-statistic under the null hypothesis that the manager has no skill. Once the distribution is simulated, we can decide if it seems likely that the t-statistic computed for the original data comes from this simulated null distribution or not. One method to simulate the distribution of the t-statistics under the null uses the vectors of factors $\mathbf{x}_t$, the factor loadings $\boldsymbol{\beta}_p$ and the vector of residuals $\hat{\boldsymbol{\epsilon}}_p$ – both vectors are estimated from the original data – to generate artificial return rate series

$$r_{pt}^{b} = \hat{\boldsymbol{\beta}}'_p \mathbf{x}_t + \hat{\epsilon}_{pt}^{b} \tag{16.13}$$

for $b = 1,\ldots,B$. The artificial return rate in Equation (16.13) is generated under the null hypothesis that the manager has no skill, i.e., $\alpha_p^b = 0$. The residual $\hat{\epsilon}_{pt}^{b}$ in Equation (16.13) for period t is drawn from the elements in the vector $\hat{\boldsymbol{\epsilon}}_p$.[11] For each draw, the full set of residuals is used (sampling scheme with replacement). Bootstrap refinements should be applied if there is evidence of dependencies in the unsystematic return rate component over time. For instance, it is reasonable to assume that there is no or only small autocorrelation in the unsystematic component. However, volatility clustering points to dependencies of the unsystematic component over time. The so-called *block bootstrap* is a refinement to deal with this problem. Instead of drawing only single elements out of the vector $\hat{\boldsymbol{\epsilon}}_p$, blocks of adjacent residuals are sampled and used to generate artificial return rates under the null. The sample of artificial return rates is complete once it has the same number of observations as the original sample. The test statistic of interest, in our case $\hat{t}_p^b$, is then computed for artificial sample $b = 1$ and the whole exercise is repeated, for instance, $B = 1000$ times.

In the end, the simulated distribution of the test statistic computed with the B artificial samples is used to assess how likely it is that the test statistic from the original sample comes from the null. For instance, assume that the 95% quantile of the simulated distribution of test statistics from the artificial bootstrap samples is $\hat{t}_{0.95}^b = 1.81$.[12] This is larger than the $\hat{t}_p = 1.786$ that was obtained for the original data. We cannot reject the null hypothesis at the 5% significance level that the manager of fund p has no skills. Inference based on the bootstrap would, therefore, lead to a different conclusion than inference based on asymptotic results. In other cases, both approaches may agree or the null might be only rejected when the asymptotic approach is used. However, it would not be correct to conclude that anything goes. The essential message is that the testing procedure must be appropriate, given the data. For small samples of financial data, bootstrap methods will be more appropriate.

Simultaneous testing

Investors looking for good managers are confronted with additional statistical problems, because they compare different managers simultaneously. For example, imagine an investor who wants to test if two fund managers A and B have skills. We know that neither of the two managers is skilled. The investor does not have this knowledge and uses individual bootstrap t-tests to infer managerial skill. The investor works with the joint null hypothesis that neither managers has skill, that is, $\alpha_A \leq 0$ and $\alpha_B \leq 0$.[13] To implement this joint hypothesis, the investor would test each manager individually at a 5% significance level. This implies that the investor will reject each of the correct *individual* null hypotheses in 5% of all cases.[14] However, taken together, the type I error – the probability that the test procedure rejects the correct *joint* null hypothesis – is not 5%. To see this, assume for simplicity that the two tests are statistically independent. The type I error of the joint test is then $0.05^2 + 2 \times 0.05 \times (1 - 0.05) = 0.0975$. The first term in this equation is the probability that the investor rejects both null hypotheses incorrectly; the second term is the probability that one of the null hypotheses is rejected incorrectly. This could be the hypothesis for manager A or manager B, so this term appears twice.[15] The type I error problem can be approached with the Bonferroni correction. If the tests for each of the two fund managers are conducted individually at the significance level of 2.5% – which is 5% divided by the number of individual hypotheses – then the type I error for the joint test is slightly smaller than 5%.

The Bonferroni correction comes at the cost of a type II error once some managers have skills. A type II error is the probability that the null hypothesis of no skill is not rejected although the manager has skill. To understand this trade-off, let us assume that the investor wants to examine 1000 managers. We know – but not the investor – that 100 of these managers are indeed skilled. A perfect test procedure would ensure that the null hypothesis is not rejected for the 900 managers without skills and is rejected for the 100 managers with skills. If the investor tests the managers individually at the 5% level, we expect about $0.05 \times 900 = 45$ false rejections. If the investor applies the Bonferroni correction to the individual tests, we expect only few, if any, false rejections. It is natural to expect that more of the remaining skilled managers will be detected at a 5% level significance than at the corrected 0.005% level. The statistical analysis of managers' skill is presumably only the first of several stages used by the investor to select a manager. Under this perspective, it might seem that many false discoveries of seemingly skilled managers are not a problem. In later stages, the investor will examine all managers that were discovered in detail, for instance through personal meetings. This should weed those managers out who have no skill. However, this argument ignores that in-depth analysis of a fund manager will bring physical and monetary cost. While individual tests have the power to detect managers with skill, these tests lead also to many false discoveries. The Bonferroni correction guards against the false discoveries, but at the cost that only few of the managers with skill, if there are any, will be discovered.

Novel methods to deal with simultaneous testing are based on controlling the false discovery rate. In the example above, the individual tests led to an expected false discovery rate of 45/900 = 5%. We are able to calculate this rate, because we know the number of unskilled managers. In reality, this number is unknown. However, there are ways to estimate to proportion of correct null hypotheses in a sample of estimated p-values; see for instance Schweder and Spjotvoll (1982). The method of Storey (2002), for instance, estimates this proportion in the first step and uses it in the second step to calculate p-values that are adjusted for the false discovery rate (so-called q-values).

Empirical evidence on fund manager performance

Jensen (1968) is one of the first studies that evaluates the performance of actively managed open-ended funds in the United States. Jensen uses the CAPM as benchmark model and finds that only three of the 115 managed funds in his sample seem to have significantly positive alphas. Jensen interprets this result with care, because – given the number of tests conducted – even if no manager is skilled, a few false positives are to be expected. Jensen (1968) complements the analysis by examining whether managers are able to outperform randomly selected buy-and-hold strategies. He finds only limited evidence for this. The early study of Sharpe (1966) also finds that actively managed funds underperform passive benchmarks. Many other studies have examined the potential outperformance of actively managed open-ended funds in the United States and other countries since then. Recent studies on US funds include Kosowski *et al.* (2006) and Fama and French (2010). Both studies find evidence that a small number of funds can outperform the market. But there are also many underperforming funds. Overall, it seems that the active fund manager industry does not generate much value for investors. For UK funds, Leger (1997) and Quigley and Sinquefield (2000) find only little evidence of significantly positive alphas and, thus, outperformance relative to passive benchmarks with similar risk characteristics. The literature includes also several studies that have examined the performance of active funds that invest in real estate related securities. Such securities are mainly listed and private REITs, but can also include stocks of real estate operating companies and real estate developers. While a couple of studies (Gallo *et al.*, 2000; Kallberg *et al.*, 2000) have found that actively managed open-ended real estate security funds in the United States outperformed the market and have significantly positive alphas, more recent studies provide little or no evidence of such outperformance (O'Neal, 2000); Chiang *et al.*, 2008; Hartzell *et al.*, 2010). Kallberg *et al.* (2000) attributed the outperformance to the opaqueness of the real estate market, which could be exploited by well-informed managers. The results of the more recent studies indicate that such informational disparities have been competed away as the sector has become mature.

Studies on the performance of unregulated collective investment schemes such as private equity and hedge funds have to deal – in addition to issues common to most fund data, which will be discussed below – with the availability of data and the lack of standardised performance measurement and reporting (Ackermann *et al.*, 1999). Using a comprehensive fund-of-hedge funds database, Fung *et al.* (2008) found that a few of these funds seem to be able to produce consistent outperformance. As Brown (2016) discusses, due diligence and close monitoring of hedge funds can lead to positive alphas. Funds of funds have thus the potential to harvest good returns for their investors. However, Brown (2016, 7) observe also that many funds of funds are too small to exploit scale economies and have 'disappointingly poor after-fee performance'. Farrelly and Stevenson (2016) examine the performance of private equity funds that concentrate on value-added and opportunistic real estate investments. They find that these funds underperform relative to the listed real estate sector measured by a REIT index and that the performance is not much different from those of open-ended real estate funds. While it might be still possible that actively managed private real estate funds have lower risk that these other related investment opportunities, it does not seem that real estate differs from other actively managed funds.

Overall, there is not much evidence that sticking with an active fund manager brings extra benefits for investors. The majority of active managers do not seem to have the skill to outperform the market consistently over the long term on a risk-adjusted basis.

If investors were able to detect *ex ante* the managers who will outperform the market over the short-term, appropriate selection and deselection of managers could generate benefits. Such a strategy will work if actively managed funds show some performance persistence. Grinblatt and Titman (1992) find evidence for open-ended funds in the United States that winners tend to continue to perform well, at least over the near term of three to five years. Other studies correct this performance persistence downwards to a most two years (Hendricks *et al.*, 1993; Brown and Goetzmann, 1995; Malkiel, 1995). If investors switch appropriately between different actively managed funds, this short-term persistence of outperformance in fund return rates might not be sufficiently strong to provide monetary benefits. The influential study of Carhart (1997) shows that this seems to be the case. Part of the persistence outperformance can be explained by the respective manager's style and disappears once the correct risk premiums are considered. Transaction costs and loads cancel the rest. Any switching strategy is confronted with the task of identifying *ex ante* which actively managed funds will show persistence and which ones will not. Busse and Irvine (2006) provide evidence that novel approaches can be useful. They use daily data and a Bayesian estimation method to identify active funds that are likely to outperform. They find that their identification approach performs better than the standard approach that uses monthly data and frequentist estimation methods.

Data issues

The performance evaluation of actively managed collective investment schemes requires transparent and standardised return rate data and sufficient market information to construct appropriate benchmarks. Return rate data for funds that invest in liquid securities usually fulfil these criteria. It is also usually possible to find or construct appropriate benchmarks for such funds. Matters become more complicated for private funds, in particular, once these invest in highly illiquid assets such a direct real estate. Return rate calculations have to rely on appraisals and are often computed with approximation formulas. Indices available for performance benchmarking might be exposed to appraisal smoothing and unrepresentativeness. There have been several steps to improve this situation, such as the standardisation of performance measurement and academic research on de-smoothing. The computation of return rates for infrequently traded real assets will presumably always be tenuous.

Fund databases have to deal with several additional issues. The first issue is the *survivorship bias*. A fund can close down and this is more likely if return rates are poor. If a database does not keep record of closed funds, then an analysis based on only the surviving funds will inflate the industry's measured performance. Several professional databases keep track of funds that cease to exist and are, thus, essentially free of survivor bias. The second issue is the *backfilling bias*. Funds that are newly included in a database are usually those that are successful and reached a critical size of AUM. Unsuccessful funds are not included. Fund companies may start many new funds, but open only those to investors that are successful. This leads to the *incubation bias*, where open funds show a good return rate history, because the dead funds were never visible to investors. In the private fund segment, fund managers may decide to report return information only for those funds that are successful. This *selection bias* implies that databases and indices will not be representative for the whole industry. These biases can have sizeable effects on performance evaluation – see, for instance, Fung and Hsieh (2000) and Brown *et al.* (1995).

Conclusion

This chapter has provided an introduction to the theory and practice of active fund manager performance evaluation. Such evaluation is not easy. The difficulties start with availability of data on fund performance, the quality of the data, and the proper use of the data. Data are fairly easy to obtain for registered funds, but not so for private funds. Even if data are easily obtainable, several biases can prevent that the data are fully representative. The liquidity of the assets active fund managers invest in may also bring difficulties. For instance, whereas the market value of listed securities is observed directly, the value of real assets such as commercial real estate is not. Return rate calculation has then to rely on appraisals and can be conducted only at low frequencies. At times, investors know exactly the target rate they want their investments to achieve. This target can then be included in the mandate to an active manager. At other times, investors will be focussed on the relative performance of active managers. This requires that active fund performance is benchmarked. This could be done relative to competitors or relative to the market. Our discussion of the choice of an appropriate market benchmark has shown that this is difficult.

Notwithstanding of all these difficulties, there is robust empirical evidence that the average active manager does not bring additional value for investors. This is what we should expect from a highly competitive industry with free entry. There is evidence that some funds can outperform persistently over the short-term, but it is usually difficult to spot these managers *ex ante*. Even if an investor could spot such funds, the costs of switching may cancel out most of the outperformance.[16]

Notes

1 Given its private nature, exact numbers on the sector are not available.
2 In this chapter, we use the terms 'collective investment scheme' and 'fund' interchangeably.
3 The following four federal laws are particularly relevant: the Security Act of 1933, the Security Exchange Act of 1934, the Investment Company Act of 1940 and the Investment Advisers Act.
4 According to the Investment Company Act of 1940 18(f).
5 Sharpe (1966) ranks managed funds with the Sharpe ratio for two separate periods and analyses the correlation between the rankings. The correlation is rather weak and persistence therefore low.
6 For instance, assume two managed portfolios A and B that have identical expected return rates in excess of the risk-free rate. The total risk is such that $\sigma_B > \sigma_A$. It follows that $SR_A > SR_B$. The risk related to the market is such that $\beta_A > \beta_B$. It follows then also that $TR_B > TR_A$.
7 According to Grinold and Kahn (2000), an information ratio of 0.5 is good, of 0.75 is very good and a ratio of 1 exceptional for an actively managed fund.
8 Asymptotic means that the distributional results will hold if the sample size is sufficiently large.
9 A test of the null hypothesis needs a decision rule regarding what should be perceived as unlikely. Common cut-off levels are 1%, 5% and 10%.
10 Consistency means that the standard error of the unbiased alpha estimator tends asymptotically towards zero.
11 This implies that the bootstrap residual for period t can be the residual from the regression fit to the original data, but it can also be a residual from the latter fit for a period different than t.
12 Ordering the simulated t-statistics from smallest to largest, $\hat{t}^b_{0.95}$ is element 950 in the case of $B = 1000$. In case of a significance level or a B that do not match to a single simulated t-statistic, interpolation between the two closest test-statistics has to be applied.
13 The reader may ask why the investor does not use a regression *system* for both funds and to use a joint F-test for all alpha coefficients. Return rate histories may start at different dates and short histories may make precise estimation of covariance matrix impossible.
14 To clarify: *we* know that the manager has no skill, but the investor does not. The investor will either accept the null correctly or reject incorrectly. The investor knows, however, how the test is constructed: if the null is true and the test is conducted many times for *different* samples, all else equal, the correct null will be rejected for about 5% of all samples.
15 The remaining event is the case where neither of the individual hypotheses are rejected, which has a probability of $(1 - 0.05)^2 = 0.9025$.
16 Bacon (2013) and Christopherson *et al.* (2009) are dedicated to the performance analysis of fund managers and are recommended for further reading.

References

Ackermann, C., McEnally, R. and Ravenscraft, D. (1999) The performance of hedge funds: risk, return, and incentives, *Journal of Finance*, 54, 833–74.
Bailey, J. V., Richards, T. M. and Tierney, D. E. (2007) Evaluating portfolio performance, in Maginn, J. L., Tuttle, D. L., McLeavey, D. W., and Pinto, J. E. (eds.) *Managing investment performance: a dynamic process*, 3rd ed., John Wiley, Hoboken, NJ.
Bacon, C. R. (2008) *Practical portfolio performance measurement and attribution*, 2nd ed., John Wiley, Chichester.
Bacon, C. R. (2013) *Practical risk-adjusted performance measurement*, John Wiley, Chichester.
Brown, S. J. (2016) Why hedge funds?, *Financial Analyst Journal*, 72 (6), 5–7.
Brown, S. J. and Goetzmann, W. N. (1995) Performance persistence, *Journal of Finance*, 50, 679–98.

Busse, J. A. and Irvine, P. J. (2006) Bayesian alphas and mutual fund persistence, *Journal of Finance*, 61, 2251–88.

Carhart, M. M. (1997) On persistence in mutual fund performance, *Journal of Finance*, 52, 57–82.

CFA Institute (2012) *Global investment performance standards (GIPS®) handbook*, 3rd ed., CFA Institute, Charlottesville, VA.

CFA Institute (2017) *Exposure draft of* GIPS® *guidance statement on benchmarks*, CFA Institute, Charlottesville, VA.

Chiang, K. C., Kozhevnikov, K., Lee, M.-L. and Wisen, C. H. (2008) Further evidence on the performance of funds of funds: the case of real estate mutual funds, *Real Estate Economics*, 36, 47–61.

Christopherson, J. A., Carino, D. R. and Ferson, W. E. (2009) *Portfolio performance measurement and benchmarking*, McGraw Hill, New York, NY.

Elton, E. J., Gruber, M. J., Das, S. and Hlavka, M. (1993) Efficiency with costly information: a reinterpretation of evidence from managed portfolios, *Review of Financial Studies*, 6, 1–22.

Fama, E. F. and French, K. R. (1993) Common risk factors in the returns on stocks and bonds, *Journal of Financial Economics*, 33, 3–56.

Fama, E. F. and French, K. R. (2010) Luck versus skill in the cross-section of mutual fund returns, *Journal of Finance*, 65, 1915–47.

Fama, E. F. and French, K. R (2015) A five-factor asset pricing model, *Journal of Financial Economics*, 116(1), 1–22.

Farrelly, K. and Stevenson, S. (2016) Performance drivers of private real estate funds, *Journal of Property Research*, 33, 214–35.

Fung, W. and Hsieh, D. A. (2000) Performance characteristics of hedge funds and commodity funds: natural vs. spurious biases, *Journal of Financial and Quantitative Analysis*, 35, 291–307.

Fung, W. and Hsieh, D. A. (2004) Hedge fund benchmarks: a risk-based approach, *Financial Analysts Journal*, 60(5), 65–80.

Fung, W., Hsieh, D. A., Naik, N.Y. and Ramadorai, T. (2008) Hedge funds: performance, risk, and capital formation, *Journal of Finance*, 63, 1777–803.

Galkiewicz, D. P. (2014) *Similarities and differences between U.S. and German regulation of the use of derivatives and leverage by mutual funds – what can regulators learn from each other?* SFB/TR 15 Discussion Paper No. 474, Collaborative Research Center Transregion 15: Governance and the Efficiency of Economic Systems, Munich.

Gallo, J. G., Lockwood, L. J. and Rutherford, R. C. (2000) Asset allocation and performance of real estate mutual funds, *Real Estate Economics*, 28, 165–84.

Goodwin, T. H. (1998) The information ratio, *Financial Analyst Journal*, 54 (4), 34–43.

Grinblatt, M. and Titman, S. (1992) The persistence of mutual fund performance, *Journal of Finance*, 47, 1977–84.

Grinold, R. C. and Kahn, R. N. (2000) *Active portfolio management: a quantitative approach for providing superior returns and controlling risk*, McGraw-Hill, New York, NY.

Hartzell, J. C., Mühlhofer, T. and Titman, S. D. (2010) Alternative benchmarks for evaluating mutual fund performance, *Real Estate Economics*, 38, 121–54.

Hendricks, D., Patel J. and Zeckhauser, R. (1993) Hot hands in mutual funds: short-run persistence of relative performance 1974–1988, *Journal of Finance*, 48, 93–130.

Hendricksen, J. and Stout, C. (2014) *A closer look at real estate under the GIPS standards: challenges and solutions for real estate managers considering the Global Investment Performance Standards (GIPS®)*, ACA Compliance Group Performance Services, New York, NY.

Investment Company Institute (2017) *Investment Company Fact Book: a review of trends and activities in the investment company industry*, 57th ed., ICI, Washington, DC.

Ippolito, R. A. (1993) On studies of mutual fund performance, 1962–1991, *Financial Analysts Journal*, 49(1), 42–50.

Jensen, M. C. (1968) The performance of mutual funds in the period 1945–1964, *Journal of Finance*, 23, 389–416.

Kallberg, J. G., Liu, C. L. and Trzcinka, C. (2000) The value added from investment managers: an examination of funds of REITs, *Journal of Financial and Quantitative Analysis*, 35, 387–408.

Kosowski, R., Timmermann, A. G., White, H. L. and Wermers, R. (2006) Can mutual fund 'stars' really pick stocks? New evidence from bootstrap analysis, *Journal of Finance*, 61, 2551–95.

Kreiss, J. P. and Lahiri, S. N. (2012) Bootstrap methods for time series, *Time Series Analysis: Methods and Applications*, 30, 3–26.

Leger, L. A. (1997) UK investment trusts: performance, timing and selectivity, *Applied Economics Letters* 4(4), 207–10.

Liu, W. (2006), A liquidity-augmented capital asset pricing model, *Journal of Financial Economics*, 82, 631–71.

Malkiel, B. G. (1995) Return from investing in equity mutual funds 1971 to 1991, *Journal of Finance*, 50, 549–72.

MSCI (2017) *MSCI global methodology standards for real estate investment*, MSCI, New York, NY.

O'Neal, E. S. (2000) Industry momentum and sector mutual funds, *Financial Analysts Journal*, 56(4), 37–49.

Pastor L. and Stambaugh R. F. (2003) Liquidity risk and expected stock returns, *Journal of Political Economy*, 111, 642–85.

Quigley, G. and Sinquefield, R. A. (2000) Performance of UK equity unit trusts, *Journal of Asset Management*, 1, 72–92.

Sharpe, W. F. (1963) A simplified model for portfolio analysis, *Management Science*, 9, 277–86.

Sharpe, W. F. (1966) Mutual fund performance, *Journal of Business*, 39(1, Pt 2: Supplement on security prices), 119–138.

Schweder, T. and Spjotvoll, E. (1982) Plots of p-values to evaluate many tests simultaneously, *Biometrica*, 69, 493–502.

Storey, J. D. (2002) A direct approach to false discovery rates, *Journal of the Royal Statistical Society B*, 64, 497–8.

Stulz, R. M. (2007) Hedge funds: past, present, and future, *Journal of Economic Perspectives*, 21(2), 175–194.

Travers, F. (2004) *Investment manager analysis. A comprehensive guide to portfolio selection, monitoring, and optimization*, Wiley, Hoboken, NJ.

Treynor, J. L. (1965) How to rate management investment funds, *Harvard Business Review*, 43(1), 63–75.

Treynor, J. L. and Black, F. (1973) How to use security analysis to improve portfolio selection, *Journal of Business*, 46, 66–86.

Wooldridge, J. M. (2013) *Introductory Econometrics. A Modern Approach*, 5th ed., Cengage, Mason, OH.

17 Fund management and governance

Pat McAllister

Introduction

In recent decades, poor or weak governance has been associated with many of the major scandals in the financial sector. While there are numerous notorious examples in consumer finance (such as insurance, mortgage and pensions mis-selling in the UK), global investment banking (such as LIBOR rate fixing, biased stock advice during the dot.com bubble and money laundering) accounting and auditing practices (such as Arthur Anderson), corporate malpractices (such as Enron and WorldCom in the United States, Olympus in Japan), such high-profile cases have perhaps provided rather extreme examples of governance failures as well as involving criminal and fraudulent behaviour. Part of the explanation for the now infamous collapses of multiple major banks and other financial institutions in the global financial crisis (such as Royal Bank of Scotland in the UK, Anglo-Irish Bank in the Republic of Ireland, and Lehmans and Bear Stearns in the United States) has also been attributed to problems of corporate governance.

While disentangling the causes of such major corporate failures can be complex, unethical and/or self-interested behaviour tend to be pervasive problems for, and in, organisations who are managing resources or funds on behalf of others. Principal–agent and moral hazard problems have long been noted features of situations where individuals who act either as employees, advisers or managers are paid to use their efforts to provide advice to, or to act on behalf of, another. Conflicts of interest can commonly arise, since company directors, fund managers or external advisers are paid professionals with their own interests, which may not necessarily be aligned with the interests of 'principals'. However, in a fund management context, such conflicts of interest can be numerous and varied and can be hard to delimit. In a speech in 2012, the US Securities Exchange Commission's Director for the Office of Compliance Inspections and Examinations highlighted that:

> Conflicts of interest exist throughout the commercial world. They are a particularly important challenge for large and complex financial institutions, which can have affiliations that lead to a host of potential conflicts of interest. If these are not carefully managed, this then leads to failure to protect the client's interests, with attendant regulatory and reputational risks that could be disastrous.
>
> (di Florio, 2012)

In the fund management sector, key issues tend to concern how funds and their boards (the clients of the fund manager) are informed of procedures for dealing with conflicts of interest and how such conflicts are handled and reported. In the funds themselves, board members, trustees and/or directors may also have conflicts of interest which may need to be recognised, recorded and supervised. Where asset management is outsourced, side-by-side arrangements involving the management of a number of accounts can create conflicts of interest where an investment manager may favour one account over another. Potential problems can occur where different fee structures may incentivise managers to prioritise certain clients. If the manager has co-invested in only some funds, there are clear incentives to favour the funds where they have more 'skin in the game'. While less likely in illiquid real estate markets, investment strategies for one client may affect the performance of other clients. Cross-trading between clients also needs to be managed. Many approaches can be used to resolve such conflicts. With a range of costs and benefits, they can include firm or team specific trading strategies, creating 'silos' that limit information sharing about clients, and mandatory consultation with compliance teams or oversight groups. As we see below, a primary concern of governance is with ensuring that the costs and risks potentially created by such conflicts of interest are minimised.

Although poor, negligent and sometimes fraudulent real estate lending practices have been significant in headline-making corporate banking scandals, a number of high-profile governance failures have also occurred in the commercial real estate investment sector. Early in the 2000s, the so-called 'Frankfurt real estate scandal' involved a whole range of problems including systematic bribery of fund managers by real estate developers, architects and construction companies to obtain contracts and/or buy buildings on corrupt terms. For instance, buyers and sellers of real estate assets were found to have engaged the services of real estate agents *after* a sale was completed and to have then split the agent's fee among themselves. It was also suggested that bribes were paid among fund management organisations to influence corruptly the outcome and level of bids in sales transactions. In 2007–08 in the Netherlands, the Philips pension fund was investigated by the Dutch regulator. Sixteen real estate professionals were arrested and accused of being involved in an illegal scheme believed to have cost the Philips pension fund millions of Euros. The investigation focussed on fraudulent real estate transactions involving internal asset managers agreeing relatively low values for assets with external valuers, before properties were sold to business connections. The properties were then later 'flipped' for the market value, with the price difference being divided among the participants. Of course, these examples are fairly extreme. In reality, individual and organisational self-interested actions will tend to be more subtle and nuanced. However, while the individuals themselves remain primarily culpable, the organisational decision making and risk management processes that 'permitted' such behaviours are the essence of governance in the commercial real estate investment sector.

While the scope of these terms has been mutating and is contested, governance-related issues are often central to the bundle of interrelated factors that are increasingly used to measure the ethical performance of businesses. In the last two decades, a plethora of new abbreviations such as 'ESG' (environmental, social and governance), 'CSR' (corporate social responsibility), 'RPI' (responsible property investment) and 'SRI' (socially responsible investment) have become increasingly mainstream within the real estate investment community. In this chapter, we explore how governance issues affect real estate investment markets and processes. In terms of outcomes, the empirical evidence on the relationship between governance performance and financial performance is reviewed. In the first section, the concept of governance is discussed and its key dimensions are identified. This is followed by a brief examination of the real estate investment sector identifying some of the key areas that need to be 'governed'. Specific areas where governance issues emerge in real estate management, brokerage, appraisal and unlisted real estate fund management are discussed. There is, then, a discussion of the evidence and expectations regarding governance and investment performance in the listed real estate sector. Finally, conclusions are drawn.

Concepts of governance

The concept of governance is used in a wide range of contexts and has been described as a broad term that 'can convey a slightly different meaning depending on who uses it' (Aubut, 2004, 8). From a broad sociopolitical perspective, governance broadly concerns the rules and structures that societies use to organise themselves. Terms such as power, accountability, stakeholders, control, decision making, authority, interests, risk management, equity and transparency tend to be central to theorisations of governance. On their website, The Institute on Governance succinctly states that 'Governance determines who has power, who makes decisions, how other players make their voice heard and how account is rendered'.[1] More specifically, *corporate governance* is concerned with:

> the system of rules, practices and processes by which a company is directed and controlled. Corporate governance essentially involves balancing the interests of the many stakeholders in a company – these include its shareholders, management, customers, suppliers, financiers, government and the community. Since corporate governance also provides the framework for attaining a company's objectives, it encompasses practically every sphere of management, from action plans and internal controls to performance measurement and corporate disclosure.[2]

The emphasis is then on the framework of procedures, regulations and guidelines by which senior management ensure accountability, equity and transparency in relationships with stakeholders such as employees, investors, suppliers and customers. This framework will often need to involve practices for managing the sometimes diverging interests of stakeholders. Its scope is influenced by different types of informal and formal contractual arrangements between companies and their stakeholders to configure the distribution of obligations and rewards. The basics of corporate governance structures consist of a board of directors, which appoints managers, and external auditors, who are responsible for a range of decisions on disclosure of information to shareholders, board members and the public, remuneration of senior managers and supervisory structures.

'Demand' for governance in the commercial real estate investment sector, like any other investment sector, is related to the largely inevitable incompleteness of contracts between the various stakeholders. Since it is usually not possible fully to allocate financial surpluses in every possible contingency, particularly in outsourced structures, contract incompleteness can create scope for opportunistic behaviour. Such problems tend to be exacerbated by the larger degree of asymmetric information. It is an inability to contractualise all possible contingencies that creates the need for some type of governance process. Rajan and Zingales (1998) identified two necessary conditions for a governance system to be necessary. First, the relationship must generate some potential for abnormal gains from the transaction. Second, the abnormal gains are not perfectly allocated in advance. Without specific contractual terms, outcomes respecting the distribution of potential gains has to be determined during the period of the contract. This is essentially the role of the governance process.

To inhibit 'agents' from taking decisions that favour their own interests, organisations tend to introduce checks and balances. Often, attempts to achieve some element of separation of powers are at the core of governance. The emphasis of *internal* governance tends to focus on setting organisations' objectives, risk control, organisational structure, the allocation of authority and responsibility, reporting lines, compliance and internal auditing. For instance, covering the financial services sector Article 22 of Directive 2006/48/EC, required that:

> every credit institution has robust governance arrangements, which include a clear organisational structure with well defined, transparent and consistent lines of responsibility, effective processes to identify, manage, monitor and report the risks it is or might be exposed to, adequate internal control mechanisms, including sound administrative and accounting procedures, and remuneration policies and practices that are consistent with and promote sound and effective risk management.
>
> (European Union, 2006)

Clearly, the potential scope of governance is wide ranging and contextual. The relative importance of the various dimensions of governance will vary with the nature of the relationships or processes that are being governed.

Governance and the real estate sector

Like most business sectors, the real estate sector can be analysed as a network of relationships, contracts, knowledge, capital and assets. Although in most real estate markets, and with marked variations, a large proportion of real estate is owner occupied, in many countries a substantial proportion of commercial real estate is owned directly by investors or indirectly by investors in various 'pass-through' vehicles as a quasi-financial asset. These pass-through vehicles such as real estate investment trusts (REITs) and unlisted real estate funds are essentially asset management organisations. An important market shift in the first two decades of the twenty-first century has been the transformation in the range and scope of real estate investment organisations and their support service providers. In addition to the longstanding occupational pension funds, insurance companies and listed real estate companies, many of whom have themselves evolved significantly, relatively new categories of real estate investment organisations have become increasingly prominent. Sovereign wealth funds, specialist open- and closed-end real estate funds, investment banks, specialist real estate investment managers, private equity groups and endowments funds have emerged as significant market participants. While sometimes engaging in real estate development, their core activities tend to focus on the assembly and management of portfolio of tenanted real estate assets.

Each type of real estate organisation will be exposed to different types of operational risk – the risk of losses stemming from inadequate or failed internal processes, people and systems or from external events – and will, therefore, focus on different aspects of governance. While the boundaries between the different sub-sectors can be blurred as they sometimes attempt to enter their competitors' markets, it is clear that the real estate investment sector comprises a variety of market operators with a range of different time horizons, investment objectives, client types and business models. This diversity of asset managers and asset holders reflects the proliferation of intermediation in the investment chain. An array of intermediaries – nominees, 'fund of fund' managers, investment consultants, distributors, asset and property managers, appraisers – are part of the network of real estate investment principals and advisers that requires internal and external governance. Both occupiers and investors need to procure a range of real estate support services from third parties to hold real estate assets. While many organisations will deliver some support services 'in-house', acting for both investors and occupiers there is a sector of third-party real estate services providers to whom many real estate support functions are outsourced. The main types include a wide range of real estate management, legal, brokerage and appraisal services. These organisations are important in that they are often the 'instruments' through which real estate investment policies are executed.

The nature of the governance issues pertinent to real estate investment will also be affected by the method of real estate investment. REITs and listed real estate companies share most of the regulatory and governance regimes with the more broadly listed sector. In the literature on REIT governance, the emphasis has consequently been on 'standard' governance variables such as board independence, disclosure, and insider ownership. Unlisted real estate funds represent one of the fastest growing real estate investment routes over the last two decades. They are often called 'private' funds since they are not quoted on any public exchanges. There is a large number of different fund structures which are based in a wide range of regulatory jurisdictions. As a result, it can be difficult to categorise and classify many of the funds in the unlisted sector. Across global real estate markets, there is a large array of unlisted, private vehicles (such as limited partnerships, trusts and private companies) with different legal structures in a range of regulatory domiciles that are used to pool real estate assets. After discussing some of the governance-related issues that can emerge in acquiring and holding real estate assets, we then look at governance issues in the unlisted and listed sectors in more depth.

Governance issues in the real estate management process

As in many other business sectors, professional and industry body regulations are common elements of governance in the real estate sector. Professional bodies typically set standards of professional qualifications and practice and maintain databases of qualified persons. They confer the appropriate designations, provide guidance on conduct and practice, investigate grievances and misconduct penalties. Internationally, there is a variety of models for governing professional organisations which, in turn, are themselves part of the range of governance regimes that monitor and supervise real estate professionals. In the UK, and in a growing number of other international real estate markets, the Royal Institution of Chartered Surveyors (RICS) has been the most prominent professional body. There is an ongoing debate within the European Union about the balances between local and international regulation, state and voluntary self-regulation. In the UK, there has been a long tradition of professional self-regulation. The RICS is a good example of a self-regulating profession in the real estate sector. While it is independent, significant changes to its constitution have to be ratified by the UK government. The membership of the European Association of Real Estate Professionals provides a good database of the main professional associations in Europe.

The RICS, in its professional standards and guidance on real estate agency and brokerage (Royal Institution of Chartered Surveyors, 2016) sets out key principles which echo the governance concerns that are found in other areas. A number of the key principles are outlined. Real estate managers should:

> ensure that clients are provided with terms of engagement which are fair and clear, incorporate details of complaints handling procedures ... do the utmost to avoid conflicts of interest and, where they do arise, to deal with them openly, fairly and promptly ...]

> ensure that all communications are fair, clear, timely and transparent in all dealings with clients … ensure that any client money is held separately from other monies, and is covered by adequate insurance.
>
> (Royal Institution of Chartered Surveyors, 2016, 4)

Many of the themes in governance can be seen in apparently prosaic issues such as services charges (common area maintenance fees in the United States). Problems can arise from a basic conflict of interest between the owner's concern with maintaining the property in the long term and the occupier's shorter-term perspective. The tenant typically does not want to pay for works from which they may derive little benefit, not least because they may intend to vacate. In addition, compounding the misaligned incentives problem, the owner is typically spending the occupiers' money and may have little incentive to ensure 'best value'. A number of problems have occurred:

- the use of service charge income on capital expenditure to improve rather than maintain the asset;
- poor procurement practices and failure to procure 'best value' providers of services;
- failure to pass on commissions obtained on insurance policies to the occupiers;
- where the service charge is 'bundled' with rent in a single payment, owners provide poor quality services in order to maximise their income;
- inadequate justification of expenditure by the owner and/or poor transparency in costings.

The key issue requiring robust governance was summed up in a legal case in the UK. The judge stated that:

> Tenants who agree to service charge clauses … rely upon the professional people involved performing their roles with professional scrupulousness, diligence, integrity and independence and not in a partisan spirit, supposing their only task to be to recover as much money as they can for the landlord.
>
> (Princes House Ltd v Distinctive Clubs Ltd [2006] All ER (D) 117)

The RICS Code of Practice for service charges in commercial property (Royal Institution of Chartered Surveyors, 2014) has become a key mechanism through which the service charge process is governed. It provides lengthy and specific guidance on a wide range of service charge issues. However, it is well summed up in the introductory section which states that:

> In incurring costs in the provision of services, the manager is spending the occupiers' money. Managers are therefore expected to demonstrate a high degree of competence, professionalism, integrity, diligence, objectivity and transparency in dealing with the service charge accounts.
>
> (Royal Institution of Chartered Surveyors, 2014, 6)

A key decision for investors in real estate investment portfolios is how to structure their procurement and delivery of property management – specifically whether to deliver in-house or to outsource to property management service providers. Anecdotal evidence suggests that, over the past two decades, it has become increasingly common for real estate investment organisations to outsource property management which many have come to regard as a non-core activity. Like many outsourcing arrangements, operational risks generated by principal-agent issues have meant that the governance of this type of interfirm relationships has tended to involve a wide range of highly contractualised control mechanisms. Outsourced property management agreements are used to set out in detail the specification of the service, pricing and financial performance penalties (or incentives), service levels and performance metrics, delegated decision rights and responsibilities, conflict resolution procedures and provisions for contract termination. For UK funds, key performance indicators – such as percentage of rent collected within three days of due date or percentage of service charge collected within three days of due date – tend to be the main mechanism of monitoring performance. In a market characterised by a limited number of large-scale services providers, information leakage is an issue and investors/fund managers – themselves prone to conflict of interest problems – have had to ensure that they are comfortable with internal confidentiality procedures put in place by their providers who are often delivering similar services to other real estate investment organisations.

Governance issues in the real estate acquisition process

Buying and selling commercial real estate assets involves a process of exchange that occurs over an extended period and incurs risks and costs of a character and order that differ from those involved when trading mainstream equity and debt securities. This stems from the private and dispersed nature of commercial real estate markets and the fact that real estate assets are heterogeneous, with varying physical, spatial and legal characteristics. Buyers normally have to spend significantly more time searching for suitable assets and sellers normally must spend time attracting buyers. Often there is a range of professionals working in different organisations involved in the real estate stock selection and acquisition process – fund managers, researchers, asset managers, brokers and acquisition specialists. Individuals influencing stock selection and pricing decisions will be prone to different pressures and have a range of motivations which may, in turn, bias their actions and advice both consciously and unconsciously. For instance, Graff and Webb (1997) explain return persistence in real estate assets as a consequence of agency costs arising from incentives (bonuses, fee structures) for managers to acquire assets and to overbid for rarely available assets. In the UK, McAllister, Hughes and Gallimore *et al.* (2008) identified a number of potential problems that investing organisations need to consider in governing real estate asset acquisition processes.

- Employed by third party firms, brokers acting for investors may be primarily motivated to generate fees from transactions rather than to ensure appropriate asset selection and pricing by their clients.
- Internally employed individuals who are responsible for the buying process for their investment organisation may be incentivised to acquire high quantities of stock rather than high-quality stock at appropriate prices.
- Fund managers who are remunerated on the basis of portfolio size may be incentivised to acquire assets to increase the size of the portfolio under management and, consequently, increase the size of their fee income.
- Fund managers often have to decide how to allocate high quality assets offered to them among different clients and may allocate assets to maximise benefits to themselves or their organisation rather than to their clients.

This is essentially a concern with different operational risks within the real estate asset acquisition process. Gallimore *et al.* (2006) concluded that, for large UK investing institutions, the real estate investment processes were relatively well governed. The potential for poor decision making at the individual asset level was limited by a number of 'checks and balances'. Institutional buyers tended to be expert and were aware of brokers' misaligned incentive structures. They had, therefore, sufficient knowledge to critically evaluate brokers' advice. Brokers had counterincentives in terms of repeat business and potential reputational damage. Within the investing organisations, it was acknowledged that individual buyers should not be rewarded by volume of transactions. Their remuneration was normally linked to corporate and team performance rather than just individual performance. In addition, the decision-making process was invariably joint – initial recommendations and evaluations were closely scrutinised by fund managers and/or committees of senior, experienced experts. The central role of joint decision making in controlling operational risks is illustrated in Figure 17.1, which provides a schematic representation of the various participants in the real estate acquisition process for institutional investors.

In institutional investment organisations, systems of consultation and approval are a vital part of operational risk management in the stock acquisition process. The fund manager is often the key pinch point in the process. In consultation with the professional responsible for buying new stock, the fund manager typically contributes to the evaluation process. This tends to involve oversight of the testing of assumptions and modifications to cash flow models. Commonly, once a fund manager decides to pursue an acquisition, there are further formal layers of approval in place. Most institutional investment organisations have some form of investment committee comprising senior fund managers and, usually, the head of research, which needs to approve proposed acquisitions. Key issues concern how much delegated authority should be given to fund managers. These processes and delegated levels of approval are part of the investment management mandate agreed with the client.

The amount of client involvement in individual buying decisions will often depend upon the investment management agreement and the degree of discretion that this gives.

The demand from investors for high quality stock can produce moral hazard for sellers' brokers. While it is difficult to demonstrate that there are systematic problems, anecdotes exist of various poor practices including acting for buyers as well as sellers, accepting inducements from buyers to provide 'inside information' on competitors' bid levels and/or providing biased advice to sellers in return for tangible benefits from the buyer. The Investment Property Forum's (IPF) *Protocol on Open Market Investment Agency* provides a case study of a professional self-regulation model to handling conflicts of interest in the brokerage sector. The IPF identifies that:

> The potential for conflict of interest has become a fact of modern investment agency. Such situations should always be managed proactively and transparently to ensure trust and confidentiality is maintained at all times.
>
> (Investment Property Forum, 2014)

Common governance themes are outlined in the protocol, focussing on clarity and fairness in terms of engagement, maintenance of conflicts of interest databases and reference to complaints handling procedures and redress schemes. Most of the protocol is concerned with multiple introductions (where multiple individual agents in a firm 'introduce' an asset to multiple potential buyers) and dual agency (where other individual agents from the firm of the seller's agent acts also for the buyer). The protocol emphasises the role of a maintaining

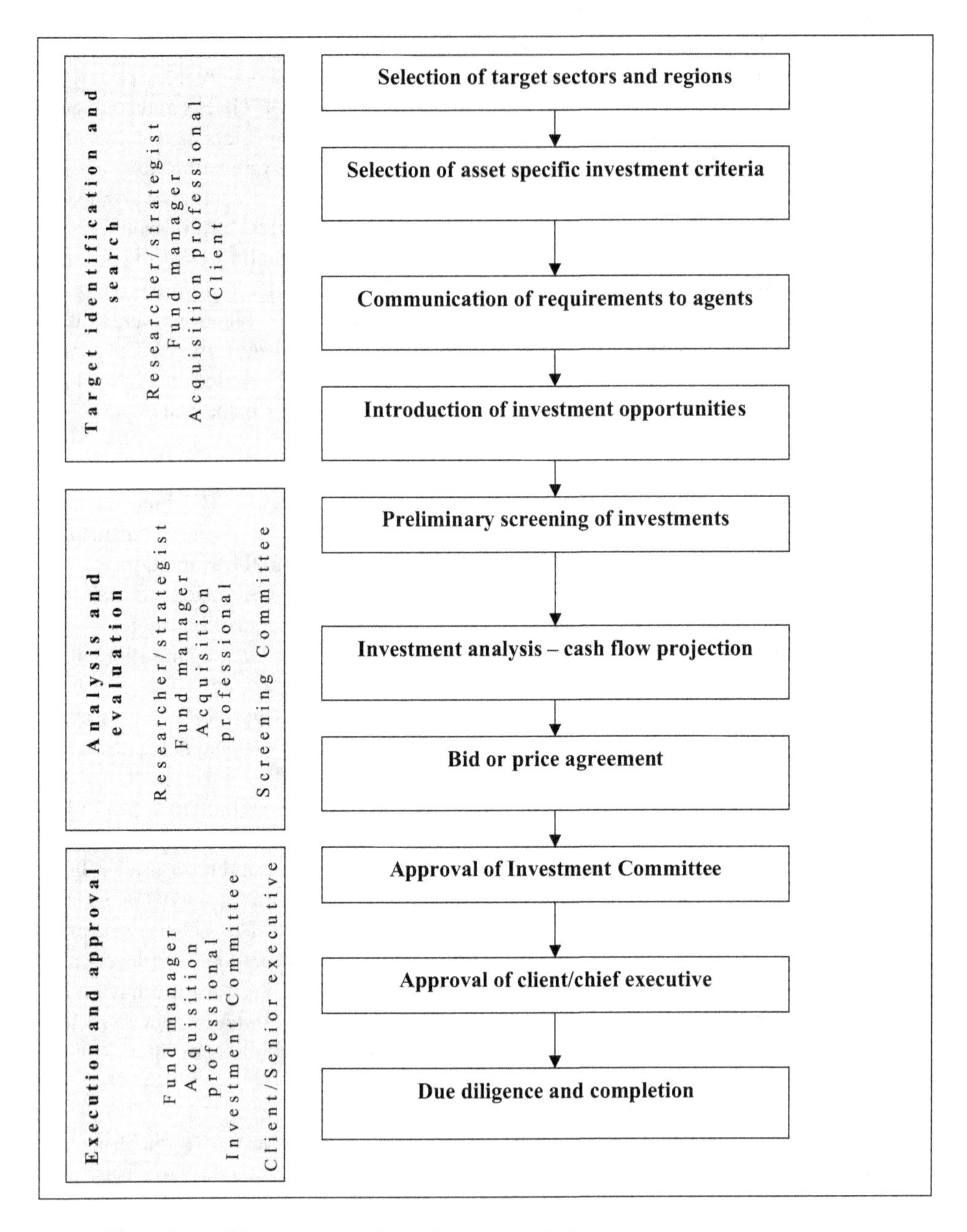

Figure 17.1 Joint decision making in the real estate acquisition process

a 'barriers policy' that seeks to ensure that 'deal teams' from within the same firm acting for different clients on the same transaction have strict separation of information flows. Effective from 2018, the RICS released its own professional statement on *Conflicts of Interest – UK Commercial Property Market Investment Agency* (Royal Institution of Chartered Surveyors, 2017), which addresses similar issues in the brokerage sector.

Governance issues in real estate appraisals

With broad implications for interrelated issues, such as data quality, approaches to portfolio construction strategies and market performance measurement among others, a key feature of commercial real estate markets is the requirement for appraisals to act as substitutes for observed prices. For listed securities, the price of assets is observable and performance and values can be monitored in real time. In marked contrast, given the absence of continuously traded and deep markets, real estate appraisals perform a vital function in real estate markets by acting as a surrogate for prices. Appraisers provide key information estimating the trading prices of real estate assets.

Appraisals may need to be commissioned for a number of purposes. A proportion consists of single, transaction-related appraisals in which the appraisal can be critical to the completion of the transaction. Periodic, repeated appraisals of the same asset tend to take place for investment performance measurement and for financial reporting. Typically, they are used as a metric to measure financial ratios and fund managers' bonuses. Clearly, when remuneration is linked to investment performance which, in turn, is based on appraisals; there are obvious incentives for fund managers to attempt to bias appraisals. Appraisals are also used to set unit pricing for unlisted real estate funds where bid and ask prices are set on a net asset value basis. Accurate appraisals are particularly crucial to this type of fund manager when demand to redeem units is high. In addition, appraisals can be used to assess whether investment funds or real estate companies that are geared are compliant with minimum loan-to-value ratios.

Similar to auditors, accountants, equity and rating analysts, real estate appraisers act as information intermediaries. In particular, they can add value by providing credible information related to financial performance. There is a large body of academic research on information intermediaries to suggest that their advice may not always be independent. For example, for equity analysts, Lin and McNichols (1998) and Michaely and Womack (1999) found that analysts' recommendations were affected by their firm's business relationship with a company. In the real estate literature, there is a body of work that has identified different types of influence (coercive, covert, reward, information) of different categories of appraisal (transactional, periodic) at different stages of the process (instruction, information collection, calculation, reporting and so on). The vast majority of existing research has been either quasi-experimental (Hansz, 2004; Amidu and Aluko, 2007; Amidu *et al.*, 2008), interview based (McAllister *et al.*, 2004; Levy and Schuck, 2005) or postal survey based (Smolen and Hambleton, 1997; Worzala *et al.*, 1998; Gallimore and Wolverton, 2000; Yu, 2002). A stylised fact that emerges from this body of work is that appraisals are often not independent.

Most appraisers have anecdotes of attempts by clients to influence the outcome of an appraisal and, as noted above, the academic literature is replete with evidence of this influence. The appraisal process facilitates high levels of interference by clients. This ranges from the selection of the appraisers to the discussion of the outcome at draft appraisal meetings. The bonus structures of clients are sometimes based on short term outcomes tied to performance targets. Additionally, the fee structure of clients is also often tied to appraisal outcomes. In the bank lending sector, there are more stakeholders in addition to the lender, such as brokers, other professionals and, possibly, providers of insurance, guarantees and indemnities. According to Crosby *et al.* (2010), even though the appraiser should have the aim to produce an objective independent valuation, they can be subjected to pressure by other stakeholders in the transaction (including the individual banker). They may all have a vested interest in the deal going ahead and a lesser interest in the performance of the loan and/or the asset.

This discussion raises issues of internal supervisory relationships within organisations, including fee structures, appointing and reporting mechanisms between the appraiser and client, and professional supervisory processes and their effectiveness. In mature real estate markets, the requirements and conduct of appraisals are typically governed by a blend of governmental legislation and professional institutions. In the UK, the most important professional regulatory body is the RICS, which produces guidance on professional standards. The RICS (2012) states that an appraiser must act independently and objectively at all times and their professional standards provide some examples of threats to their independence or objectivity. The valuation standards also identify the particular threat to objectivity of communication with a client before a report is produced:

> A threat to the valuer's objectivity can arise where the outcome of a valuation is discussed before its completion with either the client or another party with an interest in the valuation. While such discussions are not improper, and indeed may be beneficial to both the valuer and the client, the valuer must be alert to the potential influence that such discussions may have on his or her fundamental duty to provide an objective opinion.
>
> (Royal Institution of Chartered Surveyors, 2012, VS 1.7, para 7)

Following problems of client influence in appraisals identified in the UK through academic research, professional regulatory requirements to record meetings on 'draft' appraisals were introduced (Baum *et al.*, 2000). After the Carsberg report in 2002 (Royal Institution of Chartered Surveyors, 2002), the RICS developed a compliance team to monitor client influence. However, to date we know little about how it is operating and whether it is effectively countering any influence issues which remain.

Governance issues in unlisted real estate funds

As noted above, a notable feature of the unlisted real estate sector is the diversity of the vehicles. In the UK, investment in unlisted real estate funds is generally undertaken through employing one of three legal formats: partnerships, unit trusts or companies. Broadly speaking, the range of funds can be seen as lying on a continuum in terms of size, trading volume, number of investors, sector focus, gearing and rigour of regulatory framework. The vehicles can range from joint ventures – vehicles with two or three investors pooling capital and expertise for a fixed period to acquire a clearly defined asset base – towards open-ended property funds with a high proportion of retail investors and a large portfolio of assets (in value and number). While joint ventures are normally customised towards specific investor needs, retail property funds can be highly regulated to decrease investor risk and, as a result, have relatively homogenised formats. Such diversity makes it difficult to generalise about the governance issues in unlisted real estate funds.

It is also clear that an investment in unlisted real estate funds will have different characteristics relative to a direct acquisition of the underlying real estate assets. These characteristics may be perceived as both negative and positive. Relative to direct ownership, there are significant differences in liquidity, trading and price formation, search costs, financial structuring, holding costs, management control, lot size, taxation and transaction costs *inter alia*. However, just as importantly, there will be significant inter-vehicle differences in all of the qualities listed above. Most of the unlisted real estate structures have in common the delegation of fund and asset management functions to third party managers. While the length and size of the investment chain can vary, the result can be a range of potential misalignments of interests that need to be 'governed'.

Many of the potential moral hazards are implicit in the European Association for Investors in Non-Listed Real Estate Vehicles corporate governance guidelines (INREV, 2018). INREV's corporate governance guidelines provide a useful and comprehensive description of the scope of the issues that can fall within the remit of corporate governance in the unlisted funds sector. Fuller details can be found in the INREV guidelines. With apologies for such a lengthy list, the broad headings relate to provisions for:

- amendments to the constitutional terms of the fund agreement;
- handling of defaulting investors;
- composition of the investment committee;
- investor approval rights over third party service providers;
- vehicle documentation on control mechanisms and risk control procedures;
- codes of ethics;
- provision for manager removal;
- the extent, disclosure and pattern of co-investment;
- voting rights;
- the existence, composition and powers of a non-executive board;
- transparency and rights of investors to obtain information;
- quality and frequency of investment reports;
- rights to inspect accounts and records;
- investors' engagement with appraisals;
- use and appointment of external valuers;
- the use and disclosure of side letters or agreements;
- investors' rights in the event of changes to key personnel;
- fee and carry structures;
- protocols for conflicts of interest;
- exclusivity on investment opportunities; and
- the terms of confidentiality clauses.

Even within some of these broad headings, there can be a numerous ways in which potential conflicts of interests between managers and investors need to be governed.

Governance and investment performance in the listed real estate sector

From the conceptual discussion of governance above, it is clear that an expected outcome of good governance is expected to be improved financial performance mainly through reduced risk and better risk-adjusted performance. Improvements in financial performance can be directly linked to rationales for allocating resources to high quality governance. Governance has been analysed through a number of theoretical lenses which generate contrasting expected relationships between governance performance and business performance. For instance, instrumental stakeholder theory stresses the contribution of relationships with key stakeholders (other than shareholders) such as employees, suppliers, unions, customers and the local community to business performance. Closely related stakeholder–agency theory emphasises how high quality governance can reduce the agency costs within corporate structures by improving interest alignment and monitoring of the actions of employers, managers and employees. Similarly, firm-as-contract theory also highlights the significance of, often implied, contracts with stakeholders as drivers of firms' financial performance. Hence, the expected causal relationship is that the quality of governance should be a determinant of business performance.

In contrast, slack resources theory implies the opposite relationship – that business performance is a determinant of the quality of governance. It proposes that surpluses generated by strong prior business performance release resources for governance activities. While theories are often presented as mutually exclusive, it is possible that, similar to the issue of motivation, the relative importance of resource availability and the salience of relationships with stakeholders may vary between sectors or firms and/or over time. Russo and Perrini (2010) report that firm size is a decisive factor and argue that a social capital approach is more relevant for understanding governance commitments of small and medium-sized enterprises, whereas stakeholder theory is more apt for explaining the actions of large firms.

The mechanism by which a strong commitment to good governance is value-adding in terms of improved corporate financial performance can be difficult to disentangle. The direct costs of allocating capital to governance activities are relatively straightforward to measure. The direct costs are associated with the implementation, monitoring and reporting of governance processes. Indirect costs are also produced by the rejection of potential profitable business opportunities that may conflict with good governance-related objectives. It is not axiomatic that benefits are dominated by costs. Analyses of how corporate governance performance affects corporate financial performance in terms of returns, risks and company value tend to focus on more nebulous (but possibly no less important) factors. Linking back to stakeholder and firm-as-contract theories, the arguments for a positive effect on financial performance tend to emphasise increases in relational wealth, see Luo and Bhattacharya (2009). Factors broadly related to trust, such as increased transparency and reduced information asymmetry, may create reputational and branding benefits that improve key relationships with employees, shareholders, customers, suppliers and the community. A strong governance commitment implies more information about the expected cash flow distribution, reduced principal-agent costs and lower investors' risk premium. More directly, the cost of capital may be reduced because a lower risk premium may be placed on well-governed businesses.

Clientele effects are another possible mechanism by which governance performance may lead to a range of different effects on prices, returns and risk. The key transmission mechanism is that a decrease in the size of the investor base produces a neglect effect associated with exclusionary screening, lower demand for interests in poorly governed investments, a consequent negative effect on prices and a positive effect on returns. The body of work on the performance of securitised socially responsible investment funds is broadly consistent with underperformance in terms of returns (Bauer *et al.*, 2005; Geczy *et al.*, 2005; Renneboog *et al.*, 2008). The outcomes are a higher cost of capital and lower security prices for 'sin' stocks, albeit their returns can be higher. Another strand in this argument focusses on the role of differences in investor beliefs about the expected performance of well and poorly governed investments. One argument is that good corporate social performance sends a signal of high quality management.

In the listed real estate sector, transparency and disclosure in financial reporting have been highlighted as key governance issues. Creating potential adverse selection problems, a lack of transparent financial information can result in greater information risks for investors who, in turn, experience increased uncertainty about the true economic value of the firm. Without sufficient controls and monitoring, investors will tend pay the same prices for 'lemons' and 'good' companies. In this context, the European Public Real Estate Association's

(EPRA) best practice recommendations on financial reporting (European Public Real Estate Association, 2016) can be interpreted as an association-based mechanism that is intended to improve corporate governance in the listed real estate sector and reduce the information risk borne by investors. The best practice guidance from EPRA attempts to standardise many financial performance metrics and to overcome discrepancies in reporting within the European real estate sector with the intention of improving the consistency and transparency in financial reporting. In the United States, in a study of the effect of similar industry initiative by Nareit on reporting of *Funds From Operation*, Baik *et al.* (2008) found that industry guidance curtailed manager opportunistic reporting and investors perceived less manipulation and greater reliability.

Such agency problems may have two effects on a firm's stock price: they can influence expected cash flows accruing to investors and the cost of capital (Drobetz *et al.*, 2004). It is expected that the extent of these effects will depend on the quality of governance. There is a substantial body of theoretical work to suggest that high-quality financial information can reduce the cost of equity capital by increasing market liquidity or increasing the demand for a firm's securities and by reducing investors' information risk reducing shareholders' monitoring and auditing costs. While it is possible to hypothesise various linkages between governance and investment performance, empirical evidence or any effort towards ascertaining that is fraught with formidable challenges. Part of the difficulty relates to the fact that there are so many complex links in the causality chain. Does quality of governance affect investment performance or does quality of investment performance affect quality of governance? Is there a self-reinforcing pattern – does an improvement in business performance cause an improvement in governance which causes further improvements in business performance and so on? Alternatively, is there an omitted variable that is causing both improvements in both investment performance and governance performance? Such issues create difficult problems for researchers attempting to address the research question: all else equal, what is the effect of governance performance on investment performance? The other part is the severe lack of good-quality information and data on aspects of the whole process. While quality of governance is at least measured for listed firms, there are few such measures for many other real estate investment organisations.

A particular problem of research on corporate governance is the measurement of governance performance. Researchers have focussed on individual variables such as remuneration, board independence and insider ownership. There is also a number of composite indexes that attempt to measure corporate governance performance. Although governance can be quite broad in scope by itself, it is often bundled with a number of other activities (social and environmental) as a corporate attribute. It is then blended with other measures of corporate environmental and social performance to create ESG performance metrics. While incorporating a large number of variables, in the listed sector the key category headings in corporate governance performance tend to focus on disclosure and auditing, remuneration, board structure and shareholder rights with numerous sub-categories. It is notable that a number of 'rating the ratings' studies have found that different indices are corporate governance can be weakly (and sometimes negatively) correlated with each other (Daines *et al.*, 2010; Brown and Caylor, 2006). Variation between the various governance indices has been explained by a lack of consistency and theoretical justification for the inclusion and weighting of different variables in the different indices. Clearly, the quality of governance can then be difficult to measure.

Inconsistency in empirical findings regarding the relationship between governance and corporate financial performance has been attributed to the range of metrics of corporate financial performance used. This does not include operational performance issues such as staff turnover or numbers of patents. A key problem is that there are large variations in the timescales in the transmission of the governance activities to different outcomes. Share prices can be affected by new information on governance almost instantaneously. However, the lags and processes between improvements in governance and improvements in profitability or turnover are likely to be much more lengthy and intricate.

Governance and investment performance: some evidence

Outside of the real estate sector, there is a voluminous empirical literature examining whether corporate ESG performance predicts corporate financial performance. Not surprisingly, it has produced an assortment of findings (for reviews see Orlitzky *et al.*, 2003; Margolis *et al.*, 2007; van Beurden and Goessling, 2008; Cai *et al.*, 2011). While a detailed review of this literature is outside the scope of this chapter, it is clear that the topic is fraught with problems owing to potential publication bias, differences in sampling periods and potential endogeneity of corporate ESG performance. Ruf *et al.* (2001) propose that causes of the identified lack of consistency in empirical studies include weak theoretical foundations, inadequate and inconsistent measurement of corporate ESG performance and corporate financial performance, weak methodology and sampling problems. In direct real estate, poor data is also a key issue.

Supporting the theoretical predictions regarding information disclosure, there is also substantial empirical evidence that disclosure quality or earnings transparency lowers firms' cost of capital. A number of studies have found a negative relation between various proxies for disclosure quality or earnings transparency and cost of equity capital (Botosan, 1997; Botosan and Plumlee, 2002; Bhattacharya *et al.*, 2003; Barth and Landsman, 2003; Francis *et al.*, 2004). There is also a fairly established body of research suggesting that discretionary disclosure lowers the cost of debt (Sengupta, 1998), increases stock liquidity, stock performance and institutional ownership (Healy *et al.*, 1999), increases analyst following (Lang and Lundholm, 1996) and decreases bid-ask spreads (Welker, 1995). Essentially, transparency and disclosure in financial reporting and corporate governance may enable companies to signal quality in management and control. These signals may have a potential to lower agency costs by reducing conflicts of interest and investors' costs of monitoring management and searching for information.

Given the greater availability of data, it is to be expected that the vast majority of the empirical work on the relationship between governance and performance has been in the listed real estate sector – and mainly on the US real estate listed sector. There is a body of work, most of which looks at US REITS, on the relationship between corporate governance and firm performance (Ghosh and Sirmans, 2003; Feng *et al.*, 2005; Bauer *et al.*, 2010; Bianco *et al.*, 2007; Hartzell *et al.*, 2008). In most of these studies, the researchers tended to focus on individual governance variables to identify which of the conventional corporate governance mechanisms, be it board size and independence, insider ownership or ownership concentration play a significant role in the governance structure of US REITS and the REITs performance and market value. Results have been mixed. Bauer *et al.* (2010) used an index of governance strength rating as a proxy for the corporate governance system and examined its relationship to the performance of US REITs. They failed to find that corporate governance had a significant influence on REITs' performance. They suggest that, since the result contrasts with previous findings from studies of wider corporate performance, due to the requirement to distribute at least 90% of operational earnings, there are reduced agency costs for REITs and governance is, consequently, a less important factor.

In these studies, financial disclosure transparency by US REITs as one of the corporate governance variables was not explicitly examined, although it is an important governance issue. In the European listed sector, Muller *et al.* (2011) examined the effects of the adoption of accounting standard IAS 40 on fair value reporting in the European listed real estate sector using bid-ask spreads as the dependent variable (International Financial Reporting Standards Foundation, 2003). Muller *et al.* argued that this allowed them to assess perceived differences in information asymmetry across investors and thus directly to measure the impact of fair value reporting on the information environment. Comparing mandatory provision of fair value information to voluntary provision, they found that mandatory adopters experienced a larger reduction in their information asymmetry as indicated by lower bid-ask spreads, following the adoption of international financial reporting standards (IFRS). This evidence is consistent with the improvement of the information environment for investors by mandatory provision of fair values. However, they also found that differences in bid-ask spreads persisted. In the post-IFRS adoption period, firms that did not provide investment property fair values prior to IFRS continue to have higher bid-ask spreads than firms that did. This was interpreted as being consistent with investors continuing to have concerns about the reliability of mandatory adopters' fair value disclosures due to the variation in those firms' institutional structures and implementation.

Kohl and Schaefers (2012) is probably the most relevant and robust previous empirical study of European listed property companies. They test whether the principal corporate governance mechanisms, such as board size and independence, insider ownership and institutional ownership have significant effects on book-to-market ratio. They also include a disclosure variable, a self-constructed transparency index based on the EPRA best practice policy recommendations as one of the significant corporate governance variables. They find a significant positive effect of better disclosure and firm value as measured by book-to-market ratio. However, it is notable that they do not include controls for variables that may affect book-to-market ratios such as focus on real estate development as opposed to investment assets.

Conclusion

One of the main difficulties of analysing governance in the context of real estate markets is that it is such a broad, multi-dimensional, even nebulous, concept. Perhaps it is too obvious a point to make but it may be worth reiterating that problems of misaligned incentives, moral hazard and conflicts of interest are far from unique to commercial real estate markets and tend to raise difficult issues for all public and private sector organisations. Governance in this commercial context is mainly about identifying and mitigating the potential costs of such problems. In different contexts, different emphasis tends to be given to different aspects of governance. Even when the concept of governance is explicitly defined to evaluate its quality, there are major challenges in then measuring and quantifying it. In a commercial real estate investment market characterised by chains of intermediaries and typically outsourced support services such as brokerage, appraisers, asset managers, and fund administration, mitigating principal-agent costs can become a key business performance issue.

A number of features seem to be at the heart of the concept of good governance. Broadly, the focus is on the protection of the interests of 'principals' such as investors and trustees, and clients from self-interested behaviour by 'agents' such as fund managers and service providers. Aspects of governance such as fairness and equity are essentially concerned with normative ethics. The typical stress on communication, transparency and disclosure can be interpreted in the context of mitigating problems of information asymmetry. The emphasis of codes, guidance, procedures and processes that are related to the identification and management of moral hazards. Robust governance should then produce reductions in operational risk, improvements in quality assurance and decreased potential for reputational damage. A whole range of approaches to oversight and formal and informal regulation are used. Oversight can typically involve joint decision making with peers, audits and independent directors. Procedures and processes are often governed by professional or internal codes of practice and/or guidance. There are then strong grounds for expecting a positive relationship between good governance and business performance. The level of disclosure is expected to be negatively associated with information risks and monitoring costs for investors. Robust risk management procedures tend to be regarded positively by investors since they should make the organisation more resilient to external shocks. Fairness and equity with key stakeholders is expected to build trust with stakeholders with the literature highlighting the multitude of benefits that trust can create for firms.

Clearly, there are good reasons to expect a positive relationship between governance and business performance. However, even where data are available, there have been major challenges in investigating the relationship between governance and business or investment performance. Given the multitude of factors that determine the performance of a listed company and the often intricate linkages between these factors, it can be difficult to isolate the effect of a single variable such as governance. It is also worth bearing in mind that governance metrics are usually based upon a composite measure of a range of attributes such as the quality of disclosure and board independence. It is notable that different governance metrics can produce quite different rankings. Perhaps more problematically, in private commercial real estate investment markets many of the governance issues have remained relatively unscrutinised in terms of research.

Notes

1 Institute on Governance: https://iog.ca.

2 Investopedia have drawn upon a range of sources to create this comprehensive definition: www.investopedia.com/terms/c/corporategovernance.asp.

References

Amidu, A. and Aluko, B. T. (2007) Client influence in residential property valuations: an empirical study, *Property Management*, 25, 447–61.

Amidu, A., Aluko, B. and Hansz, J. (2008) Client feedback pressure and the role of real surveyors and valuers, *Journal of Property Research*, 25, 89–106.

Aubut, J. (2004) *The good governance agenda: who wins and who loses. Some empirical evidence for 2001*, Development Studies Institute Working Paper No. 04-48, London School of Economics, London.

Baik, B., Billings, B. K and Morton, R. (2008) Reliability and transparency of non-GAAP disclosure by real estate investment trusts (REITs), *Accounting Review*, 83, 271–301.

Barth, M. and Landsman, W. (2003) *Cost of capital and the quality of financial statement information*, Working Paper, Stanford University, University of North Carolina, Chapel Hill, NC.

Bauer, R., Eichholtz, P. and Kok, N. (2010) Corporate governance and performance: the REIT effect, *Real Estate Economics*, 38, 1–29.

Bauer, R., Koedijk, K. and Otten, R. (2005) International evidence on ethical mutual fund performance and investment style, *Journal of Banking and Finance*, 29, 1751–67.

Baum, A., Crosby, N., Gallimore, P., Gray, A. and McAllister, P. (2000) The influence of valuers and valuations on the workings on the commercial property market, Report for the Education Trusts of the Investment Property Forum, Jones Lang LaSalle and the Royal Institution of Chartered Surveyors.

Beurden, P. van and Goessling, T. (2008) The worth of values – a literature review on the relation between corporate social and financial performance, *Journal of Business Ethics*, 82, 407–24.

Bhattacharya, U., Daouk, H. and Welker, M. (2003) The world price of earnings opacity, *Accounting Review*, 78, 641–78.

Bianco, C., Ghosh, C. and Sirmans, C.F. (2007) The impact of corporate governance on the performance of REITs, *Journal of Portfolio Management*, 33, 175–91.

Botosan, C. A. (1997) Disclosure level and the cost of equity capital, *Accounting Review*, 72, 323–49.

Botosan, C. A. and Plumlee, M. A. (2002) A re-examination of disclosure level and the expected cost of equity capital, *Journal of Accounting Research*, 40, 21–40.

Brown, L. and Caylor, M. (2006) Corporate governance and firm valuation, *Journal of Accounting and Public Policy*, *25*, 409–34.

Cai, Y., Jo, H. and Pan, C. (2011) Vice or virtue? The impact of corporate social responsibility on executive compensation, *Journal of Business Ethics*, 104, 159–73.

Crosby, N., Lizieri, C. and McAllister, P. (2010) Means, motive and opportunity: disentangling the effects of client influence of periodic performance measurement appraisals, *Journal of Property Research*, 27, 181–201.

Daines, R., Gow, I. and Larcker, D. (2010) Rating the ratings: how good are commercial governance ratings?, *Journal of Financial Economics*, 98, 439–61.

di Florio, C. V. (2012) Conflicts of interest and risk governance, www.sec.gov/news/speech/2012-spch103112cvdhtm (accessed 20 August 2018).

Drobetz, W., Schillhofer, A. and Zimmermann, H. (2004) Corporate governance and expected stock returns: evidence from Germany, *European Financial Management*, 10, 267–93.

European Real Estate Association (2016) *Best Practice Recommendations Guidelines,* EPRA, Brussels.

European Union (2006) Directive 2006/48/EC of the European Parliament and of the Council of 14 June 2006 relating to the taking up and pursuit of the business of credit institutions (recast), *Official Journal of the European Union*, L 177/1, https://eur-lex.europa.eu/eli/dir/2006/48/oj (accessed 20 August 2018).

Feng, Z., Ghosh, G. and Sirmans, C. F. (2005) How important is the board of directors to REIT performance?, *Journal of Real Estate Portfolio Management*, 11, 281–93.

Francis, J., LaFond, R., Olsson, P. M. and Schipper, K. (2004) Costs of equity and earnings attributes, *Accounting Review*, 79, 967–1010.

Gallimore, P., Hughes, C. and McAllister, P. (2006) *Property stock selection: organisation, information and incentives*, Investment Property Forum, London.

Gallimore, P. and Wolverton, M. L. (2000) The objective in valuation: a study of the influence of client feedback, *Journal of Property Research*, 17, 47–58.

Geczy, C., Stambaugh, R. and Levin, D. (2005) Investing in socially responsible mutual funds. *SSRN*, October. Available at https://ssrn.com/abstract=416380 (accessed 20 August 2018).

Ghosh, C. and Sirmans, C. F. (2003) Board independence, ownership structure and performance: evidence from real estate investment trusts, *Journal of Real Estate Finance and Economics*, 26, 287–318.

Graff, R. and Webb, J. (1997) Agency costs and inefficiency in commercial real estate, *Journal of Real Estate Portfolio Management*, 3, 19–36.

Han, B. (2006) Insider ownership and firm value: evidence from real estate investment trusts, *Journal Real Estate Finance and Economics,* 32, 471–93.

Hansz, A. (2004) The use of a pending mortgage reference point in valuation judgment, *Journal of Property Investment and Finance*, 22, 259–68.

Hartzell, J., Kallberg, J. and Liu, C. (2008) The role of corporate governance in initial public offerings: evidence from real estate investment trusts, *Journal of Law and Economics*, 51, 539–62.

Healy, P. M., Hutton, A. P. and Palepu, K. G. (1999) Stock performance and intermediation changes surrounding sustained increases in disclosure, *Contemporary Accounting Research*, 16, 485–520.

INREV (2108) *Corporate governance*, available at www.inrev.org/guidelines/module/corporate-governance#inrev-guidelines (accessed 20 August 2018).

International Financial Reporting Standards Foundation (2003) *IAS 40 Investment Property*, IFRS, London.

Investment Property Forum (2014) *Protocol: open market investment agency*, Investment Property Forum, London.

Kohl, N. and Schaefers, W. (2012) Corporate governance and market valuation of publicly traded real estate companies: evidence from Europe, *Journal of Real Estate Finance and Economics*, 4, 362–93.

Lang, M. H. and Lundholm, R. J. (1996) Corporate disclosure policy and analyst behaviour, *Accounting Review*, 71, 467–92.

Levy, D. and Schuck, E. (2005) The influence of clients on valuations: the client's perspective, *Journal of Property Investment and Finance*, 23, 182–201.

Lin, H. and McNichols, M. (1998) Underwriting relationships, analysts' earnings forecasts and investment recommendations, *Journal of Accounting and Economics*, 25, 101–27.

Luo, Y. and Bhattacharya, C. B. (2009) The debate over doing: corporate social performance, strategic marketing levers, and firm-idiosyncratic risk, *Journal of Marketing*, 73, 198–213.

Margolis, J., Elfenbein, H. and Walsh, J. (2007) *Does it pay to be good? A meta-analysis and redirection of research on the relationship between corporate social and financial performance*, Working paper, Harvard Business School, Boston, MA.

Michaely, R. and Womack, K. (1999) Conflict of interest and the credibility of underwriter analyst recommendations, *Review of Financial Studies*, 12, 653–86.

McAllister, P., Baum, A., Crosby, N., Gallimore, P. and Gray, A. (2004) Appraiser behaviour and appraisal smoothing: some qualitative and quantitative evidence, *Journal of Property Research*, 20, 261–80.

McAllister, P., Hughes, C. and Gallimore, P. (2008) Principal-agent issues in asset acquisition: UK institutions and their investment agents, *Journal of Property Research*, 25, 269–83.

Muller, K. A., Riedl, E. J. and Sellhorn, T. (2011) Mandatory fair value accounting and information asymmetry: evidence from the European real estate industry, *Management Science*, 57, 1138–53.

Orlitzky, M., Schmidt, F. L. and Rynes, S. L. (2003) Corporate social and financial performance: a meta-analysis, *Organization Studies*, 24, 403–41.

Rajan, R. G. and Zingales, L. (1998) Power in a theory of the firm, *Quarterly Journal of Economics*, 113, 387–432.

Renneboog, L., Ter Horst, J. and Zhang, C. (2008) Socially responsible investments: institutional aspects, performance and investment behaviour, *Journal of Banking and Finance*, 32, 1723–42.

Royal Institution of Chartered Surveyors (2002) *Property valuation: the Carsberg report*, RICS, London.

Royal Institution of Chartered Surveyors (2012) *The RICS appraisal and valuation standards*, RICS, London.

Royal Institution of Chartered Surveyors (2014) *RICS Professional guidance: UK service charges in commercial property*, 3rd ed., RICS, London.

Royal Institution of Chartered Surveyors (2016) *Professional standards and guidance, global: real estate agency and brokerage*, 3rd ed., RICS, London.

Royal Institution of Chartered Surveyors (2017) *Conflicts of interest – UK commercial property market investment agency: professional statement*, RICS, London.

Ruf, B., Muralidhar, K., Brown, R., Janney, J. and Paul, K. (2001) An empirical investigation of the relationship between change in corporate social performance and financial performance: a stakeholder theory perspective, *Journal of Business Ethics*, 32, 143–56.

Russo, A. and Perrini, F. (2010) Investigating stakeholder theory and social capital: CSR in large firms and SMEs, *Journal of Business Ethics*, 91, 207–21.

Sengupta, P. (1998) Corporate disclosure quality and the cost of debt, *Accounting Review*, 73, 459–74.

Smolen, G. E. and Hambleton, D. C. (1997) Is the real estate appraiser's role too much to expect? *Appraisal Journal*, 65, 9–17.

Welker, M. (1995) Disclosure policy, information asymmetry, and liquidity in equity markets, *Contemporary Accounting Research*, 11, 801–27.

Worzala, E. M., Lenk, M. M. and Kinnard, W. N. (1998) How client pressure affects the appraisal of residential property, *Appraisal Journal*, 66, 416–27.

Yu, Shi-Ming (2002) *Client pressure in residential valuations – evidence from Singapore*, Working Paper, Department of Real Estate, National University of Singapore.

Index

Printed in the United States
by Baker & Taylor Publisher Services